NOW, MORE TH[...]
THIS IS A MUST-READ BOOK
FOR EVERY THOUGHTFUL
PERSON IN AMERICA . . .

For almost twenty-five years former Congressman Jerry Voorhis, Richard Nixon's first victim, kept a self-imposed silence about him.

Now, out of a troubled conscience and the deep conviction that the course being pursued by the President and his Administration is completely disastrous, Mr. Voorhis can keep quiet no longer.

"To one practice," writes Mr. Voorhis, "Richard Milhous Nixon has been faithful. He has done whatever at any given time would advance his political fortunes. This alone explains the strange gyrations of his strange case."

THE STRANGE CASE OF RICHARD MILHOUS NIXON

BY JERRY VOORHIS

POPULAR LIBRARY • NEW YORK

THIS BOOK IS DEDICATED TO
THE PROPOSITION
THAT GOVERNMENT OF THE PEOPLE,
BY THE PEOPLE, AND
FOR THE PEOPLE
SHALL NOT PERISH FROM THE EARTH

CONTENTS

PREFACE

The author of this book was the first victim of the Nixon-Chotiner formula for political success. It may, therefore, be thought that "sour grapes" have prompted its being written. But such is not the case. The first shock on election night was hard to take. It meant that ten years of earnest effort and a record generally judged at least good were of less consequence in deciding the outcome of an election than some cleverly turned phrases.

But as events developed, my defeat was, from a purely personal point of view, almost a blessing. It gave me three months of unharried time to finish writing my book, *Confessions of a Congressman*. And at the end of that short period of unemployment, I was selected for the very job I had most wanted. The job was that of Executive Director of the Cooperative League of the U.S.A. It gave me opportunity to work at building "grass roots" economic and social organizations and enterprises—a satisfying and rewarding task.

As time passed, I came to feel that perhaps Mr. Nixon and Mr. Chotiner had done me a personal favor in 1946.

For a period of 22 years I observed a self-imposed rule not to make any public reference to Richard Nixon. But when, in 1968, he was elected President of the United States, I could no longer in good conscience remain silent.

I remember a comment made in 1954 by the *Sacramento Bee* on a speech of Mr. Nixon's: "There was little policy and no principle in Nixon's words, but there was displayed infinite adaptability and caution, qualities which may carry the young man far if all there is to American politics is smart jockeying for power and preferment."

I hoped then, as I still hope, that the *Bee* was not prophetic in its observation. But as time passed, as Mr. Nixon's tactics did not change, as he advanced to the presidency by the use of those very tactics, and as I observed the devious and often

9

dangerous practices of his administration, my hope turned to fear that the *Bee* may have been right in its somber prediction.

So I decided to write this book and to dedicate it to the proposition that American politics can be rescued from the low state to which it has fallen in the Nixon years.

Looking across this land and beyond it I am concerned that the crisis in man's long history is upon us, now, today. I see a deterioration in the quality of our country's life that is frightening indeed. I believe I know the reason why this is so. General Omar Bradley, one of our country's finest soldiers, stated it better than I can do when he said:

We have grasped the mystery of the atom and rejected the Sermon on the Mount. The world has achieved brillance without wisdom, power without conscience. Ours is a world of nuclear giants and ethical infants. We know more about war than we know about peace, more about killing than we know about living.

It is time we began to do, individually and as a nation, what is right, simply because it is right—and leave the issue to a Greater Power than this world contains. But that, I fear, we shall not do without clear, good moral leadership and inspiration from a president of our country.

Such leadership is not forthcoming now. Nor will it be until another than the present occupant sits behind the White House desk.

Jerry Voorhis

Claremont, California
June, 1973

1. WHAT IS PAST IS PROLOGUE

Mr. Nixon's experience in politics must have been disillusioning for a clean-cut American boy, because everybody he has ever campaigned against has turned out, on his investigation, to be linked to something sinister.

Reporter Magazine

The strange case of Richard Milhous Nixon is not without its elements of pathos. Strangely, almost anyone who stood in Richard Nixon's way in the years of his ascension to higher, bigger and more lucrative positions seems to have been more or less tinged with the red brand of communism. At least that was what Mr. Nixon and his followers were engaged in telling the electorate.

Whatever other facts may have pointed to an exactly opposite appraisal of these opponents, there was one assumption that never for a moment was questioned—the assumption that anyone opposed to Richard Nixon, representing as he did all that was pure and holy in free enterprise Americanism, must be in some manner or another subversive. How could there be any other explanation of why anyone would oppose him?

And having reached this assumption Mr. Nixon and his followers felt justified in using any methods and tactics that might seem necessary to defeat his "subversive" opponents.

Mr. Nixon's general thesis was restated as late as 1968 in his interview with Kenneth Harris—widely publicized in the United States and Great Britain—in these words:

America's political leaders, statesmen, Senators, Congressmen and even mayors of towns, should owe no allegiance and have no ties, knowing or unknowing, to groups influenced by men politically hostile to the United States.

With the statement that no American public official should be hostile to the United States no decent person could possibly disagree.

It seems strange that a president-elect of the United States would feel it necessary to make such a statement. Unless, indeed, he wished to leave the impression that there were, and are, some such officials who "owe allegiance to groups hostile to the United States." Just how they could do this "unknowingly" Mr. Nixon, for obvious reasons, does not explain. For this clever word leaves the field wide open for charges that even if an opponent was not knowingly "subversive," nevertheless he might be "unknowingly" so and hence almost equally vulnerable to guilt by association.

And this is typical of the tactics consistently employed by Richard Milhous Nixon in his meteoric rise.

To be perfectly fair to Mr. Nixon, it should be stated that the tactics he employed were not his own discovery. They were, and still are, the product of the facile brain of a once obscure Los Angeles lawyer—now a major White House official—by the name of Murray Chotiner.

The Chotiner formula for political success is fairly simple. First one discredits his opponent in every possible way. For unless he is thoroughly discredited there is no safe ground on which to demand of the voters his replacement.

Second is by associating one's opponent in the public mind with an unpopular idea, concept or—better yet—organization. And if that organization or concept can be a subversive one— perhaps with just a suggestion of treason—so much the better.

Third—attack, attack, attack, never defend. When one's opponent tries to defend himself against untrue or distorted charges, learn to whimper. Above all learn to whimper and accuse him, your opponent, of using unfair political tactics by calling you a liar!

On November 28, 1945, a strong and representative committee of Republican leaders in the 12th district of California selected Richard Milhous Nixon as their candidate for Congress in the 1946 election. This was the first step in a career that led in 1968 to the White House itself.

The next step had to be to defeat the incumbent Democratic Congressman, Jerry Voorhis. For the successful taking of this second step up the ladder, the guidance of Mr. Chotiner was enlisted as early as December, 1945.

I was in the midst of my fifth term as the 12th district's representative. I had tried hard to write a creditable record. The Washington newsmen had been kind enough to vote me first in integrity among the 435 members, and the House itself had voted me its hardest working member and second in putting the nation's welfare ahead of personal political interests.

Among my assignments had been membership on the Committee on Un-American Activities and on the Committee to Investigate Executive Agencies of Government and their relation to the Congress.

The impact of the Committee to Investigate Executive Agencies had been to point out the danger to American constitutional government from too much concentration of power in the executive. The dean of newspaper writers, Mark Sullivan, in an article appearing in the *Pasadena Post* for December 5, 1944, had been kind enough to write as follows:

> The philosophy of the present step, and the temper in which it is approached, are put in especially thoughtful words by Democratic Representative Jerry Voorhis of California. What should be avoided, he says, is "continuous extension of the power and authority of the government, the abandonment by Congress to the executive department of the admittedly difficult and detailed job of conceiving precise legislation . . . and the reduction of the Congress to the position of a mere ratifying body, either approving or disapproving executive acts and proposals, and occasionally making broad and undetermined grants of power to the executive. I doubt that more than a mere handful of Americans would consciously favor such a course for our country's government."

I had accepted with some reluctance the appointment to the Committee on Un-American Activities because I believed the Committee—then popularly known as the Dies Committee—had been guilty of unfair accusations against perfectly loyal Americans and that its tactics left a great deal to be desired.

Once on it, however, I tried—and with some success—not only to inject more judicious practices but also to do my part in exposing for the nation's information the facts about such actually disloyal organizations as the Communist Party, the German-American Bund, and a number of essentially fascist outfits that had sprung up during the depression and the war years. I believed then, as I do now, that the one safe and proper method by which a democratic society can protect its freedoms from being undermined or even destroyed by totalitarian movements is by laying before the people the actual facts about the purpose and operations of such organizations.

To that end I had introduced and seen unanimously passed by the Congress the Voorhis Act, which requires the registration with the Department of Justice of pertinent facts about any political organization that is controlled by a foreign power or which engages in military activities aimed at subversion of

13

our form of government. This law was on the statute books in 1946. It still is.

The Voorhis Act was, so far as the records show, the only piece of legislation enacted by the Congress which was opposed by both the Communist Party and the German-American Bund. As a result of its passage the Communist Party publicly declared that it was severing its ties with the Commintern, the international organization of Communist parties.

For a short time during the 1920s, I had been registered as a Socialist, feeling that neither of the major parties was offering a workable solution to the growing problems which ultimately led to the 1929 crash. I had seen the Communists virtually destroy the Socialist Party of California committed as it was to constitutional democracy and peaceful political action and, therefore, constituting an obstacle to the Communist program of violent overthrow of the government.

I had seen also how Communist infiltration of some labor unions had brought destructive internal conflicts, discredited them in the eyes of the public, and rendered them incapable of benefitting the loyal American worker.

I knew that in California at that time, 1946, some CIO unions had suffered from Communist infiltration and I had therefore told my friends in the "clean" unions that I did not want the endorsement of the CIO Political Action Committee and would not accept it if offered. Nor did I ever receive such an endorsement.

I expected a tough campaign in 1946. The Democrats had been in power a long time—during the war and its aftermath. They were held responsible for the difficulties and frustrations of those years.

I also expected that the campaign would be fought around the vital issues of the time as had been the case with all my five previous campaigns. What I did *not* expect was the kind of Chotiner-directed campaign which it turned out to be. I did not expect my loyalty to America's constitutional government to be attacked. Least of all, considering all the facts about my record, did I expect that I would be labelled by my opponent as the "CIO-PAC candidate."

But I was. Indeed this became the principal refrain of the Nixon campaign, with overtones and undertones questioning my loyalty to American principles.

One Nixon campaign leaflet proclaimed that "A vote for Nixon is a vote against the PAC, its Communist principles, and its gigantic slush fund."

14

Just before the primary election, Mr. Nixon declared:

> If the people want bureaucratic control and domination with every piece of human activity regulated from Washington, then they should not vote for me but for my opponent. The day of reckoning has arrived. The issue is clear. Next Tuesday the people will vote for me as a supporter of free enterprise, individual initiative, and a sound progressive program, or for my opponent who has supported by his votes the foreign ideologies of the New Deal Administration.

On September 18 the *Whittier News* published on the same page two articles. One was headlined "Voorhis raps Wallace for Russ speech. Takes stand squarely in support of policy put down by Byrnes." The other article quoted Mr. Nixon: "It should be a matter of great concern to the voters of the 12th district that the National Citizens Political Action Committee which so loudly applauded Wallace's proposal that Russia be given a free hand, is the same radical organization that has endorsed my opponent."

A half-page advertisement appeared shortly before the election:

> Don't Be Fooled Again!
> Five times Jerry Voorhis has had the support of the radical groups because he was at one time a registered Socialist. . . .
>
> Voorhis has the endorsement of the National PAC because he voted their viewpoint 43 times out of 46 opportunities during the past four years.
>
> While he has been carrying the Democratic colors in recent years for his political purposes, REMEMBER, Voorhis is a former registered Socialist and his voting record in Congress is more Socialistic and Communistic than Democratic.

At first my reaction to this was one of amazement. I could not quite believe that Mr. Nixon would stoop quite so low as the language of that advertisement.

But I did not yet fully realize one simple fact. Mr. Nixon *had* to win. Nothing else would do at all. If it took ads like this to accomplish it—so be it. I had not yet grasped the idea that what was good for Richard Nixon *must* be good for the United States.

As for the 46 votes included in my "Communistic" record, they amounted to a compilation of four lists of votes, selected in *some* cases by the PAC, in other cases by quite different organizations. And not until October 23 did Mr. Nixon reluctantly reveal what lists he was using. Only then, on the very eve of the election, could we analyze those votes for the information of the district.

There were nineteen duplications in the four lists. So the actual number of votes on which I was "condemned" was 27, not 46.

Here is what those votes were about.

I had voted FOR continuing the Reciprocal Trade Agreements, a wartime loan to Britain, abolition of the poll tax, establishment of the school lunch program, unemployment insurance for federal workers, travel pay for war workers compelled to move their homes, separation of the Reconstruction Finance Corporation from the Department of Commerce, the abolition of certain price subsidies, and the imposing of ceilings on the cost of homes sold to returning veterans. *All these I had voted for.*

I had also voted *for* the Hobbs Anti-racketeering bill which included labor leaders in its provisions and which the CIO-PAC bitterly opposed.

I had voted AGAINST a "gag" rule which prevented amendment of an important bill, denial of relief to people in countries not having a free press, deferment of all farm workers from the draft, dismantling of the employment service at war's end, making the Un-American Activities Committee a permanent committee, giving away federal rights to tidelands oil a poorly drawn bill attempting to regulate labor's right to strike, a motion to kill the bill for control of atomic energy development, a bill to exempt insurance companies from antitrust laws, the freezing of social security taxes, and a number of amendments that I thought would make the price control program ineffective. *All these I had voted against.*

In most cases I had voted with a majority of the House of Representatives. And whatever anyone's judgment might have been as to whether I was right or wrong in my votes, to call them "Communistic" or to say I had followed a PAC "line," was clearly an arrant deception of the voters and a tactic unworthy of a responsible politician.

But Mr. Nixon had to win. And he did—by 15,000 votes.

He might even have beaten me fairly, given all the circumstances of 1946, with the simple appeal that it was time to change parties in power—a slogan he did in fact use. But he and Mr. Chotiner decided to use these other tactics. As I contemplated my defeat, I was heartened to receive a telegram from a conservative Republican who had served with me in the House. It went a long way to compensate for all that Mr. Nixon had done and said. That wire read:

OFF THE RECORD I AM TERRIBLY SORRY YOU ARE NOT GOING TO BE WITH US IN THE 80TH CONGRESS. WE NEED MEN BADLY IN THE HOUSE WITH YOUR INTELLIGENCE AND SPIRIT.

I thought this answered Mr. Nixon's charges pretty well. Some ten years later, in a biography of Mr. Nixon, he was quoted as having said, "Communism was not an issue at any time in the 1946 campaign. Few people knew about Communism then, and even fewer cared."

2. THEY HAVE TO BE SUBVERSIVE

Ninety-six percent of the 6,926 Communists, fellow travellers, sex perverts, people with criminal records, dope addicts, drunks, and other security risks removed under the Eisenhower security program were hired by the Truman Administration.
—Richard M. Nixon, Denver, Colorado
November 1, 1954

Actually I had comparatively little to complain about. What Mr. Nixon and Mr. Chotiner tried to do to me was mild compared to the treatment accorded later opponents.

Their tactics had been successful in 1946. Why not use those same tactics in 1950 and 1952 and in years to follow?

Mr. Nixon was re-elected to Congress in 1948, partly at least because he succeeded in representing himself as a Democrat to Democrats of the district. Postcards bearing Nixon's picture were mailed to thousands of Democrats. They bore the salutation "Dear fellow Democrat" and urged the recipient to "re-elect Congressman Nixon." The Republican-owned newspapers—meaning every major paper in the 12th district —strangely and obediently failed during the primary campaign to mention that their candidate was a Republican. As a result Mr. Nixon was nominated not only in the Republican, but in the Democratic primary as well.

17

Here we find our first important evidence of a developing source of political strength—a wondrous flexibility. Richard Milhous Nixon could even be—albeit very temporarily—a "member" of the party he made a practice of accusing of action highly detrimental to the nation, if not actually subversive.

Then came the campaign of 1950.

In 1950 the Republican committee chose Mr. Nixon as the candidate for the Senate to fill the place being vacated by Senator Sheridan Downey.

His opponent was Helen Gahagan Douglas, who then represented the 14th California district in the House of Representatives. Mrs. Douglas had, during her service in the House, supported progressive legislation. She had written a record that was as genuinely anti-Communist as that of any House member. While Communists inveighed against such measures, she supported the Marshall Plan, the Point IV program, Reciprocal Trade Agreements, and aid to Korea.

But since the trick with respect to Jerry Voorhis' voting record had worked so well in 1946, it was tried again even more extensively in 1950. A "pink sheet"—that color seeming appropriate—was published and given state-wide circulation; it purported to show that out of some 350 votes cast by Mrs. Douglas, she had voted many times in the same manner as Vito Marcantonio, a New York City representative with actual Communist leanings. Needless to say, the "pink sheet" failed to note that, on occasion, Mr. Nixon had done the same thing. For example, he and Marcantonio voted together against economic aid to Korea and for a 50 per cent cut in aid to Western Europe, with Mrs. Douglas in both cases on the other side. The truth was not told that in almost all cases the votes of Mrs. Douglas were on issues where substantial majorities of House members, including some Republicans and sometimes Mr. Nixon himself, had voted as Mrs. Douglas did. Guilt by association was at work again—and with a vengeance.

Mrs. Douglas simply *had* to be "subversive," else why would she run against Richard Nixon? He was fresh from his triumph over Alger Hiss, a publicity gold mine which was to stand him in good stead for years to come. Had Nixon not, as a member of the Un-American Activities Committee, stolen every headline from his fellow members of that committee? Had he not, with the indispensable aid of ex-Communist Whitaker Chambers, unearthed evidence about Hiss which was to lead to his conviction for perjury—but not, be it noted, for treason.

So why should anyone presume to run against Richard Nixon?

There may have been times when Helen Douglas wished she hadn't. Such as the occasion when young Nixon supporters sprayed her face and dress with red ink just before a speech to a college audience.

An interesting sidelight on the Nixon campaign, as detailed by *Reporter Magazine*, was that a Mr. Case, representing Chiang Kai-shek's Bank of China (the Taiwan one), directed the Independent Voters for Nixon in 1950.

Nixon was again elected in 1950 and became a Senator.

He served a profitable two years in the United States Senate. To help him along, some of the biggest names in California industry collected a special fund for his use. It was variously estimated at $18,000 to $29,000. For a while there was indignation in the land over this. It did seem difficult for a Senator receiving such generous gifts from such well-heeled friends to forget all about them when he cast his votes.

Campaign contributions were one thing. There was enough chance for those with great wealth to make candidates feel beholden to them by acceptance of large campaign gifts. But for those who could afford it to, in effect, support "their" Senator financially after he was safely in office seemed to many people a questionable practice, to say the least.

But they had not reckoned with one of Mr. Chotiner's main devices—the whimper.

And Richard Milhous Nixon won the championship in that field—hands down. He won it over nationwide television with his famous "Checkers" speech. What Mr. Nixon did in that speech was to recite his life history, to tell of the struggles he had had, to say his wife had only a cloth coat and to say that he had used the fund for political rather than personal expenses. He succeeded brilliantly in arousing the sympathy of millions of people.

And he followed up in speech after speech by charging that "Communists and crooks" had been "smearing" him about the fund. Who else indeed would question Mr. Nixon?

True there were some convenient omissions from the "Checkers" speech. Had the entire story been told there would have been less appeal for sympathy for the poor and righteous lad, persecuted by subversive forces, and struggling out of his poverty toward the vice-presidency. Nothing was said of the fact that in his very first campaign ample funds had been provided, the district saturated with bill boards, five or six campaign workers paid $500 a month each, or a top-flight public relations firm hired for an undisclosed sum. Campaign expenditure in California Congressional districts in the Thirties and Forties seldom exceeded $10,000, even on the part of well-to-do candidates. The financial records have been destroyed, but Mr. Nixon's campaign manager and treasurer have both estimated that some $32,000 to $35,000 were spent on his behalf. Pretty good for a "poor" boy! And even better was the rather ample amount of money provided to Richard Nixon for his campaign for the Senate in 1950. This sum was estimated at $1,600,000. No one, of course, kept track so no one knew exactly.

The "Checkers" speech was an important milestone. For Richard Nixon was at the time a candidate for the vice-presidency. This nomination had been won at the expense of Earl Warren, popular and efficient Governor of California to whom the state's delegation was pledged to vote. But Mr. Nixon had conducted a private poll of California voters at taxpayers' expense using his convenient franking privilege, and had "reluctantly" let it be known that the poll results favored General Eisenhower over Governor Warren. Thus armed, Nixon and friends had persuaded a considerable number of California delegates to desert Warren and support Eisenhower. Under these circumstances what more logical choice for a vice-presidential candidate could the General make than Richard Milhous Nixon?

True to form, he was elected. And so was the well-beloved "Ike."

Again true to form the Nixon campaign was conducted against forces of "subversion" if not outright "treasonable conduct" on the part of the Truman Administration, whose successor Illinois Governor Adlai Stevenson sought to be.

Dean Acheson, then Secretary of State and probably the most virulent opponent of Communism ever to hold that position, was characterized by Nixon as follows: "Dean Acheson has a form of color blindness—a form of pink eye—toward the Communist threat in the United States." The exemplary Adlai Stevenson fared even worse. Of him the Republican candidate for vice-president declared "Mr. Stevenson has a degree all right—a Ph.D. from the Acheson College of Cowardly Communist Containment."

Regarding China, Mr. Nixon referred to "Dean Acheson's spineless school of diplomacy which cost the free world 600 million former allies in the past seven years of Trumanism."

This was the same Richard M. Nixon who, in 1971 speaking as President of the United States, made dramatic announcement on nationwide television that he would shortly visit the leaders of Communist China for the purpose of "normalizing relations with that country . . . in the cause of peace."

It is, however, too bad that Mr. Nixon did not realize some years earlier the wisdom of flexibility with respect to the Chinese de facto government. For during the struggle between Chiang Kai-shek and Mao for control of China there were two foreign service officers—old "China hands"—in that country who pointed out Chiang's corruption and urged that the revolutionary forces be given a hearing by the United States. Had the counsel of these two men, John Stewart Service and John Paton Davies, been heeded, history might have been different; the rift in the Communist world might have become much wider, even, than it is; and relations between the United States and China might have been "normalized" many years ago.

Instead they were charged with something approaching treason in the early 1950s and drummed out of the State Department in disgrace. They were among the people to whom Mr. Nixon referred in a speech in Denver on November 1, 1954 in these words:

Ninety-six percent of the 6,926 Communists, fellow travellers, sex perverts, people with criminal records, dope addicts, drunks, and other security risks removed under the Eisenhower security program were hired by the Truman Administration.

Today Service and Davies are completely exonerated and asked to give guidance to Congressional Committees.

But in the heyday of "McCarthyism" it was a different story.

And Richard Nixon was, next only to Senator Joseph McCarthy himself, the prime writer of that story.

For example: "The Eisenhower Administration has kicked out the Communists, and security risks, not by the hundreds but by the thousands," declaimed Mr. Nixon in the 1954 campaign. And again: "There is nothing the Communists would like better than a return to the Truman loyalty program under which Communist agents were cleared and hired."

How anyone could interpret those words other than as an accusation that the Administration of President Truman had *deliberately* hired Communists for government positions, it is

21

hard to understand. That such was not the case every reasonable person knows full well. It was Harry Truman who met the Communist threat to Korea head-on and who inaugurated the policy of defense of Greece and Turkey against threats from the Soviet Union.

But Richard Nixon's oratory, along with the unproved accusations against thousands of people by Senator McCarthy, was "good politics" in the 1950s. It enabled Republicans to defeat, for example, the arch-conservative Millard Tydings in Maryland by publishing widely a contrived photograph of Senator Tydings "talking" with Earl Browder, secretary of the Communist Party. The fact that those two men had never met each other in all their lives was of no consequence. Winning elections was the "game plan" then as now. These same tactics even enabled the Republican candidate to unseat Senator Scott Lucas, past commander of the Illinois American Legion, in the election of 1950.

President Eisenhower was deeply concerned about the excesses of Senator McCarthy's investigations. But his vice-president, Mr. Nixon, stumped Wisconsin for McCarthy's reelection in 1952.

Eventually, of course, the nation had had its fill of these efforts to tear it apart. Conscientious conservatives took the lead. Senator Watkins of Utah introduced the resolution for the censure of McCarthy and the Senate passed it by an overwhelming majority on December 2, 1954.

But, strangely, little of this rubbed off on the vice-president. Guilt by association seems to work only against those concerned for the welfare of the people whose needs are greatest.

Actually the Senate's censure of McCarthy was a victory for President Eisenhower, who had become more and more opposed to McCarthy's broad-axe character assassination. But "Ike's" own vice-president did not say that his chief had won an important moral victory for the cause of decent government. Instead, in a press conference in Denver, Mr. Nixon simply remarked that "Our political history shows that when an individual takes on the top man and wins, he (the individual) grows. But when you make a frontal assault, if you lose you are through. That is what happened on this issue."

Whereupon the *Sacramento Bee* commented:

Nowhere in Nixon's talk was there any suggestion of indignation over McCarthyism, no rebuke to that craven, brutal era char-

22

acterized by such odious excesses as anonymous telephone calls to defame political opponents with lying charges of communism. . . . There was little policy and no principle in Nixon's words but there were displayed infinite adaptability and caution, qualities which may carry the young man far if all there is to American politics is smart jockeying for power and preferment.

The *Bee* was, obviously, far more prophetic than it could then have known.

Came the campaign of 1956 with Nixon again running as Eisenhower's vice-president. It was as important as ever to win. But there was a difference now. President Eisenhower was prevented by the recently passed constitutional amendment from running again in 1960. And who might be his most logical successor but his vice-president? And there was indeed some question whether the same tactics that had thus far elected Mr. Nixon to Congress, the Senate and the vice-presidency would prove acceptable in a campaign for the nation's highest office.

So some of the roughest of the Chotiner tactics were being softened this time.

But there was a good deal left. If Adlai Stevenson was not accused this time of belonging to the "school of cowardly Communist containment" nonetheless the implication was still there. For in speech after speech Mr. Nixon urged his audience not to "settle for second best leadership of expedient politicians who offer false hopes of ending the draft and restricting military research—all in the face of Communism."

Some 12 years later, it was Mr. Nixon who appealed for votes on the ground that he was for ending the draft and having a volunteer army instead. Only to change his mind completely about the matter once he had been safely elected.

It had been 4 years since Harry Truman had stepped down from the Presidency. But in 1956 he was still the principal target of the Nixon oratory. Referring to Stevenson, Nixon said: "Anyone who puts his arm around Harry Truman shouldn't be talking about anybody else taking the low road."

What was it then that strangely changed Mr. Nixon's feeling about Mr. Truman? Something must have. For one of the first acts of Richard Milhous Nixon as President of the United States was to ask Congress to pass a bill increasing the pension of ex-presidents from $25,000 to $60,000. He asked this for the sake of poor Mr. Truman who was then in his middle eighties. That someone else—a much, much younger man whose middle name was Milhous—would one day be an ex-president, of course, never entered Mr. Nixon's mind!

In 1968, when Richard Milhous Nixon had been elected President of the United States and had overcome all his "subversive" opponents, it was logical to expect that he might turn his back on the very tactics that had brought him to that eminence.

But such was not the case. The Democrats still controlled the Congress. Something had to be done about that. There were still victories that *had* to be won and as the Congressional elections of 1970 approached, plans were made to that end. Murray Chotiner was by this time a Presidential advisor with an office in the White House itself, having been advanced through a number of sinecure jobs by executive orders and appointments. Some place along the way it must have been decided that the "soft on Communism" accusation was becoming slightly thread-bare and that a variation of that means of discrediting opponents was called for.

The new variation was not far to seek. Young people, deeply concerned over the indefensible war in Vietnam and the corresponding neglect of home problems were protesting—sometimes violently. Crime rates were rising at an alarming rate. A quarter of a million people had marched for peace in the nation's capital and, with obvious relish, Attorney General Mitchell had found one instance of violence in that long and otherwise entirely orderly day. Many older people were unable to understand the new life styles of the young and some were fearful of them. The generation gap was widening. The Ohio National Guard had shot and killed four students at Kent State University and sheriff's deputies had done the same with students at Jackson State, causing Mr. Nixon to remark that, when students threaten, this is what you have to expect.

In these circumstances an unbiased observer might have expected the President of the United States to do what he could to mitigate the tension, to remove the causes of discontent and protest, and to pull the country closer together.

Strangely, such an idea seems not to have entered the Presidential head. It would have been a gross violation, anyway, of every Chotiner political "principle." For it would not have been an attack. Instead, in this national distress was found the very stuff of the 1970 campaign. The particular form of "subversion" would be "soft on violence." Opponents of Mr. Nixon's generally hand-picked Republican candidates were to

24

be branded as "permissive," "soft on violence," enemies indeed of "law and order." And that "great silent—and affluent—majority" was to be made as fearful as possible of the young, the poor, and the minorities.

Mr. Nixon's Attorney General—and law partner—started the ball rolling in an interview with *Woman's Day* in which he declared that the "ignorant bastards" who taught in and administered our schools and colleges were the cause of all the nation's troubles. And that truly great and wise woman, his wife, echoed his sentiments in even stronger terms a few days later.

Vice President Agnew urged crowds of hearers to "vote Republican to show your patriotism"—thus making it "perfectly clear" that any vote for candidates other than Republicans would be an unpatriotic, hence a "subversive" vote.

Nor was Mr. Chotiner exactly silent. He was, after all, a full member of the President's personal White House staff. What was more, he was a principal advisor on strategy for the Republican Party as a whole. Perhaps his classic contribution to the 1970 campaign was his advice to the Republican opponent of Senator Edward Kennedy.

The Senator had been involved in the tragic accident where his automobile had plunged off a bridge into Chappaquiddick Creek and a young secretary had been drowned. The shadow of that accident hung over Senator Kennedy's campaign for re-election.

Chotiner's advice was as follows: "This is a classic case where the Republican candidate should say over and over again that he will not make Chappaquiddick an issue in the campaign. If he says this enough times, I think the voters of Massachusetts will understand all about Chappaquiddick."

Most presidents of the United States, out of respect for their office if not for themselves, have refrained from active or ostensible campaigning in off-year elections when they themselves were not candidates.

But in the strange case of Richard Milhous Nixon this was not to be the case. He plunged with all his well modulated invective into the most basic—not, of course, to say "low"—levels of campaigning. Nor were Democrats alone his targets. In New York and Virginia he supported candidates of third-party and ultra-conservative persuasion, against Republican candidates for the Senate. He was, quite frankly, out to get a Congress "ideologically" in tune with his own ideas.

In his own words, delivered on the steps of the Ohio State Capitol, this was the way to get that kind of Congress. Mr. Nixon said:

All over this country today we see a rising tide of terrorism, of crime, and on the campuses of our universities we have seen those who instead of engaging in peaceful dissent, engage in violence. It is time to draw the line and to say we are not going to stand for that. On November 3 in the quiet of the polling booth, consider the candidates. And if that candidate has given encouragement to, has condoned lawlessness and violence and permissiveness, then you know what to do.

Just what candidates had, in fact, condoned lawlessness and violence was not made clear. Probably because no candidate, or decent citizen for that matter, had or would be foolish or irresponsible enough to do so. But the implication was clear enough. Quite obviously Mr. Nixon, the President of the United States, was not referring to the candidates he was supporting but to those who dared to oppose them.

Wrote James Reston in the *New York Times* for October 28, 1970:

No amount of public indifference to the dirty tricks of politics can remove the plain fact of this campaign: Mr. Nixon has not treated the American people in this election as they need to be treated and deserve to be treated in this troubled time. They are profoundly anxious about the moral and economic problems of the period, but he has not helped them put these problems in perspective. He has not dealt with them responsibly or nobly, but narrowly and cleverly. . . .

He is both the President and the leader of his party, but he has confused and reversed the proper priorities of his two jobs, using the majesty and trappings of the Presidency as if he were back running a cheap-jack Murray Chotiner campaign against Jerry Voorhis.

In short, he is asking for the trust of the people, but he is not trusting them to deal seriously and responsibly with the staggering problems that affect their lives. Instead, he is using their anxieties for partisan gain, and arguing the preposterous proposition that the moral confusions of the age are somehow a party issue, and that human frailty, human violence, selfishness, war, crime, drugs and smut are somehow the fault of the Democratic Party and can be minimized by the election of Republicans.

All of this seemed in the best of Chotiner tradition and almost sure, once more, to prevail on election day. For who, after all, was *for* violence and against civil peace? Certainly not a majority of the nation. Certainly not more than a misguided, irresponsible few.

There was, however, one problem. For this tactic and these accusations of the new brand of "subversion" to be successful there had to be violence as a backdrop. There had to be clear and present danger to the safety of the Republic. And if there could be instances where the defenders of law, order, and non-permissiveness—above all Richard Milhous Nixon himself—were the objects of acts of violence, then the election should be "in the bag."

The problem was a disappointing absence of violence—especially on the campuses. Things were quiet there. Such protests as did take place were orderly. Windows were no longer being smashed on downtown streets as had previously—and inexcusably and very foolishly—sometimes been the case.

At some of the presidential speeches there were hecklers at whom Mr. Nixon could point as horrible examples of the kind of dangerous persons against whom he was crusading. At one outdoor meeting in Burlington, Vermont, a rock was thrown in the general direction of the platform where Mr. Nixon was speaking. Whereupon an aide is reported to have observed that "every rock is worth 10,000 votes."

But this was not always the case. On the occasion of the President's speech in Columbus his rhetoric was blunted by the fact that only one small boy in the entire crowd seemed to pose any conceivable threat to the presidential dignity. He held up, briefly, a home-made sign which likened Mr. Nixon's remarks to a substance found in barnyards and pastures. He was quickly ejected and his sign destroyed.

This was not enough. And it began to be observed that the crowds which heard Mr. Nixon had a certain number of long-haired youths who were always present and boisterous. Cartoons appeared showing the President behind a microphone shouting "I need four volunteers—two to holler obscenities and two to throw rocks." At one very closely guarded meeting in Orange County, California, citadel of the John Birch Society, newsmen observed that the guardsmen and special police deliberately admitted an apparently pre-determined number of rather obvious protestors before enforcing an order that only the closely cropped and well-dressed were to be admitted into the audience.

An appropriate climax seemed to take place in San Jose, California, where missiles of various kinds were actually thrown at the presidential bullet-proof limousine in response to his having stood up and given, almost surely in derision, the peace sign. At last the President had been attacked. Resentment, naturally, ran high among many people. But there were disturbing factors. The San Jose chief of police, who was the responsible official, let it be known that the route of the Nixon procession had been changed without notice to him and that the trouble had occurred in the unscheduled part of the route.

This suggested at least that . . .

But the suggestion was overwhelmed by the statewide distribution of leaflets by Republican Senatorial candidate George Murphy, which read as follows: "Anarchy or law and order? Senator George Murphy has supported every law and order bill. Representative John Tunney has not. It's that simple."

Mr. Nixon's election-eve television speech was an unrestrained polemic against the forces of crime and violence which had shown their ugly heads in San Jose and which, in the absence of Republican victory, would surely tear at the vitals of the nation itself.

Unfortunately for the presidential strategy, Senator Muskie followed Mr. Nixon on television that night with a quiet affirmation of equal dedication to civil peace plus a concern for the underlying problems that lay at the root of the national distress.

The contrast was a dramatic one.

On election day, 1970, the voters of the nation reaffirmed their confidence in the institutions of democracy and in their own ability to deal with the nation's problems. They refused to panic. They did not "buy" the Chotiner message. With three or four exceptions, major races were won by the very candidates who had been accused of being "soft on violence" —which the average voter simply knew they were not. Tunney beat Murphy by 600,000 votes.

For a time after the 1970 election, even Mr. Agnew was silent. And the voice from the White House spoke in a different tone. Whether from a change of conviction or as a result of the election outcome only future events could determine.

An indeterminate amount of damage had been done, however, both to the dignity of the office of President of the United States and to the hope for unity among the people. The scars of the 1970 campaign were not of the kind that could quickly heal.

Nor, as the time for the 1972 campaign approached, was

there much evidence that Chotinerism had suffered any permanent disability as a result of the 1970 elections.

In the light of all this, it is sobering to recall what the *New York Times'* James Reston, with prophetic insight, wrote during the 1968 presidential campaign won by Mr. Nixon.

BASIC PROBLEMS REMAIN

How much order will we have between the races if Nixon as President does not see that the school desegregation law is enforced?

How much order will we have in the cities if we go on with the same gulf between the rich and the poor, the same unequal tax laws and inadequate police budgets, and the same moral indifference to private and commercial cheating?

How much order in the world if we have another expensive round in the missle and nuclear races?

Nixon's weakness as a President is that—with the exception of George Wallace—he starts with the least trust among the young, the Negroes and the Soviets.

Candidates, of course, often change as Presidents. Nevertheless, Nixon is dealing with the effects of lawlessness and disorder, but not with the causes, and, if he follows the policies he is proposing in the campaign, the nation could easily come out in the end with less law and order than we have now.

Do we have more or less "law and order" in the land than we had in 1968? Have the causes of lawlessness and disorder, of crime, poverty and social conflict been dealt with? Is the United States in fact a healthier nation in the broad sense of social as well as physical health than it was when Mr. Nixon took office? Or is the reverse true?

As we try to answer these questions as honestly as we can, remember that we live in times of ultimate crisis and danger for all mankind, that they are times when man possesses the means of his own instant annihilation, that they are times when nothing less than great moral leadership has much chance to bring us through. Let it be remembered also that the so-called "issue" between an orderly, law-abiding society, and one plagued with crime and social conflict is an utterly false issue as between political parties or political candidates. No one with a grain of sense or a scintilla of concern for his own

29

future, let alone that of society, favors crime, lawlessness or violence.

The only legitimate issue is how, by what means and where applied, to move most effectively to cure the ills that now beset our nation.

And deep seated ills they are. Neither rhetoric on television, nor well-orchestrated news releases, nor dramatically changed "game plans" will cure them.

For the people to whom the "issue" of civil peace and safety and freedom from fear truly belongs are the people of the barrios and the inner cities, not those of the affluent suburbs. And it is there, in the barrios and the core cities and the decaying rural areas, that the remedies must come if they are to be effective.

It is in this light that the Nixon record must be judged.

3. THE SLOW DEATH OF RURAL AMERICA

> I have always found when I have spoken to agricultural audiences as farm families, farm audiences, and the rest that they are, of course, very, very close to the soil.
> —Richard M. Nixon, Washington, D. C.
> May 7, 1971

The heritage of rural American culture is a priceless and irreplaceable one.

Tragically, in the years that followed World War II, that heritage began to dim. The number of farms and the number of people employed in agriculture began to decline—at times drastically. Whereas before the war there had been some six million farms in the nation, by the 1970s there were barely three million. The percentage of farm and rural people in the population decreased correspondingly. There were many factors that drove farm families off the land and forced them into overcrowded cities—sometimes to swell the ranks of the unemployed. Basic to all of these was the cost-price squeeze—low prices received by a still highly competitive agriculture and high costs dictated by increasingly monopolized industries and agencies with which farmers had to deal. The ever-increasing application of new technology to farm production meant the need for greater and greater amounts of capital and, in the case of some crops, the need also for larger acreage per farm. Smaller farmers unable to command the needed capital or to acquire added acreage were forced out of business. The escalation of interest rates in the late 1960s hurt still more.

Most sinister of all was the invasion of farming by large industrial corporations and conglomerates as well as by wealthy individuals seeking tax losses through "hobby" farming. In some places such as Kern County, California, corporation farming, much like the collective agriculture of Russia, had already forced almost every individual farm off the land. There was hardly a genuine rural community in the county.

In 1960 there were 108,000 farms in California averaging 359 acres each. By 1971 there were only 56,000 farms, averaging 654 acres. The U.S. Department of Agriculture admitted that in 1970 just 45 corporations owned 61 percent of California's prime agricultural land.

The independent farmer was not being pushed off the land because he was less efficient than the corporate collectives. Studies by the Federal Reserve Bank of Kansas City, land grant colleges, and others showed repeatedly that *other factors being equal* the owner-operated farm could out-produce the corporation on the same acreage of land. The "small" farmer cares far more what happens to the land. He uses less water, pesticides and fertilizer per acre than do his corporate competitors. And he puts more nutrients back into the soil.

The trouble is that other factors are not equal. The corporations are favored by huge government subsidies, by tax advantages, by their leverage in the market-place, and by their access to vast amounts of capital. On the other hand the individual farmers' market bargaining power is approximately zero.

To some of these handicaps the independent farmer has an answer—if he applies it broadly and intensively enough. That answer is cooperation. Particularly in the Middle West where farmer-owned cooperative businesses produce, process, refine, and deliver to the farm every important input the farmer needs except machinery. Marketing cooperatives can, grown large enough and sufficiently integrated toward the consumer markets, make the independent farmer almost the equal of the corporation in the market-place. Electric cooperatives not only give the farmer ownership of an important business but keep the costs of his electric power within bounds. And the cooperative Farm Credit institutions have put an end to the worst abuses that once were the hallmark of agricultural financing.

Against the conditions he faced in the late Sixties and early Seventies, the independent farmer would have been in sad shape indeed had it not been for such protection as his marketing, supply, electric and financial cooperatives afforded.

Long-standing government price support and soil conservation programs were in effect, and they too helped to stem the tide. Without them, typically American agriculture would have been at the mercy of industrial monopoly and the drift to the cities a mass migration.

The school lunch, school milk, and food stamp programs helped to expand the market for the abundance which American farmers, by the very nature of their operations, always produce.

Mr. Nixon did very well in the Middle Western farm states and on the Great Plains when he won the election as President in 1968.

In his campaign he repeatedly declared that a parity price index of 74 was "intolerable" and that under his administration farmers would fare much better.

It was logical to expect that Mr. Nixon, devoted as he professed to be to basic American institutions and ideals, would do everything in his power in defense of the independent farm and the American pattern of agriculture.

Such, however, did not turn out to be the case. Instead the Administration's basic policy has been to reduce farmers' dependence on government programs by decreasing if not eliminating price supports and thus casting farmers adrift to make their own way as best they can in what is allegedly a "free market." This might not have been such a disastrous policy from the farmers' point of view had there been—then or now —anything approaching a "free market" on the other side of the farm fence. But farm prices, except where somewhat protected by marketing cooperatives, are subject to competitive market manipulation; and the abundance produced by farmers becomes the cause of disastrously low prices. On the other hand the rest of the economy, and particularly those segments of it with which farmers must deal when they buy or when they sell, is more and more controlled by monopolistic power. One striking evidence of this is the fact that prices paid by consumers for food go right on up, even when prices received by farmers are going down. Farmers' cooperatives are not yet sufficiently integrated vertically to enable them to deal directly with consumer markets. Consequently, the policy of the Nixon Administration has been one under which only the biggest and best capitalized farm plants could expect to live. It has favored, furthermore, the biggest of the big, namely, the corporation farms.

During the years of the Nixon price inflation almost the only group in the nation except the very poor whose income in current dollars did not substantially increase was the farmers. Meanwhile their costs zoomed upward with the general inflation.

On the average, incomes received by farmers are barely half as much as the national average.

In the single month of August, 1970, farm prices dropped by three percent—largest monthly decline in 22 years. Since costs continued to rise, the parity ratio went down to 71, lowest level since 1933!

Lights in farm houses all over the nation were going out. Every time this happened precious values inherent in the family farm experience were being lost. So was the economic independence of another family—as they moved into overcrowded cities to look for work that was not there.

The bulletin of the Farm Credit Administration for September, 1971, noted that 1970 had recorded the highest number of farm foreclosures in many years. This was apparently "according to plan," since the Nixon Council of Economic Advisors had openly advised the policy of reducing farm income in order to force "the surplus resources of agriculture, primarily human, off the land."

This policy had succeeded all too well. So much so that in the fall of 1970 the Field Foundation made a grant of $75,000 to three public interest groups for a study of 18,000 big corporation farms. This was sparked by the fact that these huge feudal estates were by then making sales totaling $4.5 billion per year. That was one-fourth as much as all the marketing of all the farmers' cooperatives in the country.

The Administration's so-called "farm bill" in 1970 called for empowering the Secretary of Agriculture to fix loan and price support levels at anywhere from 0 to 90 percent of parity. This would have allowed the Secretary to abolish price supports altogether.

Congress tried to correct the situation. The Senate Agriculture Committee approved a bill in the summer of 1970 that would have recognized the parity principle and set floors under the price protection levels for wheat, cotton and feed grains. But Secretary Hardin wrote the committee that this was not acceptable to the Administration. A weak compromise bill was the result.

Despite President Nixon's repeated assertions that he proposed to end hunger in America, his Administration tried repeatedly to kill completely the school milk program which had been established many years before.

The first such attempt came in the summer of 1970, in a proposal to cut off funds for the children's milk as a means of helping to balance the budget.

Congress responded with vigor. Led by Republican Senator George Aiken of Vermont and Democrat William Proxmire of Wisconsin, both houses passed a bill making the school milk program permanent and mandatory on the Agriculture Department. $120 million was authorized and subsequently appropriated for the program. President Nixon refused to sign the bill. It became law without his signature.

Exceeding its authority under any reasonable interpretation of the Constitution, the President's Office of Management and Budget froze $16 million of the appropriation.

Whereupon Secretary Hardin arose in a meeting of dairy farmers and dramatically announced that "the Nixon Administration" (sic!) had provided $104 million for the continuation of the school milk program.

Nine months later, under even more strange circumstances, somewhat the same drama was enacted. We will come to that.

The election results of November, 1970, must have been something of a shock to Mr. Nixon and his Administration. For the very farm states which had supported him for the presidency in 1968 turned generally to the Democrats in 1970. For example, not a single Republican governor in the states of the Great Plains survived that election.

So according to one of two unbreakable "principles" among Mr. Nixon's otherwise flexible ones, something had to be done. For Mr. Nixon *had* to win again in 1972, else the times would be completely out of joint.

In December, 1970, the parity index had fallen to 67, lowest point in thirty-seven years. Consequently it seemed wise to do something about that. Not that farm income was to be raised or support prices boosted; rather that the parity index should be made to look better.

This was, indeed, a simple operation. Without a scintilla of improvement in the condition of American agriculture, the Nixon Administration simply changed the base on which parity was calculated! By selecting a period of very low farm income as the base and proclaiming the new "instant formula," the Administration simply informed American farmers that their parity index had zoomed from 67 to 93—overnight. Whether this sort of arithmetical magic impressed very many farmers was a matter of doubt. The Nebraska Legislature, disregarding the new parity formula, passed unanimously a resolution calling on the President to set farm price supports at 90 percent of the old parity, based on the relation of farm to other income in 1910-14. That formula had been in effect for decades, until the Nixon trickery changed it.

Needless to say, there was no response to the Nebraska resolution. Perhaps the fact that Mr. Nixon had carried Nebraska by almost 2 to 1 in 1968 made his political advisors believe that the state could be taken for granted in the Nixon column in 1972.

Meanwhile in the months of March 1971, two very interesting events had taken place.

The first of these was a second attempt by the Administration to kill the school milk program. This, despite the fact that the Department of Agriculture itself admitted that the school milk program provided the only milk which thousands of children in low-income families ever received.

Again it was the Congress that blocked this "humanitarian" move by the Nixon Administration. One hundred members of Congress signed a letter to the Chairman of the sub-committee on Agriculture of the House Appropriation Committee urging that the school milk program be funded by Congress, despite refusal of the Administration to request any money for it. Congressman Whitten, Democrat of Mississippi, responded with vigor that this would be done. And it was.

The second attempt in less than a year's time to kill the school milk program seemed difficult to understand. Except for the sharp action of Congress, the market for fluid milk would have received a severe blow, thus hurting the dairy farmers as well as the children.

Other events were taking place in this same month of March which were aimed at assuring Mr. Nixon of dairy farmer votes in 1972. As reported by the *Wall Street Journal*, the *Madison* (Wisconsin) *Capitol Times*, the *Minneapolis Tribune*, and the *Los Angeles Times*, here is the story:

On March 11, 1971 the Secretary of Agriculture, Mr. Hardin, announced that the price support figure for manufacturing milk was to be $4.60 per hundredweight in the coming year. This was the same figure that had prevailed during the preceding year. The Secretary gave his reasons. A higher price, he said, would cause over-production and obligate the government to make huge purchases of milk which would pile up in government warehouses. His action was approved, formally by the President's Council of Economic Advisors and by the Office of Budget and Management, the President's own agency that watches government expenditures and programs.

On March 22 a subsidiary organization of American Milk Producers, Inc. with interlocking directors made five-figure donations for the 1972 campaign to four Republican money raising organizations. American Milk Producers, Inc. is a huge organization of milk producers in the South and Middle West.

On March 23 leaders of AMPI met privately with Mr. Nixon at the White House for several hours.

On March 24 several additional—and larger—contributions were made to Republican committees for Mr. Nixon's reelection from the dairy farmers' money.

On March 25 the Secretary of Agriculture announced that "he" had changed his mind and that the support price would be raised to $4.93 a hundredweight.

The only possible conclusion to be drawn from this rather amazing story was that the policies of the Nixon Administration were for sale and that the AMPI bought those policies with cold cash.

But this was not the whole cost to dairy farmers of their higher prices. A few weeks later AMPI spent an estimated $7 million of the farmers' money to pay all expenses for a crowd of 40,000 people to come to Chicago to hear Mr. Nixon make a speech to them. Presumably he sewed up several thousand votes for 1972 in that speech.

It may well be that dairy farmers should have had the higher price for milk. But it is sad commentary on political morality that they got their higher price in the way they did; especially when it came from an Administration that had twice tried to reduce their market for milk at the expenses of needy children.

The next chapter in this story represented some kind of poetic justice—or perhaps not-so-poetic injustice.

Early in 1972 Mr. Nixon's Justice Department brought an anti-trust suit against AMPI for monopolistic control of the price of milk.

The suit could not have been better timed.

The dairy farmers' money was securely in the hands of

the Nixon compaign committees. There was no way it could be returned.

So it was wise, politically, to show that, after all, the American Milk Producers, Inc. had not "bought" all they may have thought they did.

There can be not the slightest doubt that the one way in which American farmers can survive in the present-day economy without complete dependence upon government is through their ownership of their own off-the-farm businesses. That is to say marketing, supply, credit, electric, and other kinds of farmer-owned cooperative businesses.

Any administration which honestly desires to lessen farmers' dependence on government programs and still leave them able to farm will encourage cooperatives in every way it can.

In this connection it is important and fair to observe that the Farm Credit Act of 1971, a landmark piece of legislation to strengthen the cooperative Farm Credit System, was passed in Congress without opposition from the Nixon Administration. It did not have anything like vigorous support from the Administration. But at least it was not opposed.

On the other hand stands the record of Mr. Nixon's Administration with respect to rural electric cooperatives. Ever since the mid-thirties, these cooperatives have been the one means of keeping the cost of electricity at reasonable levels for farmers and rural people. They have "brought back home" to rural communities ownership of a part of the otherwise monopolized power business.

"Now "Power to the People" was the theme of Mr. Nixon's message wherein he appealed for his revenue-sharing proposal.

The rural electric cooperatives have brought some real power to six million rural families.

One would think that anyone sincerely concerned about "power to the people" would do everything possible to advance the progress of such worthy enterprises of the people.

But not so today.

The electric cooperatives must meet the needs of their member-customers. This means they must expand their supply of electric energy as the needs of their growing numbers of members expand.

This takes money—more money by far than the cooperatives can readily command, despite their dedicated effort to establish and capitalize their own financing agency.

Through decades the electric cooperatives have borrowed from the Rural Electrification Administration billions of dollars, and their record of repayment of those loans is one of the best in the history of American finance. This is one program that has not cost the American taxpayer anything.

Yet, Nixon's Administration policy has clearly been to make it as difficult as possible for the electric cooperatives to do their assigned job. With power use by rural consumers doubling every eight years it is obviously necessary for the cooperatives to "heavy-up" their lines, increase the capacity of their transformers and otherwise keep pace with the need.

But whereas some $800 million of urgent loan applications were expected in the fiscal year 1971-72, only $345 million of loan authorizations was included in the Administration's budget.

Furthermore the cooperatives have been compelled to operate on a one year—sometimes even a six months'—future planning schedule, instead of the two years formerly allowed. This increases expenses and hurts relations with contracting firms.

A policy of advancing loan funds, even those already committed, only in relationship to loan repayments coming in has been followed. This is a NO GROWTH policy if there ever was one.

The electric companies used to be certain that once REA made a commitment on a loan, the money would be available as needed. No longer is this the case.

Probably most serious of all has been the virtual embargo on loans for generation and transmission cooperatives. Whether deliberate or not on the part of the Administration, this means that the electric cooperatives lose their bargaining power when they must negotiate with profit-making utilities for power supplies. Without at least the possibility that they could do their own generating, the cooperatives are helpless bargainers and the result is that they are being compelled to pay higher and higher rates for wholesale power.

In early 1972 another interesting—and typical—game was being played.

Congress, recognizing the desperate need for substantial loan funds if the electric cooperatives are to live, authorized $545 million of loan funds for fiscal year 1971-72. This was less than needed but an increase of more than $200 million above the Administration's budget request.

But as the fiscal year passed it was found, not surprisingly, that Mr. Nixon's office of Management and Budget was releasing the funds provided by Congress not in proportion to the Congressional $545 million, but only in proportion to the Administration request of $329 million.

Seventy Congressmen wrote to President Nixon as follows:

> It is particularly disturbing to us that the $85 million appropriated for rural electric loans in the first quarter of this fiscal year was almost exactly one-fourth of the $329 million you requested for this purpose and did not even approach one-fourth of the amount actually authorized by Congress.
>
> If this rate of apportionment is continued through the year, the result will be to freeze virtually the entire $216 million by which Congress increased your budget requests for the rural electric loan program.

If the Nixon Administration could not squeeze down the electric cooperatives by inducing Congress to do so by law, then it was apparently going to do it by the unconstitutional device of freezing part of the money. There was always the hope that as November 1972 drew nearer, the President would release some of the frozen funds in a dramatic gesture that would make it appear that he, not Congress, had actually provided them.

This is exactly what happened. In January 1972, Secretary Butz announced that "because of the President's deep concern for the welfare of the rural electric cooperatives" about half of the frozen funds were then being released and that the other half would be released during the next fiscal year, beginning July 1, 1972. In other words, somewhat closer to election time than even the law allowed.

When President Nixon presented his budget for 1973, the cleverness—not to say deceptiveness—of his maneuver became evident. For he *said* he was budgeting $438 million for the rural electric cooperative loan fund in 1973. But of this, $107 million was to be the very $107 million withheld until after the end of fiscal year 1972 but appropriated by Congress for that prior year. All that Mr. Nixon really proposed of loan authorization for 1973 was $331 million. This compared to the clear need of well over $800 million if the cooperatives were to meet the most pressing needs of their members.

And what of the problem of hunger in a land where farmers suffer economically because of their abundant production? The basic phase of the battle against hunger, the school lunch program, was made a permanent program by an Act of Congress in 1946.

"The moment is at hand," declared Mr. Nixon, in May, 1969, "to put an end to hunger in America itself." And on Christmas of that year he pledged that no child would go hungry after Thanksgiving 1970.

Mr. Nixon's Department of Agriculture did use most of the money appropriated by Congress for the school lunch program, and it did increase the number of children benefitting from it. At least this was the Department's claim.

By the summer of 1971, the Department estimated that 8 million poor children would be receiving free or reduced-cost lunches.

It was still true, however, that there were more needy children outside the program than there were benefitting from it, despite a law passed by Congress in May 1970 which made mandatory the extension of the school lunch program to every school in the country.

For fiscal year 1971-72, Congress appropriated $33.8 million more for the children's lunches than the Administration requested.

But on August 13, 1971 the Department of Agriculture announced a drastic reduction in its contribution to the schools. Despite rising costs for food which was already causing problems in the schools, the Department proposed to provide only 35¢ for each free or reduced-price lunch as against the approximate 50¢ previously provided. This was defended as a measure of "fiscal discipline" and a means of relieving the budget deficit. However, at the very same time the Nixon Administration was requesting an increase of some $2 billion in the military appropriations.

The reaction of Congress was swift and decisive. Members heard from their schools to the effect that the new regulations would force the closing down of the entire school lunch program in many communities. Protests from all over the nation were sent to the USDA as well. Some protestors suggested that the Nixon Administration was proposing "revenue sharing in reverse."

The Senate met in emergency session and on October 1 passed by a vote of 75 to 5 a bill requiring the Secretary of Agriculture to assure a school lunch "for every needy child." The House did not need to act, for the Department of Agriculture rescinded its regulation and promised to provide 45¢ per lunch instead of 35¢.

The battle, however, was not over. For along with the correction in the amount of Federal payments went a new regulation from the Department limiting eligibility for free or reduced-cost lunches to children in families with incomes of less than $3,940. It was estimated that some 600,000 children would be eliminated from the program if this regulation stood.

Senator Talmadge of Georgia and Congressman Perkins of Kentucky, both Democrats, introduced legislation making mandatory a 46¢ Federal payment for each lunch and requiring the Department of Agriculture to restore to eligibility all children who would have been cut off by the $3,940 limitation order.

The Talmadge-Perkins bill was passed by the House 350 to 0, and by the Senate on a voice vote without a single "nay."

Mr. Nixon signed the bill into law.

Senator Humphrey of Minnesota, however, was not satisfied. He introduced a bill entitled "Universal School Lunch Program." He pointed out that if even a fraction of the waste constantly occurring in the procuring of military weapons were eliminated, the billions saved should be enough to finance a meal a day for every school child.

Not lost on Senator Humphrey or his listeners was the fact that a Universal School Lunch Program would expand the market for American farm products in the best conceivable way.

Destruction of the independent farms and farmers plus consequent over-urbanization killed the Roman Empire.

It could happen here.

To an extent, it already has.

In the fall of 1971, Senator Gaylord Nelson, Democrat of Wisconsin, held hearings on the growth of corporation farming in the United States. Witnesses gave unchallenged testimony to show that the poultry industry had fallen almost completely under corporate control with poultry farmers working, in effect, for wages for huge feed and supply companies. Greyhound Corporation was heavily in the turkey business, Dow Chemical in the business of growing and marketing lettuce, Boeing Aircraft in the potato business, and much of the fruit juice business controlled by Coca-Cola. Fifty-seven percent of American farms classified as "small" produced 7.8% of all farm sales while less than 1% of the largest farms produced 25%.

Senator Nelson commented that "Corporate farming not only has displaced farm families, but the corporate manager

41

often tries to by-pass local merchants to purchase machinery and materials directly from the manufacturer. The small businessman simply is unable to maintain a viable operation, and the demise of the small businessman together with out-immigration of farm families is destroying the social and economic structure of this country."

Alive to the situation, the Wisconsin state legislature in its 1971 session passed a law forbidding industrial corporations or conglomerates from owning farm land or carrying on farming operations. The Commissioner of Agriculture of neighboring Minnesota urged passage of a similar legislation in that state, logically pointing out that farm family corporations should be excluded from the prohibition. He said that 500 corporations were farming in Minnesota, only one-third of which were legitimate farm family corporations.

Senator Nelson and Congressman Abourezk, Democrat of South Dakota, introduced the "Family Farm Act of 1972," to prohibit any corporation or conglomerate from engaging directly or indirectly in farming or controlling agricultural production through ownership or leasing of land for agricultural purposes. As was to be expected, the Nixon Administration opposed this legislation on the strange ground that it might hurt farmers' cooperatives, none of which owned farm land or engaged in farm operations. Furthermore, farmers' cooperatives were in all cases specifically exempted from the prohibitions, as were farm family formed corporations. Logically so. For as Dr. Eric Thor, Administrator of the Farmer Cooperatives Service observed: "Cooperatives are the only thing that can preserve the owner-operated farm."

On July 7, 1971, Senators Humphrey of Minnesota and Talmadge of Georgia introduced the "Consolidated Farm and Rural Development Act." This was a well-conceived proposal, providing for a Rural Development Credit Bank through which both venture and mortgage capital would be provided for a broad spectrum of development projects in rural areas. The objective: To improve not only its economic vitality but also the quality of life in rural America. The bill was co-sponsored by a majority of the members of the Senate Committee on Agriculture and Forestry, including leading Republican members. It received immediate and enthusiastic support from all parts of the nation.

But when invited to present testimony on this legislation, the Nixon Administration refused to do so. A possible reason was that Mr. Nixon had advanced a proposal of his own based on his concept of revenue sharing, and that he regarded as "irrelevant" this attempt on the part of Congress to exercise its legislative function instead of simply obeying the wishes of the Executive. Senator Talmadge's office reported that Administration spokesmen were lobbying against his bill, along with banking interests.

It was not long before the answer came loud and clear. Having done all he could to kill the Talmadge-Humphrey bill, Mr. Nixon made another dramatic announcement. It came just a few days after his $25 billion deficit-budget message of January, 1972 had received its mixed, bewildered, and rather cool reception.

It called for a $1.3 billion program to consist primarily of revenue sharing and credit sharing with the states. It was not possible to find any item in the budget to implement the presidential proposal. So it had to be assumed, as Chairman Poage of the House Committee on Agriculture did, that what Mr. Nixon had in mind was taking money away from existing programs in order to "revenue share" with the states in financing his own package. The only other possibility was that the President's proposal was not even seriously proposed for 1973, but might be considered for 1974. It was a weak substitute for the comprehensive Humphrey-Talmadge measure. But it was Richard Nixon's!

It did get headlines. Which, after all, was the main consideration in an election year. But the life of the Nixon proposals was short and none too sweet. The House Committee on Agriculture voted it down by a decisive margin only a couple of weeks after the President announced it.

Instead the Agriculture Committee, by a vote of 32 to 4, approved a far more comprehensive bill of its own authorship. The Committee bill would broaden the lending operations of Farmers' Home Administration, and provide funds for rural development, community services improvement, and environmental protection. It passed the House with a substantial majority. In April the Senate passed similar legislation.

The Nixon Administration showed no concern over the feudalization of rural America through the growth of corporation farming. Just the opposite. By the autumn of 1971, prices of farm crops had sunk to levels which were in many cases below the cost of production. Corn was selling at 90¢ a bushel. For this and other reasons, dissatisfaction with Agriculture Secretary Hardin was rife in the farm states. Republican as well as Democratic Senators and Representatives from those states were "hearing from home" in no uncertain terms.

So it was decided by the White House that Secretary Hardin had to go. Accordingly, he resigned in November and promptly accepted the vice-presidency of Ralston-Purina Company, one of the largest feed and farm supply corporations in the nation, and one of the bitterest opponents of farmers' cooperatives.

There was a certain logic about this, for Mr. Nixon reached into the directorate of Ralston-Purina for Mr. Hardin's replacement. Apparently without consulting the Republican leaders in the Senate, the President named Earl Butz to be the new Secretary of Agriculture. He could hardly have found a more convincing way of reaffirming the complacency of himself and his Administration with existing trends in rural America.

For if anyone personified the biggest of big "agribusiness" it was Earl Butz. It was significant that to clear the way for his confirmation Butz had to resign not only his directorship of Ralston-Purina, but his place on the boards of such other "farmer-farming" enterprises as International Minerals and Chemical Corporation and Stokely-Van Camp (canning) Company.

Farm State Senators assailed Butz as "an agent for giant agribusiness corporations dedicated to driving farmers off the land." Said Senator Proxmire, "We need more than merely a caretaker who will oversee the final death of the family farm."

Butz' long-time advocacy of big-scale agriculture, his ridicule of the concern for protecting and conserving the environment, his near contempt for the small family-type farm were all a matter of clearly written and spoken record. Under his Secretaryship the trend toward corporation agriculture would certainly continue.

For the first time in long memory a number of farm organizations came out openly against Senate confirmation of Butz' appointment. The Farm Bureau representing as it does, especially in the South and Far West, the big farmer, come to his support. Despite the traditional practice of the Senate in giving the President whomever he wants in his cabinet, there was real doubt as to whether Earl Butz could be confirmed. His protestations of sudden devotion to the independent owner-operated farm were somewhat less than convincing.

Midway in the controversy, however, President Nixon demonstrated again his miraculous flexibility when under pressure. He publicly abandoned his earlier proposal to abolish the Department of Agriculture. This was a great relief to farm state senators who had been under great pressure to save the USDA as the only voice of the farmer in the Executive Branch of the government.

This timely move, plus tradition—only eight times in the nation's history had a cabinet appointment been rejected by the Senate—were barely enough to secure confirmation. Earl Butz was confirmed on December 2, 1971 as the new Secretary of Agriculture by one of the closest votes in history, 51 to 44.

Misgivings of those concerned for the independent farmer were soon confirmed. A spokesman for the USDA told the Ohio Farm Bureau that under Butz farmers should expect support prices to continue to drop. In his very first confrontation with Congress, the new Secretary called on senators to defeat a bill that would have increased by 25% supports for sagging prices of wheat and feed grains. At the same time he opposed reduction of the $55,000 ceiling on the amount of government payments that can be made annually to any farm for any single crop.

Secretary Butz' method of trying to raise the price of corn was typical. He bought corn not from farmers or their cooperatives, but on the open market from grain dealers. Since the dealers had already bought the corn from the farmers at the distressed prices, it was dealer profits, not farmers' incomes, that were immediately increased by this move. In the longer run, if enough corn was bought and held off the market some benefits might filter down to producers.

Much was made by the new Secretary of a projected sale of 140 million bushels of grain to Russia. But here, too, the sale was to be made, out of stocks presumably already on hand, by two of the biggest grain dealing companies in the country—Cargill and Continental Grain Company. Furthermore, only half the 140 million bushels had to be purchased in the United States. This was good for the grain companies. For the farmers, the help would be approximately zero.

As the nation entered the fourth year of the Administration of Richard Milhous Nixon there was no reason, whatsoever, to expect that Administration to alter its course with respect to farmers, hunger in the land, or rural America's slow death. Nothing was more consistent with Mr. Nixon's whole political career than continuing practical support for big interests and continuing expressions of verbal sympathy for "little people" such as working farm families.

Farmers are few now, in proportion to total population. They are less important, therefore, to ambitious politicians.

Perhaps this is why Mr. Nixon changed his mind again regarding the Department of Agriculture. He undertook to ram through Congress a bill which would put the Rural Electrification Administration and the Farmers Home Administration in a new Department of Community Development. These two agencies, among all those that had traditionally been part of the U.S.D.A., were the very ones on which the smaller, independent working farmers depended most and from which they derived most benefit.

To attempt to bury them in a completely urban-oriented and brand new department was—if anything could be—a kind of "last straw."

4. POVERTY, "WELFARE" AND MIDDLE AMERICANS

"Keep, ancient lords, your storied pomp!" cries she with silent lips. "Give me your tired, your poor, your huddled masses yearning to be free, the wretched refuse of your teeming shore. Send these, the homeless, the tempest-tossed to me. I lift my lamp beside the golden door."

—Inscription on the Pedestal of the Statue of Liberty

Do these words still represent the spirit of the American nation?

In the first eight years of the decade of the sixties the number of people living in poverty declined. The average reduction was 4.9% per year.

In 1969 and 1970 almost the exact opposite was true. The numbers of the poor increased in each of those years by 5.1%.

These are Census Bureau figures.

Mr. Nixon took office as President in January, 1969.

As increasing numbers of families fell into the ranks of the poor in the Nixon years, so did the welfare rolls increase. During the year 1970, 20,000 additional people became dependent upon welfare in Los Angeles County, California alone. Some of these were solid middle-class, hard-working people for whom dependence on welfare was a new and deeply resented experience. In other large metropolitan areas the story was much the same.

There were—and are today—certain basic causes for this distress. Three among them are paramount. First, the bankruptcy of thousands of farm families due to low farm income and ever-rising farm costs. These families, forced off the land, have gone to the cities to seek employment that was not there.

Second, automation of production and the destruction of most of the unskilled and even semi-skilled jobs that, in years past, were the primary reliance of the less educated, the deprived, and the near-poor. This has affected both urban and rural employment. The mechanical "cotton picker" alone is estimated to have displaced 2 million harvesters.

But these trends had been at work in the eight earlier years of the decade. Their effect then had been markedly lessened by compensating factors and policies.

In 1969 things became different. A third factor was added. Workers in increasing numbers were losing their jobs. Automation was the cause of some of this. The growing recession was of course another. The people affected were not the long-time poor. They were people who had built up a modest stake in the economy by hard work, people who owned a little property, people who had always regarded themselves as solid citizens.

To add to the distress, prices were rising—sometimes precipitously. Sparked largely by the Vietnam War and military extravagance, plus high interest rates, price inflation was a serious problem for everyone, but especially for the poor and the newly unemployed.

Mr. Nixon and his administration adopted the deliberate —and incredibly cruel—policy of trying to dampen the inflation by increasing unemployment. One high Nixon official made the classic remark that "we can tolerate an unemployment level of 6% of the working force."

The question was *who* could tolerate it. Mr. Nixon and

his officials no doubt. But not the unemployed millions on the burgeoning welfare rolls.

Nonetheless it was administration policy to pursue a tight money policy, and interest rates—which enter into the cost of practically every business in the country and hence into their selling prices—were forced still higher until they reached the highest levels in a century.

But this was only part of the story.

Measures passed by the Democratically-controlled Congress which might have increased employment and eased the distress of the poor were promptly vetoed by Mr. Nixon. Among these were appropriations for vital education and health needs, measures to install or improve water and sewage facilities, appropriations for education, hospitals and urban renewal in the beleaguered cities. In some cases Congress was able to override the vetoes. But in all too many cases they were sustained.

And even when the will of Congress prevailed through an override, much of the money appropriated by it was "frozen" by action of Mr. Nixon's office of Management and Budget. The funds were simply not put to use for the purposes for which the Congress intended them. They were held idle in the White House. The President was clearly usurping the powers and prerogatives of the National Legislature.

The "War on Poverty" with which President Johnson had challenged a complacent country was not forgotten by the Nixon Administration. It was deliberately sabotaged, and in many respects turned into a war against the poor. Unable to liquidate outright that Democratic program which had caught the imagination of the nation and given it, for a time, a sense of noble purpose, Mr. Nixon and his minions attacked it piece-meal.

To document that fact is not difficult.

From the beginning of the "War on Poverty" it was recognized that one of the principal reasons why the poor could not break out of the cycle of poverty was the burden of unpayable debt in which most poor families were compelled to live. And that debt—generally to food or furniture merchants—bore extortionate, incomprehensible, interest rates. If only this vicious circle could be broken there could be "light at the end of the tunnel."

Clearly then what was needed was a way to encourage some savings on the part of poor people, and more immediately to provide them with a decent source of credit at reasonable rates.

Credit Unions answered both needs. Consequently the Credit Union National Association, an organization with more than 20 million members and a half century of experience behind it, was contracted with by the Office of Economic Opportunity to organize credit unions among the poor. O.E.O. provided funds for necessary start-up capital and for competent management in the early months as well as for training of managers drawn from the ranks of the poor themselves.

Needless to say not all such credit unions were successful. Poor people find it hard to make the kind of meaningful savings which can develop an adequate pool of lendable funds. But many of them did succeed. Experience was being gathered. And the program was offering real, basic hope.

Then in the fall of 1970 the program was suddenly terminated. O.E.O. refused to renew its contract with Credit Union National Association and left that organization to do the best it could to carry forward without the critically needed government help.

Budgets for the Office of Economic Opportunity were trimmed by the Nixon Administration to the extent it could. Funds for Head Start, that program which had enabled millions of children from deprived homes to start school with somewhat more nearly an equal chance to learn, were cut substantially. Once, 750,000 poor children had benefitted; by 1972 only 380,000. Local sponsors and the devoted work of volunteers kept Head Start alive and working in many places.

The Job Corps received similar shrift as did other action programs of O.E.O.

There was a time late in 1970 when President Nixon considered complete abolition of vista—Volunteers in Service to America. Critics of such a move charged that the Nixon Administration wanted to get rid of vista because the young volunteers were learning too many facts about poverty in America and because they were "stirring up" the poor to action on their own behalf.

In his budget for the fiscal year 1972, Mr. Nixon proposed to cut the funds for the anti-poverty program by 23%, a move opposed by many within his own administration. They pointed out that such a cut would mean the discharge by O.E.O. of some 60,000 employees, most of whom would be then back on the relief rolls. There was opposition—violent this time—from Democrats in Congress, who charged that such severe cuts would, as Senator Mondale put it, "remove the last vestige of credibility in the war on poverty." Part of the budget proposal was that no funds at all be provided for VISTA.

In the end there was compromise. VISTA was grouped with the Peace Corps in a new agency called ACTION, which could bear the Nixon stamp and, hopefully, help people to forget what Presidents Kennedy and Johnson had done.

But the aim and purpose of the Nixon Administration became more and more clear as the months passed. The fact gradually emerged that what the Administration actually intended was to put an end to all action programs of O.E.O. and to reduce it to a research and advisory agency.

This seemed a backward step, to say the least. For certain programs aimed directly at one of the root causes of poverty and of the growing welfare rolls had been begun in the previous Administration and were continued at first by O.E.O. after Mr. Nixon took office. For example, there had been taking place in the rural South a very considerable development of cooperatives of various kinds among the poor —especially among the Black poor. Some of these were credit unions, some consumer cooperative stores. But the more important ones, the ones most directly aimed to stem the outmigration into city ghettos, were cooperatives among poor farmers and farm laborers. Outstanding example of this movement was the Federation of Southern Cooperatives and its sister organization, the Southern Cooperative Development Foundation. Inspiration, leadership and example for both these organizations had come from the successful struggles of a Black priest, Father A.J. McKnight and his helpers in Southern Louisiana. There, in an area where average incomes were $1400 per family per year they had built painstakingly over the years the Southern Consumers Cooperative. Its educational, savings & loan, fruit cake manufacturing, credit union, and farmers marketing activities had all borne fruit, though not without their ups and downs.

Out of this experience and with the indispensable help of O.E.O. there sprang up other cooperatives in the rural South. Particularly important were cooperatives of poor farmers which taught them to grow new specialty crops instead of cotton and developed markets for these crops. The Cooperative League of U.S.A. gave its help and guidance. But funds from O.E.O. and its defense of these cooperatives' right to exist was the key factor.

By 1967 there was enough development to justify organization of the Federation of Southern Cooperatives and the Southern Cooperative Development Foundation. To the latter financing organization O.E.O. granted $500,000 as seed capital. Individuals as well as cooperative insurance companies and other foundations then came in with investments and loans.

By the time Mr. Nixon took office the Federation had some 100 cooperatives in its membership with more than 25,000 members, mostly Black farmers. The Foundation was helping them to get started, carrying on educational programs and preaching constantly its objective.

That objective was to enable poor farmers and formerly-employed farm laborers to make a decent living on the land in the South where they and where they wanted to stay and thus help stem the tide of movement to the Northern cities—and, in most cases, the welfare rolls.

To its credit O.E.O. did not abandon this effort as the Nixon Administration took hold. It was for this very reason, however, that the attempts to down-grade O.E.O. seemed so serious a mistake.

Even as much oratory emanated from the White House about revenue sharing, its proposal so far as the anti-poverty program was concerned was revenue sharing in reverse. For when, in the spring of 1971, the director of the Office of Economic Opportunity presented the Administrations program to the House Committee on Education and Labor, he proposed that the legislation require a 25% cash contribution from local Community Action Programs as opposed to the existing 3%. Nor was this all. He revealed that under Mr. Nixon's revenue sharing proposal the entire $346 millions then going direct to O.E.O. programs such as Community Action would be given instead to local political subdivisions, to do with as they saw fit. Committee members were certainly "on target" when they charged that the Administration was proposing in effect to dismantle O.E.O. Coupled with violent attacks upon the Legal Assistance program of O.E.O. which fought the court battles of the poor, these proposals made it very plain that the underlying purpose of the Administration was to silence the voice of the poor and stifle their participation in the struggle against their own poverty.

Enough has been said about poverty and "welfare" to require an examination of just who are the people on welfare, and what their attitudes are.

In mid-1971, for example, there were some 917,000 persons in Los Angeles County who were dependent to a greater or less degree upon payments from the County welfare department.

Who were these people?

118,000 of them were aged people who received some supplements to their meager incomes to bring them up to bare subsistence.

71,000 were persons permanently and totally disabled.

5,000 of them were blind.

15,000 of them were orphan children being cared for in foster homes.

30,000 were single adults dependent for one reason or another, such as ill health, absence of education, or mental disturbances.

531,000—well over half the total number—were dependent children in families without a breadwinner.

And just 22,000 were unemployed, able-bodied breadwinners—*less than 2½% of the total.*

Except for a possibly larger number of old people, and a somewhat smaller percentage of employable heads of families, these Los Angeles County figures were probably typical of other metropolitan areas and a fair sample of the national condition.

One wonders if it was surprising to such ardent devotees of the work ethic as President Richard Nixon and California's Governor Ronald Reagan to learn of some of the actions and attitudes of the people whom they had been holding up to shame and ridicule.

A survey of mothers of dependent children revealed that 4 out of 5 of them declared they would prefer to work and earn the children's livings, instead of accepting welfare if only there were a way for their children to be cared for at costs they could afford. Congress was, as we shall see, about to provide precisely such a way for them—only to have it vetoed by Richard Milhous Nixon.

On October 8, 1970 the *Los Angeles Times* reported on its front page: "More than 700 persons . . . lined up for four $133-a-week jobs in West San Fernando Valley as meter readers for the Southern California Gas Company."

Shortly thereafter the city of San Francisco advertised for

people to apply for 30 street maintenance jobs. This time 5,000 people stood in line—some of them all night—in hopes of landing one of those jobs.

And in New York City where the dependency problem was probably most acute, a plan was tried in the fall of 1971 whose success should have opened even the eyes of the dullest of the "reverse demagogues." For the city, in accordance with a new state law, called upon its able-bodied welfare recipients to work out the amount of their grants. Thousands responded and were put to work cleaning parks and playgrounds. There was little or no complaint or grumbling. Menial though the work was, the newspapers reported that the workers seemed to like doing it and to be positively grateful for the opportunity to feel that they were serving a society that had, until then told them, in effect, that they were "surplus."

There are, of course, always those among us who cheat, who receive welfare checks to which they are not entitled. Others are in high places. As to the unjustified recipients of welfare, it would seem to be the province of political executives, who have it constantly in their power, to eliminate them from the rolls.

Senator Ribicoff of Connecticut, having made his own careful investigation told the Senate that: "Figures show that fraud is detected in less than 1% of all cases, a figure corresponding to midde-class fraud in areas such as filing income tax returns."

Beyond a shadow of a doubt the real and basic problem of the welfare rolls can be described in one word: Unemployment. If jobs are available the overwhelming majority of those now on welfare who are physically able to do so will jump at the chance to take them. It is in the light of this evidence that "welfare reform" proposals, Mr. Nixon's among them, must in part at least, be judged.

It seemed a pity therefore that when Mr. Nixon presented to Congress his defense of his Game Plan III in the late summer of 1971, he should have returned to the attack on the *people* who depend, for want of a better independence, upon welfare. Among his remarks were these: "The thing that is demeaning is for a man to refuse work and then ask someone else who works to pay taxes to keep him on welfare."

The Washington Post commented after the President's speech that he seemed to be appealing to the basest and meanest values of the American people to gain support for his program.

But there was to come the proposal of Richard Milhous

Nixon, himself. And it did, in the grand manner and with the self-styled label of the most epoch-making proposal for Welfare Reform ever presented by a chief of state.

In many respects this was no idle boast.

Mr. Nixon's Family Assistance Plan, or FAP, as it was called, was a landmark proposal in three important respects. First, the federal government would recognize a responsibility for meeting the welfare problem on a national scale. And it would do it by providing a floor under welfare payments throughout the nation. At first Mr. Nixon proposed that this be $1600 a year for a family of four. Then he raised it to $2400. Second, the program would provide allowances to the working poor to bring their incomes up to the federal floor if their earnings were insufficient to do so. And then following the example set by some states, people dependent on welfare would be given the right to earn additional income and to keep a part of it without reduction of their welfare allowance, up to the point where their total income was at the poverty level of some $4,000.

There was criticism, of course, some of it from conservatives to whom the idea of a federal minimum allowance was anathema. Some of it from liberals—and from people closest to the welfare recipients themselves—who called for an allowance somewhere near the $7,000 which the Labor Department itself declared to be the minimum upon which a family of four could decently live.

There were counter-proposals, naturally enough, from the Democrats. The one which had most prominence was that advanced by Democratic Chairman Lawrence O'Brien and Chairman Mills of the House Ways and Means Committee. Mills contended that a better plan would be for the federal government simply to assume the entire cost of welfare, thus relieving the states and localities of the crushing burden they were carrying and making possible the establishment of nationwide standards.

When H.R.I. of the 92nd Congress passed the House of Representatives, it contained the proposals of Mr. Nixon but it also bore the unmistakable stamp of Wilbur Mills and his Democratic colleagues. The bill provided the $2400 annual income floor for families of four, correspondingly smaller amounts for smaller families and nothing for single or unattached poor people. But it also provided for complete assumption by the Federal Government, in future years, of the entire cost of aid to dependent children, the aged, the blind and the disabled. In addition the Ways and Means Committee had added on its own motion an increase in social security payments, effective in June 1972 and automatic cost-of-living increases in such payments.

Probably because the bill provided too much for the conservatives and too little to suit the liberals, it was stalled in the Senate until well in 1972.

But there was an additional reason for lack of action by the Senate. When Mr. Nixon dramatically announced his Game Plan III on August 15, 1971 he declared his principal objectives to be the dampening of the inflationary spiral. And he called for sacrifice to make this possible—sacrifice, unfortunately, almost wholly on the part of workers and the poor. For he proposed that action on his Family Assistance Pan be postponed for an entire year!

Did this mean that he had lost interest in it? Or that he had never intended actively to push it? Doubt on both these points seemed justified. But in his State of the Union address of January 1972, with his year delay less than half over, Mr. Nixon berated the Congress for not having completed action on his welfare reform proposal.

Some further observations with respect to FAP are necessary. It was, as we have said, a landmark proposal, coming from the President of the United States. But it was also a second-best proposal from the human point of view. It was second best for those groups who must rely on welfare—the old, the blind, the disabled, the dependent children—for it gave them all too little for a decent, hopeful life.

And it was even more a second best for those now dependent on welfare who as we have seen, desire nothing so deeply as to be rid of welfare and go back to work.

In the light of the utter failure, if not the lack of desire, of the Nixon Administration to deal effectively with unemployment, the "work or lose your welfare" requirements seem almost cruel. Especially since there is nothing in the proposal to require that the proffered job pay even the minimum wage. And even more especially so when applied, as the Nixon plan does, against mothers of school-age children.

And it must be suggested that what many in Mr. Nixon's "silent majority" of the affluent are most interested in—what indeed every affluent group in all history has, we fear, been interested in with respect to the poor—is that they be given just enough to keep them quiet.

When the Senate Committee finally acted, it proposed a

work-acceptance requirement, but it also proposed to finance enough public service work so there would be jobs to take.

And what about the "middle Americans"?—those to whom the "American dream" means more than it does to either the very poor or to the affluent. Many of them are the children of families who had come to America from other countries expecting here to find that better life which the quotation on the Statute of Liberty promised. They are hard working people, devoted church members in most cases, and people of solid moral standards which they have expected to find observed by everyone—especially the nation's leaders.

But they have begun to feel a certain helplessness and sense of neglect. They have seen politicians deny desperately needed aid to their parochial and public schools. They see tax laws enacted that favor the wealthy and saddle a disproportionate share of the burden on their own middle-income group. They see little done to provide the cheap, efficient mass transportation which they so greatly need. Worst of all, they have seen an insensitive national administration pursue a policy which seems positively to welcome increasing unemployment of workers as its principal means of "combating inflation," while hardly a word was being said about the high interest rates or the monopolistic pricing which are among inflation's root causes. They have been and are followers, not leaders. And amid all the excitement about the struggle of minorities for justice and the intense drive of the young people for change, this great group of "middle Americans," the backbone of the economy, feel they have been forgotten.

Clearly what these "middle Americans" wanted and surely needed was devoted moderate leadership that would once more unite the people and drive toward justice and fairness for everyone.

Congress had not surrendered to the Administration. It was not about to permit the War on Poverty to die. It demonstrated this with emphasis when it enacted the bill for continuance of the Office of Economic Opportunity in the fall of 1971. That bill provided for a two-year extension of the work of O.E.O. It authorized $900 million a year for the Community Action Programs, $950 million for the manpower training program, and $500 million for the neighborhood youth corps. It created, in its own right, a corporation to provide legal services to the poor, hoping in this way to immunize this essential service from attempts by Mr. Nixon or Mr. Reagan to bring such services to an end. The bill forbade the transfer of any more of the programs of O.E.O. to other government agencies—a fate which had befallen Head Start and Job Corps already.

But most important to anyone in earnest about helping people to escape the welfare dependence, Congress wrote into the bill a new Title V, designated "Child Development Programs." It contained a broad spectrum of services to children. These included health and nutritional services, afterschool and vacation educational programs, and all-day care for pre-school children. $100 million was authorized in 1972 for planning and $2 billion in fiscal year 1973 for establishment of child-care centers throughout the nation. These were to provide care and health education without charge for children in families with less than $4300 annual income, and for modest fees for families with incomes up to $6960.

Proponents of the measure spoke of it as representing one of the most significant forward steps ever to emanate from the Congress of the United States. It was conceived to accomplish two purposes: First, to give deprived children a better start in life; second, in the words of 24 Senators who wrote to the President, urging him to sign the bill, "to enable low-income parents with children to accept gainful employment and end their dependence on public assistance." Four of those 24 Senators were leading Republicans.

The bill as a whole passed the Senate 49 to 12, and the House by 210 to 186. The Conference Committee quickly resolved minor differences and sent the measure to President Nixon for his signature.

It received no such signature. Despite all he had declared about the virtues of work, and despite the requirement in his own FAP proposal that mothers accept any proferred employment or lose their right to welfare payments, Richard Nixon on December 9, 1971 vetoed this creative piece of legislation.

The veto message was belabored and unconvincing. The Senate failed by a scant 7 votes to override the veto, Senator Muskie commenting sadly: "We tried to put together a bill that in a meaningful way would have come to grips with the problems of the working mother, to open careers now closed."

Difficult as it was at first blush to understand the veto, this should not have been so. For Title V provided that the child-care program be governed and guided by boards and committees composed of parents and community representatives rather than by local politicians. This would have involved a meaningful kind of participation by lower-income people in developing to their own problems. And that, as had been amply demonstrated, was something Mr. Nixon did not want. Furthermore, here was an opportunity to kill, at least temporarily, the entire War on Poverty Program along with the child-care title—an opportunity which for some reason best known to himself Mr. Nixon did not wish to miss.

But what may have been most persuasive of all to candidate Nixon was the appeal his veto would have to the Republican far-right. There had been disturbing noises from that direction ever since the apparent reversal of Mr. Nixon's violent anti-Communism and announcement of his trip to China. There was even talk that the Right-wingers might enter a candidate against him in the primaries—as indeed they later did.

Here was a chance to appease these restless erstwhile strong supporters. It must not be neglected.

Whereupon the *Washington Post* commented editorially that "This veto message is a bone he has tossed to his critics on the Far Right, with next November in mind, and at the expense of mothers and children and of a day-care program which the President would have us believe he really supports."

On page one of the same December 12, 1972, issue of the *Post* was a story which noted that the new military budget being proposed by Mr. Nixon was expected to be $2 billion higher than the last one.

$2 billion would have been the cost of the child-care centers.

Congress was not to be stopped. As soon as it reasembled in January 1972, the committees went to work on legislation to replace the bill the President had killed. One interesting feature of the legislation being prepared in the House was a $1.5 billion item to expand the Head Start program. And the Senate was ready to challenge Mr. Nixon again with a child-care program. All the force of the Administration was being used against both the House and Senate bills and the ultimate fate of the drive against poverty was still in doubt.

In 1971 welfare rolls and costs grew sharply and alarmingly —27% overall throughout the country. Nineteen states had to cut back already below-poverty-level payments to dependents. 1972 looked like a repetition since jobs were simply not opening up to more than a fraction of the unemployed.

So perhaps, looking ahead to November, the Administration offered an unprecedented advance of an extra month's allowance of the federal share of welfare costs to the states. This was to be paid in June and on condition that the money be paid back at some future time. This would mean that in June 1972 the states would have twice the amount they normally received.

Obviously this would improve conditions in the months immediately before the election—which was good so far as it went. But the other side of it was that later on, and after the election, the states would have to cut back on their welfare payments to repay the pre-election bonus.

The heart of the economic problem in the United States can be stated statistically as follows: the poorest fifth of our people receive just 3.2% of total national income, while the richest fifth receive 45.8%. This is not only the rankest kind of inequality but also fundamentally unhealthy for the economy as a whole. It is a danger to the hold on life of the middle Americans, that 20% of the people who receive only 10% of the income.

Until a massive attack is made on this maldistribution of income in the United States, the problems of poverty and welfare will be with us in serious form.

Such an attack should begin with a sweeping reform of the tax system and the very opposite kind from the one the Nixon Administration is pushing. For the Nixon tax program, if such it can be called, means lower taxes on big businesses and less revenue from the reasonably progressive income tax and a bigger burden on regressive taxes such as the payroll tax and sales taxes. Instead of this the gaping tax loopholes should be plugged, yielding an estimated $60 billion. An excess profits tax should be enacted. The income tax should be based more accurately on ability to pay. And taxes on consumption—except for those on tobacco, liquor, luxury items, and exhaustible resources—should be avoided altogether.

Reform of taxation is only the beginning of what needs to be done. The Social Security System should be expanded and improved so that minimum income payments are more nearly adequate for a decent life. A well-conceived and large-scale program of public service employment to get the unemployed off the welfare rolls should be put into effect, as it would have been had Mr. Nixon not vetoed the Nelson-O'Hara bill in December, 1970. An all-out drive to rehabilitate our core cities, abolish the slums and develop good, cheap mass transportation should be part of the drive. Farmers' market bargaining power should be increased, primarily by strengthening their cooperatives through low-interest loans, perhaps; and creative, long-range legislation for rural America community development should be constantly pressed.

Finally the War on Poverty should be resumed, in the spirit in which it was originally conceived, and along the line of the legislation passed by the Congress but vetoed by Nixon.

The United States of America has been, as nearly as any nation in history, a land of opportunity for all people. That is, sadly, no longer true. It should and could be made true again.

By a government that really cared.

5. THE POLICY OF UNEMPLOYMENT

We can tolerate an unemployment level of 6% of the working force.

—High Nixon Official

A few days before Mr. Nixon vetoed the bill for continuance of the anti-poverty program, a shipment of food had arrived in Seattle, Washington from its sister city, Kobe, Japan. The food, consisting of 100 pounds of rice and canned goods, had been collected through voluntary contributions from the people of Kobe in response to an appeal by their city officials.

The food packages were sent for the relief of hungry, unemployed workers in Seattle.

There was need for it. For the United States Department of Agriculture had refused a request from Washington State officials for direct distribution of surplus food to "newly poor" unemployed workers. There were people whose assets were too great for them to be eligible for the food stamp program, but who had exhausted their unemployment insurance and whose families were hungry.

Senator Magnuson of Washington called the Department's action "callous and cruel." He said further: "In one simple humanitarian gesture, Japan had made a mocking of our pious claims of being a nation dedicated to serving the cause of human dignity and concern for the welfare of our citizens." The Senator said that, to make the matter even more unbelievable, customs officials had at first decided to confiscate the food and that only angry protests had finally induced them to release it for distribution by a church organization called "Neighbors in Need."

Magnuson introduced a resolution urging the Administration to provide food requested by Washington State officials to help the hungry in Seattle.

Only then did the Department of Agriculture relent and release some of the needed food.

During the Administration of Richard Milhous Nixon unemployment became a major tragedy in the United States. The Seattle story is but one bit of evidence of that fact.

When Mr. Nixon assumed the presidency of the United States, unemployment of workers stood at 3.3 percent. By New Years Day, 1971, after two years of his Administration 6.2 percent of America's workers were unemployed. Among young Black people the jobless rate was more than 30 percent. In poor neighborhoods one-third more employable people were out of work than the year before.

Almost five million families were deprived of the earnings of their breadwinner. Almost five million workers were being told that their country had no need of their talents, their brains, or their brawn.

As the year 1971 progressed there was no significant change in this tragic condition. In December 6.1 percent of the nation's work force was still unemployed. As 1972 dawned, there appeared no solid reason to expect any appreciable change. The stock market was on the rise in anticipation of greater profits for the industry. But men and women were not going back to work. In May the Labor Department reported an unemployment rate of more than 6% in one-third of our cities.

The Joint Economic Committee of the Congress scheduled hearings on the unemployment problem as the second session of the 92nd Congress prepared to convene. As is customary in such hearings the Nixon Administration was requested by Senator Proxmire of Wisconsin, Chairman of the Committee, to present the first testimony and to present its case.

But the Administration refused to do so and the hearings had to be cancelled.

Senator Proxmire's brief comment was: "I'd be reluctant to appear also, if I had to defend the kind of record this Administration has made." After three years of Mr. Nixon's Presidency and the operation of three Nixon "Game Plans," the unemployed workers of the nation were still being compelled to pay the major part of the price for the Nixon program of trying to control inflation.

The casual observer might be tempted to say that unemployment had increased to its highest level in decades and then remained there *in spite of* the Nixon "Game Plans."

But this was not so.

Unemployment had soared *because of* those "Game Plans" and *because of* a policy, which could only be regarded as deliberate, of using unemployment as the principle anti-inflationary device. The one method whereby inflation could be fought and employment opportunity increased at the same time was sedulously avoided by the Nixon Administration. That was the method of increasing the buying power of the families at and near the bottom of the economic scale. When that is done those families are certain to spend every dollar available to them. They have to; and such measures, therefore, are certain to increase market demand, to activate idle productive capacity, and thus put more goods upon the market and bring about downward pressures upon prices.

But this was what the Nixon Administration did not do. When Congress tried various approaches to such a policy, it was accused by the President of acting "irresponsibly," its bills opposed and, in many cases, vetoed.

One cause of the large volume of unemployment was the recession in business activity that had settled upon the land as a result of Nixon Game Plan I. It seemed paradoxical, but what was happening—for the first time in the nation's history —was an economic recession accompanied by a severe price inflation. How and why such a strange combination of circumstances could take place will be examined later.

Unskilled and semi-skilled jobs in the private sector were being progressively abolished by automation. On the other hand, the need of society for vast amounts of work to be done in the public sector became more and more evident each day.

But much of the work required, of those doing it, at least a modicum of training of kinds which the unemployed people had never had.

For these reasons Congress as early as the fall of 1969 began to prepare legislation to meet this very situation. The work was led by Senator Gaylord Nelson of Wisconsin and Congressman O'Hara of Michigan. Extensive hearings were held. Witness after witness, especially those from the overcrowded, underfinanced cities, demonstrated the critical need for great numbers of workers in such fields as environmental protection and clean-up, hospital and health ancillary services, teachers' aids, urban rehabilitation, fire protection, law enforcement, and the like. The trouble was that the money was not there, in the localities, either for the training of workers for such employment or for payment of their salaries once they were employed.

The result of those hearings plus arduous drafting and redrafting work on the part of Senators and Congressmen was the Nelson-O'Hara bill which passed both houses of Congress by comfortable majorities in the fall of 1970. It was a comprehensive, well-conceived, and tightly-framed piece of legislation. It was no "emergency" or "make-work measure." On the contrary, it provided a four-year program of training and employment for some 400,000 of the unemployed. $9.5 billion was authorized. $2 billion was for manpower training, specifically directed to prepare people for the types of work in public service of which society was in greatest need; $2.5 billion to provide 80% of the wages and salaries to be paid by local authorities—to the newly employed workers in the early years. $3 billion was authorized for further training to step up the skills of people and prepare them for special federal service program. The remaining $2 billion was authorized to carry the program forward until 1974. Recognizing the Spanish-speaking, the older people, and those forced out of agriculture, the bill required that all such groups receive their fair share of the work opportunities created.

It was a measure calculated to take hundreds of thousands of people permanently off the relief rolls, equip them for needed work, and employ them at jobs for which they were trained.

The Nelson-O'Hara bill was endorsed by the National League of Cities, the U.S. Conference of Mayors, the National Association of Counties, the Urban Coalition, the AFL-CIO, the National Council of Senior Citizens and many other responsible and concerned organizations.

All through the hearings and consideration of the bill, Nixon Administration representatives tried to bring about such changes as would make the jobs temporary, limit the training, and frame it as emergency legislation.

The Congress refused. It sought to begin the task of developing a lasting solution to the unemployment problem. The New Careers Development Center of New York University commented that "Unlike the highly touted Family Assistance Plan with its training without jobs and forced work requirements, the manpower bill provided a break with the welfare state mentality and began to move in the direction of a human services society."

On December 16, 1970 Richard Milhous Nixon vetoed the Nelson-O'Hara bill. He vetoed it because it would have created permanent jobs for the unemployed and trained them for such jobs. He said in his veto message that he would accept "transitional and short-term public service employment" but not the Nelson-O'Hara concept. Then he reversed his field completely and said he was vetoing the bill because it would create jobs similar to the New Deal's WPA.

Senator Mondale of Minnesota expressed the view of many people when he said "It is both tragic and incredible that the President vetoed a bill which would have created 400,000 vitally needed public service jobs at a time when 4.6 million Americans are jobless."

Senator Javits, Republican of New York, urged that the veto be overridden. The Senate tried, 48 to 35, but could not muster the necessary two-thirds vote. One of the most constructive measures to be passed by the Congress in many years was dead. Mr. Nixon had killed it.

But reaction to the veto must have caused some consternation among the White House public relations staff. The President's Family Assistance Plan required that persons dependent on welfare register for and accept employment whenever offered. But even White House advisors knew that the jobs just weren't there. So it was becoming a little hard to explain why Mr. Nixon should have vetoed a measure that would have answered, in part at least, his own dilemma.

Accordingly, just two months after his veto of the Nelson-O'Hara bill and without reference to that bill or his veto, Mr. Nixon made banner headlines by calling upon Congress to add to his Family Assistance Plan a title providing $800 million to put an estimated 200,000 able-bodied welfare recipients to work at—of all things—work in parks, hospitals and other public sector jobs! There was no provision for training such as the Nelson-O'Hara bill would have provided. The jobs would be "short-term and transitional"—quite different again from the Nelson-O'Hara objective of developing lasting skills and permanent jobs. But these inadequacies aside, two months did seem rather a short time in which Mr. Nixon completely changed his mind about public service employment.

His marvelous flexibility was, however, once more to stand him in good stead, three months later.

For in June the Congress completed action on another attempt realistically to deal with the problem of unemployment. This was a $2 billion bill to give unemployed workers jobs in an accelerated public works program. Congressional committees reported that this would mean some 400,000 jobs; and Representative Blatnik of Minnesota, Chairman of the House Public Works Committee, pointed out that "There are hundreds of applications from cities and states sitting on the shelf now with plans filed and ready to go and all they need is funding."

This time Mr. Nixon had his veto message on the tip of his tongue. The public works jobs, he said, would be "a poor and distant second" to public service employment! What he wanted, he declared, and what he would sign was a watered-down version of the Nelson-O'Hara bill.

This brought from the St. Paul (Minnesota) *Pioneer Press* this comment:

> Last December Nixon vetoed a similar bill to the one he says he will now approve on the grounds that it would have created "dead end jobs," amounting to government-subsidized employment.

The Public Works Employment bill was killed by the Presidential veto, since the Senate failed by five scant votes to override.

The Public Works Committee went back to work, reported a bill a quarter as big as the vetoed one; and perhaps because this would, after all, not put "too terribly many" of the unemployed to work, Mr. Nixon signed it.

Meanwhile the Congress had made one more attempt to get something—almost anything—that would help the jobless past the President. The Emergency Employment Act of 1971 was the result. It was sponsored by Senators Nelson of Wisconsin, Cranston of California, both Democrats, and Senator Javits, Republican of New York. In the hope that a veto could be avoided, it was designated as an "emergency employment" measure. Its training provisions were minimal. It was expected to create only about 150,000 public service jobs over a two-year period in contrast to Nelson-O'Hara's projected 400,000 jobs for four years.

Despite these substantial concessions to Mr. Nixon's objections, his Labor Department Secretary, James Hodgson, told the Senate Committee that its bill invited another veto.

But when the bill came before the Senate, only eight Republicans and two Democrats voted against it. The House passed a similar measure 244 to 142 on June 3. Despite the familiar threat of a veto, Congress was obviously in no mood to retreat further.

It was probably fortunate for the unemployed of the nation that Mr. Nixon had the Public Works bill on his desk when the Emergency Employment Act was dispatched to him by a determined Congress. For had this not been the case, it is at least questionable whether he would not have carried out the threat made by his Labor Secretary. But to veto both these bills almost simultaneously would have been too great a political risk for as canny a politician as Richard Nixon. Furthermore the substantial majority by which both houses of Congress had passed the Emergency Employment Act made it doubtful that a veto would have been sustained.

So his promise to sign the modified public service employment bill was used as an excuse for his veto of the Public Works bill. On July 12, 1971 he signed into law the Emergency Employment Act, his first and only concession in the persistent efforts of the Democratically-controlled Congress to act against the cancer of unemployment.

But it was not nearly enough even to begin to meet the problems faced by the more than 5 million unemployed. Almost 2 million of these had been out of work for so long that all their unemployment insurance benefits had been exhausted. To meet the basic bread-and-butter needs of these destitute families, Congress passed, in November 1971, a bill to provide federal funds for payment of an additional 26 weeks of insurance benefits to jobless workers in states suffering from chronically high unemployment.

The Nixon Administration testified against this Democratic-sponsored measure, giving the illuminating argument that it would result in higher taxes for business at a time when Mr. Nixon was trying to stimulate the economy by lowering business taxes.

Better, it seemed to the Administration, to let the unemployed go without *any* income than to fail to give big industry precisely what it wanted.

In the end, however—indeed during the very last hour before the bill would automatically have died without his signature—Mr. Nixon relented and signed the bill. He stated that he was signing it reluctantly and "only as a temporary expedient."

Which, indeed, it was. But a rather important one to two million hungry families.

6. OUR FESTERING CITIES

Despite the Kerner Report's widely accepted finding that one major cause of the ghetto disorders of the '60s was the shameful conditions of life in the cities, most of the changes in those conditions since 1968 . . . have been for the worse.

Commission on the Cities
September, 1971

Richard Nixon ran for President in 1968, and carried on his campaign for Republican and Conservative candidates in 1970 as a "law and order" candidate.

After three years of Mr. Nixon's presidency there was, if anything, less "law and order" than there had been when he took office. True, the college campuses were relatively quiet and no major riots had taken place. But many a high school was in ferment, and even the casual observer could look at our inner cities, read the metropolitan newspaper—and weep for the nation's future.

Schools were being vandalized by angry, hard-to-reach students who no longer felt that the schools were their friends. Citizens of such cities as Detroit feared to walk downtown streets even in daylight. The national capital itself was considered unsafe for women alone, day or night. There were reports of people being raped, attacked, even murdered while onlookers refused to lift a finger to help them. Policemen on duty were killed in larger numbers than ever before. Slum and ghetto mothers were afraid to leave their children alone in their own homes even for a few hours. Children died of lead poisoning from eating paint peeling off the walls of their dilapidated dwellings. Drug addiction mounted and the drug traffic became a way of life for many people. Crime rates were rising as sharply as they had ever done. Where there had been places of employment in the cities, there were vacant plants and factories. The jobs had moved to the suburbs and there was no adequate or reasonably-priced mass transportation in most cities to take job-seekers to where the jobs were. Idleness

67

and alienation spread among many millions, especially among minority groups. Hopes were dying.

It is not intended to lay all this at Mr. Nixon's feet. The cities have been deteriorating for many years. No president—even a great one—can cure quickly the maladies that afflict the cities of our country.

But it must be said that the Nixon Administration has paid little, if any, heed to the warnings of either the Kerner or the Eisenhower Commission reports concerning the *causes* of alienation, crime, and violence.

It is largely because millions of families live in unfit housing in this supposedly "affluent" land that our cities are in their present state.

The worst of the evils that beset our overcrowded cities could be overcome if the slums were replaced with livable housing, a little grass, a few trees here and there, adequate street lighting, some parks, and police protection comparable to that accorded other parts of metropolitan areas. The best of the cooperative housing communities have shown that this is so. Good housing is a key—*enough* good housing.

President Johnson stated as a goal of his Administration "a good house for every American family." He asked, and got from Congress, legislation for the development of "Model Cities" and the rent supplement program, whose purpose was to enable poorer families to live outside public housing projects and still enjoy decent homes through government aid.

In line with the Johnson goal, and obviously deeply concerned about the situation, Congress passed the Housing Act of 1968. It established in that Act, as national policy, the construction of 26,000,000 new dwellings in the following decade, or 2,600,000 housing starts a year. A number of "tools" were available to move toward that goal: Urban Renewal [slum clearance], Model Cities, and rent supplement programs among them.

Then, in the Housing Act of 1968 the Congress did more. To the housing programs already in operation, it provided in new sections of the housing act for a number of new programs, calculated, it was hoped, to create the needed housing and to rehabilitate the core cities. Section 23 was aimed to provide federal money to assist local authorities to rent houses from their owners, put them in livable condition, and then to enable lower-income families to pay an economic rent for them. Section 235 was intended to assist lower-income families toward home-ownership, through government subsidy of interest rates. And Section 236 was directed at assisting cooperatives and other non-profit builders to develop multi-family projects for rental to, or cooperative-ownership by, medium and lower income families. This too was to be accomplished through government subsidy of interest charges. If 25% of a family's income was not enough to enable it to pay the full economic cost of occupancy at prevailing interest rates, then the plan was to have the Department of Housing and Urban Development pay to the money-lender a sufficient proportion of the interest payment to bring the effective rate for the family down to where it would be paying no more than 25% of income for its housing.

There could be no doubt whatsoever that something desperately needed to be done about interest rates. They were too high when Mr. Nixon took office. And his "Game Plan I" policies drove them clear through the roof—to the highest point interest rates had ever reached in the nation's history except during the Civil War.

In fact, high interest rates were a cardinal part of the Nixon economic policy.

Viewing with alarm what was taking place, Congress gave President Nixon power to control and lower interest rates and to direct the Federal Reserve to channel credit to areas of need. Almost contemptuously, he declared he would never use that power. And he never did. Not in any of the three "Game Plans."

In 1968 the interest rate on mortgages insured by the Federal Housing Administration or the Veterans Administration was raised to 6¾%. At that rate a working family buying a house worth $17,000 with a 30-year mortgage had to be prepared to pay $21,678 in interest alone, for a total cost of $38,678. The *average* cost of new "moderate-priced" houses in that year was $22,000.

By May 1969, median sales prices for new houses had risen to some $25,000 and Sidney Margolius, dean of the nation's consumer economists, wrote in his weekly column that "individual new homes are well out of reach now of families earning average industrial pay." Interest rates had gone up again to 7½%.

In June the president of the National Association of Home Builders predicted a severe drop in housing construction for the year. And Secretary Romney of the Department of Housing and Urban Development stated that "at present rates of production we will fall more than 10 million units short of our housing needs." He admitted at the same time that the federal government was demolishing more housing than it was building.

The Secretary based many of his hopes for improving the situation on an imaginative idea which he called "Operation Breakthrough." It envisaged inducing large-scale community developers to work out plans for mass factory-built houses, for the assembling of large areas of land, and for sharply reducing the cost of housing in such newly-founded communities. A number of proposals were submitted and a few rather small projects carried to completion, some of them by cooperative housing agencies. But the total impact of the Secretary's program to date has been disappointing, especially, no doubt, to the Secretary himself. It has been said that a major roadblock has been the unwillingness of the Department to offer sufficient guarantees against loss if large-scale projects were undertaken. If so, the Secretary has his chief largely to blame; for in his budget for 1971-72, Mr. Nixon cut the funds for Operation Breakthrough almost in half, thus making it impossible for Secretary Romney to implement his program.

By July of 1969, housing costs in New York City had risen to such a point that a census survey showed that only 7% of the city's population had incomes sufficient to afford even publicly-assisted newly-built housing.

It was little wonder then that housing starts fell in 1969 to less than 1,400,000, a severe reduction from the previous year's figure.

In January, 1970 housing starts, according to the *Chicago Sun-Times* [January 7, 1970] were taking place at an annual rate of only 300,000, and as the years progressed, home construction in many parts of the country ground to a virtual stand-still.

The interest rate on FHA and Veterans Administration guaranteed loans was by this time at the unprecedented figure of 8½%. The *Los Angeles Times* estimated that the one percent increase, from 7½% to 8½%, had added $6,210 to the cost of a $25,000 home with a 30-year mortgage.

For the average family able to afford housing at $15,000 or less, the market was limited to mobile homes or trailers. They constituted 80% of the homes being bought by moderate-income families.

In April, 1970 Mr. Nixon's HUD Department itself stated that monthly charges on medium-priced homes at the 8½% interest rate had to be $290 to $300 and that no family with an income of less than $14,000 could afford such a burden. Fewer than one family in five had that high an income. The other four-fifths of the people were priced clear out of the market.

The reason was not far to seek. A house worth $20,000 for all the brick, mortar, labor, architectural work, plumbing, equipment, contractor's fee—everything *real* about the house —required interest payments on a 30-year mortgage at the 8½% then prevailing of $38,000, almost twice the cost of the house itself.

The plain fact was—and is—that builders in the United States cannot construct housing at costs the average family can afford if the interest cost is more than 3%.

The entire year 1970 found the home-construction industry in what even the chairman of Mr. Nixon's Council of Economic Advisers described as a severe recession.

One would have thought that the President of the United States would have taken some corrective action.

Not so.

He vetoed the appropriation bill for the Housing and Urban Development Department because, he declared, the appropriation for the Model Cities program was $350,000,000 "too much" and that the same was true of the amount appropriated for grants to municipalities for cleaning up and improving their water and sewer systems.

These were the days when Congress was beginning to discover that cost overruns on military contracts had mounted to the tens of billions of dollars and when Mr. Nixon was, nonetheless, asking increased appropriations for the Pentagon.

Not content with his veto, Mr. Nixon was proceeding on another front. If he could not persuade the Congress to stop appropriating money to save the cities from further deterioration and to bring about revival of home construction, then he would simply instruct the Office of Management and Budget to refuse to release for expenditure the money which the national legislature had provided for these purposes.

All through the years 1969, 1970 and 1971, this violation of the Constitutional right of the Congress went on. In early 1971, the colossal sum of $1.5 billion of funds duly appropriated by the Congress for urban renewal and rebuilding of the slums, for Model Cities, for water and sewer grants, and for public housing for the very poor remained frozen by Richard Nixon's order.

It was not only by vetoes and the freezing of funds that

housing for the less-than-affluent was being minimized. Another method, typical of this Republican Administration, was also being used. This was the abandonment of certain programs which had the stamp of previous—and Democratic—Administrations.

The Nixon Administration was pushing legislation to "streamline" the entire housing program and coupling this with the President's proposal for his particular kind of "revenue sharing" with the states and localities. For good reason that legislation was not quickly acted upon by the Congress. For in its original form it contained provisions which would have compelled the very poor—the occupants of so-called public housing—to pay considerably more than had been required of them.

The Administration however was not waiting for the passage of its legislation. Already two programs which had proved most successful in meeting some of the housing needs of the medium and lower-income families were being "phased out."

One of these was the program provided for in section 221(d)(3) of the Housing Act. And especially the below-market-rate-interest part of the program. Remembering that 3% interest is about all that builders can afford if they are to construct housing which is within reach of the majority of the American people, the Congress had provided, during the previous Administration, for that very rate of interest on non-profit projects whose occupancy was limited to families with incomes below the median in their communities. This program was available to private developers, to local housing agencies, and to cooperatives. It had proved remarkably successful, so much so in the case of cooperatives, that their record of repayment under this program was one of the best, if not the very best, in FHA history.

Nonetheless very early in his secretaryship, Mr. Romney announced that 221(d)(3) was to be discontinued. Congress passed more than one resolution which would, under other presidents, have required continuance of the program. But the dismantling of 221(d)(3) went right ahead. The Nixon Administration preferred to limit programs for lower-cost housing to the interest-subsidy method provided for in the new sections 235 and 236 of the Housing Act of 1968.

Another casualty of Nixon Administration policy was the section 202 program. This had provided 50-year direct government loans at 3% interest to private non-profit organizations undertaking to build housing for senior citizens, 65 years

72

of age and over. It had proved outstandingly successful. Not only had tens of thousands of older people obtained good housing in true communities but as of March, 1969, the president of the National Association for Non-profit Retirement Housing was able to write to President Nixon pointing out that not a single 202 project was in default to the government.

In August, 1970 Congress, in an attempt to rescue the 202 direct loan program, passed a bill appropriating $10 million specifically for 202 projects.

It was promptly vetoed by President Nixon. Thus housing for senior citizens was forced into the section 236 interest-subsidy program which was already proving so costly to the taxpayers and such a bonanza to the mortgage lenders.

It was little wonder then that in October 1971 Senator Charles Percy of Illinois, a staunch Republican, told the Senate Committee that: "I am all for profit, but not when it comes out of the hides of the elderly. We can't continue to allow the building of cheap, shoddy housing for the elderly just because someone can make a profit."

Accordingly Senator Percy introduced for consideration by the 92nd Congress Senate Bill 1584 to revive the section 202 program of direct 3% loans for senior-citizen housing. It received no support from the Nixon Administration, and its fate, taking into consideration a probable veto, continues to hang in doubt.

When President Nixon presented his fiscal 1972 budget at the opening of the 92nd Congress, his policies with regard to housing had become "absolutely clear." Especially those policies as they affected homes for the poor, the near-poor and middle Americans.

This was Mr. Nixon's "Game Plan II" budget. It reversed most of his previous conservatism and proposed to spend money as if the economy were running full blast, with little idle plant and low unemployment. Gone was the objective of a balanced budget. Instead economic expansion was to be the primary aim.

In line with this "brand new Nixon"—third or fourth edition, at least—the budget called for an increase in the overall spending by the HUD Department of about a half billion dollars.

But when it came to programs affecting the lower-income people of the country, the story was different. Contract authority for low-rent public housing was to be reduced from $320 million to $201 million, a 50% cut from the previous year. As to interest subsidies for sections 235 and 236 programs, the supposed favored programs of the Administration, Mr. Nixon asked only $175 million for each of these, whereas Congress had already authorized $200 million. As for urban renewal, the budget called only for the release in 1972 of the $200 million appropriated by the Congress for 1971 but frozen by the White House. And this compared to applications from the cities for slum eradication of no less than $3 billion. Because of his revenue sharing proposal which would, if passed, lump a number of programs together into one pot, not a cent was asked in the budget for the Model Cities program. And for water and sewer grants, Mr. Nixon proposed only to unfreeze half of the Congressional appropriation of the previous year, every cent of which had been impounded by the Executive.

In summary, the National Housing Conference said of Mr. Nixon's budget that it would "provide *less* in total funds for housing and urban programs than had already been appropriated by the Congress and would result in cancellation of $3.75 billion authorized for the programs."

To be fair at this point it should be said that Mr. Nixon did have a portion of a good excuse for failing to propose a stimulant for housing. For during the year 1971 the housing picture became definitely brighter for the construction industry and for the affluent segment of the population. Business conditions generally continued in a depressed state throughout the year despite "Game Plans II" and "III." And savings on the part of families reluctant to spend their money because of doubts about their future grew to unprecedented volume. It is an interesting fact that under such circumstances money tends to flow into housing more than is frequently the case in times of general prosperity.

And this is what apparently happened in 1971. The Savings and Loan Associations were bulging with money, as were the banks. Furthermore late in the year interest rates began to decline, though mortgages lagged behind other reductions.

In any case, 1971 turned out to be a year when Secretary Romney could make the encouraging announcement that 2,000,000 housing starts had taken place—a figure "only" 600,000 short of the annual goal set by Congress in the Housing Act of 1968. He could also report that more than 400,000 of the starts had been government-subsidized units, an all-time high figure.

As was to be expected, however, most of this recovery took

place in the field of luxury or semi-luxury housing for the affluent. In fact the time came when California newspapers, for instance, began to print lists of communities in the state where the higher-cost housing had actually become so over-built that vacancies were developing at an alarming rate.

The situation in the core cities, the slums, the ghettos and the barrios was, to say the least, somewhat different. "Redevelopment" had here and there taken place; but in all too many cases it was "redevelopment" of things at the expense of people. In city after city freeways or other types of highways had been built through the ghettos and barrios—or *over* them —to enable suburbanites more readily to reach their city jobs. In all such cases the result had been less, not more, housing for the residents of those neglected areas. Perhaps this is what Secretary Romney had in mind when he said that the federal government was demolishing more housing than it was building.

Moreover, the plain fact was that poor and even moderate income families simply could not afford decent housing at prevailing costs. The only way they could possibly enjoy the benefits of decent housing was through government subsidy of that cost.

And for reasons already suggested the subsidies just weren't there—not in amounts large enough to meet the tremendous need.

It is not surprising therefore that a distinguished "Commission on the Cities" set up by the National Urban Coalition issued a discouraging report in September, 1971. The Commission was co-chaired by Senator Harris of Oklahoma and Mayor Lindsay of New York. Its membership included the president of the League of Women Voters, the director of the Catholic Center for Urban Ethnic Affairs, the Governor of the State of Washington, the president of Boise Cascade Construction Company and many other distinguished people.

The Commission observed, in part:

Despite the Kerner Report's widely accepted finding that one major cause of the ghetto disorders of the '60s was the shameful conditions of life in the cities, most of the changes in those conditions since 1968 . . . have been for the worse.

At least in the cities we visited, housing is still the national scandal it was then. . . . Schools are more tedious and turbulent. . . . The rates of crime and unemployment and disease and heroin addiction are higher. . . . Welfare rolls are longer. . . .

75

And, with few exceptions, the relations between minority communities and the police are just as hostile.

Answers there were to the needs of the cities and of the average American for a home at costs he could afford, if only they could have been broadly applied.

In his column for January 19, 1970, Sidney Margolius pointed out the extortionate interest burdens which 8½% to 9% mortgages created, raising as they did the total cost of a house to three times its actual value. Then he concluded: "The only solution to the interest grab may have to be direct housing loans by the federal government."

And the Consumer Federation of America, in April 1969, had called for the same solution. The resolution to that effect read in part as follows:

> We propose a program similar to that of the U. S. Rural Electrification Administration, permitting direct Federal lending at interest rates of 1, 2 or 3 per cent a year, depending on need or circumstances, to public and non-profit private agencies, including public bodies and cooperatives, for construction on a massive scale of homes for middle and low income families.

Needless to say the proposal of the nation's major organization of consumers brought no response from the Administration. It came from the "wrong side of the tracks."

Another at least partial answer to the housing problem lies in cooperative housing. For such housing is constructed not to make a profit but solely to meet the need of specific groups of people for decent homes. This approach, and the non-profit agencies engaged in using it, received good support from the HUD Department under Secretary Romney as it had during the preceding Administrations. In fact Mr. Romney selected what was, on the whole, the best staff to administer the cooperative housing program that had ever been assembled. And their efforts to promote the progress of cooperative housing under all the existing circumstances left little to be desired.

By New Year's Day, 1970 a million or more Americans were living in cooperatively-owned apartments, town-houses, or groups of homes. A number of non-profit agencies experienced in developing such communities were responsible for this—principal among them the Foundation for Cooperative Housing, the Mutual Ownership Development Foundation on the West Coast, and the United Housing Foundation, working almost wholly in metropolitan New York City.

Over the years these agencies had shown that where large numbers of homes are built without profit for an already assured market, some 20% to 30% of what they would otherwise cost could be saved. This meant opening the gate to home-ownership to a whole segment of lower-income families who could not expect to own their homes under other circumstances.

From their very beginning the cooperative housing communities have been open to all families of every race, creed, and economic status. And always the families living in them become owners not only of their own town houses or apartments but of shares in the entire community of homes. Thus, where once there were slums, or no houses at all, there have grown up centers of social and economic health, to act as a leaven in the surrounding parts of the cities. In cooperative housing, the owners, the occupants, and the members of the cooperative home-ownership corporation are—and must be—always the same people.

But as interest rates rose, as fuel costs escalated, and other expenses increased, it became more and more difficult to keep the cost of even cooperative housing within the ability of families of modest income to pay. Fuel oil costs alone zoomed from 5¢ a gallon in mid-1970 to 14¢ in December, 1971. Monthly charges had to be raised by as much as 15% or 20% —sometimes even more. Many retired people were forced to move out of their cooperatives, unable to afford the increased charges.

United Housing Foundation had been asked in 1970 by the city of New York to build a 6,000 unit cooperative housing community in Brooklyn. United Housing wanted to do it, but it found that if the new project were to offer home ownership to even moderate-income families, an interest subsidy of some $11 million a year would be required. This was typical of the general situation.

By September, 1971 the highest interest "chickens" had come home to roost. So had the Administration's policy of liquidating sections 221(d)(3) and 202 and putting total emphasis on the interest subsidy programs, 235 and 236. For in that month Secretary Romney announced that programs of housing for lower-income people could not continue to expand since his Department was already committed for some $3 billion of interest subsidies.

The cause of the Secretary's concern was not difficult to comprehend. For the interest subsidy program projected by

77

sections 235 and 236 involves open-ended commitments over periods of as long as thirty and forty years.

Under the 221(d)(3) and 202 programs the projects are provided loans at 3% and that is the end of the government's contribution. From that point on the non-profit developers and the residents are "on their own."

But because of a rather irrational accounting procedure employed by the government, the total amount of the loans is included in the current budget as if it were outright expense, instead of the investment which it actually is. So section 221(d)(3) and 202 projects make the budget *look* bigger than it really is. And the present generation pays its own bill.

On the other hand the interest subsidies paid to private lenders under 235 and 236 appear in the budget only to the extent of the current year's expenditures. So the current budget *looks* better—and the continuing burden is passed along to our children. The commitment is "open-ended" because its amount depends upon what the going rate of interest is at any given time—something over which the Secretary of HUD can have no control. The money lender reaps a considerable bonanza when interest rates are high, as is now the case. And the government pays the bill. But because the *current* cost *appears* to be less, it has been possible to realize a larger volume of subsidized housing from these programs.

In January, 1972 the Undersecretary of HUD announced that the department was "taking a very hard look at housing allowances as an alternative strategy" to the FHA mortgage insurance programs. One probable reason for this was that too many families were being forced to abandon houses which they had presumably been helped to buy under the section 235 program. Congressman Monagan, Democrat of Connecticut, observed: "This program gives free enterprise its head. But with real estate speculators, incompetent or crooked appraisers and welfare mothers with no home ownership experience as the only players in the game, is it realistic to give free enterprise its head in the inner city?"

The fact was that many of those welfare mothers, as well as others better off, had been sold shoddy housing, overcharged and otherwise cheated.

Apparently the Administration of the Section 235 program left a good deal to be desired. By March, 1972 abuses in the interest subsidy programs had become so widespread and profiteering by middlemen so common that an organization of central city residents was formed to demand better administration of the programs. And Congressman Patman, Banking and Currency Committee Chairman, even suggested abandonment of these programs altogether. Maybe it was time to revive sections 221(d)(3) and 202.

When President Nixon presented his budget for fiscal year 1973 to Congress in January, 1972, he projected a huge deficit of $25 billion for the coming year. He budgeted a substantial increase in war appropriations and in a number of programs calculated to make popular appeal. But when it came to housing, it was a different story.

New contract authority for assistance to middle and lower income families was to be cut if Mr. Nixon had his way, and cut substantially. The figure was down to $551 million, some $130 million less than the $685 million of the previous year.

For low-rent public housing for the very poor Mr. Nixon proposed a reduction from the 1972 figure of $259 million to $183 million. Rent supplement money was reduced to $48 million, from $55 million; and the interest-subsidy fund for section 236 projects was proposed by the President to be cut 25%, from $200 million to $150 million. Secretary Romney tried to excuse this cut on the ground that he was having difficult administering the program.

Only as to the section 235 subsidies—where the exploitation of the poor had been taking place—was there no reduction. Mr. Nixon recommended the same $170 million as for the previous year.

This was the first time since the 1950s that an administration had proposed an overall reduction in the budget for housing.

These budget cuts would of course not become effective, even if Congress agreed to them, until July 1972.

What was actually to happen meanwhile was still a matter of conjecture. But there were straws in the wind. The wind blew straight out of the bulging vaults of the Office of Management and Budget in the White House, where hundreds of millions of dollars, appropriated by Congress for housing and other purposes had lain in deep freeze. Whereas up to the end of 1971, offices of the Federal Housing Administration were telling prospective applicants for section 235 and section 236 projects that there was no money at all available, these same officials were also indicating that in 1972 the situation would be different.

It was.

The money flowed much more freely as election time drew near.

But one sad note, typical of Nixon Administration policy, was struck by Secretary Romney himself. He told the House Appropriations Committee that in his opinion the slum eradication program was a waste of time and money and that he was considering its virtual abandonment.

To this Congressman Barrett, Chairman of the House subcommittee on Housing, replied that if slum clearance was a failure it was due to poor administration. The Congressman further pointed out that the Secretary had made no recommendations for changes in the program which he was denouncing.

It was altogether apparent that if anything substantial was to be done about the slums it would take a different Administration than that of Richard Nixon to do it.

7. HEALTH PLANS—AND PROMISES

We have been encouraged by the rhetoric of recent months. We find the substantive responses astonishingly poor.
　　　　　　　　　—Executive Board of the American
　　　　　　　　　　Public Health Association

The one financial reverse which American families most fear is a costly illness. Repeatedly surveys of opinion have confirmed this fact.

And no wonder. In 1960 the nation spent $26 billion for medical care. In 1970 it spent $70 billion, almost a 3-fold increase. In the year 1970 alone the bill zoomed from $63 billion. Hospital costs rose five times as fast as the cost of living generally.

Moreover much of this money was, to say the least, not well spent. Some of it went for unnecessary operations, hospitalization, and exorbitant drug costs. A good many millions of dollars of it were spent by people who were confused by the multiplicity of medical specialties and went to the wrong doctor for what ailed them.

Fewer and fewer families had the interested care of a

"family doctor," and the number of doctors and nurses was woefully inadequate for the nation's needs. In some rural areas and in the inner cities that "inadequacy" became almost total absence.

Once in a leading position, the United States had, at the time Richard Nixon took office, fallen behind most other industrial nations in infant mortality, life expectancy and the incidence of certain dread diseases. We stood 18th in infant mortality, just ahead of Hong Kong.

Demand for change had long been in the air. Medicare, enacted after years of struggle, had been passed in the Johnson years and was proving a boon to those over 65—despite the fact that too little preparation had been made for adequately servicing the needs of those who could now have long-neglected care. Medicaid was proving a help to poor families in most states, though the level of care left much to be desired in many parts of the country, and in California the State Administration was doing all it could to sabotage the program.

Group-health direct-service plans of many kinds were operating here and there, demonstrating, sometimes brilliantly, the advantages of continuous and preventive *health* care over the prevailing system of indemnity "sickness" insurance and fee-for-service treatment of advanced disease.

For years the demand for some form of "national health insurance" had been growing. Now, in 1969, it was demand also for fundamental change in what some called the "no-system" of delivery of medical care.

Above all considerations was the fact that most American families found it quite impossible to pay for the almost miraculous care which the medical profession at its best was able to provide.

As the 91st Congress assembled in January 1969 members began to introduce bill after bill aimed at improving the availability of health care for the American people. And President Nixon, like other presidents before him, promised action during his Administration in this all-important field of social need. He said he would have a comprehensive proposal to make as soon as it could be worked out.

In the first 2 years of his presidency, however, there was far more talk than action. And some of the action was, to say the least, rather negative.

For six entire months the position of Assistant Secretary for Health and Scientific Affairs in the Department of Health, Education and Welfare remained vacant. This was because

81

Mr. Nixon took six months' time in which to decide to reject, under pressure from the American Medical Association, the appointment of Dr. John H. Knowles. Dr. Knowles was the excellent choice of Mr. Nixon's long-time friend, Robert Finch, the Secretary of HEW.

At long last Dr. Roger O. Egeberg was persuaded to leave a distinguished career at the University of Southern California and to accept the Assistant Secretaryship.

Dr. Egeberg tried his best. But after a year and a half of service to the Nixon Administration he resigned. Commenting on his resignation the Executive Director of the American Public Health Association had the following to say:

It has been widely and reliably reported that Dr. Roger O. Egeberg will leave his post as Assistant Secretary for Health and Scientific Affairs in HEW after an 18-month stint. Through no fault of his own, Dr. Egeberg's tenure has seen governmental health programs fall under the anti-inflationary axe, and the morale of career health workers in federal service fall to an all-time low. Dr. Egeberg—an experienced health administrator of proven competence—came to a job which had been vacant for many months while the "Knowles Affair" was played out. During this period, HEW policy formulation and decision-making in health matters passed from professional hands into those of the grey legion of businessmen brought in to "manage" the federal government's health affairs. Dr. Egeberg was never really able to reestablish professional, rather than political, values as a basis for policy decision. Many were amazed that he has hung on this long in the face of these difficulties. It is even more amazing that he has been able to retain his sense of humor and perspective throughout very difficult days.

The reasons for the unhappiness of Dr. Egeberg as well as others concerned for the nation's health were, in these months, not hard to find.

Game Plan I was in full force and effect. And one of its major features was curtailment of *certain kinds* of government services.

One of these was medical research. The Nixon budget for fiscal year 1970 proposed a 20%, or $290 million reduction and brought about the closing of 19 centers of the National Institute of Health which the Johnson Administration had established. For fiscal year '71 an additional cut of $26 million was imposed at the expense of research into heart disease, arthritis and other chronic ailments.

Mr. Nixon vetoed the HEW appropriations bill in January,

1970 and as a result $21 million were cut from cancer research. Yet only a year and a half later he was to dramatically announce establishment of a new cancer research agency directly under the President, and a "brand new" war on cancer. No mention was made of his January, 1970 forced reduction of funds that might have been pushing cancer research ahead during all the intervening time.

Funds for medical schools were cut by $100 million in 1970, partly it now appears because his own particular plan for aid to medical education wasn't ready yet. Meanwhile Dr. Egeberg was pointing out the nation's crying need for 50,000 more doctors and 200,000 more nurses.

In June Mr. Nixon vetoed the legislation passed by Congress for continuation of the Hill-Burton hospital construction program. He called it "fiscally irresponsible." Congress thought otherwise. It was, perhaps, thinking about its responsibility for the health of the American people. So it overrode the veto by 279 to 98 in the House and 76 to 19 in the Senate. Congressman Donald Fraser of Minnesota gave his reasons for voting to override in these rather convincing words:

> The Nixon administration seems to believe there is enough money in the national coffers to bail out the Pennsylvania Railroad, to subsidize Lockheed Aircraft Corporation, to build an antiballistic missle system that won't work and isn't needed, and to develop a supersonic transport plane that would cause serious new environmental problems, but there isn't enough to finance this ongoing program of federal aid for health facilities.

Despite the appeals of his own Assistant Secretary of Health and despite the nationwide shortage of physicians, Richard M. Nixon vetoed the very bill which would have most directly attacked that shortage, in December 1970. This was a bill that would have provided $238 million to train and educate "family doctors." This was precisely where the most serious shortage had developed, as a result of the rush of most physicians into the higher-paid specialties. Among all his multifarious vetoes of acts of Congress this was one of the most difficult to defend. It appears that Mr. Nixon knew this. He must also have feared that Congress would override his veto, for the bill had passed the Senate by 64 to 1 and the House by 364 to 2. So he resorted to a trick. He declared that a short recess of Congress was equivalent to an adjournment; he did not sign the bill, and claimed it dead by a "pocket veto." (The term

83

used when a bill is passed late in a session of Congress, delivered to the President shortly before adjournment, and allowed to die on the President's desk while Congress is not in session and when therefore it is not possible for him to return it to Congress with a veto message and the chance of an override.) This illegitimate use of the pocket veto was, if anything, another evidence of the virtual contempt in which Nixon, now in power, had come to regard the Congress of the United States, in which he himself once had served.

The record of the Department of Health, Education, and Welfare must not be confused altogether with the general policies of the Nixon Administration. In many ways the Department was doing a good job. Particularly was this true of its carrying forward with a program that had been gradually growing in the previous administration.

This was the approach to health care of keeping people well instead of simply treating them after they were sick. In more specific language this departure had four principal elements: (1) the provision of continuous, preventive as well as curative care to a defined population, (2) by a balanced group of doctors and nurses, working as a team, (3) with average costs of care paid by the patients in regular monthly installments, and (4) with participation by the consumers of the care in financial responsibility and ownership, in some cases, of the physical facilities. In short, these were group practice prepayment health plans.

Through many decades those believing in this cooperative approach to solution of problems of health care had struggled to establish their plans, to staff them with doctors willing to brave the wrath and discrimination of organized medicine, and to provide to growing numbers of people at no extra cost beyond their monthly payments whatever care they might require.

The government of the United States was somewhat slow in "discovering" this new development. But when it began to do so the Department of HEW commenced to enter into contractual relations with the Group Health Association of America, national organization of the plans, and to provide the funds necessary to bring about the establishment of similar plans in various cities. This began in earnest during the Johnson Administration. It expanded in the Administration of Richard Nixon—a development on which, as we shall see, the President himself looked with favor.

During all of 1969 and 1970 hearings were in progress in

84

the Congress on the many bills which had been introduced to improve and reform the nations health care system, which Mr. Nixon himself had declared as in a state of crisis.

The most thorough-going of these bills, authored by Representative Martha Griffiths in the House and Senator Edward Kennedy in the Senate, became a principal target of Administration attack. The bill was popularly referred to as a National Health Insurance bill—as indeed it was. Detailed description of its provisions we will go into later. Suffice it to say here that the bill, if enacted, would provide needed health care as a matter of right to every citizen of the United States.

Feverishly Administration witnesses attacked the bill as "improper, unworkable, too costly, and alien to our basic traditions."

Another trouble with the bill, not stated by the Nixon witnesses, was that it was sponsored by the wrong people. That is, not by Mr. Nixon himself.

By this time there was confusion in the public mind as to why, after having promised action to meet the "national crisis in health care," Mr. Nixon was, by all the evidence, apparently moving in the opposite direction. But only a short couple of months after his veto of the Family Practice of Medicine Act the President himself provided the answer to that confusion.

The simple fact was that not until February, 1971 was Mr. Nixon ready with his own plan for curing the nation's ills.

To say that he had deliberately sabotaged most of the existing programs in order to make the introduction of his own more dramatic, would perhaps be stating the case too harshly. But surely he had not been engaged in forwarding those programs.

Be that as it may, President Nixon performed one of his better feats of "flexibility" when he delivered his Health message to Congress on February 18, 1971. If anyone had thought he was against the training of doctors just because he had vetoed a bill for that very purpose, or that he was opposed to aid to medical education just because he had cut its funds by $100 million, or that he disliked medical research because of the blows he had struck at it—well, they were simply mistaken.

For here in his February message were proposals regarding all these matters and a number more, brought before Congress with the Presidential imprint. This was what Congress was supposed to have been—but fortunately had not been—waiting for.

The President's message was a carefully prepared document,

in some respects an imaginative one. He recited the facts about rising costs, stated that they had become "prohibitive" for growing numbers of people, deplored the lack of preventive care, and stated that "Good health care should be readily available to all of our citizens."

To accomplish that goal Mr. Nixon presented a six-point proposal under these headings: Reorganizing the delivery of service, Meeting the special needs of scarcity areas, Meeting the personnel needs of our growing medical system, Malpractice suits and malpractice insurance, New actions to prevent illness and accidents and A national health insurance partnership.

With much of what the President proposed there was little argument. Congress had already tried to take constructive action with respect to meeting personnel needs and preventing illness by means of research programs. In many areas of special need neighborhood health centers had been in operation for several years before Mr. Nixon took office.

When it came to "reorganizing the delivery of service" Mr. Nixon went beyond what any previous president had ever done. Taking his cue from the progress already made by group-practice, prepayment, direct-service health plans, he coined a phrase: "Health Maintenance Organizations" or HMO. And came out boldly for a manifold expansion of such plans as a matter of national policy. In doing so he said that what was needed was a "true health system, not a sickness system."

His argument for this could have been, perhaps was, written by one of the most experienced persons in the Group Health Movement.

It is true that Mr. Nixon's proposals for implementation fell considerably short of what was needed to develop HMO's as rapidly as he appeared to want. Those who had labored through the years in various cities and rural areas to establish cooperatives and labor-sponsored group health plans were flabbergasted at the prospect of trying to put 100 new HMO's into operation in the first year. It was evident that the $23 million proposed by the President for planning grants to potential sponsors would not stretch very far. The $300 million in hoped-for private loans which he proposed to guarantee for capital, construction of facilities and the covering of early operating deficits was woefully inadequate for 100 HMO's. And, anyway, those who had gone through long months of establishment of just one really good prepayment health plan were compelled to regard the President's goal of 100 in a single year as completely unrealistic. On the other hand Mr. Nixon recognized the necessity of removing the barriers to HMO development which restrictive laws in 22 states presented. He properly called such laws "archaic," and proposed to "pre-empt" them by federal government contracts and the promotion of model enabling acts.

The strange case of Richard Milhous Nixon thus became stranger still—this time to his credit. For the same man who had so shamefully knuckled under to AMA pressure in the Knowles affair was now advocating a vast expansion of a new and constructive approach to the delivery of medical care which had until very recent times been bitterly opposed by organized medicine.

One serious danger became apparent as the Administration tried to draft legislation for the promotion of HMO's. For it was proposed to make federal aid available to promoters of profit-making HMO's. The danger in such a motivation, as contrasted to non-profit, service motivation was evident to everyone experienced in the field. For third parties running HMO's for profit will obviously have quite opposite motivations from those to which Mr. Nixon had pointed in his message. Profit-seeking promoters will, quite naturally, seek to provide as few and as inexpensive services as they can to subscribers and to pay professional staffs as little as possible. Quite the opposite from what the cooperative plans belonging to their member-subscribers are motivated to do. Unless this hole in the Nixon program is plugged there will be trouble ahead.

But to expect Mr. Nixon to rule out the opportunity for private profit is of course to expect far too much.

Good as were the President's proposals for the first five parts of his program, his sixth and by far most important proposal was controversial to say the least. This was his "National Health Insurance Partnership," his thrust against the far more comprehensive legislation already pending in Congress such as the Kennedy-Griffiths bill.

Here Mr. Nixon departed completely from the unanswerable philosophy he had set forth earlier in his message in advocacy of HMO's. For what he proposed was an indemnity insurance program almost entirely. This meant a return, with a vengeance, to the "sickness" insurance which he had spoken against. Under any cash indemnity insurance plan the insured person or family simply receives a certain amount of cash after they are already sick and they may spend that money in any way they see fit. They may buy good medical care with it. They may, in the confusion of the prevailing "no-system," come close to wasting it.

Mr. Nixon revealed his overall national program as one whereby all employers would be compelled to buy health insurance for their employees—to be paid for, after the first two years, 75% by employers and 25% by the workers, if indeed those workers chose to be covered. This, as was quickly pointed out by advocates of other proposals, would constitute a tremendous bonanza for the insurance companies. It would also provide no control whatever on the quality of care which insured people would buy, nor any effective way of preventing providers of medical care from further escalating its costs.

Mr. Nixon proposed a Family Health Insurance Plan for poor families who would not be covered otherwise. But even here his proposal was that the government simply buy insurance policies for them. This was supposed to replace Medicaid which, despite its inadequacies was supposed at least, to provide such services as the poor needed, whatever those might be. Under the Nixon plan poor families would be cast adrift in ghettos, barrios, and depressed rural areas to try to find someone to care for them and to attempt to spend their insurance cash benefits as best they could. They would also be limited to only 30 days of coverage in a hospital.

There was no reform of the delivery system of health care in the United States in these indemnity proposals of the President. He simply proposed to extend the system that has proved so inadequate.

Having climbed the HMO mountain to high ground Mr. Nixon had descended to the plain from which he started.

Spokesmen for the aged and the poor were quick to discern the inequities in the Nixon plans.

Senator Kennedy pointed out that the Nixon Family Health Insurance Plan left out completely anyone not a member of a family with children. Further he said that "under the Nixon program, a worker with a $5,000 hospital expense would be obliged to pay about $1,800 out of his own pocket or 25% of his entire year's salary."

Nelson Cruikshank, President of the National Council of Senior Citizens termed the reliance of the Nixon plan on private insurance carriers as "nothing short of shocking from the point of view of anyone having experience in the field." He said he had been assured by the Secretary of Health, Education, and Welfare himself that adequate controls would be imposed on the insurance carriers—only to find that same Secretary proposing to the Ways and Means Committees that reliance be placed upon the states to provide the admittedly necessary controls.

Ed Murphy, Director of the National Council of Senior Citizens charged that while the President proposed to eliminate the $5.30 monthly charge for Part B of Medicare, that would be more than offset by the requirement that the aged pay a substantial part of the cost of hospital care after only 13 days, plus $50 for doctor's services. He termed this "an outrageous attempt to save money at the expense of people least able to pay."

One of the more temperate but also most definitive critiques of the Nixon Plan came editorially from the American Public Health Association. Here are some excerpts:

There were several "messages" in the President's Health Message of February 18. Some were positive and even innovative. The majority were disappointments, particularly in view of the high promise of the State of the Union message.

The National Health Insurance Standards Act proposed falls far short of the standards set by this Association as required of a national program for personal health services. Coverage is spotty and categorized rather than universal. The working poor will be hit particularly hard . . .

The Family Health Insurance Plan is offered as an improvement on Medicaid, but again provides benefits substantially below those offered the poor in the States with the best Medicaid programs . . .

The Health Maintenance Organization . . . is now elevated to the status of a "vehicle for responding to all health care problems." The HMO . . . is offered as a "solution" even before it is adequately defined as a concept.

The welcome thrust toward improved systems for financing professional education is blunted by the lack of attention to nursing, to health administration, to environmental health, indeed, to basic support in any fields except medicine and dentistry.

Finally, the Health Education Foundation, the major venture into preventive medicine in the President's proposals, is presented as an isolated fragment and underfunded. There will be no federal funding, a fact that must raise real questions as to federal commitment. Rather, the insurance industry will be called upon to bankroll the effort—a small price in view of the windfall they would receive were the National Health Standards Act to become law.

The Executive Board telegraphed the President expressing the

Association's concerns with the equity and effectiveness of the proposals. They said, in part, "We have been encouraged by the rhetoric of recent months. We find the substantive responses astonishingly poor." That says it all.

While the President's proposal was not yet in legislative form there were before the 92nd Congress even more bills in the health field than had been the case in the 91st. Senator Javits, New York Republican, had one which, generally, provided for expansion of Medicare to cover many more people. The American Medical Association sponsored a measure for extensive tax deductions to help people pay medical bills. The American Hospital Association presented a proposal.

But the most comprehensive bill was an only slightly modified version of the National Health Security Act which had been the Kennedy-Griffiths bill in the 91st Congress.

It was reintroduced by Senator Kennedy of Massachusetts and co-sponsored by 21 other Senators of both parties. It was introduced in the House by Congressman James Corman of California ably supported by Representative Griffiths. This measure, numbered S.3 in the Senate and H.R. 22 in the House, was the result of years-long studies by a broadly-based body calling itself the Committee for National Health Insurance. It had the unqualified support of organized labor, the National Council of Senior Citizens and many other concerned organizations.

This measure contrasted sharply with the President's proposal. First it provided for a 2 year preparatory or "tooling up" period before the program itself would be established, to be used for training of medical personnel, development of prepayment, group-practice plans (HMO's in the President's language), health education and other means of improving the delivery of health care.

Once in operation the Kennedy plan would provide to all the American people about 70% of all health care needs including personal health services, prevention and early detection of disease, doctor's care, hospitalization, and medical rehabilitation. There would be no separation between the poor and others in the population. All would be included in the one program. The plan would be financed 50% from general tax revenues, 30% from a payroll tax on employers, 12% from a 1% tax on workers' wages and unearned income and 2% from a tax on the self-employed.

States and local governments would be relieved of about

$2.5 billion annual expenditures for health, these being assumed by the Federal Government.

The money collected by the various taxes would be placed in a Health Security Trust Fund from which all providers of health care would be paid as they rendered services. Patients would not be charged for covered services.

First payments out of the fund would go to group practice prepayment plans (HMO's) as one means of encouraging their formation.

As it did during the 91st Congress, the Nixon Administration fought the Kennedy bill tooth and nail. It charged that the cost of the plan would be exorbitant and estimated it at $77 billion, whereas sponsors said it would be $58 billion. Sponsors countered by pointing out that the money to be spent under the Kennedy plan was being spent already by the people or by various governmental bodies and claimed that the same amount would simply be better spent under their plan.

Another argument used by the Administration was that the National Health Security Act would replace private health insurance. Proponents have replied that to an extent this was not only true but precisely what they wanted to accomplish. People would receive health *care* as needed—not simply money after they had become seriously ill. Furthermore, since the Health Security Trust Fund would be paying providers of care, it would be possible to exercise control over both costs and quality of that care—an utter impossibility under indemnity insurance.

The contest goes on. Whether a bill will be passed and what kind of bill it will be remain matters of doubt.

But some kind of "national health insurance" is certain to come to the United States before very long. Ours is the only advanced nation on earth that does not have some such system in effect.

As the year 1971 passed, some of the same rather tragic absurdities of the Nixon Administration continued. Money appropriated by Congress for health purposes was continuously held back by the White House office of Management and Budget. Projects for which funding had been promised were told instead that there would be indefinite delays before the money could be made available. For example: Congress appropriated $8 million for research into kidney disease, but the entire amount was frozen by Presidential order. Protests from the National Kidney Foundation fell upon deaf ears.

The closing months of 1971 and the early ones of 1972 were a period of considerable action—much of it constructive. Senator Nelson of Wisconsin introduced a comprehensive bill designed to bring about sweeping reforms in the development, testing, marketing and use of drugs. His bill was the result of 4½ years of intensive study and hearings by the Senator's sub-committee. If passed, the bill was calculated to protect the people against harmful and useless drugs and to save them large sums of money as well.

Spurred by Senator Nelson's action the Food and Drug Administration, after years of procrastination moved at last to do something about non-prescription over-the-counter drugs sales for which the American people spend some $3 billion a year—much of it for utterly useless medications. The FDA even proposes to test such drugs for both effectiveness and safety, to act against false and misleading advertising and to move generally to protect the public.

On November 11, 1971 Congressman William Roy of Kansas, himself a physician, introduced a carefully prepared and comprehensive bill to provide for the organization and development of Health Maintenance Organizations. Unlike administration bills, Congressman Roy's measure would limit federal aid and financing to *non-profit* plans, thus avoiding the certain danger that many of them would become exploitive instead of serviceable. His measure is also realistic as to the problems to be faced, and solved—as to the financing, manpower training and other factors of impact that will be essential to their solution.

On November 18, 1971 President Nixon signed into law a bill which combined the features of the doctor-training bill which he had vetoed a year before with some of his own proposals and those of members of Congress. The measure authorized funds for the construction of facilities for the training of doctors and other medical personnel and to provide substantial federal aid to students in the form of reduced tuition payments and scholarships for students from low-income families.

But as the New Year came in a battle brewed on Capitol Hill over the enforcement, or lack of it, of the Occupational Safety and Health Act after its first nine months of operation. The charge was made by organized Labor and by consumer advocate Ralph Nader that the Labor Department was permitting states to adopt standards less stringent than the federal law allows and still to assume enforcement of it. The Labor

Department's own report stated that during the first five months of operation only 5633 establishments had even been inspected, out of a total of four million, and that violations of the law had been found in 80% of those inspected. But, charged Ralph Nader, average penalties had been only $18 for some 19,000 of such violations.

Senator Harrison Williams of New Jersey opened hearings on implementation of the law, which had been passed by Congress without support from the Nixon Administration.

Promises have been many. None more golden than those of Richard Nixon. Some action has been taken. But the promise of transformation of the present "no-system" of health care into a national one and one that will answer the people's present inability to afford good health care remains unkept. Before long it will have to be. Mr. Nixon's rhetoric, his critique of what is wrong, his word picture of what ought to be—all these are good to excellent. But his practical "partnership" plan is by no means geared to do that job. Rather it is mainly calculated to perpetuate the very present system of "sickness insurance" and fee-for-service medicine whose virtual bankruptcy he himself has eloquently described.

8. THE FUTURE OF THE PLANET EARTH

I have no intention of making "scapegoats" of the industrial community in the fight against pollution.

—Richard M. Nixon

The nearest man has ever come to "solving" the mystery of his own, and the universe's, existence is still contained in the words of the Book of Genesis: "In the beginning God created the Heavens and the Earth."

Thousands of years have passed since those words were first set down by a person willing to be humble, and hence to begin to understand.

In all those thousands of years nothing new has been added to man's knowledge of *Original Creation* or the *reason* for it. The wonder, the awe, the mystery and the majesty of Original Creation and the *why* of it remain as far from man's grasp as they were when Genesis was written. For the realm of that wonder and the mystery is where knowledge fades and merges into Faith. And it is where we can hope to understand only as we are willing to be still and wonder why we should exist at all.

Science tells us that all matter comes from previously existing matter. If this be so, then Existence can have no beginning nor ending in time and there can be no boundaries to space. And we may perhaps speak of God as the Essence of Eternal Existence.

Science tells us *how*, but not *why*, the Earth came to be. It pushes knowledge back through incalculable eons of time to when there was only a boundless diffuse gas. Why it existed, what lay beyond it, how it had come to be, science does not, perhaps need not, say.

The gas was "there."

Then "from some cause," portions of the gas congealed and became gigantic nebulae of less diffuse matter. Again, "from some cause" those nebulae did not stand still but whirled through space in tremendous flaming masses. And as they did so, and out of trillions of years of time and through limitless oceans of space, nodules of yet more congealed matter formed and became galaxies of stars, or "suns" as man came to call one of them. A force called "gravity" held them together. What it was, and is, and why it has existed—such questions can only be answered with "from some cause."

Gravity was "there."

The stars rotated at immeasurable speed upon their axes; and as they did so bits of them flew off and began to orbit around their "mother" stars.

One of those stars, born of an eternity of creative process— or the plan of God, as you will—threw off a piece of itself that was destined to become a home for life. Through more eons of time—some scientists say five billion years—this little satellite of this particular sun cooled. Around it there formed, in time, an envelope of atmosphere. And after much more time, a thing called water fell upon the steaming planet. It cooled still more to become a place—the only place we know of in all the vastness of the known and unknown universe— where a miraculous thing called *Life* could come to be.

The beginning of that life was one tiny cell. But within it "from some cause" lay a power to grow, to reproduce, to change, to evolve. Until, after millions of years and only because a countless multitude of events and circumstances all fit perfectly together, the absence of any one of which would have stopped the entire creative process, there came upon the Earth a form of life called Man.

Earth was made for him. He—*and she*—for Earth. And the time came when men and women grew full of scientific knowledge: knowledge of *how*, not *why*, they had come to be, knowledge of the nature and structure of the universe and of Earth's place in it; knowledge of the riches of the Earth, of how the intricate matter that formed Earth was put together.

And of how it could be torn apart.

With that knowledge there came arrogance, and forgetfulness. Arrogance born of man's growing power to create and destroy. Forgetfulness of the travail of creation, that had prepared the Earth as a home for life and human life. Forgetfulness, too, of the fact that Earth was the one home man could ever have—man today and his children and children's children in whatever tomorrows there might be.

Our Earth is a precious place.

But within the past very few years people have begun to wake up to the fact that it is not an indestructible one.

In fact, our young people, with their Earth Day and other protests, have helped to teach us that the process of destruction of our precious Earth is already far advanced.

Young people, with longer lives—they hope!—ahead of them simply cannot understand the criminal apathy of their elders who seem content to depend on a frightful balance of terror as the only protection of all humanity against death in an atomic war.

But in the unlikely event that this balance of terror actually holds off the annihilation of war, there is the growing danger that the Earth will, in the not distant future, be rendered unable longer to sustain human life.

Man is killing his own planet, and none too slowly. Unless the direction of technology is turned from measures that pollute and destroy the air and water—and soon—the hope for survival of man as we now know him is dim.

We have the power radically to transform the environment. Not merely locally, but world-wide. It is not alone over cities like Los Angeles and New York that the atmosphere is being rendered lethal, but all over the world. The Atlantic Ocean is on the same road that led to the death of Lake Erie.

The evidence of impending disaster to planet Earth has been accumulating for a long time.

Dr. Paul Ehrlich, of Stanford University, stated the grim prospect in an interview with *Playboy* magazine in these words:

There are many species that have vanished because they could not adapt. It's not at all inconceivable that man will follow these creatures into extinction. If he continues to reproduce at the present soaring rate, continues to tamper with the biosphere, continues to toy around with apocalyptic weapons, he will probably share the fate of the dinosaur. If he learns to adapt to the finitude of the planet, to the changed character of his existence, he may survive.

If not, nothing like him is likely to evolve ever again. The world will be inherited by a creature more adaptable and tenacious than he.

Such a creature exists—the cockroach.

Evidence was not hard to find. In 1930, 6000 people became sick and 60 died in one polluted pocket in industrial Belgium. In 1948 in Donora, Pennsylvania, half the population was stricken and 20 people died when a heavy fog, combined with stagnation of the air, prevented escape of the industrially polluted air. And during a 10-day period of fog and lack of wind in London in 1952, 6000 more people died than would normally have done so.

Despite the fact that modern medicine has dramatically reduced the death rate from infectious diseases, the length of life of people in the United States is *not* increasing and has not been for the past 10 or 15 years. Air pollution is a major reason why this is so.

The biggest single source of air pollutants is the automobile —especially in warm climates where there is little wind. Carbon dioxide from automobiles weakens and adds strain to the heart, thus making people less able to resist the impact of other diseases.

The United States of America with only 6 percent of the world's population, consumes today about half of the exhaustible resources of the earth and causes half of its pollution. This present generation of Americans is guilty of criminal violation of the right of all future generations to a life-sustaining earth. It is rich nations and rich people, *not poor* nations or poor people, who are destroying the earth by increasing consumption of power.

The environment was not a major issue in the campaign for the presidency in 1968. But Dr. Barry Commoner and his associates at Washington University, St. Louis, were being listened to more and more as they warned of the dangers ahead unless the thrust of technology were reversed. Rachel Carson's book, *The Silent Spring*, once dismissed as extreme alarmist writing, was being taken seriously; and Senator Muskie was in demand as a speaker on environmental subjects. His address to the 1969 Consumer Assembly, titled "The Last Clear Chance," likened the present generation to a person who had the last clear chance to avoid a fatal accident. He plainly told his audience that the next very few decades would decide whether Earth would have a bright future or none at all as a home for human life.

By the year 1970, the second year of the Nixon presidency, Congress, the President, newspapers, magazines, television and radio were competing with one another for leadership in the fight against pollution.

So were an increasing number of popular organizations. Some of these, like the Sierra Club, cooperatives and organizations of consumers, had been at it for some time. Others were brand new associations, formed for the specific purpose of fighting one part or another of the battle.

Much of the attack was levelled—quite properly—against corporations which had for decades been fouling the air and water with smoke and wastes. Governmental action was obviously called for. But increasingly it was realized that a basic culprit in the piece was the very high standard of living of the American people. Emphasis was on material satisfactions, comforts and luxuries. And these were demanding more and more power from the Earth.

How long the world's resources of fossil fuels would last at accelerating levels of consumption became an openly discussed question. So did the safety, or lack of it, of the much-promised power source from nuclear reactors. How long could the great American "love affair" with the automobile be allowed to continue? Was it not long past the time for a massive drive to develop the cheap, efficient mass transportation systems which workers so badly needed to get to jobs, and which the nation needed to replace half the automobile traffic? Was the craze for air conditioning an indulgence of the present generation which would be a major factor in robbing future generations of their rightful heritage? Were certain fertilizers and pesticides—DDT for example—the lethal danger to the environment which some scientists contended?

These and other questions were being asked. And answers

demanded—especially by the young people who had most at stake.

There were those who asked another question, this time a political one. Why was the Nixon Administration neglecting completely government development of the one time-tested method of producing power which did not pollute at all? This was—and is—hydro-electric power. Out of its deference to the private power monopoly, no doubt, the Administration was then, and continued throughout its course, refusing to inaugurate any significant hydro projects at all.

It was true that in his state of the union address of January 1970, Mr. Nixon had dramatically pledged himself to a $10 billion program of environmental clean-up, modestly labelling it "the most costly and comprehensive program in the field ever in history." Mr. Nixon declared: "I shall propose to this Congress a $10 billion nationwide clean-waters program to put modern municipal waste treatment plants in every place in America where they are needed, and get them built in five years." Only $4 billion of this was to be Federal money, the rest to come from the hard-pressed states. And his own Secretary of Interior, Walter Hickel, was joining Senator Muskie in saying that some three times the President's figure would be needed just to bring municipal water and sewer systems up to date.

The President did create a number of commissions, chief among them the Environmental Protection Agency. And before his first term was over he had recommended the spending of considerably more money on environmental programs than had ever been done by previous administrations.

But his performance on the practical front of action against polluters and pollution was, in general, a different story.

Congress was way ahead of him. In 1969 it had passed the National Environmental Policy act, authored by Democratic Senator Henry Jackson of Washington. And in part to provide staff for the Council of Environmental Affairs, created by the Jackson bill, Senator Muskie had authored the Water Quality Improvement Act of 1969. Strangely, Mr. Nixon had supported the Jackson bill but declared that the Muskie bill "would be a mistake."

In 1970 President Nixon requested just $214 million for water and sewer grants to cities and towns, whereas Congress appropriated $800 million. In August, 1970, Mr. Nixon actually vetoed the HUD appropriation bill because, he contended, it contained $350 million "too much" for water and sewer grants. And he kept some $200 million of funds actually appropriated by Congress for this purpose impounded in the Office of Management and Budget.

In June 1970 other events transpired which it seemed hard to reconcile with the high-level oratory of Mr. Nixon's state of the union message of six months before.

Newspapers reported on June 7 that actual work on anti-pollution projects had been sharply reduced because of an order from the Administration to cut expenditures. Jacob Dumelle, head of the Federal Water Quality Administration for the Lake Michigan region, called the order "unfortunate" and said it "jeopardizes vital summer programs." At the time there were only 2,200 people employed in the Federal anti-water pollution program compared to 1,500,000 *civilian* employees in the Defense Department.

At this same time—the summer of 1970—President Nixon was demanding that Congress appropriate $290 million as first installment on development of a supersonic air transport plane, the total cost of which was estimated to be $4 billion. This money was to be a virtual gift of taxpayers' money to a private manufacturer. Furthermore from the standpoint of environmental pollution, it was, to say the least, undesirable. Environmental scientists feared that such planes would upset natural meteorological balance in the upper atmosphere where they would fly, and thus expose the Earth's surface to excessive radiation. No one even attempted to deny that the plane would subject Earth, its people and its other living things, to a bombardment of sonic booms. Its only conceivable use would be to get a handful of rich travellers to Paris in a couple of hours' less time. The President's ad hoc task force on the project, the Federal Council on Environmental Quality, and the President's Science Advisory Committee had all recommended against the SST. And a number of state legislatures had passed laws forbidding such planes to land on their soil.

Nonetheless the Administration persisted. Mr. Nixon made this a major personal recommendation to the Congress.

But Congress refused to obey in the 1970 session.

A year later the project was pushed again by the President. And again after long and bitter debate, the Congress refused to authorize it. Whereupon Mr. Nixon declared he would find some other way to get a supersonic air transport built in the United States. There the matter rests.

In December, 1970, House and Senate conferees agreed on the final form of the Muskie bill to require automobile manufacturers to produce a nearly pollution-free automobile by 1975. The bill did empower the Administration of the Environmental Protection Agency, which President Nixon had established, to grant a one-year extension, to 1976, if it was persuaded, by evidence, that this was necessary. The bill contained another important provision. It required the Administrator of the EPA to take into account not only the technology developed by the petitioning automobile company but also any better technology developed by independent engineering concerns.

The Nixon Administration joined the automobile companies in opposing the Muskie legislation. The Secretary of Health, Education, and Welfare wrote to the Senate committee considering the bill urging that a later deadline than 1975 or 1976 be put into the bill.

As well he might have done. For the Administration's own bill in the same field merely set 1980 as a "goal" for achievement of nearly pollution-free cars and contained no requirement whatever that the goal be met!

It was becoming less and less difficult to tell whether the real defenders of planet Earth were in the Congress or the White House.

Losing his battle against the tough actions of Congress, Mr. Nixon tried an "end run" around it. He, or his staff, discovered to their credit that the Refuse Disposal Act of 1899 forbade discharge of industrial wastes into the nation's waterways without a Federal permit. If the Administration could not win the contest with Congress in the air, perhaps it could do so in the water. Accordingly Mr. Nixon signed an executive order directing the U.S. Army Corps of Engineers to begin to issue permits to industries whose discharges met state or Federal standards.

At first blush this looked like a victory for President Nixon over his rival Senator Muskie, who was working on a bill to impose strict—and exclusively *Federal*-government—controls over water pollution.

But troubles developed with the Nixon plan. Manufacturers were extremely slow in applying for permits. Some complained of the cost of doing so; others said the applications themselves would expose the worst aspects of their practices.

Furthermore, environmentalists were quick to point out a fatal weakness. Since the Nixon plan provided that Federal standards would not be applied if states had established their own, this was an open invitation to the states to compete against one another for location of industries by deliberately setting their standards low.

The Nixon plan was described, not altogether unjustly, as "license to pollute." The magazine *Environmental Action* ran an article in February, 1971 which concluded: "The Administration is embarking on a program that may cause critical delays in the fight against pollution."

It would be unjust to lay at President Nixon's feet too much blame for what was happening to the future of planet Earth. In his budget message for fiscal year 1972, he proposed to almost double his request of Congress for appropriations affecting the environment. He abandoned his $10 billion, nine-year program which Congress had rejected as inadequate and proposed instead a three-year $12 billion program, half to be put up by the states, for waste-treatment grants to cities. And for his Environmental Protection Agency he budgeted almost twice the amount of the previous year.

Furthermore Mr. Nixon appointed, as head of the Environmental Protection Agency, William D. Ruckelshaus, a thirty-nine-year-old Indiana Republican who proceeded to surprise and delight many environmentalists with his energetic concern for actually moving to protect the environment. The trouble was that in doing so, Mr. Ruckelshaus stirred the wrath and opposition of powerful forces within the Administration and apparently even incurred the displeasure of the President himself, who had, after all, assured the industrial community that he had no intention of making "scapegoats" of them in the fight against pollution.

Money in the budget was one thing. Offending some of the best contributors to Republican campaign funds was quite another. Secretary of Commerce Stans, who was to resign in 1972 to become collector of funds for the Nixon re-election campaign, led the fight to prevent Mr. Ruckelshaus from "going overboard" for clean air and water. On July 15, 1971, Mr. Stans made a speech to the National Petroleum Council in which he pictured the economic life of the nation grinding to a halt under the lash of the environmentalists. Stans was joined by the Office of Management and Budget in applying the brakes to the efforts of the Environmental Protection Agency. And under pressure from the White House the EPA was forced to weaken its rules on air pollution, to drop its plans for a nationwide permit system as opposed to a state-by-state one, and to abandon plans for imposing inspection standards on automobiles now in use. EPA also agreed to allow exceptions to its standards in cases where industries claimed that it would be "too costly" to cleanse the air and water.

In November, 1971 Secretary Stans actually presided at a meeting of the National Industrial Pollution Control Council, an industry-formed body concerned not so much with "control" as with its absence. Out of that meeting came a joint effort of industry and the Administration to dilute the strong water pollution bill which the Senate had passed by a substantial majority. Members of the House of Representatives began receiving callers from the Stans meeting.

Efforts of the Administration to water down the pending legislation or to defeat it if that could be done, were understandable.

President Nixon's clean-water proposal was for a $6 billion, three-year program, with $2 billion to be devoted to the job each year.

The bill already passed by the Senate carried authorization of $14 billion to be spent over four years' time for the purpose of making the waters of America safe for swimming by 1981. Thereafter the intent of the Senate bill was to end the discharge of *all* pollutants into the waters of the United States by 1985.

The House bill, opposed by the Administration, authorized $20 billion to be spent by 1975 for grants to municipalities for construction of waste-treatment plants. By 1976 all municipalities participating in the program would have to have secondary treatment processes in operation.

The contest between members of Congress and the President over action to save the environment has not always been a clean or fair one. As Senator Muskie began to emerge as a likely opponent to Richard Nixon in November, 1972, strange events began to take place in the Senator's home state of Maine.

The Senator was the acknowledged national leader in the battle to save planet Earth. So if his home state of Maine could be "shown up" as having a bad pollution record this might tarnish Mr. Muskie's image right where it was brightest and thus improve Mr. Nixon's chances of re-election.

Perhaps it was coincidence but on the very next day after Senator Muskie announced his candidacy for the office of President of the United States, Mr. Nixon's Department of Justice brought suit against a Maine industry for pollution of the St. Croix River. The company thus charged replied publicly that this was "an obvious hoax to embarrass one of the nation's leading anti-pollution campaigners" and that it objected to "being placed in the middle of political in-fighting."

But this was only one in a series of strange circumstances. The record for the years 1970 and 1971 is interesting. The state of Maine has one-half of 1% of the nation's population and less than 1% of its land area. Yet in 1970 10% of all anti-pollution suits brought by the Justice Department were against alleged polluters in Maine, and in 1971 it was 3%.

Meanwhile, not a single anti-pollution charged was filed in those two years in Oregon, for example. And the number of such suits in Maine exceeded that in such classic centers of pollution as Ohio, Pennsylvania and Alabama. In fact, of the eight judicial districts of the nation which the Justice Department itself selected as most likely to require anti-pollution action, only one—that of New York—exceeded Maine in the number of suits filed. While all this vigorous prosecution was going on in Maine, two-thirds of the 93 U.S. attorneys were filing not one single action during the years 1970 and 1971.

Are industries of Maine some ten to twenty times as likely to pollute as are those of other states in proportion to population and land area? This seems a little doubtful, to say the least.

The President had failed to observe even a minimum of traditional courtesy toward Senator Muskie. In early 1971 Congress passed the historic Clean Air Act. Senator Muskie was author of that bill and it was he, more than anyone else, who had guided it to final enactment. But when Mr. Nixon signed that bill, he not only failed to invite Senator Muskie to the signing but took full credit for the passage of the Act and did not even mention Muskie's name.

Nowhere was the scale of priorities of the Nixon Administration more clearly demonstrated than when as part of his Game Plan III package Mr. Nixon called for repeal of the 7% tax on automobiles. Here was the agent responsible for 85% of the air pollution in crowded centers. Here was $2 billion of revenue to be lost and made up—someday—by taxes on other payers. Yet as a major feature of his new game plan the President called for repeal of the 7% tax on automobiles.

Senator Cranston of California, where the automobile is a terrible offender, countered with imagination. He proposed that instead of repealing the tax on automobiles it be kept in effect and the money put into a Federal trust fund for the development of mass transportation systems. Senator Cranston estimated that if this were done, the work to follow would open up 140,000 new jobs.

But the President, not the Senator, had his way.

Our account of the struggle for a future for planet Earth would be an unbalanced one if we failed to point out that the obstacles to assuring that future are not all to be found in inadequacies of governmental measures. We, the people, bear equal responsibility. And we too often fail the test.

Some 35 acres of prime California land are being paved with concrete every day. The benefit of rainfall in the Los Angeles basin is diminishing as the years pass and as the trees and other vegetation are destroyed to make way for highway pavement and buildings. A massive program of *urban* as well as rural reforestation is critically needed in the state.

But when in the fall of 1970 it came time for voters in California to approve a referendum that would have devoted a quarter of the highway fund to development of mass transportation, they were not listening to scientists.

Instead they were reading deceptive billboards put up by fronts for the oil companies and cement contractors who had made very large secret contributions to fight "Proposition 18" as it was called. The voters defeated the proposition and decided to keep on building freeways so more automobiles could clog them, and so more smog could be created to stifle the lungs of the inhabitants.

A few months later some of the same oil companies that had financed the billboard campaign were assessed fines of just $500 each—yes, five *hundred* dollars—for their part in polluting Santa Barbara Channel with giant oil spills from off-shore drilling.

But in other action the oil companies fared not so well. "Pat" Brown, Jr., California's Secretary of State and son of the last Democratic Governor, brought suit against Gulf, Standard and Mobil Oil Companies on the ground that they had violated the law in making secret contributions to the fund to defeat Proposition 18. Gulf confessed to this and agreed to contribute, as penalty, $25,000 to a University research project studying the pollution problem. Secretary Brown dismissed his suit against Gulf. But not the ones against Standard and Mobile which were reported to have admitted to contributions of $45,000 and $30,000 respectively.

And what about atomic energy and its effect for good or evil upon the environment?

Ever since the people of Hiroshima and Nagasaki had had

their lives snuffed out by single atomic bombs, the United States has had a bad conscience.

One way of trying to console ourselves has been to talk about the great potential for peacetime benefit that lay in the newly-freed universal energy. To date, precious little has come of this.

Great "progress" has been made in developing "bigger and better" bombs and weapons at fabulous cost to the taxpayers of the Soviet Union and the United States and one or two other countries.

But very little progress in practical production of power for peaceful uses has, thus far, taken place. Always, however, there has been the promise.

In what the immediate post-war Congress thought was a wise and prudent move, the Atomic Energy Commission was established and given two functions. One was protection of the nation, its people and its environment from the evident potential perils of nuclear energy. The other was the development of peacetime uses of that energy.

I bear my share of the blame for having voted at one time to place those two conflicting duties in one and the same agency.

For what has happened is that vastly more effort has been put into the development phase of the Commission's work than into the protective one. A lion's share of the development, furthermore, has been directed toward greater military frightfulness rather than civilian benefit.

Correspondingly neglected, shrugged off, or "swept under the rug" have been the duties of the Atomic Energy Commission to prevent developments of nuclear power from rendering the earth a poisoned planet.

As is now plain, this result was inevitable. In its desire to make an impressive showing of nuclear power development the Commission is at every point tempted to cut corners on safety.

The two functions should be lodged in separate agencies. And at least one lawsuit has been brought by concerned citizens to compel such a division of functions.

As the nation began to wake up to the fact that increasing use of power was itself a basic threat to the environment, and as it came at last to realize that the supply of fossil fuels was something less than infinite, a widespread interest grew in the possibility of having, someday, a clean source of power production through nuclear energy.

The Atomic Energy Commission was not slow to grasp its opportunity. It allied itself with the private power companies of the nation and began to license the development by them of more and more nuclear power plants. By 1970 there were some 90 such plants either in operation, being built, or in the planning stage. Although the American taxpayers had invested tens of billions of tax dollars in the developments of atomic energy, all but one or two of these 90 installations were being developed for private profit. That meant, considering both "human nature" and the nature of the profit economy, that costs would be cut wherever possible and expensive safety features eliminated wherever the Commission was willing to consent. As in all too many cases it was.

All 90 of the plants were admittedly experimental. The AEC was anxious to find out which particular kind might work best. This was understandable. But knowing even the little they did about the awesome destruction power of atomic weaponry, the average citizen began to feel a little uneasy at the prospect of experimental nuclear power plants near his front door. And some of them were being located very close to multitudes of front doors in major cities.

The bold advocates of nuclear power development, with AEC at their head, were quick to contend that no major accidents had occurred in any of the plants thus far. This was true. But a number of minor ones had taken place, and some of these could have become serious.

Then on September 26, 1971, President Nixon, fresh from inspections at the Hanford, Washington, Atomic Works, gave forth with one of his many dramatic announcements. His Administration, he said in effect, was embarking upon a program for the development of a large number of "fast-breeder reactors." The President pointed out, with truth, that such reactors produce more nuclear fuel than they consume. He also referred to the energy to be expected from them as a "clean" source of power.

This was not so true.

For while if no accident occurs these reactors appear to be a cleaner source of power than most conventional ones—except hydro—they are far from clean. For they produce the most lethal kinds of atomic waste materials known to science —plutonium principally, one of the most poisonous substances yet known. Its half-life, that is the period of its greatest virulence, is 24,000 years! Furthermore, in all the debate over the safety or lack of it of nuclear power development, on one

106

point there is no disagreement. That point is that no one—repeat, *no one*—has as yet worked out any satisfactory or really safe way to dispose of atomic wastes. And while the containers now being used may last through the lifetime of this generation, this period of relative safety is almost certain to be at the expense of the future of planet Earth and those who hope to live on it in the tomorrows.

For this and other reasons citizen protests had been growing almost as fast as the Atomic Energy Commission was rushing into production with its power company partners. In city after city, protests were lodged and law suits filed to prevent location of nuclear power plants nearby.

There was deep concern lest the safety standards of the AEC were far too lenient, and some scientists formerly employed by AEC resigned to speak their minds about the inadequacy of the standards.

At one point some eleven states had suits pending to compel the AEC to raise its standards for any plants to be located within their boundaries.

There was solid reason for the worry.

It was discovered that great peril was involved in the mining of uranium, the essential raw material for nuclear power production. "Tailings" from the mines were found—and not by AEC—to contain vast quantities of highly dangerous radioactive particles.

Stories circulated, and were verified, of horrible suffering endured by workers at some atomic plants where minor malfunctions had taken place.

The continuous underground testing by the AEC in Nevada was reported to have contaminated a large area of that state, almost for perpetuity. And law suits were filed in Salt Lake City charging that an increase in infant mortality and leukemia in Utah had been caused by fall-out from leakage at the Nevada test grounds.

In Denver, Colorado, it was discovered that the AEC had stored large quantities of radioactive waste near Stapleton airport, directly in the path of planes taking off and landing.

At Hanford, Washington, the wastes from that plant were stored in huge containers almost directly over a known earthquake fault.

And yet the Atomic Energy Commission had tried to license a nuclear power plant at Point Reyes, California, which would have been only feet away from the famous San Andreas fault.

The need for clean sources of power is critical to man's

survival. If nuclear power can give mankind such a clean source, its blessings will be incalculable. Whether it can do so or not remains an open question.

But some facts we do know.

One is that unless the strictest conceivable standards are applied to every step in nuclear power development, there will have been criminal neglect. Dr. Edward Teller who has been called the "father of the hydrogen bomb" has told us this: "Nuclear reactors are clean only so long as they function as planned, but if they malfunction in a massive manner they can release enough fission products to kill tremendous numbers of people."

We know that there are other sources of power which are far less dangerous to the environment than nuclear fission can possibly be today. Among these are thermal power—from the steam within the earth—which Mexico has exploited with apparent success almost on the United States border. Another is harnessing of the tides which France is doing with marked success. Another, of whose practicability our own experience tells us volumes, is hydro-electric power. And still another, which scientists tell us would be completely clean and produce no radioactive waste at all, is fusion power.

The question, therefore, arises as to why so little effort or substance is being devoted to development of these power sources. That question goes to the heart of another question: whether it is possible to turn technology around and direct it toward a monumental drive to save planet Earth, and away from its present course of devising more and more "sophisticated" and cruel ways to destroy it. On the answer to that question probably hangs our fate.

It is time to change our life styles, time to learn again the joys of walking, time to learn to do without air-conditioning, time to learn to plant trees and to stop destroying them, time to recycle paper, cans and bottles, time to reject the whole sterile idea of conspicuous consumption, though advertising urges it upon us wherever we look or listen.

It is time to be careful.

It is time to use less power, not more of it.

It is time to begin to cherish our good green planet Earth as it deserves to be cherished. It is time to think—to think that unless we change our ways we could destroy five billion years of creation of the Earth in the tiny span of one generation.

The stakes are life and death. And they are too great to be

subjected to the play of petty policies. Or—what is worse—"great power" politics.

This brings us to a final question. What of Amchitka, of the nuclear blast which our country set off on that Alaskan island?

We are told by the Atomic Energy Commission and by the Nixon Administration that it was a "great success." It gave us another weapon system, we are told. It is pointed out that no major disaster took place, as many of us had feared.

But the question lies deeper. The Council on Environmental Quality which President Nixon himself appointed, recommended against the Amchitka blast—and its report was suppressed. A great many scientists warned of what *could* result from this underground explosion—250 times as powerful as the bomb that decimated Hiroshima. It could have resulted in a disastrous earthquake and even more disastrous tidal waves. It could have—indeed perhaps it *has*—destroyed fish life in a great part of the ocean. It could have affected the very crust of planet Earth.

It was with knowledge of these risks that President Richard M. Nixon decided the charge should be detonated. His decision gave him another bargaining chip in the game of power politics. He chose in the name of his country to risk a major violation of the balance of nature itself for the sake of one more weapon with which to destroy human life.

In the light of the questionable future of planet Earth, was his decision a right one?

That is the question.

9. GAME PLANS AND THE AMERICAN ECONOMY

> We are not going to change our game plan at the end of the first quarter of the game. We are not considering wage and price controls. Nor are we considering putting the government into the business of telling the working man how much he should charge for his services or how much the business man should charge for his goods.
>
> —President Nixon

The three "games plans" of Richard Milhous Nixon make up one of the strangest aspects of his strange case. They run the gamut from the most reactionary aspects of traditional Republican Party philosophy to a policy of wild deficit-financing coupled with the most drastic government controls over imposed upon the United States in peacetime.

Yet, in both their positive and their negative aspects, all three of the game plans had certain features in common—strange as this may seem. In what they did do for the privileged and the powerful and in what they did not do for the unemployed, the farmers, small business and the poor, the three game plans have been the very soul of consistency.

Game Plan I was pursued during the first two years of Mr. Nixon's presidency—that is, until the results of the elections of November, 1970 had been "read, marked, and inwardly digested" by Mr. Nixon and his advisors.

Game Plan II was in effect for the eight months from January, 1971 to August 15 of that year.

Game Plan III was suddenly and without warning unveiled on that fateful August day.

All three plans were rooted and grounded in the "trickle down" theory of economics—the theory, holding that if enough government largesse is poured in at the top of the economic pyramid, if measures are taken to reduce taxes and increase profits of big business, then somehow benefits will trickle down to the people who support the pyramid's broad base.

The only trouble with the "trickle down" theory is that it

doesn't work. Certainly it did not do so under Richard Nixon's direction.

On the other side of the coin—the other side of the tracks —none of the three game plans contained the one course of action which can be depended upon to increase the demand for goods, to reactivate idle productive machinery, and thus to restore general health to the economy.

That course of action is to increase the buying power of the people at or near the bottom of the economic pyramid. They are the ones who are sure to spend whatever they have in hand. They must do so in order to live at anything like an American standard of life.

But for some strange reason this rather elementary fact did not occur to Mr. Nixon and his advisors. Or else it was, for political reasons, rejected. Probably the latter.

One announced objective of Game Plan I was the dampening of inflation. The rate of inflation was substantially less when Mr. Nixon took office than it later became. But considering the life-long orientation and basic loyalties of Richard Nixon, it is easy to understand why he chose to fight inflation as his primary aim.

Inflation affects everyone. No one likes it. It reduces, somewhat, the buying power of every dollar anyone possesses. In a free market economy, price inflation normally stimulates employment. But it is otherwise undesirable for people generally. And for those who enjoy the privilege of creating the nation's money, as the commercial banks do today, or for anyone in the business of lending money, inflation is not simply undesirable or harmful, but absolute anathema. For inflation, whatever, its other undesirable features, does make debts easier to pay, since they are repaid in dollars of less real value than that of the dollars that were borrowed.

So the decision to combat inflation was not only appealing to home-makers, it was also popular with the financial interests which had, from the beginning of his strange career, always been Mr. Nixon's most ardent supporters.

In general there are two ways to combat a price inflation. The constructive one is to increase the supply of needed goods and services to the point where that supply equals or exceeds the effective demand and thus exerts a downward pressure on prices. In the long run this is the only sound economic cure for price inflation.

The Nixon Administration did not choose to pursue that course.

The other method of combating inflation is by deliberately slowing down economic activity, reducing buying power and thus "dampening the fires" that have supposedly been causing an upward spiral of prices and wages.

This was the course chosen by Mr. Nixon and his advisors for Game Plan I. The fact that it involved planned disemployment of workers was no detriment of them since a loose labor market is regarded as desirable by large scale employers—even though few of them will openly admit this.

One basic rule of Mr. Nixon's Game Plan I was laissez-faire. The government would not attempt to interfere with or control business. There was to be faith in the American economic system and confidence that once the brakes had been put on inflation by application of a tight-money, high-interest policy along with a "tolerable" level of unemployment, prosperity would inevitably result.

Mr. Nixon expressed this philosophy plainly indeed in an address delivered in the early months of his presidency. He said: "We are not going to change our game plan at the end of the first quarter of the game. We are not considering wage and price controls. Nor are we considering putting the government into the business of telling the working man how much he should charge for his services or how much the business-man should charge for his goods."

Lest those strong words sound too strange in the light of certain subsequent events it must be borne in mind that this is a strange case we are dealing with.

In line with the policy of economic restriction, tight money was a cardinal rule of the game. Interest rates, key to that policy, continued to soar. Up went the Federal Reserve rediscount rate. Up went the "prime rate" charged by banks to most favored customers.

Facts set forth previously are worth summarizing briefly here. In 1968 the rate on FHA and Veterans Administration guaranteed mortgages had been an all-too-high 6¾%. By May, 1969 it had gone to 7½%. Meanwhile in April an alarmed Congress had empowered President Nixon to control and lower interest rates. But he stoutly declared he would never use that power.

By January, 1970 the rate on government *guaranteed* loans was an unbelievable 8½%, the highest level since the Civil War. Borrowers not helped by the Federal Government guarantees paid, of course, much more. Loans to small businesses were made at 9% and 10%. Those to farmers would probably

112

have been even higher had the cooperative farm credit system not been in the picture providing the kind of competition which user-owned business always gave. The impact in the construction industry which almost always operates on borrowed money was predictable and devastating. Housing starts fell sharply in 1969 and continued to decline throughout 1970. Other businesses suffered correspondingly if somewhat less severely.

Having declared he would never use "jawboning" as Presidents Kennedy and Johnson had done, Mr. Nixon stood by, deliberately speechless while monopolistic industries like steel and automobiles boosted prices, cut production, laid off workers, in order to maintain per-unit profit margins. Attorney General Mitchell's Department of Justice brought few antitrust actions.

In consequence of all these factors—especially of the extortionate interest rates and tight-money policy—Game Plan I worked all too brilliantly in one of its aspects. It did slow the economy. In fact it reversed it. In 1969, for the first time in many a year gross national product actually declined in the fourth quarter, and declined drastically—by more than $5 billion—in the first quarter of 1970. Unemployment which had been at a low 3.5% when Mr. Nixon took office stood at 5.8% by November, 1970 and was on its way to a more than 6% figure, where it remained virtually unchanged until well into 1972.

On the anti-inflation front, however, the record of Game Plan I was less impressive. Instead of going down from its 4.8% where it was when Mr. Nixon took office, the rate of inflation climbed to 6.1% during the first Nixon year, 1969.

The reasons for this were apparent enough, but unrecognized or unheeded by the Nixon Administration. The three major ones were (1) the very large military, space, and other economically nonproductive expenditures, (2) monopolistic-administered pricing, and (3) the declining volume of production.

As the year 1970 dawned, Game Plan I entered its most virulent phase. Still determined to balance the budget, Mr. Nixon resorted to his two devices: the veto and the freezing of appropriated funds. In January he vetoed, and forced substantial reductions in the appropriations for the Health, Education and Welfare Department, on the ground that it contained "too much" for education and health programs. He vetoed the Hill-Burton hospital construction bill but was overridden. When he vetoed another bill for aid to education in August, 1970 he was again overridden by Congress. But his veto of the appropriation for Housing and Urban development on that same August 11 was sustained. He had objected to an appropriation of $350,000,000 above his budget for urban renewal and a like amount for water and sewer grants. Even disabled veterans were not spared. The Administration cut back the budget for Veterans hospitals by $41 million.

The other device used by Mr. Nixon to dampen the economy and to attempt to "save money" was his, probably unconstitutional, freezing of monies actually appropriated by Congress for various socially-needed purposes. This practice reached, at times, the peak figure of more than $12 billion.

Not despite, but primarily because of the Nixon policies, inflation continued to worsen. In the single month of April, 1970 prices rose at an annual rate of 7.2%.

Welfare rolls all over the country rose—as the inevitable result of unemployment and the refusal of the Administration to spend the needed funds appropriated by Congress.

Neither the President nor his economic advisors nor members of his cabinet had a word to say about the two root causes of the nation's growing plight, namely, the huge expenditures for war and space exploration and the hamstringing of the economy by administrative pricing.

The whole price of the alleged fight against inflation was being paid by the unemployed workers, the millions of people in need of homes, the farm families forced off the land, and the small businesses going bankrupt. In his annual report to his constituents Senator Percy of Illinois was moved to write: "In 1970 thousands of small businesses failed with total losses amounting to $1.9 billion. Yet the Federal Government was not called upon to rescue these firms, nor was it asked to aid the thousands of farmers who went out of business." In September, 1970 industrial production actually declined by 1.7%. Third quarter growth rate was only 1.4%.

By October, 1970 unemployment had deprived 5.6% of American workers of their jobs, and just one month later the figure was 5.8%. October saw the cost of living rise at an annual rate of 7.2%, equaling the previous record set in April.

Then came the November elections. In the nation as a whole the result was a resounding defeat for Mr. Nixon and his policies.

This was the kind of language that Richard Milhous Nixon understood.

The result was Game Plan II, launched at the opening of the 92nd Congress in January, 1971.

It was dressed in the trappings of a Monarch. Game Plan II was, according to its author, going to transform the United States into the image he had proposed for it.

The program as a whole was labelled by Mr. Nixon as "The New American Revolution," the genesis of which was to be "power to the people."

It was immediately evident that the "people" he had in mind were by no means the American people as a whole, but rather local politicians.

Game Plan II was to have six objectives: (1) Welfare reform, (2) full prosperity, (3) enhancement of the environment, (4) national health care, (5) revenue sharing and, (6) reorganization of the Federal Government.

Mr. Nixon projected a budget deficit of $11.6 billion in his message, a diametric reversal of field from his previous insistence on a balanced budget.

Examination of the budget revealed that the President's actual proposals were hardly calculated to bring about full prosperity or a dampening of inflation, much less any return of "power to the people."

The budget called for an increase of $1.5 billion in appropriations for the Pentagon's current expenditures for war, thus increasing inflationary pressure from that source.

It called for appropriations of $235 million for the supersonic airplane or SST—this to be a virtual gift to private industry, and the beginning of a program that would eventually cost some $4 billion. Its benefit to the American people as a whole seemed hard to explain.

So far as the poor of the nation were concerned the Nixon budget failed to accord with the "power to the people" concept. On the one hand there was the welfare reform program under which Mr. Nixon proposed to provide a minimum family allowance—but only for families with children—of some $1600 to $2400 per year, a figure far below the poverty line. Humanitarian as this was from a certain point of view, and precedent-breaking as it was for a President to propose it, nonetheless, if enacted, this proposal meant dependence on government for millions of people. On the other hand Mr. Nixon proposed further to take from the War on Poverty seven of the ten programs then carried on by the Office of Economic Opportunity, and among these was the Community Action Program. That CAP program had been aimed through the years at giving to the poor meaningful participation in, and decision-making power over, their own struggle for economic and social betterment. All CAP programs, if the President had his way, were to be put into the hands of local authorities, most of whom had been hostile to them from the start. Here, certainly, the President's proposal meant less rather than more "power to the people."

The budget was not in all respects an expansionary one. Certain savings were proposed. The reductions were hardly at the expense of the affluent in society. Among them were downward revisions of net benefits from Medicare and Medicaid and complete elimination of the children's school milk program.

Taking the budget as a whole however, it was a classic example of deficit spending. After having cut them severely in previous years, Mr. Nixon proposed badly needed increases in items for research and development in various fields, more money for environmental controls, and other substantial increases.

Overall, the projected expenditures were almost $30 billion more than Mr. Nixon had budgeted for the previous fiscal year.

The election of 1970 had had its effect.

The time-honored Republican idea of the sacredness of a balanced budget was out the window. The pressure of events, and the expression of the voters had convinced Mr. Nixon of this. His wonderous flexibility was equal to the occasion.

But another long-held predilection of Mr. Nixon and the conservative wing of his party was not out the window by any means.

This was the "trickle down" theory of economic policy. And true to that theory the President, by unilateral executive action, granted a tax bonanza to industry at the very start of Game Plan II. This was in the form of a change in the rules for write-off of depreciation. It was estimated to be worth some $3.7 billion of tax saving to industry in the first year and some $50 billion over the coming decade, if continued in effect. This was another attempt to "prime the pump" by pouring money in at the top. That it had no beneficial effect on the nation's economy became apparent as the months passed.

A phalanx of organizations rose up in opposition to this move. Among them were the AFL-CIO, Ralph Nader's Public Interest Research Group, Republican John Gardner's new 200,000 member organization called "Common Cause," the Consumer Federation of America, and the National Rural Electric Cooperative Association. This not inconsiderable body of opposition pointed out that the tax relief given to industry had to come from somewhere. Either it would increase the deficit, thus swelling the national debt, or else others in the population would have to pay correspondingly more taxes, now or later.

Several of the above-mentioned organizations joined to seek a permanent injunction against the carrying out of the President's order. But without success.

Just how successful were the President's proposal for reorganization of the government, his plan for revenue sharing as a means of giving "power to the people," and the impact of Game Plan II on "full prosperity"?

As part of the "new revolution," Mr. Nixon proposed to consolidate eight existing Departments of the Federal Government into four new ones: Economic Development, Human Resources, Natural Resources, Community Development. Only State, Justice, Treasury and Defense Departments would be untouched should the reorganization ever be approved by Congress. The Departments of Agriculture, Commerce, Labor, HEW, HUD, Transportation, Interior, and whatever the government still had to do with the new Post Office Corporation would all be abolished and their functions taken over by one or another of the proposed four new conglomerates.

The plan was, and is, defended by the Administration on the ground that it would make the government more "efficient." To many people besides those interests immediately affected, this seems questionable. If four departments are better than eight, why not do the job completely and group all the functions of government into one, two, or three gigantic bureaus? On the other hand was it true—will it *ever* be true—that conglomerates are more efficient than single-purpose agencies? Certainly the experience of big industry was to the contrary. Decentralization had been the order of the day for some time, with greater efficiency generally resulting.

As might have been expected, neither organized labor nor farmers thought well of the organization plan. Both groups had had, and felt they deserved, a special voice in the affairs of their national government, through the Labor and Agriculture Departments. Farmers were especially violent in their opposition. Declining in numbers as they were they felt that abolition of the USDA would be a kind of "last straw" in the corresponding decline in their influence over national affairs.

Mr. Nixon finally decided—perhaps after contemplating the virtual Democratic sweep of the Plains States in 1970—to content himself with stripping the Agriculture Department of all its functions "not directly related to farming."

As Game Plan III ballooned into an Election Year Game Plan in 1972, the fate of the rest of the "New Revolution" in government structure remained in doubt.

The real core of the Nixon "Revolution" and especially of his "power to the people" theme lay in revenue sharing. As proposed in the Game Plan II package, the plan called for having the Federal Government hand over to the states and cities some $5 billion annually to be spent exactly as the local authorities saw fit. Then another $11 billion was to be passed out in large categories, into each of which would be thrown a number of the existing grant-in-aid programs. Here again, the "strings" on the money were to be loose ones since governors, mayors and county supervisors would find considerable leniency in shifting funds from one program to another within each grouping.

Thus power was to be showered on the people through the good offices of their local officials.

The division of this money, as proposed by Mr. Nixon, was to be on a per capita basis. This meant that the states with larger populations would receive proportionately more than those with fewer people.

Chairman Mills of the Ways and Means Committee was one of the first to express opposition to the Nixon proposal. He pointed out—and no one contradicted him—that it was unsound practice not to make the politicians who spent taxpayers' money assume responsibility for raising it. Mr. Mills also contended that the Nixon formula was wrong. The basis of distribution of funds should be need rather than numbers of people. Some of the states with smaller populations, like some of the smaller cities, were in far greater need of federal help than some of the more populous areas.

There was some understandable resentment, too, over the fact that Mr. Nixon had presented his revenue-sharing proposal as if he had invented the idea. Those who had labored to put into effect such revenue-sharing programs as Social Security, grants for schools and highways, urban improve-

118

ment and many another could see only one important difference between their kind of financial relief to states and localities and Mr. Nixon's.

That difference, however, was an important one around which swirled most of the debate. The Nixon proposal was branded—not without a certain logic—as a simple revival of "states rights." And Arthur Burns, the economic counsellor to the President, said it represented "an old Republican concept."

There were many in and out of Congress who believed it to be a duty of the Federal Government to see the taxpayers' money which it collected be well and carefully spent; above all that it be spent for the specific purposes and benefits to the people for which it was intended.

These opponents also felt that local politicians would be sorely tempted simply to use the federal gifts to pay part of their current operating expenses rather than for expansion of services to the people. Especially was this fear expressed with regard to the $5 billion of completely undesignated funds.

Even where some general purposes for the use of $11 billion were to be prescribed by the national government there was, said the opponents, no way to prevent certain programs from being robbed or even entirely discontinued in favor of others, perhaps less needed. For example, what would happen to Urban Renewal, Water and Sewer Grants, the Model Cities Program and Rehabilitation Housing Loans if lump sums were dished out to cities for all four of these programs put together, as Secretary Romney testified was the proposition?

This fear was colorfully expressed by Milton Semer, former general counsel of HUD, in an address to the National Housing Conference:

So we face a rather puzzling question: What exactly does this merger merge? If you merge 1800 urban renewal apples with 147 model city oranges, with 450 water and sewer kumquats in a wide variety of localities, in many instances not the same, what do you have? Some people are already wondering whether a proposal involving so much trouble and disruption, and so little identifiable benefit, may not be the result of an unannounced wish to turn these programs off—or, failing that, to bring them to a virtual halt through a procedural breakdown of unpredictable length.

This was a kind of keynote. Mr. Nixon's dislike of programs initiated by anyone but himself had been amply demon-

119

strated. The gnawing question about both government reorganization and revenue sharing was whether at least one purpose was not to get rid of many of these programs altogether.

Counter-proposals came from a number of sources. All of them involved revenue sharing in order to relieve the growing financial crisis faced by many cities and even some states.

One of these by Senator Humphrey of Minnesota and Congressman Reuss of Wisconsin contained the condition that any governor, in order to receive the federal money, must present a plan for modernization of the governmental structure in his state and its local subdivisions.

Senator Muskie's proposal contained four major points. First, the shared revenues would be distributed on the basis of relative need of the localities; second, in order to induce states to reform their own—generally outmoded—systems of raising revenue, the Senator proposed bonuses for states instituting or increasing the effectiveness of income taxes; third, federal standards would be required to prevent discriminatory use of the shared monies; and fourth, in order to bring about long-range planning, the federal commitments would cover periods of five years.

Chairman Mills advanced the proposal that the Federal Government assume the full cost of welfare, thus going one step beyond the President's Welfare Reform proposal. The final form which revenue sharing will take, beyond its present scope, remains to be decided upon.

As time wore on there was little evidence that Game Plan II was doing any better than Game Plan I had done—either in reviving the sagging economy, in reducing inflation, or in increasing employment.

In the month of February, the Bureau of Labor Statistics reported a rise of only .2% in cost of living generally, but added that food and clothing prices were up .4% and costs of medical care a whopping .9%. Apparently BLS revealed too much. It should have stopped with the "good news" of the .2% rise, for Labor Secretary Hodgson announced that the press briefings by BLS experts, standard practice for 20 years, would henceforth be discontinued.

Anyway unemployment was at 5.8%, and the less said of that the better. Especially when the office of Management and Budget was sitting on some $12 billion of funds appropriated by Congress which if released could have put a good many unemployed to work.

Industrial production declined by almost half a percent in February, 1971.

Inflation, however, did not decline. The consumer price index of cost of living registered an increase of 7.2% annual rate in May and 6% annual rate in June, to crack an all-time two-months record.

The lesson clearly had not yet been learned, by the Nixon Administration, that it may not be—probably will not be—"inflationary" to put idle workers to work in idle plants to produce more goods and increase the supply relative to the demand.

To cap some sort of climax for Game Plan II, Richard Nixon won a big victory in Congress on August 2, 1971. After all the billions that had been spent for war equipment, after all the years of favoritism which "defense" contractors had enjoyed at the hands of the Pentagon, Lockheed Aircraft Company, the biggest of all those contractors, was found to be on the verge of bankruptcy. If any event were needed to prove once and for all the utter bankruptcy of the "trickle-down" theory, this was it. Yet, in accord with that theory the President called on Congress for passage of a bill whereby the taxpayers of the United States would guarantee a quarter of a billion dollars of loans to salvage Lockheed. The bill passed the House. It squeaked through the Senate by the margin of a single vote.

This was the last major play called by the quarterback in Game Plan II.

It was a great help, no doubt, to the biggest defense contractor in the country. But it helped Lockheed's workers much less. For right after the loan guarantee bill passed, a substantial number of workers were summarily fired by the company.

All year long Mr. Nixon and his economic "wise men" had stuck resolutely to their defense of laissez-faire and the "strength of the American economic system."

The First National City Bank inserted in its monthly economic letter for August, 1971 an article written by Mr. Nixon's own chairman of the Council of Economic Advisors, Mr. Paul McCracken. The article was published in the *Washington Post* on July 28, 1971:

General price and wage control would be a serious threat to individual freedom. It is amazing that the press, so jealous of its own freedom, does not recognize what would be the implications of having the income of literally everyone in the country controlled by a government agency.

Strangest of all was the statement of Secretary of the Treasury Connally who, if anyone, should have known what was coming. At his press conference only a few days before August 15, 1971, the Secretary declared: "I have said we weren't going for a wage-price review board and we haven't. I said we weren't going for wage and price controls, and we haven't."

But they did.

By midnight of August 15, 1971, Game Plan III was in full force and effect through presidential fiat.

Game Plan III had two objectives, according to the President. The country was suffering under the unprecedented combination of sharp inflation and severe recession. So Game Plan III undertook to move in two almost opposite directions at the same time—that is, to stimulate the economy and to dampen inflation. It was like stoking the fires in the boiler and sitting on the steam valve simultaneously. The bed which Mr. Nixon's past policies had made was not a comfortable one for him nor for the nation.

Mr. Nixon's imposition of the 90-Day Wage-Price freeze and Game Plan III was obvious admission that his previous policies were unworkable if not disastrous. Characteristically he made not a hint of honest admission of this fact. But everyone else knew that for the first time in its history the nation had been suffering from severe and rising unemployment and economic sluggishness on the one hand and from a galloping price inflation on the other. Add to this a $23 billion budget deficit in fiscal 1971 with probability of an even larger one in 1972. Add also the first foreign trade deficit in several decades, deep depression of prices received by farmers, a serious threat to the "soundness" of the dollar, a progressive destruction of the environment—and we have the general picture that brought on the freeze.

It was no wonder that Mr. Nixon took drastic action. He had to.

It was, however, a matter of considerable enlightenment to find the most committedly conservative administration since Harding tacitly admitting in one short half-hour that the "free market" economy was operating in reverse and that the gold standard was operating like a ridiculous millstone around the nation's neck.

Congress, concerned about what it saw coming had, as we know, conferred upon President Nixon more than two years before the power to institute economic controls, including control of the escalating interest rates. Mr. Nixon declared then and repeatedly thereafter that he would never use these powers. And so far as controlling interest, profits, or dividends he has kept his word—unfortunately—to this day.

Had the President acted promptly when Congress conferred these powers on him his action could have been far less drastic and would almost certainly have been far more successful. It would also have saved the country from its abysmal crisis. But at the time, Game Plan I was in full, if wilting, flower.

While Mr. Nixon abandoned many of his life-long predilections on August 15, one he did not abandon was the "trickle-down" theory of economic recovery and stimulation. He persisted in the belief that if the people at the top, especially large-scale business, are given enough economic advantages, their prosperity will trickle down to the people generally—to the workers and farmers and small businesses—and cause increased employment and economic recovery.

The fact that the theory had brought the country to near disaster seems to have made no impression on the Chief Executive. Mr. Nixon had certainly given it every chance to work. Military expenditures had been maintained at fantastically high levels, with new weapons systems regularly emerging from the Pentagon woodwork to threaten the Strategic Arms Limitation Talks (SALT) with failure.

Interest rates had been allowed, if not encouraged, to skyrocket to the highest levels since the Civil War. Money-lenders had had a field day. Even short-term government bonds were costing taxpayers 6% interest and more. And interest on the national debt had gone from $14 billion in 1968 to more than $20 billion in fiscal 1971—a full 50% increase in the Nixon years.

As if this were not enough, Mr. Nixon had granted the fast depreciation tax write-off to business.

Finally not a word had the Administration had to say about the cancer of monopoly pricing. Utility rates had been allowed to skyrocket, steel prices had been boosted more than once, the same with autos, aluminum and others.

But none of this had done any good. Unemployment continued to rise. Inflation continued with a vengeance.

Then—suddenly—came the freeze: of prices, wages, and

rents. But *not*—significantly—of interest rates, profits, or dividends.

The trickle-down theory was still the basic policy of the Nixon Administration, for Game Plan III. True, the freezing of the dollar from its bondage to gold would probably benefit the nation generally. True, also that the President proposed to advance the second $50 increase in basic tax exemption, which Congress had scheduled for January, 1973, to January, 1972. But there the help to the average family and its buying power abruptly ended.

Instead, Mr. Nixon proposed, on top of his fast depreciation write-off, worth some $4 billion to industry, to add another $5 billion annual bonanza in the form of a 10% investment tax credit for money spent on new plant and equipment!

A brief glance at the economic facts of life should have shown, even to Mr. Nixon, that more productive capacity was not what the nation needed. A quarter of that capacity was lying idle. What *was* needed was a stimulation of consumer demand so the plants already in existence would go back to work and employ people. And there were several ways to bring about that stimulation of consumer demand. The most obvious one was by *an immediate and substantial reduction in family taxes.* Another was by a really effective program for training and public service and public works employment of the unemployed. Congress had passed no less than three such bills in the past few months, all of which Mr. Nixon had vetoed, only finally to sign a badly emasculated version of a bill he originally had castigated when he vetoed it.

A third and badly needed method was an increase in prices received by farmers. The most constructive way to accomplish that was by measures that would strengthen the market bargaining power of farmers' cooperatives.

Mr. Nixon's new game plan did not include any of the measures to increase the mass buying power of the people.

Again, and hardly noticed amid all the excitement about other measures, Mr. Nixon announced abandonment for one year, at least, of his proposal to provide the poor with a minimum of $2400-a-year per family as a measure of "welfare reform." *The Christian Science Monitor* observed that Mr. Nixon was asking those least able to do so to make the sacrifices he demanded for the success of his game plan. There was no hint that he might cut, even temporarily, his own $200,000 salary.

So what Mr. Nixon's package amounted to was hardly any

increase in the people's buying power, and a continued reliance on the "trickle-down" theory.

But there was more to the story. If we did not need more productive capacity, we needed more automobiles even less. It is hardly necessary to reemphasize the fact that the automobile is an arch-destroyer of our God-given air. To try to cure the recession by encouraging production, sale, and use of more automobiles by repeal of the excise tax, or in any other manner was, to speak generously, the height of irresponsibility.

And the proposal of the President to "increase employment" by firing 5% of government employees (!) requires no comment beyond the simple observation. He could easily have saved his projected $4.7 billion by cutting the budget of the Pentagon, instead of disemploying workers. But he chose to fire the workers.

As for foreign trade, we had to wait and see. Certainly the imposition of the 10% tariff on imports would increase the cost of living of the American people as long as it lasted. Prices for both imports and domestically produced goods go up inevitably behind tariff walls. If this tariff protection brings about increased employment, it may balance out the loss to some extent. But whether this policy will actually increase American exports and reduce imports remains a matter of doubt. It all depends upon whether other countries finding it harder to sell in the American market will choose to continue to buy from us, or whether they will take their trade elsewhere. As the months pass there are signs that the latter might take place. Foreign trade is a two-way street. And more than one country can play the game of tariff-and-trade retaliation.

Evidence of these facts of life was not long in appearing.

Close on the heels of Mr. Nixon's sudden change of course, Canada welcomed the Premier of the Soviet Union on a state visit and signed a far-reaching trade treaty with that country. A few months later trade talks between Canada and the United States broke down.

In October France and the Soviet Union signed what the press called an "unprecedented" 10-year economic agreement under which France undertook to assist the Soviets in production of goods ranging from heavy trucks to baby food. Russia was allowed to build factories in France, among them a refinery and a steel plant. And Renault, the French government-owned automobile company, agreed to invest $240 million in a truck factory in the Soviet Union.

In January, 1972, Japan, which had been America's best

customer, especially for farm products, entertained a trade delegation from the Soviet Union to discuss stepped-up commerce between the two countries. Japan and Canada were hardest hit by the new American policies.

Whatever the wisdom of the new Nixon policies, certain it was that the dramatic suddenness with which he chose to announce them—above all the lack of a word of consultation with U.S. trading partners beforehand—left much to be desired in the way of statesmanship.

In December, 1971, a negative note was struck when the U.S. Department of Commerce announced that the trade deficit for the nation had been at an all time record $821 million in October, followed by $227 million in November. The Commerce Department was compelled to revise its estimate for the trade deficit for the year upward to $2 billion from the $1 billion originally forecast. The last year in which the U.S. had had such a deficit was 1893.

Minutes after Mr. Nixon announced his freeze it was apparent that all sorts of inequities and injustices had been "frozen."

Certainly action was called for. But, as a number of economists said, the method employed by Mr. Nixon was a "clumsy" one.

For the major oil companies the blow was not too severe. For on July 30, just two weeks before the Nixon announcement, they had raised gasoline prices in many areas by as much as six to eight cents. Whether some friends of big oil in the inner councils of the Administration had "inadvertently leaked" the news of what was coming, no one knew for certain.

There were other groups in the population who were less happy, and severely confused.

For example, in thousands of school districts and in hundreds of institutions of higher learning, contracts had been entered into with teachers for the ensuing year. But none of these were to go into effect until the school year started in September. This was in the very middle of the 90-day freeze. Hence the increases were forbidden, at least until the middle of November. What would happen then no one knew.

Again labor contracts covering tens of thousands of workers had been negotiated to take effect during the three months period of the freeze. Practically all of them provided for wage increases. Would they be permitted to be effective when the freeze ended? And would the pay boosts be retroactive to the date fixed in the agreement, or paid only from the end of the freeze period?

None of this was clear. Attempts to get clarification failed, probably because no one knew what the policy was to be.

There was also broad speculation as to what would take place at the end of the 90 days. Would the freeze be continued for a longer period, perhaps indefinitely? Or would that "bureaucracy" which Mr. Nixon declared he would not create have to be instituted to administer some kind of selective controls? Or would the economy be turned loose again with the virtual certainty of a greater amount of inflation than ever before?

The second alternative seemed the more likely one, as turned out to be the case. This leads to the question whether it would not have been far wiser, even at so late a date, to have established an orderly system of selective controls on wages, prices, rents, interest, profits and dividends—difficult as its administration would have been—than to have imposed the freeze. Such a system would have left room for the correction of inequities and injustices, which the freeze did not. And it had to be resorted to in any case when Phase II began on November 12.

All things had not gone too well under the 90-day freeze. Unemployment, needless to say, was not alleviated at all. This was to be expected. But even inflation continued apace. In August, despite the freeze, the cost of living jumped by .3%, an annual rate of 3.6%, and double the July increase. Gasoline prices advanced more in August than at any time in the past year. In September prices received by farmers which were *not* frozen went down a whopping 5.7%. Frozen and canned foods which were supposed to be "frozen" managed to rise, and interest rates on mortgages, which of course were not controlled, were increased again as they had also been in August. Had farm prices not declined so sharply, the rate of inflation in September would have been at an annual 5%.

By October, with the freeze still in effect, the inflation rate was, understandably, considerably reduced.

On November 12, Phase II of Game Plan III began.

Two control boards had been appointed without Senate consent—one for prices, the other for wages. Five of the members of the original wage board were representatives of organized labor, though four of them were soon to resign in protest. But not a single representative of either farmers or consumers was appointed to either board, though some representation of people's organizations was allowed on advisory panels.

Wisely and properly the Price Commission was instructed to concentrate its efforts against increases on the part of large corporations doing more than $100-million-a-year volume. Many people concerned about the march of monopoly in the U.S. economy felt that control over pricing by such companies might well be a permanent function of government.

Smaller companies were subjected to less stringent control. And by January, 1972 all of the following commodities and services had been virtually exempted from controls: about half the rents in the country, and smaller food stores, raw farm products, raw seafood, real estate, custom-made goods, all used products, including used automobiles and of course interest, and financial securities.

Organized labor and consumer organizations were quick to point out two rather obvious weaknesses in the price control system, once the picture became clear.

One was that *individual* item retail prices were really not to be controlled at all, only the long-term trend of all prices in given stores. This meant that consumers finding the price of certain items to have been increased really had no valid complaint or recourse.

The other complaint, related to the first one, had to do with enforcement. This function had been given to Internal Revenue Service, but no one including the President, the Price Commission and IRS expected it to do more than spot-check for violations. There were only 3,000 staff members of IRS assigned to the total job of enforcing price control throughout the country.

Labor unions blanketed the country with "price-watchers," as a measure of citizen enforcement. But in view of the regulations, there was comparatively little they could do.

In the very first 2 weeks of Phase II some 200,000 complaints of violations swamped offices of Internal Revenue Service, not one of which had by December been referred to the Justice Department for prosecution.

It was little wonder, then, that Phase II enjoyed something less than universal approval. Polls of public opinion showed that, even among upper-middle income people, the program was regarded as inequitable. Those polled objected to the fact that profits, interest and dividends were uncontrolled while wages and prices were supposed to be. They also said that the tax favoritism shown business was unfair.

Workers' representatives went farther, saying that while wages were subject to definite and easily enforceable controls, there existed no genuine control over retail prices or half the rents at all.

The poor were, as usual, less protected than anyone else. The exemption of smaller, non-chain food stores made sense in affluent neighborhoods. There, it was true, as defenders of the Price Board's actions contended, that if the independent stores tried to raise prices their customers would quickly go to the chains where controls were, to a degree, in effect. But in the poor neighborhoods, the ghettos and the barrios, the chain stores hardly exist. The only stores left are the smaller independents whose credit practices and higher prices are notorious. The poor people were by this ruling left practically unprotected against price increases during Phase II.

What might turn out to be the most serious loophole of all in the attempt to control inflation escaped the notice of many people. But not of Senator Lee Metcalf of Montana, self-appointed watchdog for consumers over utility rates. For it was announced by the Price Commission that state regulatory bodies would have power to approve utility rate increases, subject only to "review" by the Commission. Senator Metcalf pointed out: (1) that applications for rate increases by utilities were at an all-time high of some $4 billion annually; (2) that in most states regulatory commissions were subservient to the utilities they were supposed to regulate: (3) that the Price Commission could not possibly give anything approaching an adequate review of such complex facts as utility lawyers always present in rate-increase application cases.

There appeared indeed, every likelihood that, unless Senator Metcalf's warnings were heeded, utility rate increases would go clear through the roof of the guide-lines. The rural electric cooperatives alone reported applications by their private power company suppliers for rate increases of as much as 75% and 100%.

It was understandable that consumers were doubtful about Phase II. The record of the Nixon Administration had been a disappointing one. The President's consumer message of 1969, titled "The Buyer's Bill of Rights," had been called disappointing by the Consumer Federation of America. But Mr. Nixon had, in that speech, promised administration support for legislation in a number of areas. Among these were class action suits by consumers, an independent consumer protection agency, and product warranties. All three measures had made considerable progress in Congress only to die with the 91st Congress either because of active Republican opposition or failure of the President's consumer specialist to say a word in support of them. And in the 92nd Congress the Administration had used all its influence to water-down the powers of the Consumer Protection Agency as the bill passed the House.

While all this was going on, Congress was wrestling with legislation on two fronts.

The first was the Nixon proposals for tax relief for business. Congress knuckled under and gave approval to a somewhat modified form of the fast depreciation tax write-off which the President had arbitrarily put into effect some months before. Congress also approved repeal of the 7% tax on automobiles and provided certain special tax advantages to exporters. All these the President had demanded.

From there on, however, it was a different story. Congress reduced from 10% to 7% the investment tax credit to industry for the purchase of labor-saving machinery. Then it turned to an attempt at stimulation of the economy where such stimulation was most likely to be effective.

The Bill as finally enacted by Congress provided:

(1) An increase in the personal income tax exemption to $675, not in 1972 but for 1971 taxes. (2) An increase in the exemption to $750 in 1972. (3) Complete relief from payment of income tax for some 3 million families at or near the poverty level. (4) An increase in the "standard deduction" from $1500 in 1971 to a maximum of $2000 in 1972. (5) For working families, a deduction of $400 a month for child care in the home or to send children to a day care center. (6) A tax credit of 20% of salary paid by an employer to a welfare recipient hired by him.

Whether or not tax reduction of the various kinds provided in the bill was the best attack upon the problem, it was probably the quickest one. And the extent that Game Plan III succeeds will be due far more to the action of Congress than to the President's original almost simon-pure "trickle-down" proposals.

The other job which Congress had to tackle was that of extending the power of the President to exercise control over the economy. That authority, having been legislated by Congress in April, 1969, was due to expire at the end of three years—in April, 1972.

The bill which Mr. Nixon asked Congress to pass was, in the words of Senator Stevenson of Illinois "little more than a blank check that would have empowered the President to control the economy as he saw fit."

Congress refused to pass such a bill and was publicly berated by the White House for that refusal. Doughty old Wright Patman, Chairman of the House Banking and Currency Committee, led the fight to protect the right of Congress to have something to say about how this nation is governed. His committee approved a bill that answered one of the sorest points about the wage freeze. It provided that where labor and management had signed before August 15 a contract whose provisions were to take effect during the 90-day freeze, then, in such case wages should be paid retroactively to the effective date of the contract. Contracts entered into in good faith were to be honored, said the committee, unless they would cause wages to be "grossly disproportionate" to the wage-price guidelines.

The bill gave the President, once again, power to control interest rates and to direct the flow of credit to where it was most needed. This power the President declared he did not want and would not use.

In other action the Congress gave the Administration power to roll back windfall profits, required Senate confirmation of future appointments to the Wage-Control Board and the Price Commission, exempted from control the wages of workers which were sub-standard, and authorized consumers to sue for treble damages in cases of overcharges in violation of the price-control regulations.

After the action of Congress, the Pay Board decided that employees who were due a wage increase during the 90-day freeze period could be reimbursed for the lost wages if the wage increase did not exceed 7%.

Increases in pay of military personnel were approved at a 15% figure, however, despite the Pay Board's adopted ceiling of 5.5% for wage increases.

Donald Rumsfeld, Mr. Nixon's director of the Cost of Living Council, which was the supreme arbiter over both the price and wage boards, declared on the day before the freeze ended that some increase in prices was to be expected in the coming weeks.

He was not mistaken.

For in December wholesale prices jumped by .8%, the steepest rise in almost a year, and an annual rate of 9.6%. And the consumer price index for the cost of living climbed by .4%, or at an annual rate of nearly 5%. The Administration and the country generally expressed disappointment. But the Administration for its part declared that this was probably only a temporary condition and that inflation would surely be down to 3% annual rate by the time of the fall elctions.

Late in January, 1972, the Cost of Living Council promulgated its guide lines for exemption of low-paid workers from wage controls. Congress had required in the law that this be done. But, quite in accord with Nixon Administration policy, the Council exempted wages from controls only if they were less than $1.90 an hour. This was contrary to a decision of the Wage Control Board itself. It was also, in the words of Congressman Ryan of New York, author of the provisions in the law affecting low-paid workers "a flagrant violation of the will of Congress," which had intended, clearly, to exempt all workers whose wages were below $6,960 annually—the Department of Labor's minimum for a decent living standard.

On January 24 General Motors and Ford Motor Company blandly announced price increases on their automobiles, with Chrysler expected to follow suit quickly.

In Los Angeles there occurred a grim sidelight on the "success" of Game Plan III so far as reducing unemployment was concerned. The Fire Department of that city advertised that it would accept applications for 36 positions, whereupon no less than 3,300 applicants took the Civil Service examination. 3,274 of those applicants would still be unemployed after those jobs were filled. So would several million other workers. How could it be otherwise when businesses were being given tax concessions for introducing labor-displacing machinery?

"Trickle down" just was not working.

The AFL-CIO claimed that the true unemployment ratio was more than 9% rather than 6%. The reason: Labor Department figures did not include "discouraged workers"— those who had given up believing they could ever find a job.

So the Administration changed its mind—and the rules— somewhat as it had done with farm parity. It decided that its *goal* for an "acceptable" number of unemployed people by election time would be 5% instead of 4% as previously announced. And it furthermore began to issue press releases stating that the definition of "full employment" should be changed. For years a 3% or 4% unemployment ratio had been considered to indicate "practically full employment." The Nixon Administration blandly proposed to begin defining "full employment" as a condition where "only" 5% of the workers were out of jobs. Both Game Plan III and Mr. Nixon would look better on election day if this were done.

The consumers and workers of the country were unimpressed, however, with this device. The convention of the Consumer Federation of America, held late in January, 1972, accused the Administration of "stringent restrictions" on wage increases and allowing prices and profits to increase virtually without restraint. Delegates demanded that ceilings be placed on corporate profits and dividends, that interest rates be rolled back and utility rate increases curbed.

Consumers showed their concerns in another way, too, as the year wore on. The rate of personal savings continued at a high rate, reflecting lack of confidence in the future of the economy.

Would 1972 still be a "very good year" as the President had been predicting with regularity?

But the statistics for 1971 were none too encouraging. Growth rate had been only 2.7% against a normal of 4.%. And despite the freeze and subsequent controls the rate of price inflation had been 4.6%.

One of the most serious problems that lay ahead, according to experts like Sidney Margolius, was in the cost of housing. Rents had continued to rise even during the freeze. And with the replacement of "controls" with guide-lines some landlords imposed sharp increases. Internal Revenue Service itself reported some of these at 30%. Costs of new houses were up an average of $2,000 each over a year before, the biggest one-year increase in a decade.

As President Nixon and his large party of attendants took off for China, they left behind a nation whose principal mood was one of uncertainty.

There were three major factors which doomed Game Plans I and II to their dismal failure and which made the price the nation must pay for such success as Game Plan III might achieve a staggering one.

With none of these factors has Mr. Nixon been willing to deal. Indeed the tactics his Administration has followed throughout the game plans have been such as to exacerbate the deleterious effect of all three of them upon the economy.

These three factors are high-to-extortionate interest rates, monopoly and its administered pricing, and economically wasteful expenditures such as those for war and space-exploration.

Unless these three factors are effectively dealt with and the "trickle-down" theory abandoned, the tragic combination of simultaneous inflation and recession becomes a virtual certainty.

About $2 out of every $3 of Federal taxes paid by the American people now go for war—past, present, and future. This is true if honest accounting is practiced, if expenditures like social security payments—already paid for by the people —are eliminated from the budget of controllable expenses and if items like Veterans Benefits and most of the national debt are recognized as expenditures related to war, as certainly they are. Every dollar that is spent for war and weapons of war is economic waste and a purely inflationary dollar. Tens of billions of those dollars are being dished out annually. A scandalous percentage of them wind up as contractors' profits. Several billion of them are simply wasted. Some of them go into workers' wages. But not one of those military dollars produces a dime's worth of anything useful or saleable in the markets of the nation. The entire impact of the military budget is, therefore, to drive up the prices of the goods and services produced by the wealth-producing segment of the economy.

As for employment, a billion dollars spent on military weapons employs far fewer workers than does a billion dollars spent in almost any other way. Most of the war money is necessarily used for acquisition of very expensive materials, for salaries of highly paid technicians and scientists. Furthermore, our burgeoning war establishment is robbing the rest of our economy of much of its productivity and efficiency because the military usurps so large a percentage of our best scientific and technical talent and of our exhaustible natural resources.

In the face of all of this and despite his avowed concern about inflation, Mr. Nixon's budget for fiscal 1972 called for an increase of close to $2 billion in the military budget. And the same was true of his $25 billion-deficit budget for 1973.

Until that trend is drastically reversed and the military expenses cut back to what is really needed as deterrent—without waste or profiteering—inflationary pressure will be intense. Congress did not give the President all he asked for the military in either fiscal 1971 or 1972. But the cuts were not deep ones in either case.

High interest rates have been apologized for on the false grounds that they curb inflation. They do no such thing. The cost of borrowing is a major element in the cost of production and distribution of practically everything we buy in this country. The selling prices must reflect those costs. The higher the interest rate, the greater price inflation must inevitably be.

And the record for the 10 years, 1960 to 1970, is clear as crystal. The rates of increase in prices from 1960—1965 were moderate indeed:

1960 to 1961 — 1.6%	1963 to 1964 — 1.5%
1961 to 1962 — 0.9%	1964 to 1965 — 1.1%
1962 to 1963 — 1.2%	

In December, 1965, the Federal Reserve board, by a 4-to-3 vote, decided to raise its rediscount (interest) rate from 4% to 4½%—a 12½% boost. The excuse for this action was that the higher interest rates were needed "to curb inflation."

The spiral was not long in taking effect. In the five years that followed, interest rates rose to heights unheard of.

Did high interest rates curb price inflation? Or did they *cause* it by adding to the cost of every economic transaction and every productive process in the country?

Let the record speak for itself. Here are the figures on rates of price inflation from 1965 to 1970!

1965 to 1966 — 2.4%	1968 to 1969 — 4.9%
1966 to 1967 — 3.0%	1969 to 1970 — 6.2%
1967 to 1968 — 3.7%	

Should Mr. Nixon decide belatedly to use his power to control interest rates and hold them at their present level, it will not be enough. High interest rates not only are a major cause of price inflation. But for reasons too obvious to require cataloguing, they discourage economic recovery and increase unemployment by making it more costly for farmers and businessmen to produce.

The third factor making for both recession and inflation at the same time is monopoly control of industry. To take but one example we are witnessing today a progressive monopolization of the energy resources of the nation. Over the past few years, seven out of ten of the biggest coal companies in the country have been bought up by other power-producing concerns. Four of the biggest of those coal companies now belong to major oil companies. Though the price of coal jumped some 60% in 1969 alone, and 100% in the Tennessee Valley Area,

Mr. Nixon's Justice Department has made no move to halt this ominous trend. Major oil companies are acquiring sites where thermal power might be produced, and seeking control of the Rocky Mountain shale deposits, which now belong to all the people.

The tragic fact is that most of the major industries of this nation are now subject to monopolistic pricing, which means that prices of their products always go up and never down.

Just how perilously close the American people and their economic life are to being completely dominated by a few industrial giants can be illustrated by a few examples.

General Motors Company is a semi-political state responsible to no one. It produces half the automobiles in the United States, is able to fix the price of all automobiles whenever it will. It has 1,300,000 stockholders, few of whom can possibly exercise any control whatsoever over the company. GM employs 700,000 people, has plants in most states and in 24 foreign countries.

GM is one of 100 huge corporations which among them own half of all manufacturing assets in the United States. Many of them own plants abroad from where, taking advantage of cheaper labor costs, they can ship products back into the United States to undersell American workers.

Four manufacturers of dry cereal account for 90% of all sales of that product.

Four steel companies controlling 54% of the industry raise their prices periodically and together, despite the fact that they are operating at only two-thirds capacity and are being undersold by imported steel. It was companies like this that Mr. Nixon's Game Plan III, in its international aspects, was calculated to help most.

The American Telephone and Telegraph company, a complete monopoly controlling an indispensable service which everyone *must* use, made net profits of $2.2 billion in 1969 on a volume of $15.7 billion—a 14% return.

The major oil companies are a classic example of oligopoly —that is, monopolistic control exercised by the coordinated action of a number of giant concerns. An example of their power, devastating to apartment dwellers on the East Coast especially, is this: Residual heating oil sold in New England for $1.78 per barrel in July, 1970. By May, 1971, the price was $4.92 per barrel, though the world price for crude oil was only $2.00 a barrel. Seven oil companies, two British and five American, control international marketing of oil.

When companies are as large and powerful as these, price competition comes to an end. Advertising competition which "helps" the consumer only by raising the price he must pay for the product, takes its place. Excessive prices exacted by monopoly rob all competitive industries—above all agriculture—of their just share of the consumer's dollar.

If we had anything like a competitive or truly "free" economic system any longer, our outlook could be different. For in competitive industries when there is a slack market, prices generally go down to stimulate demand; more workers are hired and the businesses try to maintain themselves by selling a bigger volume at a lower price. This is the one effective way to stop price inflation.

But in monopolistically-controlled industries—steel, automobiles, chemicals, containers, farm machinery, aluminum, electric power, and all utilities for example—prices go only one way—upward. In such industries a few managers and boards of directors are in position simply to decide how much production shall be allowed to take place and at what prices the products will be sold. They can decide this regardless of what economic conditions may be. Their consistent rule and policy is maintenance of the profit margin. To protect that profit margin, production will be curtailed to assure an excess of demand over supply. And even in times of recession when sales are slow, monopoly industries do not reduce prices to stimulate sales and increase employment as competitive industries do. Instead they lay off workers, curtail production and actually raise their prices to protect their profit margins. Examples of such action are legion.

The giant industrial empires are able constantly to expand through "internal financing." By imposing monopolistic prices on their customers they in effect compel those customers to finance their new plant and equipment, and even acquisition of smaller companies. Thus they seldom need to borrow money and are largely immune to high interest rates. Even when they do borrow they are favored with the prime rate. The advantage this gives the giants over their smaller competitors is almost incalculable.

These facts go a long way toward explaining that, despite the controls, automobile prices advanced 1.6% in January, 1972 alone and wholesale prices generally went up at an annual rate of more than 10% in the month of February, 1972. In that month alone, food prices rose by 1.7%—the largest increase in fourteen years.

What this country really needs is not a 90-day wage-and-price freeze but rather a continuing selective control of prices to be charged by monopolistically controlled industries. They should be treated as the public utilities which in fact they are. But regulation should be far more effective than present regulation is over what we now recognize as public utilities. Under such circumstances, with firm ceilings placed on the prices they could charge, monopolies would be compelled to protect their profit margins by increasing production and selling a larger volume of goods. And the only right or long-run effective way to cure a price inflation is by increasing production to the point where supply equals or somewhat exceeds demand.

If Mr. Nixon, or any President, would propose to Congress that it establish permanent machinery for the control of monopoly prices, if he would cut interest rates in two, and lop all the fat and waste off the war expenditures, then and only then could we hope to have once more a prosperous, full-employment economy without harmful inflation, and free of freezes.

Obviously, the American people deserve something considerably better than a series of hastily concocted "game plans."

10. HIGH FINANCIAL "RESPONSIBILITY"

A demagogue may find it easy enough to advocate that we allocate necessary defense dollars to social programs.
—Richard M. Nixon

On the last day of January in 1972, John Connally, President Nixon's Secretary of the Treasury, marched on Capitol Hill. His purpose was to persuade the Congress to raise the statutory limit on the national debt from $430 billion to $480 billion—a 12% increase. Moreover, this responsible head of the nation's Treasury told the House Ways and Means Committee that another increase in the debt ceiling would surely be necessary in 1973.

Asked if the Nixon Administration had any intention of recommending increased taxes as a means of checking the alarming rise in national red ink, Mr. Connally assured the Committee that it did not.

The $50 billion request of Secretary Connally was a considerably larger one than had ever been made by a national administration before—even in war time. It was the direct result of illogical monetary and fiscal policies, long pursued, combined with the strange record of the Nixon Administration in the field of national finance.

There was considerable shaking of Committee members' heads. They doubted that a tax increase could responsibly be avoided in 1973, if not in 1972.

The Congress did not jump through the Administration's hoop. It raised the debt limit by only $20 billion—not $50 billion—and it made even that a temporary increase to expire on June 30.

Mr. Nixon assumed the presidency at a time when only some 3% of the country's workers were unemployed and when the economy had enjoyed the longest period of continuous growth in its history. In fiscal year 1969—half of which was in Mr. Johnson's presidency and half in Mr. Nixon's—there occurred a budgetary *surplus of* some $3.2 billion. And few presidents in our country's history have assumed that high office with more loudly professed commitments to a balanced budget than did Richard Nixon.

It therefore seems almost incredible that one Administration—above all a supposedly conservative Republican one—could manage to saddle the American people with nearly $90 billion of additional debt in four short years. That $90 billion is one-fifth of all the debt our Federal government had contracted up to the time Mr. Nixon took office.

Yet that was exactly the prospect the nation faced when in January, 1972, President Nixon presented to Congress his budget for fiscal year 1973. He might well have claimed another "first" for himself, for he stood forth as the deficit-spending champion of all time.

Yet Mr. Nixon was the same person who had repeatedly accused the United States Congress of "fiscal irresponsibility." Especially when Congress tried to provide funds for critical needs of the people such as hospitals, water and sewer grants, slum eradication, or child care centers.

A fundamental cause of this strange set of circumstances was the dismal failure of "trickle down" to trickle with any effectiveness whatsoever.

The budget for fiscal year 1970, covering the period July,

1969 through June, 1970, was basically a Johnson budget. Mr. Nixon inherited it from the Johnson budgeteers and altered it only in a relatively minor way by a $4 billion reduction. The net result was a modest deficit of $2.8 billion.

By January, 1970, Game Plan I had begun measurably to slow the economy. But Mr. Nixon was sticking to his good Republican guns and declared he was presenting not only a balanced budget but one with a small surplus of $1.3 billion. He said he was doing this in order that the citizens could balance their family budgets. The difficulty for several million of them in accomplishing that purpose in the midst of a growing recession seems not to have occurred to the Chief Executive.

But things did not turn out according to Mr. Nixon's over-optimistic calculations. Game Plan I's planned recession settled over the land. Unemployment rose and production and the growth rate dropped. Inevitably tax receipts declined sharply. This should have been, but was not, anticipated. The result was a *deficit* of $23 billion, instead of the President's projected surplus of $1.3 billion. He was a little more than $24 billion off target.

The story of that fiscal year would almost certainly have been a far happier one had Mr. Nixon promptly used the power Congress had given in April, 1969, but which he immediately and heatedly declared he would never use. He could have brought the extortionate interest rates down to something like decent levels, saved the government several billion dollars of payments on the national debt, relieved business of utterly needless extra costs and almost certainly stopped the economic toboggan before it gathered momentum. He could also have set up machinery for providing guidelines for prices, wages, rents, profits, and dividends if he feared that more reasonable monetary and fiscal policies would turn out to be inflationary. Better yet, in order to dampen inflation, he could have recommended reduction in military expenditures and delayed, at least, expeditions into outer space.

But he did none of these things.

Instead, he pursued the same deflationary policies throughout the year 1970 and vetoed bill after bill that might have tended to retard the economic regression.

After the elections of November, 1970, the President inaugurated Game Plan II, with his state of the union and budget messages in January, 1971. He had apparently decided by then that his re-election was going to depend at least as much on

140

the state of the domestic economy as on his headline-making summitry with foreign chiefs of state. In any event, he changed course drastically.

A less "resourceful" person would have felt impelled to honestly tell the people that his attempts to balance the budget had resulted instead in one of the largest deficits in the nation's history and that, therefore, he was resorting to deficit spending in order to try to pull the economy out of the doldrums into which it had fallen.

But not Richard Milhous Nixon.

When the facts about the sharp decline in farm parity had not suited him, what did Mr. Nixon do? He simply changed the definition of parity. And when he was confronted with failure in trying to bring back employment of workers, what did he do? Why again simply changed the definition of full employment. So when he had so sadly failed to balance the budget and wanted to embark on deficit spending, the obvious thing to do was to change the definition of a balanced budget.

So a wonderful idea was developed for the Presidency by his economists. That idea was that the budget would not really be unbalanced so long as it would have been balanced *if* there had been full employment and normal economic growth. This was not exactly to say that the people had not had $23 billion added to their debt in fiscal year 1971. They would have to pay $1 billion or so in increased interest. So in a way the debt was real. But no one was supposed to think so. Because Mr. Nixon told them not to. The budget had really been in perfect balance. The only trouble was that tax revenues had not come in like they were supposed to.

No one could deny that this was a clever—but surely not to say a "tricky"—way of looking at things.

So that was the way the President of the United States presented his budget for fiscal year 1972. He called it a "balanced budget at full employment"—meaning that it would be balanced *if* there were full employment. Since even he doubted that so sudden a change could quickly transpire, he suggested that it might *look like* there was a deficit of $11 billion in the coming year, but that no one should be deceived by that appearance.

At least not until the interest bill had to be paid.

A year later, in January, 1972, with Game Plan II abandoned and Game Plan III in effect, President Nixon was compelled to report to the Congress and the nation that his $11 billion estimate had been somewhat conservative. The deficit would be about $39 billion instead, some 3½ times his original estimate.

There was more of what Mr. Nixon was now calling "strong medicine" to come. For his new budget—for fiscal year 1973 —would, he estimated, show a further deficit of $25 billion.

In order to see the total picture of the perilous—and continuously deteriorating—state of the nation's finances, we must look at the broad aspects of the way we mismanage our national monetary system. For this Mr. Nixon is no more responsible than the Congress or a long line of Presidents and Congresses before him.

Interest on the national debt of the United States was to amount to almost $25 billion in fiscal year 1973. That is some eight times the total amount provided by the Federal Government for education. It is one-ninth of our present annual Federal tax burden.

In 1970, American farmers owed $60 billion, five times their debt in 1950.

At the close of World War II, consumer debt was about $8 billion. In 1972, consumers' indebtedness stood at a staggering $133 billion.

In the midst of all our other problems, however, only a few people seem to worry much about the mountain of debt—public and private—which looms over our sick economy—and ourselves. We resemble an alcoholic after the third or fourth drink. After the first one he is afraid he will get drunk. After the third or four he is afraid he won't.

One reason why more people are not worried can be stated in one word: inflation.

In fact, until this nation's monetary system is changed to reflect the nation's credit instead of only its debt, inflation may well be the price of survival of our economic system.

One of the decisions of the New Deal period—scarcely recognized at the time—was that the nation should never again go through a period of panic and wide-spread bankruptcy. Instead, the government would go into debt to whatever extent was necessary to obviate the necessity of private bankruptcy.

This was the beginning of deficit financing to revive a sick economy.

We are still at it, only much more so. Under Mr. Nixon, $90 billion more so.

The reason why the Nixon Administration incurs these deficits is the same basic reason that prompted the action of the New Deal, which Richard Nixon made a career attacking.

Now there are valid reasons why the Federal Government should incur a deficit in periods of unemployment and shortage of people's buying power—especially when unworkable games have been played with the nation's welfare. But a serious and increasingly dangerous problem looms ahead because of *the way* in which deficit financing is handled. For if the actual desirability—even necessity—of a sharp inflation is to be avoided, deficit financing should—and must—be accomplished without these astronomical increases in the people's debt.

The Constitution of the United States—by clear implication at least, requires that this be done.

So does every decent moral consideration.

So does the survival of an even partially "free" economic system.

And there is no reason whatsoever why the Federal Government of the United States cannot inject certain calculable amounts of additional buying power into the economy when needed, without increasing the nation's debt and without the necessity of inflation.

In 1946 our national debt stood at $269 billion. Interest rates then were at reasonable levels so the interest bill was $5 billion.

When the Eisenhower-Nixon Administration came to power in 1952, all the measures which had successfully held average interest rates on government securities, short and long term, at around 2%, even during the war, were abandoned. Interest began to skyrocket. That skyrocketing has not stopped since.

According to the Administration's own estimate, the national debt will top $480 billion this year, more than one and a half times what it was in 1946. But interest on that debt will probably exceed $25 billion in this fiscal year, five times what it was in 1946!

Had President Nixon taken the measures to hold down interest rates which President Roosevelt and Truman had used so successfully even in the midst of the most terrible war in history, he could have saved American taxpayers at the very least $30 billion during those three years. This was what Congress gave him power to do in April, 1969. And a saving arrived at in that manner would have helped immeasurably to check inflation and to start the economy on an upward course.

Instead the monetary and fiscal policies pursued by the Nixon Administration forced interest rates to their highest level since the Civil War. Even short-term, 15-month U. S. bonds were for many months carrying an interest rate of more than 6%.

Even before the 1972 devaluation, the dollar had lost more than half of its buying power since 1946. In other words, each dollar represents only half as much real wealth as it did 25 years ago. This makes debts somewhat easier to pay.

Had there not been this inflation in the post-war years, the real debt burden today would be approximately double what it is. We would be paying, in terms of real wealth of the people, not $21 billion or $25 billion in interest on the national debt, but $42 billion or $50 billion.

Even the most ardent of debt merchants and debt apologists would be a bit staggered by such a figure. It would be a quarter of our total national tax payments! Be it never forgotten that the larger the debt grows, public and private, the more vulnerable our country becomes to any downturn in economic activity. So the government must resort to more and more drastic action to avoid the danger of a cycle of defaults setting in. But the remedy thus far applied has been, and is in the present crisis, still further to increase the mountain of debt!

This is indeed a gospel of despair.

Thus it almost seems that some fateful, and perhaps benign, hand has been pushing up our prices so we could live with our soaring debt and meet its exactions with cheaper dollars. But the grim tragedy of the matter is that neither the inflation nor a major part of the staggering burden of dept is at all necessary. The Constitution of the United States says: "Congress shall have power to coin money and regulate the value thereof."

Congress does no such thing, which is the heart of our trouble. Private banks coin our money and regulate its value. In doing so they take from the government and people of the United States a large chunk of their sovereignty, a large chunk of the taxing power, and the key to a prosperous economy without inflation.

For example, in testimony before the Banking and Currency Committee of the House of Representatives in 1935, Marriner Eccles, then Chairman of the Federal Reserve Board itself, said: "In purchasing offerings of Government bonds, the banking system as a whole creates new money, or bank deposits. When the banks buy a billion dollars of Government bonds as they are offered—and you have to consider the banking system as a whole as a unit—the banks credit the deposit account of the Treasury with a billion dollars. They debit their Government bond account a billion dollars; or they actually create, by a bookkeeping entry, a billion dollars."

Mr. Eccles' statement is exactly as true today as when he made it. Here is how it works: The private banking system of our country creates our money in the form of demand deposits on the banks' books. The reason it is able to do this is because no bank is required to have in its vault anything like the amount of money which its depositors think they have in the banks.

Banks are only required by the Federal Reserve System, which the banks are sure they own, to have in their vaults anywhere from $1 to $1.50 for every $10 of demand deposits on their books.

Thus for every $1 or $1.50 which people—or the government—deposit in a bank, the banking system can create out of thin air and by the stroke of a pen some $10 of checkbook money or demand deposits. It can lend all that $10 into circulation at interest just so long at it has the $1 or a little more in reserve to back it up.

This is, of course, the "fractional reserve system" of banking. It is more or less controlled by the Federal Reserve System, whose only stock is held by the private banks of the Federal Reserve System. Not a single share of such stock is held by the government or people of the United States, although if "national sovereignty" means anything at all, these banks of issue should be the property of the nation.

But what actually happens when our government engages in deficit financing?

The obvious way the government can get more buying power into the people's hands is by itself putting more money into the stream of commerce than it takes out in taxes. The tragedy of the situation is that, up to date, the only way our government has enabled itself to spend more money than it takes in has been by forcing this sovereign nation to borrow its own credit from private sources.

This has been true, despite the fact that if deficit financing accomplishes its purpose at all it will increase production and trade, enhance tax revenues, and broaden the base of government *credit*.

To the extent that government bonds are sold for cash to individuals or to institutional *purchasers other than banks* the government is taking out of circulation approximately as many dollars as it will put back in when it spends the money.

To accomplish its purpose, deficit financing must result in the creation of *new money,* and the use of it to increase mass buying power. Only if this happens will there be any stimulation of idle plants to go back into production, or more employment.

Under these circumstances what *ought* to happen is that the *credit* of this great nation should be drawn upon directly by the government—not that it should go more deeply into debt.

For the credit of this or any nation is squarely based upon and derived from the production of wealth by the nation plus the power of the government to tax. A nation like the United States thus possesses an almost unlimited amount of credit. Otherwise it could not possibly have persuaded investors to buy $480 billion of government securities.

By whatever percentage it can be anticipated that production and hence potential tax revenues will increase as a result of deficit spending, by that same amount the credit of the nation and its government will be increased. This same percentage of the volume of money previously in circulation should appear on the books of the Treasury as a *credit* entry to be drawn upon just like tax revenues. To do that would be nothing more than rational and proper bookkeeping. It would also be morally right bookkeeping. And it would make some sense out of Mr. Nixon's "full employment budget" idea.

But this is not what happens at all. Instead the sovereign government of the United States goes hat in hand to the private banking system and asks it to create the new money that the economy needs.

The government *gives*—the word is used advisedly—it *gives* to the banking system, including the Federal Reserve banks, government bonds, the debt of all the people. Interest-bearing bonds, that is, bonds bearing as high an interest rate under today's regime as the banks decide to demand. Else they won't buy the bonds.

The banks "buy" the bonds with newly created demand deposit entries on their books—nothing more. It is fountain-pen money and it is considerably *more* inflationary than would be the same amount of dollar bills created by the government.

The deposits the banks create with which to own the people's debt are backed by nothing *except the bonds themselves!* In other words, they are backed by the credit of the American people.

What the government has "borrowed" from the banks, what

the people must for years pay interest on, is nothing more nor less than the credit of the nation, which obviously the nation possessed in the first place or the bonds themselves would be no good!

At long last, a few years ago the Federal Reserve made tacit acknowledgement of these facts. As a direct result of logical and relentless agitation by members of Congress, led by Congressman Wright Patman as well as by other competent monetary experts, the Federal Reserve began to pay to the U.S. Treasury a considerable part of its earnings from interest on government securities. This was done without public notice and few people, even today, know that it is being done. It was done, quite obviously, as acknowledgement that the Federal Reserve Banks were acting on the one hand as a national bank of issue, creating the nation's money, but on the other hand charging the nation interest on its own credit—which no true national bank of issue could conceivably, or with any show of justice, dare to do.

But this is only part of the story. And the less discouraging part, at that. For where the commercial banks are concerned, there is no such repayment of the people's money.

When the commercial banks create money, as they do when they acquire government bonds, they levy a tax on every person in the United States. This is so because every new dollar that is created makes every dollar previously in existence worth somewhat less than it was worth before. This is the very heart of inflation.

It is also taxation without representation with a vengeance.

Until this system is changed, our debt will continue to sky-rocket without limit and the fixing of debt limits by the Congress will continue to be an exercise in utter futility.

What ought to be done?

Banks should lend existing money. But, as the Constitution clearly requires, the money (or credit) of the nation should never be created by any private agency, but by an agency of the nation itself. It is the duty of Congress to provide for this by a carefully drawn statute.

The stock in Federal Reserve Banks should be purchased by the government from their present private bank owners. The Federal Reserve should then become our national bank of issue. It should create Reserve Bank Credit as it does now. But that credit should be *credited* to the United States Treasury, not charged against it and the people as debt. As much such new credit *should* be created each year as is needed to keep our economy running at or near capacity—and no more than that. A stable price level could result.

Then and only then can we expect to overcome recessions, to put our people to work, and do this without the danger of inflation and the ever-increasing debt which are inescapable under the present monetary system.

But this is obviously not what we are doing. Instead, we are going into debt as a nation faster and faster as the months pass. It is questionable whether even the colossal deficits of the Nixon Administration will be enough to pull the economy out of its slump. Some improvement will probably take place as 1972 wears on. But much of the stimulus that the huge deficits might otherwise provide is blunted by the persistence of high interest rates. It is also blunted by the tremendous drains on national resources caused by the extravagances of the Pentagon. And it is blunted by the continuing basic adherence of President Nixon to the "trickle down" theory, despite much popular oratory in his various messages and some "plums" for certain groups of people in his budget for fiscal year 1973.

That budget was the election year budget.

It was the budget tailored to make Richard Nixon look good by election day.

President Nixon described his projected $25 billion-deficit budget as "strong medicine," but necessary. Administration spokesmen were remarkably frank in stating that the purpose of the strong medicine was to get the economy moving satisfactorily "by election time." That was the universally accepted target date.

The country had waited through three difficult years for "the time" to come.

The Los Angeles Times reported White House spokesmen frankly stating that wherever possible construction of flood control dams, Federal office buildings, and other money-spending projects would be accelerated and jammed into the remaining months of the 1972 fiscal year. There were, in addition to other resources for this "by-election-day" spending, the billions of previously frozen funds in the White House basement. There was little doubt that the Office of Management and Budget would suddenly be overcome with compassion for the nation's needs and release those funds with generosity. Each time this was done the President would have opportunity to announce that "he" was making those funds available—with no reference to the fact that they could not have existed had Congress not appropriated them.

Somehow as election day approached the once deep concern of the Nixon Administration about inflation was becoming less and less acute. Members of Congress were still concerned, however. They pointed out that one reason for the huge projected deficit was Mr. Nixon's failure to recommend any new taxes, such as a tax on excess profits. And Chairman Mahon of the House Appropriations Committee, remarked that: "With these whopping deficits, we cannot hope to win the fight against inflation."

As should have been expected, the principal beneficiary of Mr. Nixon's budgeting was the Pentagon. In presenting the budget the President took occasion to attack the Congress for having cut some $5 billion from his military requests for the two previous years. He branded, ahead of time, any Senator or Congressman who dared question his increases in war spending in these words: "A demagogue may find it easy enough to advocate that we allocate necessary defense dollars to social programs." A good many careful students of military matters questioned that word "necessary." And a good many members of Congress were certain that their $5 billion cuts were at the expense of Pentagon waste and "fat," not of necessary national defense.

For fiscal year 1973, Mr. Nixon demanded of Congress an increase of more than $1 billion in direct appropriations. But he also called for $6.3 billion of contract authorizations. These are actually open-ended commitments for new weapons systems whose total cost usually runs to many times the original contract authorizations.

Senator Proxmire of Wisconsin called his colleagues to arms in these words: "How can we justify spending more money for the Pentagon when the Vietnam War is being wound down? Instead of rubber-stamping the President's program, I call upon Congress to cut the military budget from last year's level and cut it hard."

At least one Senator was not afraid of being falsely called a demagogue.

Next to his war appropriations the largest increases asked by the President were in a category called "science and technology." This was to receive $17.8 billion, up $1.4 billion over the previous year. Only a detailed study of the fine print could reveal exactly how these billions were to be spent. But surely much of it would be used for space expeditions such as the brand new "space shuttle" estimated to cost ultimately some $6 billion. And the military were almost certain to benefit, directly or indirectly.

It was rather clear that the fields in which Mr. Nixon sought to bring about increased employment were in the so-called "defense" industries and the highly technical fields. These are the very fields where dollars expended create the fewest jobs—and none for the unskilled or semi-skilled unemployed.

There were in the budget a number of items for the start-up of programs whose total cost over the years would be very large indeed. To give one example, Mr. Nixon asked $5 billion for his particular form of "revenue sharing," namely, the no-strings-attached dishing out of Federal monies to local authorities to spend as they wished. But the $5 billion was proposed as only the beginning of a program that was to cost $7.25 billion in the first 17 months.

So costly were the President's proposals for advance commitments that budget director Schultz as well as Mr. Nixon himself, warned Congress that it would be guilty of fiscal irresponsibility if it dared to promote any social programs other than Mr. Nixon's own. The idea seemed to be for the President to pre-empt the field of government largesse, and woe to anyone who dared compete with him—now or for four years to come.

To his credit Mr. Nixon proposed modest increases in appropriations for abatement of pollution, for veteran's benefits, for combatting crime, and for food distribution by the Department of Agriculture.

But when it came to social needs which were closest to the average citizens' daily lives it was a different story. Mr. Nixon proposed to cut aid to education by $282 million, the school milk program by $10 million, soil conservation by $55 million, farmers' price supports by $200 million, housing by $130 million, nurses' training by $22 million, and mental health services by $72 million. Even the hoped-for increase in social security payments was proposed by Mr. Nixon to be held to five percent, considerably less than had been called for by older people's organizations.

There was, it is true, the President's dramatic offer to recommend to Congress that older people be relieved of their monthly payments for Part B of Medicare. But the way he proposed to cover this $1.5 billion loss of income to Medicare was so interesting as to warrant later discussion.

In its editorial for January 25, 1972, the *Washington Post* concluded:

Is this budget a good one? It is the best of all possible budgets, if you agree that lower income taxes and less inflation are the nation's greatest needs, that the elderly require Federal help more urgently than any other group of citizens, that an unemployment rate of five-plus percent is tolerable and that higher defense spending is necessary.

If you have doubts about these premises—as we do—then you will also doubt this budget itself as the basic guide to Federal policy for the next 18 months.

For the second year in succession, Mr. Nixon made a claim for himself so remarkable as to require comment. He said in his budget message of January, 1971: "For the first time in 20 years we are spending more to meet human needs than we spend on defense." He repeated a similar boast with respect to the budget for 1973. According to his figures some $77 billion was to be the total cost of "defense" and $104 billion the budget for "human needs."

The President's statements were, to say the least, in sharp contrast to those of other trusted sources. Senator Mark Hatfield, Republican of Oregon, had stated that in his opinion 60% of government expenses in 1971 had been military ones and only 16% for human resources. And the journal *Church and Society* arrived at the same conclusion.

So it is necessary to dig a little deeper. And here is what we find.

First, in order to make his claim look credible, Mr. Nixon has changed the accounting system. His budget for fiscal year 1971 called for $135 billion of expenditures. How then could the 1973 budget soar to almost twice that figure—that is, to $246 billion? The answer is it could not and did not. What happened was that, in order to make his claim as a great humanitarian, Richard Nixon included in the budget figures the receipts and disbursements of funds for which the government acts only as trustee and over which the President can lawfully exercise no control whatsoever. They simply have no proper place in a budget of current, controllable receipts and expenditures.

Biggest, by far, and most important of these trust funds are those of the Social Security System. Old Age and Survivors Insurance Benefits are paid out of a trust fund into which the people have paid their taxes and out of which the government must pay the benefits fixed in the law. The money in these trust funds belongs quite literally to the people who have contributed to them, not to the President to do with as he sees fit. Medicare and Medicaid payments are in the same category of fixed obligations with the government acting as trustee of the Social Security funds. In the listing of health expenditures, Mr. Nixon no doubt included the government's contributions to the Federal Employees Health Benefit Plan—again expenditures which have no place in a current budget.

For Mr. Nixon to claim personal virtue for expenditures of these kinds was, to say the least, presumptuous, since he had had nothing whatever to do with instituting any of these programs and had, on occasion, even opposed either their enactment or their expansion. Every one of the programs mentioned in the preceding paragraph was enacted into law by a Democratic Congress in a Democratic Administration.

The total of these Social Security fixed obligations for fiscal year 1973 will be approximately $60 billion. Subtracting that from Mr. Nixon's $104 billion, we have just $44 billion as a *possible* amount of controllable expenditures for human needs for which the present Administration has any reason to claim credit.

But even the $44 billion is a grossly deceptive figure. For included in it are $11 billion of Veterans' benefits, which, if anything does so, belong in the category of defense expenditures. This leaves $33 billion which conceivably could be counted as "human need" expenditures.

Interestingly, $33 billion constitutes about 14% of Mr. Nixon's projected $246 billion of expenditures for 1973, which percentage is very close to the estimate of Senator Hatfield and *Church and Society*.

If we take defense expenditures, we find other interesting facts. Mr. Nixon uses only the figure of current direct expenses by the Pentagon itself—some $77 billion. Add to that the $6.3 billion of military contract authorizations. To that sum, obviously, must be added the $11 billion of Veterans' benefits. In addition, at least two-thirds of the interest on the national debt is directly due to wars and preparations for wars. So another $14 billion needs properly to be added to the "defense" bill. How much of the appropriations asked for the space program or for the $17.8 billion "science and technology" item are in fact for military purposes can only be guessed. Certainly a considerable percentage. We thus arrive at a fair approximation of the real expense for war and find it to be not $77 billion but somewhere between $110 billion and $120 billion.

Was it true that the budget presented by President Nixon proposed to devote more of honestly budgetable expenditures to human needs than to "defense"?

It was not. To say so was nothing less than gross deception. What was true was that "defense" and war expenses were to be some four times as great as those for human needs.

At whose doorstep should charges of "financial irresponsibility" be placed? Should such charges lodge at the door of Congress for having tried on occasion to exceed the President's budget by a billion dollars or so for such purposes as education, employment of the unemployed or child care centers? During the first four years of Mr. Nixon's presidency the Congress appropriated some $20 billion less money than the President requested.

Or should there be at least a gnawing doubt about the financial responsibility of a President and an Administration which have increased the national debt of the American people by more than $90 billion and have inaugurated spending programs of great magnitude in many fields in order to have everything just right "by election." And be it remembered that the "election day" expenditures of the Nixon Administration have not been made possible—or "responsible"—by the closing of tax loopholes which enable some of the wealthiest people to escape taxes altogether, nor by an excess-profits tax on the exorbitant profits of military contractors, or by paring the waste from the Pentagon budget, or by curtailing fabulously expensive expeditions into outer space, or by restraint in giving tax bonanzas to big industry. Instead these deficit expenditures are being made at the expense of this and future generations of Americans who must carry by their tax payments the burden of a national debt of half a trillion dollars. The larger that debt becomes, the more dim grows the hope that we, the American people, can escape a perpetual bondage to deficit financing and the fiscal irresponsibility which it engenders.

To revive the hope of escape from such a fate we must learn soon to recognize the difference between legitimate national debt and debt-that-ought-not-to-be-debt, but national credit instead.

11. THE PLUSH LIFE OF THE PENTAGON—AND OUR SCHOOLS

The Military-Industrial Complex

The conjunction of an immense military establishment and a large arms industry is new in the American experience. Its total influence—economic, political, even spiritual—is felt in every city, every state house, every office of the federal government. We must not fail to comprehend its grave implications. Our toil, resources, and livelihood are all involved. So is the very structure of our society.

In the councils of government, we must guard against the acquisition of unwarranted influence, whether sought or unsought, by the military-industrial complex. The potential for the disastrous rise of misplaced power exists and will persist. We must never let the weight of this combination endanger our liberties or democratic processes. We should take nothing for granted. Only an alert and knowledgeable citizenry can compel the proper meshing of the huge industrial and military machinery of defense with our peaceful methods and goals, so that security and liberty may prosper together."

—Farewell Address of former
President Dwight D. Eisenhower

Since President Eisenhower issued his warning in the year 1960, the grip of the military-industrial complex on the nation has grown tighter. In parts of the nation where desperately needed public works and services are neglected and where a high percentage of employment depends on war contracts the grip has become almost a strangle-hold. For under such circumstances workers who would otherwise not be employed can be enlisted in support of ever-increasing war contracts as a means of gaining their livelihood.

The Nixon Administration has proved to be the best friend the military-industrial complex has ever had. As surely as Adolf Hitler ever did, this Administration has placed the emphasis of whatever re-employment program it had upon jobs in so-called "defense" or war-related aerospace industries.

Whatever the Pentagon has demanded President Nixon has attempted to give it. And while the Congress has made some cuts in military appropriations—much to Mr. Nixon's openly expressed disgust—the limitations on the expansion of America's arsenal of death have been minor indeed.

Were it any longer possible for anyone—president, general, senator or anyone to claim that the people's money is being spent for their own defense—the situation would be different. But this is not the case.

All pretense of defending our cities from probable total death should a nuclear war come has long since been dropped. We only seek with our ABMS to "defend" the sites of our own missiles—that is to defend our ability to wipe out all lives in other countries in exchange for our own.

And those who know best the lethal qualities of atomic fall-out tell us that even if any enemy dropped not a single bomb in the United States, nevertheless most of our residents would be dead, dying or deformed as a result of the fall-out if we dropped enough bombs and missiles on another country to "win" a war.

The plain fact is that it is no longer possible to defend the lives of the people of any nation by military means.

In the mid-1960's the United Nations appointed a commission to study and report on the probable effects of a nuclear war on the world. Both the United States and the Soviet Union were members of that Commission along with representatives of a dozen other countries. Its report, after some two years of intensive study, contained this language: "Civilization as we know it would inevitably come to an end if a *reasonable number* of nuclear weapons are *ever* used."

The Commission might have added that even military leaders calculate that a death toll of half the nation's population would have to be "acceptable" in a war which the United States "won."

The war system is sociologically bankrupt.

The so-called "great powers" have by their very frightful armaments painted themselves into a military and diplomatic corner. They dare not use their ultimate weapons lest they bring suicide upon themselves or, if not that, such a torrent of adverse world opinion as to be unable to maintain decent relations with any other nation. But if the war system is sociologically and diplomatically bankrupt it certainly is not so financially. The best resources, brains, and most of the tax payments of the "great powers" are devoted to a mad race to

155

see who can claim the greatest ability to wipe our mankind.

In the United States the Pentagon lives a lush life indeed, while schools are forced to close all across the nation because there isn't money enough to keep them open. Children of this time are thus, in part, denied the opportunity the older generation enjoyed for an adequate education.

In this hour the people of the United States are more insecure than they have ever been. With each new weapons system which we develop, other countries do the same. And on goes the arms race. Never once in all human history has any arms race ended in anything but war.

As Senator Mansfield, Majority leader of the Senate once pointed out in a speech, there are in many underground sanctuaries in the United States pairs of men—just two of them in each case—who hold in their hands keys that could bring nuclear war upon the world. These two men with their keys can launch our missiles at any moment when, due to mental lapse, a false signal, or any other cause they might decide to do so.

We may be sure that the Russians have somewhat the same arrangement.

In his sobering book *The Economy of Death* Richard Barnet, formerly one of the Pentagon's own experts, points out, with unaswerable logic, what the only limits are, to what the Pentagon can demand of American taxpayers. He writes:

> Since there is almost no weapons system remotely imaginable which the Soviet Union could not build if it devoted enough time, energy, and resources, the only limit to US military spending is the Pentagon's imagination. In the real world, individuals who spend most of their money to arm themselves against threats that exist only in their minds are called paranoid. In the world of national security, the system itself is paranoid.

What author Barnet refers to is an all-familiar experience of the American people. Each year when the appropriations bill for the Pentagon comes before the Congress we are told of some new weapons which the Soviet Union, or—it used to be—China, is building or thinking about building or may be building. In fear and trembling the Congress votes most if not all of what the Pentagon asks, and we the people acquiesce in silence.

Over and over the Pentagon predictions have been proved wrong, at least temporarily. But usually only temporarily. For once we, on the basis of the imagination of our military leaders, have authorized the development of the weapons systems to counteract what it has been imagined the Russians are doing, then the Russians go to work, on their part, to develop those very weapons which we were led to fear.

Just as the United States would do if the picture were reversed.

All this brings us to one clear conclusion. The future of life on planet Earth will never be assured—rather it will be certainly doomed—by the policy of "negotiating from strength." This as he has asserted over and over again is Mr. Nixon's policy. It has of course been the policy of Presidents before him. But seldom if ever with the same violence.

As long as the United States, led by its President, insists on having a constant military advantage over the Russians, nothing of consequence is likely to come out of the Strategic Arms Limitation talks which have been in progress for the last several years. The reason is that two parties can play the game of "negotiating from strength."

A former Assistant Secretary of Defense of the United States has frankly stated which country he believes is taking the lead in escalating the arms race. Mr. Paul Warnke has said:

> In each case it seems to me the Soviet Union is following the U.S. lead and that the U.S. is not reacting to Soviet action. Our current effort to get a MIRV capability on our missles is not reacting to a Soviet capability so much as it is moving ahead again to make sure that, whatever they do of the possible things that we imagine they might do, we will be prepared.

It is impossible for both the United States and Russia to "negotiate from a position of strength" at the same time. But both of them are bound to try. So every time either country develops a new and more terrible weapon the other one stalls the talks until it "catches up."

The United States Senate once saw this fact clearly. It voted 72-6 for a resolution asking the President to propose to the Russians that both nations refrain from development of any new weapons systems as long as the SALT talks were in progress. Mr. Nixon declared that the Senate vote was "irrelevant."

Instead he demanded, and got, a step-up in development of ABMS (anti-ballistic missile systems) and MIRVS (intercontinental missiles with many war-heads which can hit several cities at once).

In his budget message of January, 1972 President Nixon outdid himself. He asked for more "bargaining chips" for the SALT negotiations. Principal among them was a new fleet of ULMS—that is, Undersea Long-Range Missile Systems. These are submarines armed with multiple nuclear warheads capable of firing at long range from any part of the world. Obviously against such weapons no defense is even conceivable.

What would we do if another nation threatened us in that manner? Well, we may be sure the Russians are doing it. At least trying to.

What the Russians *said* in their official newspapers was that "certain militaristic circles in the United States are trying to block the Soviet-American SALT talks."

Negotiating from a position of strength is a gospel of mutual death, not a way to ease the frightful burden of armament.

Senator Muskie was, we may think, quite justified when he said on Christmas Day, 1971 that the SALT talks "are a story of unfulfilled promise" during which both sides have built their arsenals. He said that the talks were being used as "a political umbrella for the Administration to keep off the rain of criticism over further escalation of the arms race. Since SALT started the U.S. has begun deployment of its safeguard ABM and the Russians resumed, after a 3-year-long layoff, construction of their system around Moscow. Both nations have gained tremendous momentum while arms control is at a standstill."

The alternative to the fruitlessness of negotiation from a position of strength is obvious. It is for some truly great nation sometime along the way to have the courage to say "we will stop if you do." And then do it. Such a policy would perhaps involve some risk. But it would be a risk for peace. And without someone cutting through the vicious circle mankind is doomed. Which is probably what the Senators had in mind when they passed their "irrelevant" resolution.

Richard Nixon's entire policy has been the exact opposite of any such statesmanlike offer. In fact, a former deputy director of the Central Intelligence Agency has said that the Nixon Administration has progressively down-graded even its goals for the SALT disarmament talks and expects only a window-dressing kind of agreement.

In June, 1969 President Nixon addressed the graduating

class of the Air Force Academy in Colorado Springs. He made "absolutely clear" what his policies and his attitudes were going to be. He repeated the standard phrases in praise of the military establishment and said that any who did not share his views were something less than patriotic. One columnist, James Wechsler, compared this part of the speech to that of a high school orator competing for the prize in a contest sponsored by the D.A.R. But the President went further, declaring that anyone who opposed military appropriations of the kind he would recommend belonged to a band of "new isolationists." He accused his opponents of advocating "unilateral disarmament."

These were the days when the drive by Mr. Nixon and his Pentagon for an ABM system was in full swing. Two tactics were being used, neither of them focused on the scientific merits of the ABM. One, typical of the strange case of Richard Nixon, was to reveal the "subversive" character of opponents of the ABM. The other was the standard appeal to fear. But this time not so much to a fear of Russia, but rather of *China!*

How times have changed!

But—yes—it is quite true as even a cursory examination of the press and Congressional hearings will reveal that in 1969 and even early 1970 the taxpayers were being bludgeoned into acceptance of increasing war costs by the holding up before them of a Chinese ogre about to shoot a nuclear missile at our cities.

In those times we were also being told by the Nixon Administration that the reason the war in Southeast Asia must be carried on at whatever cost was because it was necessary to prevent Chinese domination of that part of the world.

Year after year and month after month President Nixon has asked increases in the appropriations for the Pentagon. He has not always gotten the full amount through Congress. But he got his way, substantially, about the ABM and the MIRV. And despite signs of increasing skepticism, Congress has usually capitulated and provided the President and the Pentagon almost all they demanded.

There are some 6,000 reasons why this is so.

For example when it came time for Congress to consider appropriations for the Pentagon in the spring of 1971, the 6,000 "public relations" men who are on the payroll of said Pentagon were ready to march on Capitol Hill, out into the hinterland of the nation, into the offices of newspapers and the script-writing rooms of the television networks. Their mission was to get through Congress the $5 billion increase in Pentagon appropriations provided in the Nixon budget.

The taxpayers regularly pay almost $40 million a year for the salaries of the Pentagon lobbyists and propagandists, whose task it is to persuade those same taxpayers and their representatives in Congress to give the war department considerably more than half of all the taxes paid to the Federal Government.

The strange fact is that every spring, about the time for Congress to take up the Pentagon appropriation, it is suddenly discovered that the Soviet Union or some other potential enemy has become a greater menace than before. New weapons have, it is said been developed by them and the security of the United States will be in jeopardy unless every cent the Administration and the Pentagon have asked is granted by the Congress.

In 1971, just a few short months before President Nixon dramatically announced that he would visit China, one of the principal appeals on behalf of the war appropriations was that the Chinese *may* have shot off an intercontinental ballistic missile. At the same time the Congress and the country were told that, while the Russians had apparently "levelled off" on their missile deployment this *might* well be because they were at work on "bigger and better" missiles. Senator Jackson, from a state rich in "defense" contracts, chimed in with the alarming news that the Russians were developing a new and ominous weapon. Just what it was has not yet been revealed.

No one knew for sure. That was, as always, the trump card for Mr. Nixon and his 6,000 bearers of bad news about the nation's defenses." No one knew for sure, so it was prudent to be on the "safe" side and up the appropriations so the U.S. could escalate the arms race.

In mid-1971 came the Mansfield Amendment. The Senator from Montana, Democratic Majority Leader of the Senate, had been one of the President's most effective supporters in most respects. But he was convinced that the time had come, for many reasons, to bring home some of the soldiers stationed abroad. This, he argued, would go a long way toward relieving the unfavorable balance of payments of the United States. Furthermore, since the Russians had expressed interest in a mutual reduction of troops in Europe, the time seemed ripe for a truly peace-building move.

Secretary of State Rogers labelled the Mansfield proposal

"dangerous" and President Nixon fought it to a standstill. Mansfield won in the Senate, but the President prevailed, as usual, in the House, and all the soldiers stayed in Europe.

The vehemence with which the President denounced Senator Mansfield and his amendment seemed hard to understand in view of the many times Mansfield had come to Mr. Nixon's defense. Especially so since it was to be only a few weeks' time before Mr. Nixon was to announce his bewildering turnabout of August 15, 1971 which included drastic measures to correct the very unfavorable balance of payments which the Mansfield Amendment would have done so much to cure. Could it have been that announcement of his visit to the Soviet Union was already in Mr. Nixon's mind and that he wanted to be as sure as he could to have a dramatic announcement to make in connection therewith—such as an agreement on troop withdrawal? Was this perhaps another case where the soldiers and the balance of payments problem could both wait for the coming of Richard Nixon's carefully planned "timing" of events for his re-election year?

We may never know the answers to those questions.

Richard Nixon campaigned for the presidency in 1968 with a promise to end the draft and develop a wholly volunteer army. But when it came time, in the summer of 1971, for the conscription law to expire he demonstrated once again his marvelous flexibility. He had, in fact, almost completely changed his mind. Not only did he call on Congress for a one year extension of conscription, but for two years'. Strangely this was exactly what the Pentagon also wanted. Absolute control over young men's lives by older ones is a prize not easily given up. Especially when one wants power. A bitter fight ensued in Congress, particularly in the Senate. A few Senators, having tried to amend the bill to limit it to one year and to reduce it in other ways, refused to give up the debate. They were accused of filibustering, which indeed they probably were doing. And they were also accused by the President of playing politics with the safety of the nation—especially as the date for expiration of the old law approached and passed.

For a time there was no conscription law in effect. Senator Cranston and a few Senators who stood with him suggested that this was no great tragedy and that the issue deserved a full hearing and debate.

President Nixon and other Administration spokesmen declared on the other hand that unless the draft was reenacted immediately the nation would stand in peril.

Well, the draft law was finally renewed, and for two years, as President Nixon had demanded. But it did not appear that the security of the nation had been threatened very seriously by the delay. For Selective Service announced, almost on the day the draft renewal passed Congress, that it was going to conscript only 10,000 men in the following 3 months. This was the lowest draft call since 1965. Apparently the "crisis" caused by the Senators was a figment of someone's fertile imagination.

But consider what it costs to maintain and constantly expand a war machine which is, from every point of view affecting people's lives, obsolete and useless.

Since 1964 it has cost American taxpayers more than one trillion dollars—that is $1000 billion. It is costing us, currently $200 million every 24 hours. So extravagant have become the demands of the Pentagon that even Senator Stennis of Mississippi, saltiest militarist in Congress and Chairman of the Senate Armed Services Committee refused to add a $42-million item to his committee's bill "for development of improved, high-accuracy strategic missiles."

A few details will illustrate.

The General Accounting Office is an agency created by act of Congress and responsible for keeping track of government expense and reporting its findings to the Congress. It is one of the few agencies of government which the executive cannot control. The GAO has found that in very recent years there have been some $33.4 billion of "cost overruns" on 61 weapons system. A cost overrun is the amount over and beyond the original contract price which the contractor actually collects from the government.

A classic case of one such cost overrun is the military transport plane C5A built by Lockheed Aircraft Company, the largest single military contractor of all and the one for which Mr. Nixon demanded and got a loan guarantee of $250,000,000 by American taxpayers. The C5A was originally contracted for at a cost of $3 billion. It was planned to be the largest cargo plane in the world. Its only purpose is to bring large numbers of American soldiers, supplies and equipment to the far corners of the Earth. The $3 billion was supposed to buy 115 such monster planes. But the final cost for just 81 of them will be $5 billion, a $2 billion cost overrun. But that is not all the story. The facts about this tremendous overpayment to Lockheed were carefully concealed from the Congress by the Pentagon. Those facts were partly told to Congress by an officer named Ernest Fitzgerald who at the time was cost-control expert for the U.S. Air Force. Immediately after Fitzgerald's testimony to the committee of the Senate headed by Senator Proxmire he was fired by Secretary Laird and his job abolished.

At last a few C5A's came off the production line. On the first test flight of the plane an engine fell out of it and landed in the middle of the runway! By some miracle no one was killed. Then the Air Force began to examine the planes. It found their wings cracked, the landing gear deficient.

This is what was bought for $5 billion.

But it is only one case.

The General Accounting Office reports that on 146 contracts for military weapons the contractors' average profits have been 56%. A major reason why this is so is because of the way the Pentagon lets its contracts. Often this is done without competitive bidding, which the law requires. Contracts are signed in other cases with lowest bidders whose bids however are far below what they know the weapons will finally cost. But these low bidders know that they can come back to their friends in the Pentagon and get their cost-overrun money, almost without limit.

Many of the plants in which our weapons are produced have been built entirely with taxpayers' money and then turned over to private companies to enable them to profiteer at the same taxpayers' expense.

Complaints by members of Congress about these conditions and attempts on their part to cut out some of the colossal waste of which the Pentagon is guilty have brought forth from Vice-President Agnew his classic comparison of members of Congress with Gus Hall, secretary of the Communist Party. Mr. Agnew said on September 23, 1971 that Gus Hall and those members of Congress who tried to cut military expenditures were alike "disastrously tampering with the nation's security."

Once started on their way to development with comparatively small appropriations, weapons systems become multiple time more costly than Congress was given any remote notion of. The ULMS submarines for example for which Mr. Nixon projected $15.5 billion in his budget for fiscal 1973, is estimated to finally cost as much as $100 billion.

In fact, it was in 1970 that a group of 27 Congressmen and Senators of both political parties worked out a plan to save the taxpayers $10 billion by cutting out needless Pentagon expenditures. Needless to say their efforts yielded no such salutary results. They tried—that was about all.

This same will be true of Senator Barry Goldwater of Arizona, probably the most conservative member of Congress, a retired Major General in the Air Force, and a devoted militarist. He expressed himself in colorful terms in a recent Senate hearing. The senator told Mr. Kenneth Rush, appointed to be deputy Secretary of Defense, that "defense procurement needs a head-rolling overhaul to halt the god-awful waste in money, manpower, and time."

But all these members of Congress have been, and are, up against the most powerful antagonist in the United States—the military-industrial complex.

Anyone who dares to challenge it or to suggest any reduction in appropriations for its greedy operations will be in deep, dark trouble. President Nixon served notice to that effect when he presented his record-smashing military budget in January, 1972. He said, as will be remembered from our last chapter, that only "demagogues" would presume to question any items in the Nixon budget.

The tentacles of the military-industrial complex are long and strange. They reach into most of the universities of the nation with offers of attractive contracts for research into weaponry. These have probably exceeded $1 billion in the past ten years: They reach into political campaigns with huge contributions, one contractor alone having provided, through its officers and their families, $150,000 to the party in power in a recent election. They offer lucrative—and non-existing—jobs to military officers. In the past 3 years almost 1,000 high-ranking officers left their posts to accept such offers. The Pentagon alone employs directly half of all the civilian employees of the Federal Government—1,500,000 of them. And untold but ever-increasing numbers of American families depend for their daily bread upon jobs directly or indirectly connected with the manufacture of weapons of war. Nor is this any temporary trend related to the war in Southeast Asia. It is already carefully planned as an ever-expanding burden upon the American people, their pocket-books and whatever remains of their consciences.

Mr. Nixon has fought every attempt to reduce the war appropriations. He had done all he could to accelerate the arms race. He has demanded the ABM, the Minuteman III missile, the Multiple Nuclear Missile warhead, the continuance of the draft. And in his 1973 projection he demanded the Multiple-Missile ULMS submarine at $15 billion to start, the space-shuttle at $5 billion to start, a brand new Navy, and what he calls "modernization" of the whole military weaponry. He has not raised a finger to correct the scandalously wasteful practices of the Pentagon. That waste itself is water on Mr. Nixon's wheel. Even as he announced his war on inflation and froze wages and prices the President uttered not a word about reducing the spending of the Pentagon, though it is the biggest single inflationary factor in the entire economy.

Mr. Nixon and his foreign policy decision-maker Henry Kissinger base this country's total policy on the idea that the constant threat of force and the building of an enormous military machine are the only means whereby the United States can get its way in the world.

The hopes of the unemployed for going back to work, under the Nixon program, depend more and more on expansion of manufacture of weapons—not only to add to our own arsenal of terror but also to supply half the munitions trade of the entire world. The Nixon Administration has finished the job of making the United States the most militaristic nation in the world. Tighter and tighter becomes the strangle-hold of the military-industrial complex upon the American nation.

Against this background Richard Nixon brought forth his 1973 fiscal year budget with its $82 billion treasure chest for the Pentagon and its contractors. Just what that "new Navy" was to cost Mr. Nixon did not reveal. But United Press International had, on September 3, 1971, released a story, datelined Washington and headlined "Navy Seeks Super Ships— $50 Billion Dream Fleet."

The theme of the President went far beyond the "new Navy." He called for "modernization" of the entire armed forces of the country. And as an added gift from the taxpayers the President proposed the "space shuttle" project to carry the nation's manned and unmanned civilian *and military* payloads from the Earth to orbiting space "laboratories." Thus we would gain the new ability to rain death from outer space on any part of the world. This indeed could mean mastery of all mankind.

The Secretary of Defense, Mr. Melvin Laird, went to Capitol Hill to describe in florid testimony threats to American "security." His testimony consisted, as usual, of many "mays."

He said that the Soviet Union *"may"* be developing multiple independently targeted nuclear warheads to match the United States in these weapons by next year.

He said that the Russians were working on a new supersonic bomber that "might" be ready in the mid-1970's. He said the Soviets were "perhaps" preparing to deploy two new or modified intercontinental ballistic missiles.

As for China, the Secretary informed Congress that by 1975 the Chinese "could" begin deploying intercontinental missiles.

At all costs Mr. Laird urged Congress to give him all the money he and Mr. Nixon might ask for so the United States could so increase its military power as to keep well ahead of anything the Soviet Union or the Chinese might do.

The thought occurred that this was, after all, the best possible way of making certain that the Russians and Chinese would do all Mr. Laird had predicted—if indeed they could.

Then Mr. Laird could ask for still more money.

Mr. Laird's testimony would have impressed Congress and the average citizen somewhat more had it not been for a couple of rather disturbing facts.

Back in 1970 Mr. Laird had given some surprisingly similar testimony. He had painted a picture of an imminent and increasing "missile gap" due to actions by the Russians. This was when Senator Jackson was also speaking of an "ominous" new weapon being developed by the Soviets. Mr. Laird declared that: "In 1965 there were no operational launches for the large Soviet SS-9 missiles. Today I can report to you that there are some 220 SS-9's operational with at least 60 more under construction." The Secretary had further asserted that: "The Russians are now deploying an advanced generation of offensive weapons."

The trouble with all this was a report by the Central Intelligence Agency, the redoubtable CIA, which came to light through a Republican Senator and was reported by the *New York Times, Washington Post* and other newspapers. The CIA report was based on actual observation by the SAMOS satellites. It showed that in 1965 there had been spotted 66 missile launching sites in the Soviet Union, whereas in 1969, 54 had been found. Further the report stated that the "ominous new weapon" activity in the Soviet Union consisted not of new weapons but rather of the digging of large holes around existing sites so that concrete shells could be placed around the silos to protect them against air strikes. This the United States had done several years before.

Accordingly Senator Proxmire described the testimony of Secretary Laird, on the 1970 occasion, as marking "the shortest missile gap in history."

Maybe Mr. Laird's alarm in 1972 was more justified than that of 1970—maybe. Maybe it was best for Congress to give him his money, just to be on the "safe side." Except that there wasn't any safe side. And the Secretary did suffer from something of a credibility gap as a result of past performances.

There were no doubt some among his Congressional listeners who remembered something else in Mr. Laird's background. For in 1962 he wrote a book entitled *A House Divided* in which appears this sentence: "What it means is serving notice, and meaning it, that we reserve to ourselves the initiative to *strike first* when the Soviet peril point rises above its interminable limit."

Is all this just a passing phase in our country's history? Would the end of the Southeast Asia War, whenever that took place, bring an end to our frenetic build-up of military overkill?

Not if the military-industrial complex has its way. Its plans are laid already. Time was during the Johnson Administration when the nation was assured that, once the war was over, there would occur a $20 billion increment to funds available to meet domestic needs.

This has disappeared. Very early in the Nixon regime the nation was informed that even if the fighting were to end we must not expect any reduction in military spending. New plans for new weapons systems had already taken care of that.

One of these plans, reported by United Press on February 19, 1972, was for an intercontinental missile that could dodge anti-ballistic missiles. Should such a weapon be developed by the U.S. it would of course be followed by similar development by the Soviet Union and probably China. Then all AMBs would be useless and all the billions spent on them at Mr. Nixon's insistence obviously wasted. The last pretense that the military could ever again defend anything or anybody would be gone. A grim commentary on where the arms race is taking us.

In September, 1971, the Senate Armed Services Committee reported that "Weapons systems now in development or procurement will cost at least $104.6 billion before procurement is completed. This cost does not include funds necessary for operation and maintenance of the system."

If even a fraction of the advance commitments which President Nixon asked of Congress in January, 1972, are carried to completion the Senate Committee report of six months before will be the soul of conservatism.

So-called "defense" contractors are making no moves of any consequence looking toward increasing production for other customers than the Pentagon. Confident that the military-industrial complex has an unbreakable hold upon the nation's mind as well as its economy, the makers of the 56% profits as reported by the General Accounting Office look forward to the same lush life that is enjoyed, entirely at taxpayers expense, by the Pentagon itself.

Does anyone care?

Yes. Some people do. Children and young people who seek an adequate education certainly do. So do those older people who still feel a certain obligation toward the up-coming generation. There are those among us—teachers, parents, ordinary citizens—who can recognize rank injustice when they see it. And they see exactly that kind of injustice in these facts. First our presently dominant generation will certainly leave to our children the most horrendous ganglia of unsolved problems of which any generation has ever been guilty. Second we are denying to our children the kind of adequate education which alone can possibly prepare them to meet these problems. We are robbing the schools of the money they desperately need in order to spend more than half of all our federal tax dollars on a military "balance of terror" which we hope will hold off the war during our own lifetimes. After that—well, let the children worry about it.

Certainly someone needs to worry. In the year 1971 schools were actually closing because there was not money enough to keep them open. In Independence, Missouri voters twice turned down propositions that would have financed the schools and they were closed until further notice. Los Angeles voters refused twice to approve bond issues that would have made possible repair of earthquake damage and given the children buildings in which they would have been safe from death. At one time no less than 25 school systems in the state of Ohio were either closed or on the verge of doing so. Chicago schools were forced to extend the Christmas vacation to a full month instead of the usual two weeks. California state college teachers did not receive an increase in pay for three years and the state fell from near the top to 16th place in rank among the states, grouped by per capita support of the schools by the state.

None of this needed to happen. The burdensome property tax did not need to bear almost the total cost of education. A large part of that cost could have come out of the sheer "fat" and waste in which the Pentagon rolled—and without reducing one whit the military "fire power" of the country.

Back in 1953, when costs were a fraction of what they are now President Eisenhower made a speech in which he said: "This world in arms is not spending money alone. It is spending the sweat of its laborers, the genius of its scientists, the hopes of its children. The cost of one modern heavy bomber is this: a modern brick school in more than 30 cities."

At today's prices 17 army machine-guns cost all it would require to pay the salary of an elementary school teacher for an entire year.

Six high school buildings could be constructed for the cost of just one destroyer.

But in case it were desired to give up not a single military weapon, but only to introduce thoroughly honest and reasonably tough procurement practices into the lush Pentagon, what could happen then? The cost overruns should largely disappear.

Just the $2 billion cost overrun on the infamous C5A is enough to increase the federal contributions to education by some 50%, quite a difference!

And the $33 billion of cost overruns of the past few years would if directed to education instead of sloppy contracting accomplish these purposes. That amount of money would give 1500 communities in the nation a fully equipped elementary school for 1000 children, a junior high school for 1300 students, a senior high school for 1500. And it would pay the salaries of 135,000 teachers!

It is of course unrealistic to expect either that all the ways of the Pentagon can be quickly reformed or that, if they were, all the saving would go to education.

But at the very least a $10 billion reduction in military expenses could be made at no cost whatever to true national defense. And if that were done the Federal Government could treble the amount of revenue sharing it now does with the schools of the nation.

It is altogether a question of where we wish to put our treasure—in adequate educational opportunity for our children or in a military "overkill" far greater than our country conceivably needs as an effective deterrent.

Richard Milhous Nixon and his Administration have chosen military overkill.

The choice has been clear from the earliest months of Mr. Nixon's presidency.

In the year 1969 Congress passed the appropriation bill for the Health, Education and Welfare Department. It contained $1 billion more for education than Mr. Nixon had requested and about $300 million more for health. The President waited until January, 1970, when the fiscal year was more than half gone. Then he vetoed the bill, accusing the Congress of having passed legislation that would increase inflationary pressures.

The truth was that Congress had cut the Nixon budget by $5.5 billion. It had not increased it by a single penny. But Congress had violated Mr. Nixon's priorities. For it had cut $5.6 billion from the swollen Pentagon budget and $1.1 billion from military foreign aid—a total of $6.7 billion. Then the Congress had added about one fifth of that amount—$1.3 billion—for education and health.

The difference in priorities, in where the nation's treasure should go, was plain as day. President Nixon wanted $6 billion more for weapons of war than the Congress was willing to give. The Congress wanted $1.3 billion more for the people's health and education than Mr. Nixon was willing to give. The President's proposal was almost exactly four times as inflationary as was the action of the Congress.

At the time of his veto Mr. Nixon had received—and suppressed—a report of a task force on Urban Education which he himself had appointed. That report recommended a $5 to $7 billion increase in federal aid to city schools. It might never have come to light had not Democratic Congressman Jeffery Cohelan of California got wind of it and insisted on its release.

In August, 1970, for the second time in a row Mr. Nixon vetoed the education appropriation bill—this time the bill for fiscal year 1971. He did so because Congress had appropriated $453 million more than the presidential budget called for; Mr. Nixon called this "the kind of big spending that is wrong for all the American people." But at this very same time he was asking $1.5 billion for more ABM's and $900 million to bail out the Penn Central Railroad. Presumably since these expenditures would not benefit the school children, therefore, they would not be inflationary! As for the Attorney General, his remarks in his interview with *Women's Wear Daily* were especially colorful coming from one who had expressed such shocked dismay at the use of "four letter words" by some students. He characterized the teachers and school administrators of the country as "ignorant bastards" and said they were the cause of all the country's troubles. He added that "this country is going so far to the right that you won't be able to recognize it." The wish, rather clearly, was father to the thought.

Mr. Nixon's budget for fiscal year 1972 called for a cut of $50 million in aid to elementary and secondary education. It was presented at about the same time when the President was addressing a Roman Catholic audience and promising his listeners that he was about to provide, personally, federal monies in aid of parochial schools. Just how or when he was to accomplish this was not then—nor at any later time— revealed.

By mid-1971 the President of the National Education Association had had all she, or American educators, could endure. On June 28 Mrs. Helen Bain, speaking for NEA, used plain and unmistakable words:

A lion's share of the nation's ills, frustrations, and failures must be placed at the doorstep of Richard Nixon. . . . This is the most anti-education administration this country has had in many years. This administration has repeatedly made statements which were calculated to reduce confidence in public education. On rare occasions, Mr. Nixon has asked educators to serve on such task forces as urban education, higher education, and student unrest. In each instance, he has discredited and ignored the reports. It seems that the administration attacks the schools because that is much cheaper than financing them. . . . Mr. Nixon says we need to know more about learning. He is not aware of the things you & I learned shortly after we first stepped into a classroom: that a hungry child cannot learn; that children cannot learn in an over-crowded and understaffed school; that schools cannot function in a constant state of financial crisis.

Undaunted by the pointed attack on his anti-education policy by the head of the nation's leading educational organization, Mr. Nixon proceeded to prepare his $25 billion deficit budget for fiscal year 1973. For education he asked even *less* than his figure for the previous year, while for the lush life of the Pentagon he demanded an increase of several billion dollars.

The day came however when Richard Milhous Nixon saw a popular issue coming down the road, and, as his custom was, seized it quickly and with flair.

It was widely recognized that something must be done to

relieve the local property taxpayers. Other sources of support for the schools had to be found. And this became imperative when the Supreme Court of California declared locally-levied property taxes to be an unconstitutional method of financing education. Rich school districts were able to spend much more per school child with lower tax rates. Poor school districts even with higher tax rates were able to provide far fewer dollars for the education of each child.

State legislatures began consideration of reforms—*statewide* property taxes, uniformly levied in all districts, and income taxes, new or increased, among them.

By early 1972 the situation was critical in many parts of the country. It was a good time for a dramatic proposal. Mr. Nixon was equal to the occasion. He suddenly announced that he was going to provide federal funds for support of the schools to replace local property taxes. He did not specify how, when or at what cost to the federal budget this might be done. The general promise was the main thing. And it received, at first, the hoped for acclaim. Nixon had done it again!

The general idea was an appealing one—particularly to home-owning suburbanites—and it was calculated to bring many votes in an election year.

But as time passed, it became obvious that nothing except another golden promise was likely to result. The cost of conducting the elementary and high schools of the country is $50 billion a year. Was Mr. Nixon proposing to add $50 billion to federal taxes at a time when he had warned against *any* new spending programs and when his budget was already $25 billion in deficit? How, when, and where was he going to get the money? From a value-added tax—which had raised the cost of living by 8% when imposed in Holland? From a sales tax? Either of these would amount to shifting the burden from property owners to the general population, with heaviest burden on the workers and the poor.

In any case so diametric a shift in federal, state, and local taxation as Mr. Nixon's proposal would require would take months if not years to accomplish. Meanwhile school financing would be in limbo and the children would be deprived still more.

Months passed and it became more and more evident that Mr. Nixon had, in fact, no actual proposal or plan in mind at all. He was only trying—again—to provide for his re-election.

There was a way whereby Mr. Nixon—assuming he was sincere—could provide a large share of the money needed to relieve the overburden property taxpayers. And that was to determine honestly what amount of nuclear fire-power and weapons systems was really necessary to deter the Soviet Union or any other country from starting a war. And then to have the Pentagon worry along with perhaps $20 billion less than it was being provided by Mr. Nixon. Needless to say no one in the Administration or the so-called "Defense" Department was about to make any such calculations. It was altogether contrary to the policies of Mr. Nixon. But others, concerned about the general health of the nation, had done so— among them Richard Barnet, former Pentagon expert, and Seymour Melman, Columbia University professor of industrial engineering.

Melman points out that 64% of all controllable expenses in the federal tax dollar goes for wars, past, present and future. He contends that unless this economic waste is stopped our country's economy—and more than that its life—is headed rapidly and inexorably down hill. He says that this need not happen. Not if our military policy is really what the people are told it is—namely a policy not of making war but of deterring other nations from making it.

Melman contends that our three military objectives should be effective deterrence of any possible enemy from daring to attack the United States, protection of our coasts, and participation in peace-keeping actions of an international character. He quotes the Secretary of Defense to the effect that the "Polaris and Poseidon submarines at sea can be considered virtually invulnerable today." And the destructive power of these submarines is amply sufficient to destroy all the war-making power of the Soviet Union or any other nation.

Melman points out, as have many other military experts, that the United States possesses today weapons capable of destroying Russia thirty times over. Once, it would seem, should be enough.

It is not necessary to detail the completely-developed plan which Melman presented in an article for the *Saturday Review* of October 9, 1971. Suffice it to say that his case seems absolutely conceiving and that if the policy of the American government were one of providing for the security of the United States by means of unquestionably effective deterrent power and actually seeking to promote peace we would need to spend only about one third of what we are now spending on the military establishment.

But the trouble is, that is not our policy. Our policy instead is one of having sufficient weaponry to dominate the world and fight several wars, including a nuclear one, all at the same time.

That policy is our problem.

For even aside from the overwhelming moral and religious considerations, it is wrong to rob our economy of its competence for the sake of limitless ability to kill our fellow human beings many times over.

Melman puts it this way:

> A widening network of American industries is becoming technically and economically depleted, incompetent not only in the world market, but unable to hold even domestic markets. This is true in steel, shoes, machine tools, civilian electronics, shipbuilding, typewriters, automobiles, and other industries.

A whole new world of hope is possible to us. But it will take courage and an understanding of what true love of country requires of us, if we are ever to win that world.

Those who love their country best are not necessarily those who seek to make her mighty—sincere as they may be. Rather it may be a deeper form of patriotism to seek to make your country good and to be willing to be reviled for that attempt.

There is only one way this mad race to destruction can be halted and turned around. It is not by forever trying to outdistance other nations in weapons of total destruction. It is not by "negotiating from a position of strength." It is by acts of courage. The United States once tried such an act.

When both the U.S. and the Soviet Union were testing nuclear weapons in the atmosphere, there was great alarm over the poisoning of air, water and food. For the sake of human survival, these tests had to be stopped. Our government, under pressure from Adlai E. Stevenson, then Ambassador to the United Nations, decided—to its everlasting credit —to stop those tests unilaterally and to challenge the Soviets to do the same.

It worked. The Russians stopped too.

The result was the nuclear test ban treaty, which is still in effect. That treaty, result of an American act of courage, may have saved millions of lives.

If the U.S. were to try similar tactics in connection with disarmament talks and genuine efforts to build a peace it might save the lives of our children. And it might save the Earth as a home for man.

12. "WINDING *DOWN*" THE WAR

> This is the most generous peace proposal in the history of warfare.
>
> —President Nixon on his 8-Point Plan.

What the American people once believed to be a crusade against Communism degenerated into a war to preserve a dictatorship in power. And its military aspect became a kind of cruel target practice, a handy opportunity to try out new weapons, and unintentionally, of course, an unparalleled demoralizing influence upon our own soldiers. It is difficult indeed to reconcile our national action in these two respects with the teachings of human brotherhood, mercy, and justice which are taught by both the Old and the New Testaments.

Daily we heard from Nixon Administration sources, if not from Mr. Nixon himself, about how the President was "winding down the war." We were told that the war was inherited by this Administration from that of President Johnson.

In a measure this was true. But it should not be forgotten that in his campaign for the Presidency in 1968 Richard Nixon declared himself again and again to be in support of the Johnson war policies. Furthermore the *idea* for the war— even a wish for it—was not inherited from Lyndon Johnson. The first important American official to advocate sending American troops to fight a land war in Asia was Richard Milhous Nixon himself. This he did in 1954, while he was Vice-President of the United States, at the time the French were pulling out. An editorial, appearing in the *Chicago Daily News* for April 20, 1954 makes the facts very clear. Here it is in part:

> It was Vice-President Nixon's answer to a question from the floor of the American Society of Newspaper Editors convention that made the headlines last week.
>
> The question was what the United States would do to save Southeast Asia if the French quit fighting in Indochina. The answer was that he did not think the French would quit fighting; but if they did we might have to put in our own forces even if it meant fighting alone . . .

The whole of Nixon's prepared remarks tended in the same direction as the sentence that made the headlines. It was a well-organized argument that Indochina must be saved to save Southeast Asia; that Southeast Asia must be saved to save all of Asia including India, and to save indispensable raw materials for the free world in case of global war.

Though it did not fly into the headlines, one of Nixon's prepared passages was just as alarming as any of his answers to questions.

To discharge our responsibilities, the Vice-President said, we shall have to make a new definition of aggression. Nowadays, it is "aggression" only when one power crosses the boundary of another, as the North Koreans crossed over into South Korea. Hereafter, he said, we should be prepared to punish as aggression any foreign aid to an internal Communist revolution.

Senator Ed Johnson Democrat of Colorado was blunt and forthright. He accused Vice-President Nixon of "whooping it up for war" in Indochina. And he added: "I am against sending American GI's into the mud and muck of Indochina on a bloodletting spree to perpetuate colonialism and white man's exploitation in Asia."

It is of course true that shortly after he took office as President Mr. Nixon began to withdraw American forces from Vietnam. But it is also true that the peak of our involvement and the peak number of men fighting in Vietnam occurred in the early months of Mr. Nixon's regime.

President Johnson had stopped the bombing of North Vietnam and had managed to get the peace talks started in Paris, manned by some of the most skillful and respected diplomats in this country, Averill Harriman at their head.

President Nixon discharged those men—men who might in time have brought about a settlement—and replaced them with a succession of negotiators of steadily declining ability and prestige.

One of Mr. Nixon's principal appeals to the voters when he was in process of getting himself elected was that he had a secret plan for ending the war. The people took him seriously, partly perhaps because General Eisenhower had made a somewhat similar statement in 1952, regarding the Korean War.

The difference was that once elected, President Eisenhower went to Korea and promptly carried out his pledge.

Richard Nixon did nothing of the sort. Instead it was many months before he "revealed" what his "secret plan" may have

176

been. Whether he did not have any such plan in mind when he said he did, or whether for some strange and unaccountable reason he deliberately delayed announcing it for almost a year no one can be sure. What we can be almost sure of is that had anyone imagined that there would be 120,000 American soldiers killed, wounded or missing in the first three years of Mr. Nixon's rule and had they not, on the contrary believed that Mr. Nixon did in fact have a secret plan to bring the war to a speedy end, Hubert Humphrey, and not Richard Nixon, would have been elected President in 1968.

Just what was the secret plan? Vietnamization of the war—a shift from the killing of Americans to a wider killing of the people of Southeast Asia? Was it his 8-point program which he told the country he and Mr. Kissinger had been secretly negotiating through the months and which he finally revealed in a television spectacular just in time to divert attention from his rather horrendous 1973 budget?

To this day we cannot be sure.

In any case Mr. Nixon carried on the war as vigorously as Mr. Johnson had ever done. And up to almost the very day when Mr. Nixon announced a complete reversal of his long-held enmity toward Communist China, the war in Vietnam was excused on the ground that we were "fighting Communism" and seeking to contain the "Chinese Menace" to all of Southeast Asia.

As time passed, however, certain trends in events began to become clear. To the great relief of American families, and to President Nixon's credit, he began, periodically, to announce reductions in American forces engaged in Vietnam. He was "winding down the war" and bringing the boys home. There were no unfulfilled promises here. So far as could be determined each presidential announcement was followed by actual reduction of forces on schedule. The goal was very important. It was to have all U.S. troops out of Vietnam "by election day," so that the war would not be an issue when Mr. Nixon went to the voters in November, 1972.

But in spring, 1972, while ground troops were coming home their places were being taken by more and more naval units in Southeast Asia waters.

Mr. Nixon's policy for Southeast Asia had two apparent objectives. He was determined to do what American voters most deeply desire—to get their sons out of the war—and to do it before the re-election date. But he was equally determined to win the war with American technology and

American bombing and American destruction of villages, facilities and ecology in Southeast Asia, all coupled with the army of South Vietnam.

This was the very genius of "Vietnamization."

The strange case of Richard Milhous Nixon would be stranger still if he had not wanted, all along, to be responsible for ending—not just "winding down"—the war. Of course he wanted that. But he wanted it on his own terms. And the essential element in those terms was—and is—the preservation of a center of American influence and strength in South Vietnam.

One obvious reason for this is to "save face," to make it appear that something at least has been salvaged for the United States from the disastrous course so long pursued by both the Johnson and the Nixon Administrations. But there keep cropping up other less obvious reasons. One of them is oil.

The magazine *Oil World* predicts "a production of 400 million barrels a day by 1975 from this Asian area." And *Petroleum Engineer* magazine has said: "Oil exploration could conceivably be successful enough to turn that part of the world into another South Louisiana-Texas type producing area. It all depends on the Vietnam War, how long it takes to get the job done and how well it's done."

Whatever his reasons, Richard Nixon wound down the war in one respect and one only—the withdrawal of American troops. In many other ways he wound up, accelerated, intensified, and spread the war. And even as to troop withdrawal, he resisted bitterly every move on the part of Congress either to speed up the withdrawal or to fix a final date for the end of American involvement.

Why?

Perhaps for the reasons that Richard Nixon gave in an article he wrote for the *Reader's Digest* in 1965. He said: "To negotiate with the enemy before we have driven him out of South Vietnam would be like negotiating with Hitler before the German armies had been driven out of France. We should negotiate only when our military superiority is so convincing that we can achieve our objective at the conference table—and deny the enemy his."

President Johnson refused to the end of his term of office to permit violation of the neutrality of Cambodia, despite the apparent fact that the North Vietnamese were using small areas of Cambodia as "sanctuaries."

But Richard Nixon had no such concern. In April, 1970

he ordered an invasion of Cambodia by American and South Vietnamese forces. The invasion followed close on the heels of the overthrow of the neutralist government of Prince Sihanouk and its replacement by military dictatorship headed by General Lon Nol. There have been persistent ugly rumors that this revolution was aided and abetted by American agents. The objectives of the invasion were said to be to discover and destroy a major enemy headquarters located just inside Cambodia as well as to drive North Vietnamese forces out of alleged "sanctuaries" along the Vietnamese border. Mr. Nixon promised to have all American *ground* troops out of Cambodia by June. And except for the 350 men who were killed in that invasion all ground troops had been withdrawn by the appointed date. Mr. Nixon made no such promise with regard to Air Forces, including ground-skimming helicopters. And certainly he imposed no limitation whatever on how far the South Vietnamese might carry the invasion or how long they would stay.

They are still there even though the government of Cambodia has more than once demanded that they leave, and that the South Vietnamese government close its military bases in Cambodia. The reason for this plea on the part of the hardpressed government of Cambodia is that South Vietnamese troops have been guilty of unbelievable atrocities against the civilian population of Cambodia. The worst of these have been committed against women.

When Mr. Nixon ordered the invasion, he apparently either did not know or else deliberately disregarded the bitter hostility that has existed through hundreds of years between Cambodians and Vietnamese.

This is part of the sordid story.

The much publicized secret headquarters of the enemy either never existed or, in any case, was never found. Since the invasion some two million Cambodians have been driven from their homes. There have been instances reported by United Press of American jet bombers striking populated Cambodian villages with napalm.

Most of Cambodia, not just a couple of tiny enclaves along the border, is firmly controlled by the North Vietnamese, and what remains of its military government depends for its tenuous existence upon American taxpayers' money, American bombs and American helicopters. Mr. Nixon's invasion of Cambodia continued, from the air, long after the so-called "peace with honor" was signed.

Unlike the invasion of Cambodia, which was openly announced by President Nixon, the invasion of Laos was, on the contrary, shrouded in secrecy and deception. But a very real invasion nonetheless. For as long as the Southeast Asia war has been in progress, the Central Intelligence Agency of the United States has been operating an airline in Laos, known as Air America.

It has been said that without Air America there could not have been a Royal Laotian Army to fight the Pathet Lao, counterpart in Laos of the Viet Cong in Vietnam. The pilots of Air America are supposed to be civilians. But the planes carry troops into battle and bring out the wounded. And when "necessary" Air America pilots have apparently flown many "missions" in T28 fighterbombers.

A more-or-less secret army composed of guerilla tribesmen has been trained, equipped and perhaps even led by American agents in Laos, as a means of shoring up the Royal Laotian Army.

And the official army has had its full complement of American military "advisers" for many years. Some of them have piloted light planes to spot targets for U.S. bombers flying support for the Laotian Army according to a *Los Angeles Times* on-the-spot reporter, whose article appeared in that newspaper for January 19, 1972. By that date it had become clear at last that, except for the sending in of uniformed infantry, the United States had been engaged in every kind of war activity in Laos for a long time.

Congress had passed legislation in an attempt to prevent U.S. involvement in Laos. It had placed limitations on expenditure of money there. But apparently to no avail. For the purpose for which the CIA spends its appropriations is regarded as none of Congress' business!

In March, 1970 President Nixon gave out an official statement concerning American military activity in Laos. He said: "We will continue to give the American people the fullest possible information on our involvement consistent with national security." But when Republican Congressman Paul McCloskey went to Laos in April, 1971 to try to find out what was going on he unearthed a number of disturbing facts. He interviewed a number of Laotian refugees, driven from their homes, and found that, despite repeated denials by Nixon officials, U.S. planes had been bombing villages in Northern Laos for many months. McCloskey said: "There are 9,400 villages in Laos and it looks to me like we may have destroyed thousands of them." Congressman McCloskey obtained a copy of a U.S. Information Service survey of several hundred refugees. The survey reported that bombing was the main cause of their having left their homes.

Other action in "winding down the war" in Laos by winding it up is better known. Untold tons of bombs have, for more understandable reasons, been dropped on the Ho Chi Minh Trail to prevent passage of enemy supplies to forces operating in Vietnam and Cambodia. And in February, 1971 a major invasion of the southern Laotian "panhandle" was ordered from Washington.

Its declared purpose was to cut the Ho Chi Minh Trail once and for all and thus block the flow of enemy supplies. The result was almost total disaster. Advance forces of the South Vietnamese army were caught in a trap by the North Vietnamese. They fled from the scene after suffering heavy losses. They abandoned large amounts of artillery, tanks and ammunition. It was even reported that they abandoned their own wounded as they stormed U.S. helicopters in their attempt to escape. The helicopters had been sent in to support the South Vietnamese drive, but had proved useful mainly as a means of rescuing the remnants of the advanced South Vietnamese forces.

Yet this operation was reported by the Pentagon and Administration spokesmen as having accomplished its objective. Reporters who told a different eyewitness story were accused of aiding the enemy by distortion of the facts.

So Laos had been added to South Vietnam and Cambodia as a beleaguered, war-ravaged little country, tottering "on the brink."

And the war had been spread to yet another Southeast Asia country.

Have Richard Nixon's claims that he was "winding down the war" been justified or have they not? In one respect— the welcome withdrawal of American ground forces—the answer is "yes." In almost every other facet of the tragic situation the answer is a definite, demonstrable, resounding "no."

The air war has been increased in intensity under Mr. Nixon's direct orders.

Whereas under President Johnson monthly bombing averaged 59,700 tons, under President Nixon they have averaged 95,000 tons. In fact, in the first three years of his presidency Mr. Nixon had ordered the delivery of more bomb tonnage than did Mr. Johnson in his entire term of office. This is the finding of an exhaustive study conducted by the Center for International Studies at Cornell University.

Some students of warfare have said that Mr. Nixon's bombing of civilian targets has been on a scale unequalled in the history of warfare.

The Cornell study contains this omnious paragraph: "We are manufacturing a slave army of mindless machines to police the world; the very existence of such advance technology will bring strong pressures for its use to counter 'insurgency' all over the world."

What the Cornell scientists referred to is made clear in an advertisement run by Westinghouse Electric Company. It describes an invention, or a series thereof, which have made it possible for pilotless planes aided by sensory devices scattered across the countryside to detect any kind of movement on the ground and even to drop bombs on any moving object over which they pass. The electronic sensors have been planted over many rural areas in Indochina. They are disguised as twigs of trees or animal droppings. They explode if touched. They flash signals to computers in planes flying overhead. The sensors cannot of course distinguish between a farmer, a child, a cow, an enemy soldier, or an American soldier. Thus it is important not to have any American soldiers in these places. Thus withdrawal of troops and intensification of the air war fit together perfectly. And the people of Southeast Asia became objects of "target practice" on the new American "electronic battlefields." Some enemy soldiers or Viet Cong collaborators may have been killed by these new inventions. Certainly many innocent civilians have been.

To date, in the name of the United States of America, more than four million *civilians* in the countries of Indochina who were alive and well when Richard Nixon took office have been either killed, maimed or driven into refugee camps. These are findings of an investigating committee of the United States Congress.

The reason for this mass tragedy was stated by Mr. Nixon's Secretary of State, William Rogers, on January 29, 1971, when he said: "We see no reason why there should be any limit in the use of air power. The President intends to use the air power as he sees fit. Our air power is going to be used to the maximum extent necessary."

"Necessary," that is, to win the war militarily.

And Mr. Nixon himself followed on February 17, 1971

with this: "I am not going to place any limitations upon the use of air power." Even in Cambodia *after* the "peace."

On September 21, 1971 the President personally ordered the largest air strike against North Vietnam since the Johnson bombing halt of 1968. A 35-mile stretch of territory north of the demilitarized zone was bombed by 250 U.S. planes.

Newspapers of November 10 reported the fourth consecutive day of mass bombing of North Vietnam, in retaliation for a missile having been fired at a U.S. B52 bomber over Laos. This marked the longest period of sustained attacks since Richard Nixon took office. One missile site was destroyed according to the American high command.

But the Christmas season was selected by Mr. Nixon for what was reported as the most massive air assault of the entire war. An armada of 350 planes took part, of which five were shot down. Damage was hard to estimate. But it was perhaps significant for the future that some 150 of the planes came from aircraft carriers in the Gulf of Tonkin.

Selection of the Christmas season for these raids demonstrated once again Mr. Nixon's cleverness. For at that time Congress was in recess and the university campuses were empty for the sacred holidays. So there was less opportunity for protest.

On December 26th Hanoi had announced that no American prisoners would be freed as long as the bombing attacks continued. It was on the next day that Mr. Nixon ordered the major assault.

As the time for President Nixon's much-publicized visit to China drew near, the people of Southeast Asia were called upon to pay the price for making the visit a joyous occasion. It was feared that the North Vietnamese would mount an offensive which might "embarrass' the American President while he was in Peking. Whether or not a Vietnamese peasant who came home to his village to find his house destroyed and his family dead would be "embarrassed" was, it seemed, beside the point.

On February 5th the Associated Press reported the 37th air raid on North Vietnam since New Year's Day, together with the regular bombings of Laos and Cambodia. And on February 13th, the AP told of 356 air bombardments in South Vietnam alone and "hundreds more" against North Vietnamese supply trails in Laos and Cambodia.

Richard Nixon was not winding down the war, he was

changing it from a land war into an air war. And while he was reducing the number of Americans called upon to fight and die in a war they knew wrong, he was, at the same time, making the suffering and dying of the people of all Southeast Asia more intense and frightful than ever.

This is not to minimize the cruelty with which the Viet Cong has carried on its guerrilla warfare. Nor to represent "the other side" as blameless for the continuance of the sickening slaughter. But the United States is supposed to be a great nation. We boast that ours is the most powerful nation in the world. We even at times dare to call ourselves a "Christian" nation. And we have been the invaders—not the Vietnamese nor the Cambodians nor the Laotians.

Lieutenant Calley has been tried and found guilty of murder in what Mr. Nixon once described as a "massacre"—only to come to Calley's defense when he found that to be a more popular course. But if Calley is guilty of killing innocent people with a gun, how much more guilty are those who order them killed in far, far larger numbers by bombings from the skies.

President Nixon said the war must go on until our prisoners were freed. And no one disagreed with him that the freeing of those prisoners must be a condition for the ending of the war.

The question however was how to get the prisoners freed. And the way was not by continuing the war. That has never been the case in all the history of warfare. Prisoners are freed at wars' ends—not before.

It is not to be forgotten that as part of their 7-point program for ending the war, the "other side" proposed on July 1, 1971, that they would free our prisoners simultaneously with the withdrawal of American forces, provided the American President would fix a firm date for the final withdrawal of all U.S. forces. There is considerable evidence that in the beginning at least this was the *only* condition required by the enemy for the release of the prisoners. But, so far as can be determined the proposal was not given serious consideration by the Nixon Administration. Certainly it was never given the courtesy of a formal response. Thereafter, it is true that Hanoi hardened its terms to include a cessation of American support of the Thieu regime in South Vietnam.

Neither rhetoric nor raids nor bombings nor threats of bombing could release our prisoners of war. Whoever sought to have them released would have to bring about an end to American involvement in the war.

Congress seemed to see this relationship clearly enough when it passed the Mansfield amendment to the military appropriation bill for fiscal 1972. That Amendment read: "It is the policy of the United States to terminate at the earliest practicable date all military operations of the United States in Indo-China and to provide for the prompt and orderly withdrawal of all United States military forces at a date certain, subject to release of all American prisoners of war."

The Mansfield Amendment was a solemn declaration of United States policy, adopted by the only agency—The Congress—which has the constitutional right and duty to chart the nation's policy.

The history books fail to record an instance where an American president did not accept such a policy declaration by the Congress as a directive for his action as chief executive.

But in the strange case of Richard Milhous Nixon that rather healthy precedent was broken. He himself had signed the amendment into law along with the rest of the appropriation bill. But, arrogating to himself legislative as well as executive powers, Mr. Nixon openly announced that he would disregard completely the Mansfield Amendment. No one but Richard Milhous Nixon was going to run this war. Neither Congress nor the American people were apparently supposed to have anything whatever to say about it.

Congressman Boland of Massachusetts said the President's action was "incomprehensible and indefensible." Senator Church of Idaho declared: "The Mansfield Amendment is now part of the law of the land and, as such, is not subject to dismissal by the President." But Richard M. Nixon obviously considered himself above the law.

Senator Church asked this question: "What is he going to do next? Dispatch Henry Kissinger to Capitol Hill to disband Congress?"

It was a logical question:

The action of the President in disregarding the Mansfield Amendment shed light—or was it darkness—on his repeated assurances that he was "doing all he could" to bring about the release of the prisoners.

There had been a time when those who sought an excuse for the Indochina war thought they found it in an effort by our country to assure the people of South Vietnam an opportunity

185

freely to choose their own government in a democratic manner.

On October 3, 1971 that excuse became utterly obsolete. For on that day President Thieu, aided by his military minions throughout the country and protected by acts of a supreme parliament, was reelected in a one-man contest. All his opponents had been, by one device or another, prevented from even becoming candidates. The people had no choice whatsoever. The badge of "dictator" around Thieu's neck was mild description.

For some strange reason this situation did not bother Richard M. Nixon. He dispatched Governor Reagan of California to Thieu's inauguration, there to carry the congratulations of the President of the United States. Mr. Nixon's was the *only* such message that President Thieu received. And Mr. Reagan was the only representative of any country to attend the inaugural ceremonies.

By this time it was clear enough that what Mr. Nixon was concerned about, and the reason for the devastating bombing he was ordering upon Southeast Asia, was not free elections or the right of a people to choose their own form of government. Rather it was now starkly evident that the Nixon objective was a government in South Vietnam which would be subservient to the United States and be a base for future U.S. power politics in the region.

The Business Executives Move for Vietnam Peace and New National Priorities asked this question: "Do we want to continue our support for the Thieu government or do we want all U.S. servicemen and prisoners of war home soon?"

On January 25, 1972 President Nixon staged another of his television spectaculars, only hours after his controversial budget message had been delivered. There was every reason for Mr. Nixon to wish to turn attention of the nation in a different direction. He succeeded cleverly.

He revealed that for a period of many months his Dr. Kissinger had been carrying on secret negotiations with North Vietnam. He said that an 8-point proposal for ending the war had been presented to the "other side" on October 11 and that since that time efforts had been going on in secret to try to get agreement from the North Vietnamese to that plan. He appealed for national unity, saying that he, the President, had all along been trying to do what his critics had been demanding and therefore it was time for everyone to close ranks behind their leader. Mr. Nixon further accused North Vietnam

186

of failing to negotiate in good faith in secret and said that perhaps his revealing of the secret sessions might bring the enemy to agree publicly to what they had been unwilling to agree to privately.

The President's 8-points which he described as "the most generous peace proposal in the history of warfare," were as follows according to the White House release:

1—There will be a total withdrawal from South Vietnam of all U.S. forces and other foreign forces allied with the government of South Vietnam within six months of an agreement.

2—The release of all military men and innocent civilians captured throughout Indochina will be carried out in parallel with the troop withdrawals mentioned in Point 1. Both sides will present a complete list of military men and innocent civilians held throughout Indochina on the day the agreement is signed. The release will begin on the same day as the troop withdrawals and will be completed when they are completed.

3—The following principles will govern the political future of South Vietnam:

The political future of South Vietnam will be left for the South Vietnamese people to decide for themselves, free from outside interference.

There will be a free and democratic presidential election in South Vietnam within six months of an agreement.

This election will be organized and run by an independent body representing all political forces in South Vietnam which will assume its responsibilities on the date of the agreement. This body will, among other responsibilities, determine the qualification of candidates. All political forces in South Vietnam can participate in the election and present candidates. There will be international supervision of this election.

One month before the presidential election takes place, the incumbent president and vice president of South Vietnam will resign. The chairman of the senate, as caretaker head of the government, will assume administrative responsibilities except for those pertaining to the election, which will remain with the independent election body.

The United States, for its part, declare that it:

—will support no candidate and will remain completely neutral in the election.

—will abide by the outcome of this election and any other political processes shaped by the South Vietnamese people themselves.

—is prepared to define its military and economic assistance relationship with any government that exists in South Vietnam:

Both sides agree that:

—South Vietnam, together with the other countries of Indochina, should adopt a foreign policy consistent with the military provisions of the 1954 Geneva accords.

—reunification of Vietnam should be decided on the basis of discussions and agreements between North and South Vietnam without constraint and annexation from either party and without foreign interference.

4—Both sides will respect the 1954 Geneva agreements on Indochina and those of 1962 on Laos. There will be no foreign intervention in the Indochinese countries and the Indochinese peoples will be left to settle their own affairs by themselves.

5—The problems existing among the Indochinese countries will be settled by the Indochinese parties on the basis of mutual respect for independence, sovereignty, territorial integrity and noninterference in each other's affairs. Among the problems that will be settled is the implementation of the principle that all armed forces of the countries of Indochina must remain within their national frontiers.

6—There will be a general ceasefire throughout Indochina, to begin when the agreement is signed. As part of the ceasefire, there will be no further infiltration of outside forces into any of the countries of Indochina.

7—There will be international supervision of the military aspects of this agreement including the ceasefire and its provisions, the release of prisoners of war and innocent civilians, the withdrawal of outside forces from Indochina, and the implementation of the principle that all armed forces of the countries of Indochina must remain within their national frontiers.

8—There will be an international guarantee for the fundamental national rights of the Indochinese peoples, the status of all the countries in Indochina, and lasting peace in this region.

Both sides express willingness to participate in an international conference for this and other appropriate purposes.

On first reading, the 8-points appeared reasonable to most people. Democratic candidates for president were generally mild in their first comments. Some of them commended the President for his initiative. Senator Muskie stated that he hoped that it would succeed, but that he doubted its acceptance by the other side because it contained nothing particularly different from the proposal which Mr. Nixon had publicly set forth in October, 1970.

The Washington Post, agreeing with Muskie's comment, published the text of the October, 1970 offer and stated that the only substantial difference between it and the newly revealed 8-point plan was the added provision in the latter for the working out of complicated election machinery, a process that could require a very long time.

In making his speech the President was obviously in a strong position since no one could question a report about negotiations that had been held in secret. No one, that is, except the North Vietnamese, whose version was to follow a few days later.

As the days passed some questions began to arise in people's minds and to be voiced more and more in the press and, as was to be expected, by Democratic candidates.

Among the questions:

(1) Why did the President wait until this particular time to "unify the country" and silence his critics?

(2) Since the July 1, 1971 seven-point proposal of the North Vietnamese had so many similarities to Mr. Nixon's 8-points, why was it not responded to publicly and accepted along with Mr. Nixon's own proposal of the previous October as at least a basis for negotiation?

(3) Why, if the President had been secretly negotiating about a withdrawal date for American forces, had he seen fit to insult the Congress by saying that he would disregard the Mansfield Amendment—especially in view of the fact that the Amendment did not itself fix any exact date?

(4) What precisely did withdrawal of "all" American forces from South Vietnam mean? Did it include American "advisers"? What about forces of one kind and another in Cambodia, Laos, and Thailand? What about naval forces immediately off shore?

The *Christian Science Monitor* observed that the 8-point

Nixon-Kissinger proposal did not rule out continued presence of American advisors and certainly did not contemplate any slackening of the flow of U.S. weaponry to the South Vietnamese Army during the period of negotiations. The proposal only said that the U.S. would be willing to "define" what military assistance it would provide to a future government of South Vietnam.

(5) As to the proposed election, since President Thieu's resignation was scheduled for just one month before that election was to take place and since there was no provision for removal of his local and provincial leaders, would it be possible for the supervising committee to prevent control of that election by the Thieu forces? His police and military would still be at their posts. Would people opposed to him dare to come forth and participate freely in the election, considering the manner in which they had been suppressed and, in the case of Viet Cong sympathizers, even hunted down?

(6) Surely a man like Mr. Nixon must understand the primary importance of "saving face"—especially to an Oriental. But if he did understand this, and if he sincerely was seeking peace, why then did he deliver his speech in so belligerent a tone and present his 8-point plan on so nearly a take-it-or-leave-it basis?

(7) Finally to what extent were Mr. Nixon's 8-points negotiable? At one point he had indicated they might be. But President Thieu, with considerable heat, accused Secretary of State Rogers of having violated the sovereignty of South Vietnam and "not for the first time" by suggesting that the matter of Thieu's resignation might be a negotiable matter. And Mr. Nixon immediately gave assurance to Mr. Thieu that under no circumstances would the proposal regarding him be changed without his full consent. President Nixon went further and said that no new or modified proposals would be made until Hanoi began to negotiate in good faith.

As was to be expected the immediate response of North Vietnam to the 8-point proposal was one of bitter attack. The attack centered on what Hanoi called a "breach of faith" on Mr. Nixon's part for having unilaterally revealed the secret negotiations.

But at first there was no outright rejection and hope was general that perhaps Mr. Nixon's proposal would, despite unanswered questions by critics, provide a basis for discussion that could lead to a settlement of the war.

The rejection was, however, not long in coming. The North

Vietnamese based it largely on two points—points to which they declared neither William Porter head of the U.S. Paris negotiations nor Dr. Kissinger in the secret talks had ever responded. These points were:

—The Americans refused to stop Vietnamization of the war, to pull out from South Vietnam all U.S. and other foreign troops, military advisers, personnel and war material and close down all bases. They also refused to stop all air and naval activities and "other acts of war" in North and South Vietnam.

—The Americans persisted in maintaining President Nguyen Van Thieu and his "puppet regime" in office.

Hanoi then proceeded to reveal its own 9-point plan which it said it had presented to Mr. Kissinger in the secret sessions as long ago as June 26, 1971. The 9-points were as follows:

1—The withdrawal of the totality of U.S. forces and those of other foreign countries in the U.S. camp from South Vietnam and other Indochinese countries should be completed within 1971.

2—The release of all military men and civilians captured in the war should be carried out parallelly and completed at the same time with the troop withdrawal mentioned in Point 1.

3—In South Vietnam, the United States should stop supporting Thieu-Ky-Khiem so that there may be set up in Saigon a new administration standing for peace, independence, neutrality and democracy. The Provisional Revolutionary Government of the Republic of South Vietnam will enter into talks with that administration to settle all internal affairs of South Vietnam and to achieve national concord.

4—The U.S. government must bear full responsibility for the damages caused by the United States to the people of the whole Vietnam. The government of the Democratic Republic of Vietnam and the Provisional Revolutionary Government of the Republic of South Vietnam demand from the U.S. government reparations for the damages caused by the United States in the two zones of Vietnam.

5—The United States should respect the 1954 Geneva agreements on Indochina and those of 1962 on Laos. It should stop its aggression and intervention in the Indochina countries and let their peoples settle by themselves their own affairs.

6—The problems existing among the Indochinese countries should be settled by the Indochinese parties on the basis of mutual respect for independence, sovereignty and territorial integrity, and noninterference in each other's internal affairs. As far as it is concerned, the Democratic Republic of Vietnam is prepared to join in resolving such problems.

7—All the parties should achieve a cease-fire after the signing of the agreements on the above-mentioned problems.

8—There should be an international supervision.

9—There should be an international guarantee for the fundamental national rights of the Indochinese peoples, the neutrality of South Vietnam, Laos and Cambodia and lasting peace in this region.

The above points form an integrated whole.

The differences between President Nixon's proposal and the 9-points of North Vietnam were mainly three. First, the *extent* of withdrawal of American forces. Mr. Nixon offered withdrawal of all combat forces from South Vietnam. Hanoi called for withdrawal also from all the other Southeast Asian countries. Second, the timing and extent of U.S. withdrawal of support of the Thieu government. Hanoi insisted that this be done at once and the interim government composed of all South Vietnamese factions be set up long before election-time. President Nixon did not say the U.S. would stop supporting Thieu. He proposed Thieu's resignation one month before the elections but presumably with his right to run again in those elections. Third, the timing of the cease-fire. President Nixon wanted it to take place on the day the agreement was signed. Hanoi had from the beginning and through all the negotiations in Paris refused to agree to a cease-fire before all the political questions were settled.

It is noteworthy that the North Vietnamese did not ask that the Viet Cong be included in the interim government of South Vietnam. Rather, they called for negotiations between that government and the Viet Cong after the government had been established.

As spring approached in 1972 and Richard Nixon began his summit meetings with the big Communist powers, the war in Southeast Asia still raged on. Withdrawal of American infantry was still scheduled to be virtually complete by election day. Otherwise there was to be no winding down unless someone gave ground.

There was no reason to expect that it would be Hanoi or its allies in South Vietnam, Cambodia, Laos and Thailand who would do so. They had only to wait for American ground troops to be withdrawn in greater numbers—perhaps altogether. For political, if for no far better reason, Mr. Nixon could not repudiate his commitments regarding that withdrawal. Furthermore there was no chance that Hanoi or its allies could be bombed into submission. This had been amply proved over more than a decade. As white "colonial" invaders the Americans were disliked, if not hated, more and more as the days passed—even in South Vietnam.

Hard as the decisions would be, if the war was to be ended soon—or it seemed ever—the initiative would have to come from the United States and it would have to be different in certain respects from Mr. Nixon's 8-point plan.

But the initiative for peace that was forthcoming was intensified bombing all over Southeast Asia. More bombs were dropped on Mr. Nixon's orders in the first two and one-half months of 1972 than had been dropped in all of 1971.

That bombing, as should have been expected, did not deter the North Vietnamese or the Viet Cong. In early April they launched their offensive. It swept across the demilitarized zone and captured the provincial capital of Quang Tri. It threatened Hue. It struck at An Loc, a strategic town only 60 miles from Saigon. South Vietnamese units fled in disorder. Their generals gave orders that unless they returned to their units they would be shot.

Vietnamization obviously had failed.

Richard Nixon's response was characteristic. He ordered the bombing of Hanoi and Haiphong. He announced in a television spectacular that troop withdrawals would continue, but at a slower rate; and he gave no date for announcement of any further withdrawals. At the same time, however, naval vessels were ordered to the coasts of Vietnam in such numbers that naval personnel engaged in the war was increased threefold, as were the number of ships. And the numbers of airmen in Thailand were increased to some 50,000, the highest figure of the entire war. On balance, despite the now ridiculous pretense of winding down the war, the numbers of Americans engaged was being sharply increased.

The Paris peace talks were resumed for a few days—both openly and in secret—and suddenly broke off again.

And then came the great gamble. Mr. Nixon ordered the mining of all the harbors of North Vietnam and the bombing of all railroads leading into that country. He gambled everything he may have gained by his much heralded trip to China, the whole of Soviet-American relations, indeed the very peace of the world. At the same time Mr. Nixon proposed an immediate cease-fire to stop the North Vietnamese offensive and said that American forces would be withdrawn in four months if a cease-fire was agreed to.

Protests swept across the United States, Protestors were shot in New Mexico. Thousands, including university presidents, were arrested. An attempted rally in Sacramento, California, in support of the President's actions drew just six people.

The final outcome of Richard Nixon's gamble with the fate of mankind remained to be seen. Whatever that outcome, two facts were evident. One was that Richard Nixon did not wind down the Southeast Asia war. Instead, in an attempt to win it he devastated three countries of Southeast Asia with ruthless bombing. Most of Cambodia and great areas of Laos were delivered over to Communist control. Without protest from the Nixon Administration an absolute dictatorship was set up in South Vietnam. Whatever decent excuse for the war may once have existed was gone. Mr. Nixon's visit to China rubbed out the excuse that we were resisting Communism or Chinese domination of Southeast Asia. The Thieu dictatorship rubbed out the excuse that we were fighting to give the people of South Vietnam a chance to choose their own government.

The second fact is that the day of the colonial invader is gone. Mr. Nixon has refused to recognize that fact. Or to see that by the very carrying on of this war in an attempt to maintain a power base in Southeast Asia, the United States has shut the door on that possibility.

At long last, in January, 1973, a peace agreement was signed, and the last of the American ground forces withdrawn from Vietnam. Our prisoners of war were freed when the war was officially ended—just as the much maligned peace organizations had been saying.

Until the last day before the peace was concluded, Mr. Nixon did not wind down the war. Nor did he do so in Cambodia even after that.

13. "TOMORROW THE WORLD"

It is my great privilege to announce the conclusion of the most magnificent monetary agreement in the history of the world.
—President Nixon at the Summit
with French Premier Pompidou.

This has been the greatest week in the history of the world since the creation.
—Richard Milhous Nixon
on the first moon walks.

On February 14, 1972, *Los Angeles Times* columnist, D. J. R. Bruckner, commented on President Nixon's State of the World message as follows:

The President's State of the World message this month was much more cheerful than his State of the Union message last month. That is fair enough. The world probably is better off than the nation. Mr. Nixon has long believed that his expertise is foreign affairs and if he can make it appear now that he is reordering the world well, he will be in good shape for the coming campaign.

As Richard Milhous Nixon's policies and predilections unfolded, certain characteristics of both the policies and the man became clear.

The underlying and controlling one was an apparently unquenchable desire for power—power not only for the United States, but personal power for Richard Nixon.

He had tasted it and wanted as much of it as he could get. Unhampered as he turned out to be by any guiding principles or beliefs, he was free to seek power for his country and himself in any manner that seemed to offer promise of the desired results.

Columnist Bruckner was not shy of the mark when he spoke of Mr. Nixon's program for "reordering the world." He might have added that the President was determined to accomplish this reordering personally. His "foreign policy advisor," Dr.

Henry Kissinger, would have a good deal to do with it, for as a member of the President's personal staff, he was beyond the reach of Congressional fact-finding and what he did could be as an alter-ego of Mr. Nixon. The Secretary of State, William Rogers, was to be strictly an errand boy and a remarkably silent and self-effacing one at that, since most of the important functions of his office were taken over by Dr. Kissinger.

For three years the SALT disarmament talks had been going on with the Russians. All the other nations in the United Nations had asked, by resolution, that the United States and the Soviet Union stop developing any more horrendous nuclear weapons while those talks were in progress. The vote was 82 to 0. The United States Senate asked the same thing.

Neither of the so-called "great powers" has paid the slightest heed. Led by Mr. Nixon's power politics, the three years of the SALT talks have produced not a disarmament agreement, though one may come some day, but instead these *military* accomplishments:

Thousands of new stockpiles of warheads.
Greatly "improved" nuclear submarines.
The MIRV—An airborne system of missiles capable of destroying several cities at a single firing, among others.

All of which has made any real success at the SALT talks much more difficult to achieve.

It is—or should be—an important part of the foreign policy of every nation today to work for world peace. That is what Mr. Nixon declares he is striving to do.

But he has consistently neglected, by-passed, and denigrated the most logical path toward that goal. That path is the United Nations. Not necessarily as it now exists but as it *could* be if given wholehearted support by the major nations and accorded certain essential original authority in its own right. At present the United Nations can act, in most instances, only with the consent of its member nations. It must subsist on virtual gifts from those nations. It has no revenue-raising power of its own.

Yet if there is one greatest of all needs of mankind today it is for an institution in the world that could establish, maintain and enforce peace in the world, stop aggression before it got started, and so effectively police a disarmament agreement that no nation need fear violation by any other.

The United Nations is far from such an institution today. The highest duty of true statesmen is to make it so.

During the Nixon Administration the United States has

done little to that end. On the contrary, it has done much to render the United Nations even weaker than it once was.

A few examples will illustrate the point.

In the General Assembly session of 1969, eight votes were taken which might have advanced the world along the road to a more peaceful state. India and Ceylon voted for all eight of those measures. The Soviet Union supported only three of them; the United States but two.

Every other major nation in the world has ratified a treaty signed in Geneva, Switzerland in 1925 which prohibits the use of biological or chemical weapons in any war. But the United States has never done so. President Nixon once made a speech saying we would never use such weapons. And the United Nations went to work on a new treaty to outlaw these two types of lethal instruments.

But the United States was spraying Southeast Asia with chemical defoliants, napalm and other triumphs of Western technology every week. So, contrary to his own statement, Mr. Nixon's representation at the United Nations demanded exclusion of chemical weapons from the treaty. The smaller nations were outraged. Russia supported the United States position. The hands of the United Nations were tied.

The year 1970 was the 25th anniversary of the United Nations. On May 5 of that year U Thant, the Secretary General of the United Nations, formerly called upon "all interested parties to meet together to settle the tragic wars raging in Southeast Asia." So far as can be determined the Nixon Administration did not even reply to the Secretary General. Certainly it did not agree to his proposal.

For many years there has gone on an effort in the United Nations to get a broader nuclear test ban treaty adopted— one that would forbid underground testing as well as testing in the atmosphere. As if to forestall any such move, Mr. Nixon appointed Dr. Edward Teller, the scientist who insisted on development of the H-bomb, to the Foreign Intelligence Advisory Board. He is popularly known as "Dr. Strangelove" among American scientists. Perhaps reflecting Dr. Teller's influence, the Pentagon has opposed any broadening of the nuclear test ban.

President Nixon was invited, along with other heads of state, to address the 25th Anniversary session of the United Nations General Assembly in October, 1970. He devoted most of his address to a discussion of relations between the United States and the Soviet Union. He dismissed in a few sentences the peacekeeping role which a stronger United Nations might play.

The heart of his address was contained in these two paragraphs:

> But we also know that the world today is not what the founders of the U.N. hoped it would be 25 years ago. Cooperation among nations leave much to be desired. The goal of the peaceful settlement of disputes is too often breached. The great central issue of our time—the question of whether the world as a whole is to live at peace—has not been resolved.
>
> This central issue turns in large part on the relations among the great nuclear powers. Their strength imposes on them special responsibilities of restraint and wisdom. The issue of war and peace cannot be solved unless we in the United States and the Soviet Union demonstrate both the will and the capacity to put our relationship on a basis consistent with the aspirations of mankind.

Perhaps Mr. Nixon had in mind even then the high level summitry he was to enjoy in the months to follow. It was, in any event, quite clear that he preferred to leave to the summitry of the giants the fate of mankind, rather than attempting to build a structure that would give all nations a word to say about whether they should live or die.

When President Nixon reversed his position of a lifetime and announced that he would visit the People's Republic of China, it became necessary that the United States reverse its long-held opposition to the admission of Communist China to the United Nations. Quite properly, President Nixon so stated. Support for bringing in the world's most populous country had been gradually building over the years and it was questionable in any case whether the move could any longer have been delayed.

The question was not therefore whether Mainland China should be admitted, as it should have been long ago. It was what to do about Taiwan, or Nationalist China of General Chiang Kai-shek, which had been the fifth permanent member of the United Nations Security Council ever since the founding of the United Nations. Through the years the United States had supported the government on Formosa, had maintained military forces on the island, and used it as a Naval base.

So despite the contention of the Mainland Chinese that Formosa was part of China and that they would never recognize it as a separate country, the United States took the position that both Chinas should be members of the United Nations. Communist China should be admitted, but Nationalist China should retain its membership.

Most of the rest of the world thought otherwise. It felt that if Mainland China was to be admitted at all, it should come in on its own terms—which meant that it would *replace* the Chiang government as representative of all of China in the United Nations.

The vote came on that proposition—to seat the People's Republic and, in effect, to expel Taiwan.

There were legitimate as well as sentimental reasons for American opposition to this. It would be the first time any member had been expelled. It was a bad precedent to do so, since the proper objective of the United Nations had to be universal membership.

The opposing argument, of course, was that Taiwan was not truly a nation; that the Mainland Chinese were correct in claiming it to be a part of China and, therefore, not entitled to separate status.

The United States fought hard for its "two Chinas" position —in the worst possible way. Mr. Nixon left Dr. Kissinger in China on his mission there during the very days when the vote was taken. This seemed a pretty clear indication that the United States did not want to offend Communist China. On the other hand American representatives, including the Secretary of State, went on an arm-twisting spree in the United Nations corridors. And dark threats were allowed to circulate to the effect that unless the United States had its way, financial support for the United Nations might not be forthcoming from Washington.

The reaction to these tactics was what anyone should have expected: resentment and a determination to show the Americans that they could not always control the United Nations.

The vote was a stinging defeat for the United States and its position. Not a single major nation on earth, except Japan and the Brazilian dictatorship, voted with us. All the NATO allies, all the Communist bloc, Israel, Ireland, a number of Latin American countries were on the other side. The vote was 76 to 35 to admit Mainland China on its own terms.

This was the first time in all the 25 years of United Nations history that the United States had lost on a vote of any consequence. Since that was the case one would have thought our country could have taken just *one* defeat with good grace.

Not so. Mr. Nixon expressed himself as "shocked" and was reported to be in a state bordering tantrum because some delegates had shown "glee" over the first "declaration of independence" from the United States. Secretary Rogers gave forth with the complaint that six small nations—not named—were responsible for the defeat. Conservative members of Congress vowed that they would cut off all funds from the United Nations. The Administration, including the President, raised not a finger in opposition to such a move. They were too busy insisting that Congress place no limitation on military aid to the Greek dictatorship or on expanding operations in Cambodia and other parts of Indochina.

Some people suggested that leaders of the United States were acting like spoiled children. Fortunately this was not universally the case. A substantial majority of Congress kept its head and approved the customary appropriation for support of the United Nations.

Came the summer of 1971.

Game Plans I and II had brought the United States to a condition of acute sickness. The election was less than a year and a half away. Something had to be done. It was. In fact a number of things.

First came the sudden, surprise announcement by the President in mid-July that he would visit Communist China sometime during the winter of 1971-72. Characteristically the news was broken upon the world without the slightest advance warning. Henry Kissinger knew about it, for it was he who had made the arrangements. Whether anyone in the State Department had been appraised seems doubtful. Certainly no one in the Congress had the slightest hint about it. Nor did any foreign country.

No mention was made of the fact that Richard Nixon more than any other American politician had built his active career out of attacks upon Communism and Communists, real and imaginary. Neither was historical fact alluded to—such as Mr. Nixon's close associations with Chiang Kai-shek's China lobby or his virtual leadership in the long effort to exclude Mainland China from the United Nations. Blandly, the President announced that it was time to "normalize relations" with China since it was, after all, the most populous nation on Earth. He made his U-turn from the direction he had followed all his life, without so much as a hint or suggestion that, in the past, he might have been mistaken.

There was bitter consternation among Conservatives who had voted for Mr. Nixon on his record. Most people, however, saw that, whatever the motives, and however unstatesmanlike the chosen method, nevertheless the normalizing of relations with China was not only desirable but long overdue.

The thought did occur that relations with China could be normalized quite as well—and perhaps with less risk—in a less dramatic way and without the projected visit. Mr. Nixon did not need to go to China in order to remove trade restrictions, to encourage reciprocal travel, or to reverse the position of the United States with respect to Chinese membership in the United Nations. The President's actions in taking these steps were certain to receive the general support they deserved. The visit to Peking was a separate, almost an unrelated matter. It would be summitry at its loftiest and best. It would be a stroke of power politics fit to rock the Kremlin. And for a period of weeks in an election year and during the political campaign, it would keep Richard Nixon on the front page of every newspaper and for hours on end on every television screen.

As if to keep "his" world on its toes, the President let only a little time elapse after his Chinese trip announcement before he demanded free prime network time to reveal a second 180° change of course. This was the unveiling of Game Plan III on August 15, 1971. It was done, like the China trip broadcast, with a maximum of drama, without notice to the Congress or any friendly nation, and without a word of admission that the reason for his new course was the utter failure of his previous policies.

A considerable part of Game Plan III affected foreign policy. There was the, on the whole welcome, notice that the United States would no longer promise to redeem its dollars with gold. There was the decision to let the dollar "float"—seek its own level—on the money markets of the world. And there was the very questionable imposition of a 10% duty on most imports into the United States.

All these measures were calculated to affect severely the nations with which most of the trade of the United States had been carried on in the post-war period. The blow fell heaviest upon Japan, our best customer for agricultural exports, and Canada with whom our greatest total volume of trade was carried on. A period of complete uncertainty, if not chaos, followed in international monetary relations. And not only in Japan and Canada but in the Latin American countries whose raw material exports to the United States constitute major elements in supporting their relatively weak economies, there was something like consternation. The Common Market of Western Europe was better able to defend itself—and proceeded in various ways to threaten to do so.

Of the President's two "spectaculars," neither was without its cost.

In part that cost was due to the substance of Mr. Nixon's actions. Announcement of the visit to China was cause of heightened tension between the United States and the Soviet Union, of fear of "sell-out" in Taiwan, of a mingling of anger and deep concern in Japan, and, along with other forthcoming events, total destruction of the friendly relations that had existed for many years between the U.S. and India.

The foreign policy elements in Game Plan III brought to an abrupt halt the "trading-partner" relationship that had been developed with a number of countries. It caused some of them to look elsewhere than to the United States for future economic progress.

But it was not alone *what* was done that brought about the high price at which any hoped-for benefits from Mr. Nixon's actions would be purchased. It was also the manner in which it was done. Had friendly nations been consulted beforehand, had their reactions to what he was about to do been sought by Mr. Nixon his double-barrelled blow could have been struck with far better grace and with far less damage to the foreign relations of the United States.

Unfortunately, however, that was not the way in which the man who described himself to the Pope as the most powerful man in the world was pleased to act. He much preferred to display his power, to show those who failed to act as he wished them to, that President Nixon of the United States of America was not a man to be crossed. He was in position to reorder the world and he proposed to do it in his own way.

It is possible, taking into account Richard Nixon's liking for summitry and travel, that his imperious method of procedure may have been deliberate. For it created a situation where a number of summit meetings became one attractive means of endeavoring to undo the damage.

Even the Nixon strategists could see that Canada had to come first. The Canadians had for some time felt themselves threatened with take-over of their industries by United States capital. They felt also that Canada, as the best trading partner of the U.S., was being neglected and taken for granted by U.S. policy. The Nixon bombshells brought deep and bitter resentment and fear. And not without reason. Unemployment in Canada began to increase almost immediately after the President's August 15th blow was struck. To make matters worse Mr. Nixon said in a press conference: "Japan is our biggest customer in the world and we are their biggest customer in the world." This simply was not true. Canada was, and had been for years, ahead of all other nations in trade with the United States.

So Mr. Trudeau, the Canadian Prime Minister, was invited to come to Washington to talk to Mr. Nixon. No one knows what the President said to Mr. Trudeau. Whatever it was, the Canadian leader went home in far better spirits.

But the breach was far from healed. Canada proceeded to entertain the Soviet premier and to sign a far-reaching trade agreement with the Soviet Union.

The 1971 $2 billion foreign trade deficit—biggest in U.S. history—looked even bigger than it was.

None of the other summits took place, however, until Mr. Nixon had commissioned Secretary of the Treasury John Connally to meet with the finance ministers of those nations most vitally affected by the new monetary policies laid down in Game Plan III.

These talks set the stage for the second summit and the precise announcement by President Nixon which would be most appropriate for the occasion. There can be little doubt that well before Mr. Nixon met French President Pompidou in Portugal's Azores Islands, it had been decided that the monetary crisis, for which the U.S. was being justly blamed, had to be resolved by definite devaluation of the dollar. France had been one of the nations most adamant in its refusal to revalue its franc and its insistence on a change in the "gold content" of the dollar. So what could be more dramatic than for Mr. Nixon to announce his decision to ask Congress for the dollar devaluation as if it were a result of his conversations with Mr. Pompidou? This was indeed good diplomacy as well as politically valuable drama.

So it was that Richard Nixon followed in the footsteps of Franklin D. Roosevelt, whose action in raising the dollar price of gold as an anti-depression measure had been so roundly attacked through the years by that same Richard Nixon. For the first time since 1933, the United States dollar bowed to economic necessity and admitted to a decline in its value in world trade.

Specifically the President said he would propose to Congress that the dollar price of gold be raised from $35 an ounce to

$38. The actual consequences, as the weeks passed, proved somewhat more far reaching than the Administration had counted on. The dollar sank on some exchanges to figures like $50 per gold ounce, and little was done to protect it.

As a side light on this summit meeting, held as it was in Portuguese territory, Mr. Nixon promised the dictatorship of that country some $436,000,000 of assistance—at least part of which would no doubt be used to keep the independence movements in Portugal's African colonies in check.

Fresh from his success with the French President, Mr. Nixon proposed to meet with British Prime Minister Heath. But not without a veritable chorus of critical comment in the background. Editorials at home were referring to the round of summit meetings as an attempt to make up for the "surprise and demanding tone" of his August 15th announcements. One such editorial put it this way: "Not many foreign affairs specialists would argue that the ideal way to deal with your chief world trading partners is to swat them first with a two-by-four and then show up in Bermuda or the Azores with a suitcase full of bandages and balm." *Newsweek* columnist William P. Bundy expressed "the unhappy feeling that Mr. Nixon was 'greatly overdoing' the summitry act." And the British *Manchester Guardian* went so far as to suggest that: "Mr. Nixon's summitry is mainly calculated to demonstrate that he is equal to the giants in the Communist Camp."

Few who have followed Richard Nixon's career believed that his ambitions stopped one whit short of the *Guardian's* attributed objective.

But the preliminaries had to be attended to. And next on the program was the summit meeting with Prime Minister Heath in Bermuda. The news release was, as expected, eulogistic. Mr. Nixon was well prepared and announced the removal of the 10% import duty. It had been the least acceptable part of the Game Plan III package. It had aroused justifiable fears of retaliation by other countries and of a "trade war." In all probability Mr. Nixon had viewed it as one of the "bargaining chips," like the Amchitka underground nuclear explosion, which he appeared to enjoy using.

But unlike the Pompidou summit, the Heath one had its disturbing overtones. Somewhat sadly and ominously the Prime Minister of Great Britain pointed out that the "special relationship" that had existed between his country and the United States for hundreds of years was coming to an end. Great Britain was turning eastward, joining the Common

Market and throwing her economic lot with European nations instead of the United States. Mr. Heath was considerate enough not to add that this was, at least in part, due to the "two-by-four" blow which Mr. Nixon's power politics had brought forth. But the implication was clear enough. In future the United States would face a stronger competition for free world trade than had been the case during most of her history. And British support for American policies would be uncertain.

But this was not the main point. The third summit had enabled Mr. Nixon to hold the headlines for several days. There was water on the re-election wheel.

Next on the program came Chancellor Willy Brandt of the German Federal Republic. He came to Washington, talked with the President at some length, was frequently interviewed on U.S. television.

It was reported that Herr Brandt received from the President a promise not to make a deal for withdrawal of American troops from Europe when Mr. Nixon went to Moscow for his major summit of them all. If such report were true it would have been in direct conflict with what the President had told his own countrymen when he opposed so vigorously the Mansfield troop-withdrawal amendment. For he said on that occasion that there must be no troop reduction in Europe until he himself negotiated a mutual withdrawal with the Russians—a project which he indicated was definitely "in the works."

Furthermore the impression would not dissipate that Mr. Nixon's talks with the erstwhile trading partners were aimed not so much at solving basic problems as at appeasing them in preparation for his summits with the Communist giants. Mr. Nixon was averaging 35 feats of summitry per year compared to an annual rate of only 8 "top level" conferences by either President Roosevelt or President Truman. Perhaps William Bundy was right about a "bit of overdoing."

Japan was the nation hardest hit by the Nixon reversals. Japanese leaders had a right to feel that their cooperation with the United States ever since World War II had been complete. Moreover, President Nixon had given the Japanese a firm assurance in 1969 that he would consult them about any contemplated changes in U.S. policy toward China. Japan had faithfully followed American policy regarding Taiwan and had not attempted direct dealings with mainland China, even though her trading position might substantially have been improved thereby.

Therefore, for Mr. Nixon to announce his visit to Peking

without even informing, let alone consulting, with the Japanese government was regarded by that nation not only as a diplomatic insult but as a flagrant breach of faith. When this was followed by the floating of the dollar plus the 10% import duty, the Japanese economy was thrown into a minor recession and the government of Prime Minister Sato threatened.

It was against this background that Prime Minister Sato came to San Clemente in January, 1972, to afford Mr. Nixon another summit experience. This time however there was no disguising the fact that all had not gone according to plan. The only news of a "highly successful meeting" that could be given out with any show of validity was that agreement had been reached on opening up a "hot line" between Washington and Tokyo.

Otherwise it was all too evident that another partnership which had been of great value to the United States as well as to Japan had fallen victim to Richard Nixon's game of power politics.

Prime Minister Sato, perhaps inadvertently, stated in his news conference that he thought Japan was now free of obligation to continue its guarantee of the security of Taiwan. This roused a storm from the American side and Foreign Minister Fukuda was compelled to state that: "There is no change in the Japanese thinking that the security of both Taiwan and South Korea is important to Japan." A short two months later it was Mr. Nixon himself who yielded to Chinese demands and reversed the United States position on Taiwan, leaving the Japanese holding an empty bag of made-in-America policy.

The Japanese further stated that they had asked U.S. support for a reduction in the list of Japanese products banned from export to China. Secretary Connally told the American press that that subject had never been discussed.

So it went. Prime Minister Sato and his ministers went home with a promise from President Nixon to fix a date for the return of Okinawa to Japan. But that was about all.

Japanese fear of what might come of Mr. Nixon's much-heralded negotiations with her gigantic neighbor, mainland China, were not allayed. Back home again Prime Minister Sato told the press that he would await the outcome of the Peking talks before he could conclude that no more diplomatic "shocks" were in store for his country.

Almost forgotten amid the other summits was the one which undertook to recognize that after all there was such a place as Latin America in the world. Comparatively little publicity was given to this one and no important release emanated from the White House at its conclusion.

It was probably just as well. For Mr. Nixon chose for his Latin-American summit partner, General Medici, the military dictator President of Brazil. The General came to Washington to find awaiting him a request from 19 outstanding religious leaders of the United States that he permit an impartial investigation of "reports of torture and repression coming out of Brazil so numerous, so well documented and so horrifying that we have indeed no other choice."

It was true enough that President Nixon had selected the chief of state of the largest Latin American country for the summit. But that in itself caused other countries of South America to be fearful and resentful. President Caldera of Venezuela publicly stated his alarm over the prospect of a hegemony over all of Latin America by a U.S.-backed Brazil. The Peruvian and Agentinian governments issued similar statements. President Nixon's remarks to the effect that Brazil was among the "closest friends" of the United States and that "as Brazil goes, so will go the rest of Latin America" did not serve to calm these other countries' fears.

Neither did the policy of the Nixon Administration toward Latin America in general. The lion's share of U.S. aid was going to the Brazilian dictator—much of it in the form of arms. Except for such "statesmanlike" remarks as that of Herbert Klein, White House Communications Director, when he predicted that the Chilean government of leftist Salvador Allende "wouldn't last long," the Nixon policy toward Latin America was one of studied neglect. Result of this was to give private investors—not to say exploiters—free rein in the continent.

The days of the "Good Neighbor" and "Alliance for Progress" were over and no one knew this better than the highly sensitive Latin Americans. The significance of President Nixon's speech to the United Nations was not to be forgotten.

In the midst of President Nixon's summitry he had received a sharp rebuff from the United States Senate. Under the Constitution the Senate shares with the President responsibility for the conduct of the nation's foreign relations. Mr. Nixon has over and over shown his irritation with this provision of the Constitution. And on more than one occasion his attitude toward efforts of the Senate to exercise its prerogatives has been met with something close to Presidential contempt.

At last, in October, 1971, the Senate rose up in its smoldering resentment and defeated outright, by a bipartisan vote of 41 to 27, the entire foreign aid bill as recommended by the Administration.

The reasons were many and varied. There had been, for some time, disturbing reports to the effect that much of the American foreign aid monies was lining the pockets of politicians, rather than reaching the people they were supposed to help. Again, after much digging in Congressional hearings, it was discovered that money appropriated for foreign aid was going to finance the "Nixon doctrine" wars in Southeast Asia, that is, wars financed by American money but fought by other people. This had been found to be true in Vietnam, Laos, and Cambodia. A third source of concern on the part of many Senators was the tendency to use large quantities of foreign aid funds to help military dictators buy arms. These might be used against other countries. They might also be used against the dictator's own people in case of attempted protest or revolt. Finally there was widespread resentment against what Republican Senator George Aiken of Vermont termed "over-lobbying" by the Administration against the Cooper-Church Amendment which aimed to curtail funds for the Southeast Asia war.

Having defeated the foreign aid bill and, in effect, won a victory in its uphill struggle to share in the conduct of foreign affairs with the executive, the Senate then proceeded to write substitute legislation bearing more of its own stamp.

The final result was a bill cut by about $1 billion below the figure demanded by Mr. Nixon. In various ways the legislation restricted the Presidents' free-wheeling diversion of funds intended to assist needy people to such purposes as the invasion of Cambodia.

Most significant for the long-run future, the Senate passed two bills, not one. One contained money for economic aid to depressed nations. The other was confined to military assistance. Thus the two kinds of foreign aid could be considered separately, each on its own merits.

Finally the Senate inserted a requirement that before the $2.6 billion provided in the bill could be spent overseas, the White House must release a like amount of Congressonal appropriations frozen there and intended by Congress for health, education, housing and agricultural needs of the American people.

Until Richard Nixon became President of the United States

an especially warm relationship existed between this country and India. India was and is today the most populous democracy in the world, and the most exemplary one. For India is a poor country. It is a country which has enjoyed independence for only a short time. It is surrounded by dictatorships of various kinds—some Communist, as in China and the Soviet Union, some military, as in Pakistan, some monarchical, as in Iran. Yet in the midst of her poverty and economic distress, India has clung to institutions of freedom, and the percentage of her eligible voters, many illiterate, who cast their ballots in elections is far larger than has ever been attained in the United States.

It was not only logical but also the only decent course consistent with the most elementary of American ideals for the United States to act as a faithful friend of India and the Indian people.

As indeed our country did until Richard Nixon became President.

Then things changed. Mr. Nixon has shown, throughout his ruling years, a strange predilection for foreign dictators:— Medici of Brazil, Franco of Spain, Thieu of Vietnam, the dictator in Greece, Mao of China, to name a few. This preference extended to the military dictator of Pakistan, Yahya Khan, for whom Mr. Nixon openly expressed an "extremely high regard."

On the other hand the President simply did not like Mrs. Indira Gandhi, the Prime Minister of India. Neither did he like the social democracy which was developing there.

In December, 1970, Pakistan held its first general election. In East Pakistan that election resulted in an overwhelming victory for Mujibur Rahman, and his independence party. This was not the way Yahya Khan and his military-industrial complex had planned it. And they proceeded in the most direct possible way to reverse the results of their own election. Rahman was arrested, charged with treason, and carried off to prison in West Pakistan. In March the Pakistan army began a systematic slaughter of the followers of Rahman in East Pakistan.

Conservative estimates say that between 200,000 and 500,-000 Bengalis were killed by the Pakistan army. These people died without one word of protest from the United States government. They were killed with American weapons. Mrs. Gandhi's appeals to Richard Nixon to stop the flow of arms to Pakistan fell on deaf ears. While the slaughter went on, Mr. Nixon continued the flow of arms to Pakistan. The U.S.

State Department denied that any arms were being shipped that had not been contracted for prior to March 25. But the General Accounting Office uncovered two contracts signed after that date and involving sale of some $10 million of arms to Pakistan.

When Congress appropriated funds for the relief of some of the 10 million people who were fleeing into India Mr. Nixon sent the money to Yahya Khan—some $137 million of it. It was to be used, it was said, to persuade the refugees to return to East Pakistan!

Poor as she herself was India tried with little outside help, none from the government of the United States, to care for the millions of refugees and prevent them from starving. The strain on the Indian economy was growing day by day.

Such was the situation when President Nixon made his surprise announcement that he was going to China to seek to normalize relations with that Communist country—one that had threatened India more than once.

A month later India signed a 10-year Mutual Assistance Pact with the Soviet Union. It provided that if either country was threatened or attacked the other would come to its assistance. It provided further that neither India nor the Soviet Union would enter into any agreement with any other nation which was incompatible with the provisions of the treaty.

Twenty years of careful effort and $10 billion of economic aid spent by Americans to develop the kind of relations that should exist between two great free peoples went down the drain. The most valuable ally the United States could possibly have if it believed in its own ideals was lost—perhaps irrevocably. And a major reason was that Richard Nixon liked dictator Khan better than he liked democratic Prime Minister Gandhi.

Soviet influence in South Asia was now firmly established. And the blame lay squarely at the door of the Nixon-Kissinger brand of power politics.

Through all the summer and fall of 1971 the carnage in East Pakistan went on. Millions of frightened people continued to cross the border into India, often walking as far as 100 miles to reach safety. Mrs. Gandhi appealed to Britain and the United States for help. She received none of any consequences.

In December war broke out in earnest. Driven to the point of desperation by the refugee problem and outraged by the killing, India invaded East Pakistan. Her army was welcomed by the people as liberators. In a short two weeks the war was over, East Bengal was free of the rule of Pakistan, and a new nation, Bangladesh, was about to be born.

During those two weeks Mr. Nixon's government—almost certainly contrary to American public opinion—charged India with responsibility for the war, threatened to cut off economic aid to India, despatched warships to the Bay of Bengal. Over protests from the lower echelons of the State Department the United States was aligned, in accordance with the President's wishes, on the side of Pakistan.

According to syndicated columnist Jack Anderson, Henry Kissinger himself complained that he was "getting hell every half hour from the President because we are not being tough enough on India."

Rumors were floated that India intended to turn its forces against West Pakistan and attempt to conquer it. Reports were circulated that President Nixon had called upon the Soviet Union to restrain India. Whether there was any truth to those rumors is a matter of doubt for as soon as Bangladesh was freed, India on her own motion offered a truce to Pakistan. Yahya Khan accepted and the war came to an abrupt end.

As its aftermath Yahya Khan was deposed and arrested, upon demand of the people of Pakistan. His successor freed Sheik Mujibur Rahman, who returned to what had been Pakistan, now Bangladesh, to untertake the monumental task of organizing a new nation. At his inauguration as first President of Bangladesh the only governments not represented were those of the United States and mainland China.

John P. Lewis, dean of the Woodrow Wilson School of International Affairs at Princeton University, spent years in India and surrounding countries. Of the tragic events he has written as follows:

In one series of strokes we have managed to align ourselves with the wrong side of about as big and simple a moral issue as the world has seen lately: we have sided with a minor military dictatorship against the world's second largest nation which happens also to be the staunchest of all developing countries in its adherence to our own deepest political values; we have joined the sure-fire loser in a subcontinental confrontation; and we have depleted a once abundant, durable fund of Indo-American goodwill at a sickening rate.

All the evidence suggests that within the Administration the aberrations trace directly and primarily to Mr. Nixon himself. For eight months he remained officially blind to the most massive savagery that has been visited on a civil population in recent

211

times. He has been faithful to his good friend, the chairman of the savagery, Yahya Khan . . .

A question was whether normalization of relations with Communist China would be worth the loss of the long-time friendship of democratic India.

But then, India did not have nuclear weapons. China did. So, at whatever the cost to American principles of life and government the road for Richard Nixon led straight to Peking.

In his campaign for the presidency in 1968, Mr. Nixon stated: "I would not recognize Red China now and I would not agree to admitting it to the U.N. and I would not go along with people who say 'trade with them because that may change them'."

Quite obviously by 1972 some of Mr. Nixon's views about China had changed. In fact before his trip began he had stated, wisely most people thought, to "ply it (China) with offers of trade," and the People's Republic had already been admitted to the United Nations.

So before the trip even started, the process of normalization of relations was somewhat advanced. But however much Mr. Nixon might try to deflate people's expectations of results from the visit, there was no hesitation about making the trip itself as commanding of television and press copy as could possibly be done. Long before the day of the Presidential departure, huge planes were flying across the Pacific carrying complete television equipment and personnel to be sure that the world would witness all Nixon did. An entourage was carefully selected. Not a single member of Congress was included in the list. It was to be the Chinese premier who would correct this "oversight" by inviting the Senate leaders to visit China later on. But a veritable army of newsmen was chosen to go with the President. Mr. H. R. Haldeman, White House aide, fresh from having accused Democratic candidates for president of treason because they disagreed somewhat with Mr. Nixon's peace proposal, was included. So were large numbers of personal aides to the President. Even the Secretary of State was allowed to go. He might be of some use to Dr. Kissinger.

Commentators accompanying the President did some philosophizing. Jim McManus of Group W News pointed out that the old image of China as a menacing ogre, which had in the past proved so useful in prying military appropriations out of Congress, was in the process of being changed. A chief architect of that old image had been the very man who was now attempting to change it. As Congressman, Senator and Vice-President, Richard Nixon had built the old image of China as a perennial threat to peace and to our country. He had accused General Marshall, Adlai Stevenson, President Truman of "delivering 600,000,000 people over to Communism." This had been one of his principal campaign themes.

Now this same Richard Nixon was telling his countrymen that a chief objective of his foreign policy was a rapprochment with that same China. He was painting a very different picture of that country, almost an idyllic one.

McManus wondered aloud whether the new image would be more enduring than the old one—or more true.

If, as suggested, a main purpose of the visit to China was to dominate the news for several weeks as an aid to Mr. Nixon's reelection the journey was a brilliant success. Regardless of who was speaking or where the center of attention in China might be, the television cameras always focused on Richard Nixon. Two outstanding journalists, Hugh Sidey of *Time-Life* and Peter Lisagor of the *Chicago Daily News* called the show "pop journalism," complained that the "print journalists were kept in a strait jacket." Lisagor said: "The President's trip was designed to produce spectacular pictures —and it did. Designed to produce pop journalism—and it did. Substance was lost sight of. There was a gee-whiz attitude but not much happened." In one television sequence the cameras focused for several minutes on an empty airstrip, apparently because a plane carrying Mr. Nixon had just hallowed that runway.

President Nixon remarked during one of the televised festive occasions that more people were seeing him and those in his company than had ever seen anything before in the history of the world. He was probably correct.

The "separate but equal" communiques that were issued at the end of "the week that changed the world" hardly justified that designation. Robert Troth, staff writer for the *Los Angeles Times* wrote: "There was not much in the statements, in fact, that requires a 16,000-mile trip, and of what there was Mr. Nixon appeared to have given more than he got, at least in the short run."

Clearly it had not been possible for the American President and the Chinese Premier to agree on a *joint* statement of agreement. Instead each issued in effect his own.

Agreement there was however on a number of points,

among them increased trade—a process already begun—, a program of exchanges of persons between the two countries, and further "diplomatic contacts." It had been expected by many people that formal diplomatic relations would be resumed as a result of the summit. But such was not the case.

All these were good steps toward normalizing relations. The potential for trade advantages however had been considerably overplayed. The *total* foreign trade of mainland China was about $4 billion a year, just twice as large as the U.S. trade *deficit* for 1971. And how much of the $4 billion U.S. business could get was problematical. Further, as Mr. Troth observed, every one of these measures could easily have been achieved in much lower key than the sensational summit meeting. Had normalization of relations taken place through regular diplomatic channels, it would most certainly have been accomplished at far less cost to the relations of the United States with other countries. What country among them would have objected, for example, to reopening of trade between the U.S. and China, when most of the rest of the world was trading with China already? Most nations would have welcomed an exchange of persons between China and the United States as evidence of lessening tensions in the world. And since most other countries had already recognized the People's Republic and established full diplomatic relations with it, who was there who would have been especially concerned about that?

It was not the fact of normalization that concerned Japan or India or other Asian nations—with the exception of the Soviet Union. It was the summit meeting itself that worried them. It worried them in minor part because of what the communiqués did say. It concerned them far more because of what those statements did not say.

For it was inconceivable that all that had been discussed in the week long meetings had been revealed in the formal statements.

There were of course matters of significance in these statements, in addition to those already mentioned. Principal among there was Mr. Nixon's concession to the long-held Chinese position that Taiwan is part of China and that the question of the future of Taiwan and its Nationalist government of Chiang Kai-shek is for China to settle. Furthermore Mr. Nixon agreed to the "ultimate objective" of total withdrawal of all U.S. forces from the island.

That many Americans would welcome such a withdrawal was certain. That the concession was a recognition of "reality" could certainly be argued. But the concession did seem a bit strange when contrasted with Mr. Nixon's bitterness at the United Nations for having refused to recognize two Chinas and with his repeated promises that nothing would be done at Peking at the expense of friends of the United States.

No comparable concessions were made by the Chinese, unless one could be found in the agreement that all foreign troops should be withdrawn to their own countries. It was possible to interpret this as applying to North Vietnam. It could certainly be applied to the United States in all Southeast Asia. And it was probably directed against India and her troops still in Bangladesh.

The one thing that would have justified Mr. Nixon's trip more than anything else would have been some progress toward ending the Southeast Asia war. But if any had hoped that the summit would lead to peace in Southeast Asia they were doomed to disappointment. Nothing in either statement indicated any area of agreement respecting the wars there. The Chinese statement reaffirmed its support of the "peoples of Vietnam, Laos, and Cambodia" and of the Viet Cong. It also called for unification of Korea. The United States reaffirmed its position that the 8-point proposal of Mr. Nixon should be the basis for a settlement of the Southeast Asia war. And it declared its intention to withdraw U.S. forces from the region "consistent with the aim of self-determination for each country of Indochina." The United States also reaffirmed its support of the government of South Korea.

So the highest officials of the two giant countries met to toast one another and to talk of greater collaboration. But neither budged an inch toward relieving the people of the smaller countries of Southeast Asia of the frightful suffering they had endured for so many years.

Quite the contrary. Mr. Nixon and his entourage had barely departed before the Chinese government renewed its demand for the end of the bombing and withdrawal of all U.S. forces from all Indochina "unconditionally and before a set date." In the same statement the Chinese again pledged "all-out support to the Vietnamese and other Indochinese people in their great struggle."

It is too soon perhaps to make appraisal of all the results of this historic meeting. But some of them are clear enough.

One involved the basic aim of Nixon-Kissinger policy. The meeting served notice on the Soviet Union that the United States and China were moving toward some kind of accord.

This would be one of Mr. Nixon's power "bargaining chips" when he went to Moscow for the biggest summit of them all. In his final toast the President seemed to be issuing a direct warning to the Russians when he said: "Never again shall foreign domination, foreign occupation be visited upon this city or any part of China."

Did this mean that the United States would go to war on China's side if war broke out between the Soviet Union and China? The answer was left to the imagination.

So was much else.

What, for example, did President Nixon say to Communist Party Chairman Mao Tse-tung that caused the coldness with which the Presidential party was first received in Peking to turn to warmth and to bring forth unprecedented publicity in the controlled Communist press?

What else did Mr. Nixon and Chou En-lai discuss that did not appear in the communiques? Surely a great deal.

Why did the Japanese foreign minister feel called upon to state after the conclusion of the Peking summit that nothing had happened there to ease Japan's fears and concerns. Why did Prime Minister Sato make the cynical comment: "Nixon says it was the week that changed the world so maybe it was."?

As expected, the Soviet official press came out with scorching comment to the effect that the United States and China were plotting together to dominate the world.

India, as usual, kept her own counsel, more sure of herself than she had ever been before.

From Taiwan came, as expected, cries of betrayal and expression of concern as to what would happen to their island now.

At what cost had the big "bargaining chip" to be used against the Russians and the desirable and overdue "normalization" of U.S.-Chinese relations been bought? At what price had Mr. Nixon gained such advantages over his political opponents as the Chinese summit might give him?

Some of them were heavy costs indeed and the sad part of it was that many of them might have been avoided had the new relation with China been developed at lower key and with less surprise, shock, and flamboyance.

The close partnership with Japan was pretty well destroyed. Japan and the Soviet Union were negotiating a trade agreement for developing Siberian oil. The uniquely friendly relations that had existed between the United States and India were at an end as long as Mr. Nixon occupied the White

House, and India and the Soviet Union were joined in a 10-year mutual assistance pact. The small nations of Asia simply could not know in what direction Henry Kissinger's power politics might next lead the President of the United States. The shaky government of Cambodia was asking help from—of all places—the Soviet Union.

President Nixon had said in his State of the Union message that "Our commitment to freedom remains strong and unshakeable." But was alliance with Communist China and Militarist Pakistan against Democratic India the way to defend freedom? Indeed was support for dictators in Pakistan, Brazil, Spain, Portugal, Greece, Cambodia, Thailand and—yes—South Vietnam the way to defend freedom? Was freedom defended by sudden announcements of diametric changes in course that took the nations of the free world by total surprise?

Many people said no. And so did the Congress of the United States.

Back in October, 1971, Senator Mansfield of Montana, the Majority leader of the Senate, had said on the Senate floor: "The intention of Congress has been overridden too many times and too consistently and it is about time to stand up and be counted." Coming from some other senator that statement might not have been so significant. But Mansfield, leader of the opposite party, had been one of President Nixon's most effective apologists, He was now serving notice that the high-handed manner in which Mr. Nixon was conducting the foreign relations of the United States, the bland assumption on Mr. Nixon's part that he could carry on wars as he pleased, the blantant disregard of Congressional attempts to help steer the country's course had now become too much for him to tolerate any longer.

In December, Senator Javits, Republican of New York, introduced a bill, S.2956. It was co-authored by Senators Spong of Virginia, Eagleton of Missouri, and—most significantly—Senator Stennis of Mississippi, chairman of the Armed Services Committee. The aim and purpose of the bill was to curb the war-making powers of the President. The opening paragraph stated: "It is the purpose of this act to fulfill the intent of the framers of the Constitution of the United States, and insure that the collective judgment of both the Congress and the President will apply to the initiation of hostilities involving the armed forces of the United States and to the continuation of such hostilities."

What the Senators proposed to do was to prevent any more presidential invasions of countries such as Mr. Nixon had caused in Cambodia and Laos.

They proposed to put a brake on power politics. They drew support from Republican Senators Case of New Jersey, Mathias of Maryland and the Republican leader, Hugh Scott of Pennsylvania. And Senator Sam Ervin of North Carolina, recognized as the best scholar on the Constitution in the entire Congress, remarked that the practices of the executive "reflect a certain contempt for congressional requests for information and an apparent disdain for the wish of the American people to be informed."

In May came the Moscow summit—a masterpiece of advance planning and orchestration. It enabled Richard Milhous Nixon to achieve a pinnacle of power and glory.

But not without some relief for mankind. The arms limitation agreements, two and one half years in the making, would have been consummated whether Mr. Nixon had gone to Moscow or not. This was the stated opinion of members of the American negotiating team. Nonetheless, Mr. Nixon received appropriate credit for the eventual signing. A treaty did propose to freeze development of ABM defensive systems at 200 missiles for each country. But an executive agreement on offensive weapons did no more than provide a pretense of stabilizing the mutual balance of terror because, while the *number* of land-based and missile-launching submarines was theoretically frozen, no limits were put on substitution of "improved" submarines or missiles. The arms race would go right on—only it would be a race for "quality" instead of quantity.

The agreements—all prepared in advance of the summit —regarding environmental pollution, cancer research, harassment on the high seas, and a joint space venture marked progress in relations between the two countries. The world could benefit from this too. And the entire pageant was, of course, of immense benefit to Mr. Nixon's reelection ambitions.

On the other hand no visible progress was made toward increased trade; and whatever benefits might have flowed from the expensive summit in China were pretty well erased as China charged collusion aimed at her.

And most cynically tragic was the fact that while the world rulers wined and dined one another at their taxpayers' expense, neither Richard Nixon nor the Soviet leaders had a word to say about stopping the carnage in Southeast Asia.

The summit ended with the Russians still encouraging North Vietnam to fight for their cause to the last man. They even lacked the courage to protest Richard Nixon's bombing of the cities of their ally, or his blockading of their shipping. And Mr. Nixon left the summit still determined that South Vietnam must fight to its last man to protect an American power base in Southeast Asia.

14. THE FIRST AMENDMENT

"Congress shall make no law respecting an establishment of religion or prohibiting the free expression thereof; or abridging the freedom of speech, *or of the press,* or the right of the people peaceably to assemble, and to petition the government for redress of grievances."

—From the Amendments to the Constitution of the United States

Our forefathers overlooked something when they wrote the First Amendment to the Constitution. They should have added: "Nor shall the President or any member of his Administration seek to control, intimidate, investigate or otherwise harass the press or other media of information."

Throughout modern human history, whenever any monarch, military figure, organized group or political party has sought inordinate power, the first and most essential step to such power has been curtailment or abolition of the freedom of the press. In recent years an even more necessary measure has been control of the air waves.

On November 3, 1969, President Richard M. Nixon called on all four television networks to give him free time to speak to the nation. He had been elected to his high office almost exactly one year before. A major factor in his victory over Hubert Humphrey had been a golden promise. That promise was that he had a secret plan for bringing the war in Vietnam to an end.

Whether in fact Mr. Nixon had such a plan in mind in November, 1968 we cannot know. What we do know is that the nation waited through an entire year—and news of many casualties in the war—before the President unveiled his plan.

219

He did so in these words: "In the previous administration they Americanized the war. In this administration we are Vietnamizing the search for peace."

Mr. Nixon's plan was to withdraw American forces from the war as rapidly as the South Vietnamese could be trained and equipped to carry it on successfully.

Naturally enough the plan was popular in the United States. It combined bringing our fighting men home with the prospect of having "our side" win the war at the same time. It meant shifting the fighting and dying off the shoulders of Americans and onto those of the people of Southeast Asia. Messages of support poured into the White House, and the Gallup Poll reported that four-out-of-five of those responding expressed approval of Mr. Nixon's speech.

But this apparently was not good enough for Richard I. He seemed to covet universal acclaim. Others who had sought power for themselves had felt the same way. Why not Mr. Nixon?

These may seem extreme statements—perhaps unfair ones. But how else can the subsequent events be explained?

The networks had presented, following the President's speech, panels of eminent and experienced observers of international affairs to comment on what the President had said. They were, in general, in accord with his expression. But some doubts were expressed, and a few of the commentators were unkind enough to suggest that Mr. Nixon had presented nothing particularly new.

Just ten days thereafter Vice-President Agnew spoke in Des Moines, Iowa. It was a landmark speech. In it the Vice-President attacked the television networks for having permitted what he termed biased commentary on the President's speech. He complained that there had been unfavorable comment on the President's speech and questioned the right of broadcasters to comment so immediately on a talk by Mr. Nixon. He said that American public opinion was controlled and manipulated by a handful of "self-appointed television commentators," and astonishingly he warned them and the networks that they enjoyed "a monopoly sanctioned and licensed by the government."

This last remark, coming from the second highest ranking official in the government in power, was the key not only to his speech but to the policy of the Nixon Administration toward the mass media.

That policy had already been made plain enough by the

action of the Nixon-appointed chairman of the Federal Communications Commission, Dean Burch, who two days after Mr. Nixon's speech had demanded of the networks transcripts of the commentaries.

Columnist Max Lerner, writing of Mr. Agnew's accusation that a few commentators had too much control over the news dissemination, said, "But the total power over the destinies of the nation is in the hands of an even smaller group, and the power over the Vietnamese war and peace today is in the hands of one man. In the hangman's home, be wary of talking about death."

And Mr. Frank Stanton, President of Columbia Broadcasting System, eloquently summarized the danger in a speech on November 25th to the International Radio and Television Society. "The troubled pages of this country's history are writ dark with the death of liberty in those nations where the first fatal symptom of political decay was an effort to control the news media.

"The ominous character of the Vice President's attack derives directly from the fact that it is made upon the journalism of a medium licensed by the government of which he is a high-ranking officer. This is a new relationship in government-press relations. From George Washington on, every Administration has had disputes with the press, but the First Amendment assured the press that such disputes were between equals, with the press beyond the reach of the government. This all-important fact of the licensing power of life and death over the broadcast press brings an implicit threat to a government official's attacks on it, whether or not that is the intention and whether or not the official says he is speaking only as an individual."

After less than a year in office Richard Milhous Nixon had tasted power. He was apparently determined to have it virtually without limit and he proposed to brook no criticism of any of his actions along the way

The saddest part of the story has been that the intimidation begun by Spiro Agnew at Des Moines on November 13, 1969 has worked. As the months have passed, television commentators and news broadcasters have shown unmistakable reluctance, not to say fear, of making unfavorable remarks about the actions of Mr. Nixon or his administration.

In fact two years after the Agnew speech, Walter Cronkite, recognized dean of television newsmen, testified before a Senate Committee. He spoke, necessarily out of his own experience in the years of the Nixon Presidency. His testimony was, in part, as follows: "Broadcast news today is not free, because it is operated by an industry that is beholden to the government for its right to exist; its freedom has been curtailed by fiat, by assumption, and by intimidation and harassment . . ."

The violent reaction of the Nixon Administration to the very mild criticism of the Vietnamization speech was nothing new in Mr. Nixon's career. In 1962, when he was defeated by Pat Brown for governor of California, Nixon called a press conference and angrily denounced those who attended, concluding with the now-famous words: "You don't have Dick Nixon to kick around any more."

Obviously Richard Nixon cannot stand criticism from any source, foreign or domestic.

In general, the press of the nation has shown less fear of the Administration than the television and radio, for an obvious reason: newspapers and magazines do not have to be licensed by the government.

President Nixon has demanded far more free time from the television networks than any President before him. His broadcasts have been unctuous with self-praise and he has seldom omitted attacks, veiled or open, upon his opponents. But when those who were in disagreement with the President have sought time in which to reply they have almost always had to purchase it at regular rates. This is especially true of the Democratic National Committee.

On several occasions the networks refused even to sell the time, contending that they would be airing "controversial subjects." On one occasion, in July, 1970, a bi-partisan group of 14 Senators filed a formal complaint with the Federal Communications Commission because the networks had refused to permit them to purchase time for a statement explaining the purpose of their "Amendment to End the War." One network stated: "We do not believe the public interest warrants a further presentation in a paid broadcast at this particular time."

Soldiers in Vietnam and their families might have had a somewhat different view of what the "public interest" actually was.

Meanwhile in Southeast Asia correspondents who attempted to inform the American people of what was going on were receiving strange treatment. Senator Cranston of California described some of it in an article published by the newspaper *Chicago Today* on March 30, 1970:

> Fewer American lives are being lost, the number of troops in Vietnam is going down instead of up, and the immediacy of the war begins to fade from public concern.
>
> To keep it fading the administration has attacked the mass media, which has reported the war to the American people as its reporters have seen it. At the same time, reporters in Laos who tried to tell the story found that they had thereby forfeited some of their rights to protection as American citizens.
>
> On Feb. 24, the press reported that one plane per minute was leaving the secret American-run base at Long Cheng in Laos. It also revealed that many armed Americans in civilian clothes were active in the battle then sputtering on the Plain of Jars.
>
> The plucky reporters who filed that story were arrested in Laos by Laotians. And the American ambassador there promptly declared:
>
> "The American mission has lost any interest in the press whatsoever because of what happened this afternoon."
>
> I was under the illusion that embassies overseas were supposed to protect American citizens, not to wash their hands of them.

Had those reporters been writing what the Nixon Administration wanted them to write, there is little doubt that they would, in the first place, not have been arrested, and that, had they been, the diplomats would have come immediately to their aid.

The record is plain enough. What Mr. Nixon and his Administration want and expect from the mass media is complete approbation of all they do.

The other side of that coin is an ill-concealed attempt to deny to the American people any information which might be unfavorable to Mr. Nixon, his policies, or his practices. This too is not hard to document. The "people's right to know" has been violated by this Administration as by no other in American history.

It took Senator Symington of Missouri two years to get for his subcommittee the facts about commitments of the United States to and in foreign countries. If any kind of information is vital to the American people, certainly such information is. But had the Symington subcommittee not fought a long and bitter battle with Nixon officials, the people would not know to this day what their government has committed them to do, militarily and otherwise in various parts of the world.

When President Nixon decided that the SST must be built, at taxpayers' expense, if necessary, he requested a committee of scientists to study the project and report to him. The report was in his hands six months before he publicly announced his intention to invest taxpayers' money in the project. But the report was supressed because it recommended, for a variety of weighty reasons, "withdrawal of government support." Other reports, favorable to the SST, were publicly released and delivered to Congress. But not the unfavorable and most competent one. Senator Proxmire remarked that had the scientists' report been made available to Congress it would have "stopped the SST dead in its tracks." But the fight was practically over before the people's representatives were allowed even to know of its existence.

In the midst of the controversy over the SST the Nixon Administration had demonstrated again its determination to control the news media. In March, 1971, the Dick Cavett show on WABC had scheduled a debate between Senator Proxmire and William Magruder, Nixon's staff man in charge of promoting the SST. Pressure from the White House upon the WABC network brought the usual fearful reaction. Cavett was informed that he must cancel Proxmire and give Magruder the entire time of the broadcast.

In order to prevent either Congress or the people from receiving information which the White House or the Pentagon wishes them not to have, a directive was issued to some 800,000 military personnel and federal employees in early 1971. According to the *Washington Post*'s column on governmental affairs, this directive contained these words: "There are to be no contacts with members of Congress other than responding to simple questions of fact. Casual social contacts with press, members of Congress or other political organizations are to be avoided. You are reminded that failure to obey this directive can lead to court-martial for commissioned officers and discharge for Civil Service employees."

The Pentagon has a five-year plan for military aid to foreign countries—most of them dictatorships, incidentally. The Senate Foreign Relations Committee thought, strangely to the Nixon Administration, that it really ought to know what the Pentagon had in mind before authorizing expenditure of some $4 billion of the people's money. But Mr. Nixon invoked the seldom-used doctrine of "executive privilege" to refuse to let the Senators see the documents in question. The President gave as his astonishing reason that the papers had to be kept from public knowledge in order to preserve "the full, frank, and healthy expression of opinion which is essential for the successful administration of the government."

The same sort of contempt for the American people's right to information about their government appears in matters that are purely domestic and have nothing whatever to do with "national security," so-called.

The Department of Justice, finding that crime continued to increase under the Nixon "law and order" administration has abandoned the long-term practice of the FBI of reporting to the nation the statistical figures on crimes of various kinds committed in the United States. Instead, carefully prepared releases are delivered to the press.

For decades it had been the practice of the Bureau of Labor Statistics to hold monthly briefings for the press. At those briefings the professional staff of BLS gave out the simple facts regarding progress of the economy, employment and unemployment, movements of various price levels and other information which enabled the nation to know how it was getting along. The briefings had always been conducted by career officials of the Bureau and without political interpretation of any kind.

But no more. In the spring of 1971 the Nixon Administration discontinued them. It did so, from all appearances, because one of the BLS experts gave a less sanguine interpretation of the statistical facts than the Secretary of Labor had done. The facts simply weren't as favorable to the Administration's record as it wanted them to be.

A few months later the *Washington Post* reported that the professional staff of the Bureau of Labor Statistics was being progressively fired and replaced with safe people—from the Administration's point of view.

Not content to rely on his hand-picked chairman of the Federal Communications Commission to keep television "in line," President Nixon appointed a bright young man by the name of Clay T. Whitehead to his personal White House staff. Mr. Whitehead was designated as "Director of the White House Office of Telecommunications Policy." He was given the informal title of "communications czar." He had no responsibility to anyone except the President. But he proceeded, according to *Newsweek* magazine for February 7, 1972, to "infuriate, intrigue, and occasionally bewilder virtually every sector of the vast U.S. telecommunications establishment."

One of Mr. Whitehead's principal assignments was to control the "fairness doctrine" which has been in effect in television for many years. That doctrine holds that if one position on a controversial subject is aired, the opposing one must be accorded or sold a roughly equivalent amount of time for reply. Instead Mr. Whitehead wanted television time to be sold only on a first-come-first-served basis to whomever has the money. Which of course put the Republican Party in the forefront of all potential purchases, since it has the money whereas the Democrats are—to put it bluntly— "broke." The Whitehead plan would be ideal also for President Nixon since he gets all the time he so frequently demands free of charge.

Concern over the consistent attempts of the Nixon Administration to enforce de facto censorship upon the media has by no means been confined to progressives or populists. Indeed the person most concerned in the Congress, if not in the entire nation, has been Senator Sam Ervin of North Carolina. He is a staunch Conservative with a deep reverence for the Constitution, including the First Amendment.

Senator Ervin had had numerous brushes with the Administration over its failure to honor the Bill of Rights when he decided that the situation was sufficiently critical and important to hold hearings on the matter. This he undertook in January, 1972. He billed the hearings as an attempt once and for all to determine what was the Administration's attitude toward freedom of the press.

What may have caused the Senator to act at that particular time was the case of Daniel Shorr who had been for some time assigned by Columbia Broadcasting System as its White House correspondent. Shorr carried to the job a reputation for the highest quality of journalistic reporting. But he made the mistake of giving his accounts of White House goings-on in what he deemed an even-handed manner. If he thought the President partly mistaken, he said so. This was obviously not what the Administration wanted in a White House correspondent.

One day Mr. Shorr found himself under investigation by the FBI for the purpose of determining whether or not he was a loyal American and whether or not he might be subversive as all critics of Richard Nixon are supposed to be. When this rather strange circumstance was brought to light, Ronald Ziegler, the presidential press secretary, declared the reason for the investigation was that Shorr had been under consideration for a federal appointment, but that this was no longer the case. No one, including Shorr, was aware of any such offer having ever been made.

Daniel Shorr was not the only witness to appear before the Ervin Committee. Some of them came armed with solid facts. Spokesmen for the Writer's Guild of America, for example, reported the results of a poll of 3,000 writers of television scripts. Eighty-six percent of those polled stated that they were subject to constant censorship by "nervous network executives." And 81% said they believed that because of executives' fear "a distorted picture of what is happening in America today" was being presented. Senator Ervin described the testimony as "illuminating."

And so to the strange case of the Pentagon papers—to the story of a man who once was a soldier in Vietnam, who had at first been a "hawk" about the war, but who found he could not live with his conscience unless he let the American people know what he knew about the clandestine actions of their executives . . .

This man was Daniel Ellsberg.

The story of how Ellsberg delivered the Pentagon Papers to the *New York Times* and *Washington Post*, of how these two newspapers decided as Ellsberg had that it was their duty to give this vital information to the American people is too well known to require repetition here. But some salient and disturbing points must be made.

First, the Nixon Administration did everything it could to prevent publication of the Pentagon Papers. So far as political scientists could recall this was the first time since adoption of the Constitution that a National Administration had attempted to exercise open and *prior* censorship upon the press in clear violation of the First Amendment.

The Administration tried to obtain a restraining order against the newspapers. The case went quickly to the Supreme Court which ruled in a mixed decision against the government and for the *New York Times* and the *Washington Post*.

Both Nixon appointees in the Court voted faithfully for the President's wishes. The deecision was by a 6 to 3 vote but only one or two justices wrote opinions that upheld clearly the First Amendment. Erosion of that Amendment was plainly taking place.

Meanwhile, because Senator Gravel of Alaska had read

some of the Pentagon Papers at a midnight hearing in the capitol, the Justice Department threatened him with prosecution, but did not actually bring suit.

Daniel Ellsberg was not so fortunate. He was charged by the Justice Department with a variety of crimes including possession and disposition of stolen property and something akin to treason. Penalties could put him in prison for many years.

His real "crime," however, was giving to the American people information vital to their survival as a free people—contrary to the wishes of the Nixon Administration.

The *Christian Science Monitor* has noted that the Nixon Administration had repeatedly sought to subpoena newspaper reporters' notes—especially those of *New York Times* and *Washington Post* reporters. William B. Arthur, editor of *Look* magazine before its unfortunate demise in the face of increased postal rates once wrote that the Administration was trying to create a "know-nothing" nation by "expressing and intensifying the natural resistance of the American people to acknowledging and accepting certain distasteful truths about themselves." Mr. Arthur deplored "an atmosphere of bold-faced repression of truth and unpleasant realities."

The professional journalism society, Sigma Delta Chi, brought together Mr. Ronald Ziegler, Mr. Nixon's press secretary and three top reporters for a panel discussion. The reporters were Helen Thomas of United Press International, Dan Rather of CBS, and Hugh Sidey of *Time-Life*, all of them assigned to the White House. The comments by those three reporters, on that occasion, are revealing:

Thomas: "The American people have no involvement in policy. The President outlines his policy and you take it or else . . . Attacks from the White House are systematic. Look what happened to (former Interior Secretary Walter) Hickel. If you don't say what they like, you're out . . . We still don't know what's going on in Laos and Cambodia. When we do learn anything, it's a leak."

Rather: "The record of intimidation is quite clear. How else are we to respond to Vice President Agnew's speeches? . . . The net effect, whether intended or not, of conducting an FBI investigation of (CBS reporter) Daniel Schorr without telling him what the job was and of complaining about his stories to the top boss of CBS, is intimidation."

Sidey: "The reason we crave more press conferences and fear intimidation is that we don't know enough about this Administration, the President and the men behind him. We don't see how or why he arrives at a decision. We still don't know the real story behind the Supreme Court nominations. There's a great emptiness after three years of this Administration."

Mr. Sidey's comment may be the key to the hostility of Mr. Nixon and his people toward the media. The *Atlantic Monthly* once said editorially that "more than any other President in recent memory, President Nixon governs with privacy and a remoteness from the rest of Washington—even from some of his own cabinet departments."

If we remember the strange career of Richard M. Nixon from the beginning, we see a man convinced of his own righteousness, whatever he may do. We also see a man who regards opposition to himself as enmity toward the nation. And since he expects virtually complete and unanimous acclaim for his deeds, he naturally feels abused when the response falls short of that standard.

This may explain his dislike of news people. In any event Marquis Childs was probably appraising the situation with accuracy when he wrote in his January 18th column the following:

The clamor over secrecy in government and the revelation of leaked documents owes a lot to the man in the White House. Except for carefully stage-managed television performances, communication with the media has fallen close to zero.

In 1971 the President had nine press conferences, and four of these were of the impromptu kind held on short notice where only the White House regulars are present. This is a measure of his distrust of a direct confrontation with reporters. He shies away from even the kind of East Room Press conferences that has increasingly become a television spectacular with the seats in the front row allotted to those who are familiars.

Mr. Childs went on to point out that in 1970 President Nixon held just four full-scale and one impromptu press conferences. In 1969 he held only eight. This record hardly compares with that of President Eisenhower who averaged 24 press conferences a year during his eight years in office. In three years John F. Kennedy met the press 64 times, and in six years Lyndon Johnson did so 162 times.

It is understandable that press conferences are trying upon

any chief executive. But they are part of his job if he wants to keep the nation fully informed of both the successes and the shortcoming of his Administration. This cannot be done by carefully-staged television speeches where only one side of the story is revealed.

What the United States needs in these critical times in the world's history is not a manipulation of public opinion but the challenge of a great moral leadership.

From the record of his Administration, it is only possible to conclude that Mr. Nixon wishes the mass media would dry up and blow away and let him tell the people exactly what he wants them to hear and nothing more.

The First Amendment to the contrary notwithstanding.

15. THE BUYING OF THE PRESIDENCY

At least 80% of campaign gifts are from men who could sign a net worth statement exceeding a quarter of a million dollars.
—Sen. Long of Louisiana, Chairman, Senate Finance Committee

The most lavishly financed political campaign in history by far was that which elected Richard Milhous Nixon to the Presidency in 1968. The widely respected non-partisan Citizens' Research Foundation of Princeton, New Jersey, produced a documented report which shows that the total cost of the Nixon campaign was $35,000,000. Of that amount some $12.7 million was spent for Mr. Nixon's television appearances.

Mr. Nixon has the distinction—perhaps a slightly questionable one—of being the biggest spender in American political history. The cost of his 1968 post-convention campaign alone was equal to the total amount spent by both candidates in the 1964 election.

Where did all the money come from? It came from the wealthiest people in the nation. One insurance company executive, Clement Stone by name, is reported to have contributed half a million dollars; Henry Salvatori, Los Angeles oil man, gave $83,000; and Max Fisher, Detroit industrialist, more than $100,000 according to the Citizens' Research Foundation's findings. The Mellons of Pittsburgh came in handsomely with $279,000. And from the Sun Oil Company millions, the family of J. Howard Pew spent $208,000 as their contribution to the purchase of a President. There followed an impressive list of 10 contributors with a total of $300,000 to their credit—every one of whom was appointed an ambassador of the United States to a foreign country by Richard Nixon.

More than twice as much was spent on behalf of Mr. Nixon's election as was spent by the Democrats. The Republican Party came out of the campaign with a healthy surplus—the Democrats with a $9 million deficit.

These facts are not surprising when it is recalled that for every one wealthy family which contributes to the Democrats there are ten among the super-rich who pour their millions into Republican coffers. Senator Long of Louisiana, Chairman of the Finance Committee of the Senate, has stated that "at least 80% of campaign gifts are from men who could sign a net worth statement exceeding a quarter of a million dollars."

The time has come when, in the absence of widespread agitation and concern among the people, elections can be, and are, bought with cold cash. Television "exposure" has become an acknowledged necessity for all candidates for major offices. Television time is exhorbitantly costly. The Citizens' Research Foundation study shows that $300 million was spent on all political campaigns in 1968. Only a few years ago a corresponding figure would have been a tenth as much.

There can no longer exist the slightest doubt that big money now threatens the very survival of government of, by, and for the people in the United States. Local political organizations are becoming alarmingly weaker. Whereas a few years ago political meetings and rallies were well attended, today such meetings are seldom even attempted except among the deeply concerned "core" groups whose minds are already made up.

The Democrats are trying to reform their procedures for selection of candidates and for election of delegates to their national convention. On paper the reforms look good—look as if many more rank and file party members would have a voice to be heard. But it remains to be seen how many such "rank and filers" will *try* to have their voices heard. People by the millions who once volunteered their services in political campaigns have ceased to do so. Why? Probably because they have a foreboding that the well-turned phrase, the wry smile, the Madison Avenue make-up of a candidate on a single television appearance might well cancel out the work of months of house-to-house canvassing.

Perhaps because of their overwhelming financial advantage the Republicans are making no significant gesture at reform.

That the people know the danger to their control over their own government is clear from polls which show that they favor electoral reform by a margin of more than 3 to 1.

In the summer of 1970 both houses of Congress passed by substantial majorities—and with considerable Republican support—a bill which would have put a limitation at $5.1 million on the amount which any political party could spend for television or radio time in the 1972 election. This would have been almost a million dollars less than the Democrats spent in 1968 and a whopping $7.6 million less than Mr. Nixon spent. To no one's great surprise, on October 13, 1970, Richard Milhous Nixon promptly vetoed the bill, labelling it "the wrong answer" to the problem. From his point of view it certainly was. His veto said in plain, clear, if unspoken, words that Mr. Nixon had no intention of seeing his chance to buy the Presidency in 1972 diminished.

If ever there was a cynical, politically inspires veto of an Act of Congress this was, indeed, it. Democratic leaders were understandably quick to make this point. A White House spokesman added that the Administration had no intention "at this time" to submit legislation of its own to limit campaign spending.

It is not only the sheer value of campaign spending coupled with the sources of the funds which threatens our political institutions. It is also the secrecy and essential dishonesty that surrounds the collection and expenditure of campaign funds. Seldom do candidates report fully their collections or expenditures. Former Senator Douglas of Illinois probably shocked many of his colleagues in the Senate as well as most other political figures by doing exactly that during his entire career. And there are other exceptions.

As a rule, however, committees are set up to receive and spend the money on behalf of candidates—allegedly, in most cases, without the candidate's knowledge. So when he makes his report, only a part—and often a minor part—of the money actually spent is included. While this has been standard practice for many years, the process has reached some kind of pinnacle of perfection during the years of Mr. Nixon's presidency. For example, in the spring of 1971 the Republican

Party was confronted by an embarrassment of riches in the form of the six-figure contributions to Mr. Nixon's re-election budget from milk producers' organizations—the price of the classic "change of mind" about milk-price supports on the part of the Department of Agriculture, described in an earlier chapter.

It would never do to have such substantial contributions go into any one or two campaign funds. But this was not necessary. For the *Wall Street Journal* reported (Sept. 27, 1971) that Republicans were operating—as no doubt they still are—an underground network of "voluntary associations." All of these operate in one legal jurisdiction, the District of Columbia, thus avoiding public registration, since the District has no law which governs political committees. The *Journal* story told how each of these associations receives relatively small sums of money which are deposited in separate bank accounts until needed by the Nixon re-election campaign.

Just how many such "voluntary associations" exist, or have existed, is difficult to determine. But the *Wall Street Journal* story told how in the month of August, 1971, the Trust for Agricultural Political Education (a milk producers' organization) sent a $2,500 check to each of 50 such associations. The *Journal* further reported that all 50 of them had identical charters stating that their purpose was to "work for the renomination of Richard M. Nixon." The charters also make clear that once the renomination is safely achieved, remaining funds can be transferred to committees working for Mr. Nixon's re-election. And this can be done without the necessity of any public disclosure. Thus Mr. Nixon and his friends were well prepared to avoid the toils of almost any conceivable reform which Congress might enact.

None of which is intended to indicate that Democrats have been entirely guiltless of some similar machinations. They are, however, as usual, a rather poor second where high finance is concerned.

Now the main interest of Congress, especially of the Democrats therein, was in limitation of expenditures, not in tighter reporting requirements. And for very obvious, if partly selfish reasons. Limitation on expenditures would not only give the people a greater voice in their government. It would also spare candidates and their parties such extravagant need for money. This would be a tremendous relief, especially to financially poor candidates, most of whom are Democrats.

Following Mr. Nixon's veto of the TV and radio limitation

bill, the Congress was determined to act. On both sides of the aisle members had heard from home in no uncertain terms. It was not going to be politically healthy for either Republicans or Democrats to go to the voters unless action was taken to place some limit on campaign expenditures. The result, as was to be expected, was a compromise between what the thoroughgoing reformers would have liked to pass and what, it was hoped, Mr. Nixon would sign into law.

Mr. Nixon's alleged reason for vetoing the earlier bill had been that that measure placed limits on television and radio expenses but did not affect spending in other media. So the new bill was drawn to include, along with television and radio, limitation on newspaper, magazine and outdoor advertising. The ceiling on media spending is a generous one—ten cents per person of voting age, no more than six cents of which could be spent for television. This however means, in practical terms, that some $8.5 million can be spent by candidates for television time alone.

The bill carries a limit of $50,000 on what a presidential candidate can spend of his own money—a thinly veiled but probably justifiable curb on such families as the Kennedys and the Rockefellers. But, in a rather clear concession to those able to collect large sums from the wealthy, no other limits whatever are placed on the amount that anyone can contribute. Contributors of less than $100 need not even be reported by name, which means, in practical effect, that if it is desired to conceal the source of funds, all that is necessary is to set up a vast number of committees for collection purposes. The ease of doing that has already been amply demonstrated. Thus, while the bill does establish some ceiling on certain campaign expenditures, it does next to nothing to correct the more ominous threat to the nation's political freedom which inheres in the ability of a few very wealthy contributors to purchase the allegiance of candidates to their special interests. Furthermore—and this point has been scarcely noted in the press— the bill fixes no top limit whatsoever upon the total amount which can be spent for all purposes to elect a candidate. The *only* limitation is on media spending.

These two features of the bill—rather these two omissions from its provisions—were enough to assure Mr. Nixon's signature. He got exactly what he wanted—no limit on the amount that could be spent in his behalf in 1972. He signed the bill and it is now the law.

Meanwhile things were going very well indeed in preparation for the 1972 "auction" of the Presidency. The high bidders were already posting their offers. A $1,000-a-plate dinner in Chicago raised some $2,000,000 for Mr. Nixon's use. "Salute to the President" dinners in 1971 proved successful ventures, and interestingly, were well attended by federal employees who somehow learned about them.

Receipts from 19 GOP fund raisers in November, 1971, are reported to have totaled $5 million. Having broken all previous records for campaign spending, both in 1968 and in the off-year elections of 1970—when some $11 million was spent—the Nixon forces had no intention of resting on their laurels.

There was an attempt on the part of Congress to deal with the most basic of all dangers to the health and validity of the American system of government, namely, the fact that a handful of superlatively wealthy families are able, with their money plus the influence of television to corrupt the political process and often to negate the will of the American people as a whole. The obvious remedy for this situation is to provide for the financing of campaigns by small contributions from vast numbers of people. It is as simple as that.

This was what Congress sought to do when by majority vote both houses passed a bill with these provisions: First, each tax payer, when filing his or her federal income tax form was to be permitted simply to put a check mark in a box displayed on the form and by so doing to indicate that $1 of his or her taxes was to be donated to financing the Presidential campaign. By this means it was calculated that some $20 million would be made available to both the Republicans and the Democrats, and it would relieve both parties of any obligation whatsoever to big donors. Second, if a political party accepted the estimated $20 million from all—or almost all—the American people, it was then prohibited from soliciting or collecting other funds for its presidential campaign.

It would seem to the casual—and concerned—observer that a $20 million kitty should pay for a pretty good campaign. And the beleaguered Democrats, who voted solidly for the measure, were altogether content with such a sum. Not so the Republicans. Nor Mr. Nixon. Republican members—on orders no doubt from the White House—had voted with unanimity against the bill. It had passed because, for once, the Democrats had not broken ranks, but had loyally supported the party leadership.

The reason for Republican—and Nixonian—opposition to the bill was very simple. If, already, far more than $20 million had not been collected through one channel or another for the 1972 "essential" re-election of Richard Nixon, then certainly there was every intention of collecting perhaps several times that amount. The measure would have limited the Republicans to the same amount of campaign funds as the Democrats!

So, despite the fact that this measure had been made part and parcel of the tax reduction bill—a measure desired by Mr. Nixon as part of his Number III "game plan"—he immediately, and angrily, threatened to veto the entire bill unless the Conference Committee of the House and Senate eliminated the campaign financing provision. The President declared that he was opposed not for any conceivable political reason, but because of deep conviction that the provision was wrong in principle.

The tax-reduction bill was, as finally framed by the Congress, a very different measure from the one Mr. Nixon had originally proposed and requested. The Democrats, with some Republican support, had changed it from a bill giving billions in tax relief to business and little indeed to hard-pressed family consumers, to one which was a reasonably well-balanced one and one which would give considerable relief to poor taxpayers in particular. For the entire bill to be lost, was therefore not in the interest of either party—nor certainly of the sagging economy of the nation. Nevertheless Mr. Nixon gave not an inch. His veto would probably have been sustained, since the campaign-financing portion of the bill had been adopted by far less than a two-thirds vote. What would have happened had the Democrats stood firm we will never know. For, faced with the probability of loss of this entire bill, Chairman Mills of the House Ways and Means Committee decided to accept a compromise.

The compromise was the soul of simplicity. It was to delay the popular-financing provision in the bill until after the 1972 campaign. Under the Constitution, the last time Mr. Nixon could run for president was in 1972.

For some strange reason this compromise seemed to have removed Mr. Nixon's objections. No longer did his "principles" compel him to veto it. Since it could not now affect his own personal political fortunes, he signed the bill into law. The compromise made possible the buying of the presidency once again in 1972.

Seldom was the subservience to, or fear of, the Nixon Administration on the part of the mass media more evident than in its treatment of Mr. Nixon's self-serving action with respect

236

to this bill. Comment was almost totally absent on the fact that the President had approved something he claimed to oppose "on principle," as long as it would not affect his own personal ambitions. On the contrary, most newspaper stories and television comment was in praise of his cleverness.

16. RICHARD I

Has it come to this then, that it lies within the sole province of one man, unlimited by law or opinion, whether elected by landslide or hair's breadth, to decide without let or hindrance how the military power of the United States shall be used even in a situation his own policies have done much to create?

—Tom Wicker, *New York Times,*
in an article titled "An American Emperor"

Richard Milhous Nixon built his political career on two foundations. One was relentless accusation against his opponents —accusations that stopped just short of treason. The other was shrill outcry against control of people's lives by a handful of Washington officials. Power in the hands of people other than himself was evil. But once he, himself, became President, all was changed. Power in the hands of Richard Nixon was very good. And he began to climax his career by a relentless drive to concentrate power in his own hands and those of his White House staff.

It was Richard Nixon who was pleased to dress the White House policemen in uniforms which would be appropriate only in an imperial court. On occasion his guards are said to address him as "Your Excellency."

It is Richard Nixon who follows a monarchial custom and has religious services held for him, his family and invited guests in his Executive Mansion instead of attending church with his fellow citizens.

It is Richard Nixon who has travelled to many lands at taxpayers' expense—and almost always to lands ruled by men with monarchial power where ordered pomp and ceremony would greet him and where there was no danger that the voices of free people would mar the occasion. He visited Spain where 10,000 policemen and countless soldiers lined his triumphal entry into Madrid, and where he and General-issimo Franco signed a pact providing for U. S. military bases in Spain and agreed between them that relations of their two countries would be carried forward by executive agreement, circumventing any upstart interference by the United States Senate.

Under similar circumstances he visited Portugal, Rumania, Yugoslavia, Iran, Russia, and China.

But strangely he seldom visited nations having free speech and free assembly. Once he did stop long enough in England to have luncheon with the Queen. The *London Times* described the entourage accompanying and protecting the President as a "traveling circus." It called the luncheon "one of the most expensive luncheon appointments ever undertaken," and remarked that the five-hour call of Mr. Nixon upon Great Britain involved "logistic planning worthy of a major military campaign." Six helicopters were flown from Germany to transport the Presidential party from the airport to the scene of the luncheon.

Once, too, the President went to Rome to meet with the Pope of the Catholic Church. But no chances were taken with the Italian people. Instead the President arrived at the Vatican by helicopter, landing in St. Peter's Square and taking off from that same place after his visit with the Pope. The fact that St. Peter's Square had heretofore been used only for crowds seeking a religious blessing made the contrast all the more exciting.

Not only does the President like to visit foreign countries where some brand of dictatorships holds sway, he seems simply to like dictatorships. His preference for Yahya Khan over Mrs. Gandhi is now classic. He seemed to have had no great concern when Mr. Thieu took power in South Vietnam in a one-candidate election. Over such protests as the people of Greece dare to mount he supports with lavish aid the military dictatorship of Greece. And that of Brazil. And of Portugal. And of Cambodia. And of Thailand. Yes, even of Haiti. For licenses have been granted to U.S. munitions manufacturers to sell arms to that most corrupt and tyrannical dictatorship in the entire world. No doubt this is all being done "in defense of freedom."

It is characteristic of those who seek power to control in one way or another the mass media and to use radio and television to speak directly to "their people." President Nixon is no exception. Although he has held only a minor fraction

238

as many press conferences as any of his predecessors have done, he has commanded vastly more television time than any of them ever did—most of it free of charge. The record shows that President Eisenhower spoke to the nation on television 38 times in eight years, President Kennedy 15 times in three years, President Johnson 28 times in five years, but President Nixon 53 times in just three years.

These have been no ordinary television appearances. They have indeed been appearances "fit for a king." Dozens of full-time experts in television photography are employed on the White House staff. One of them, an expert in "television angles," is said to draw an annual salary of $35,000. Mr. Ziegler, White House press secretary, has a staff of ten; Herbert Klein, communications director, employs nineteen. There are in addition five people to monitor the news media, eight speechwriters and other experts, and helpers too numerous to mention. Four full-time photographers do nothing but take pictures of President Nixon. The California Museum of Science and Industry has a display of fifty photographs of President Nixon entitled "The First Two Years: A Photographic Impression of the Presidency." It is the fruit of the work of the White House staff of photographers. Never before has such aggrandizement of an incumbent President been attempted. The staff employed to present Richard Milhous Nixon to "his people" is unprecedented in American history.

The expense of Mr. Nixon's personal publicity staff to the taxpayers is unknown. It does not appear specifically in the budget. Neither is there any available estimate of the expense of transporting Mr. Nixon and his family from White House to White House, there being several of them. But we do know that to make sure of sufficient transportation equipment for the President's travels and those of his entourage, Congress was asked in the $25 billion-deficit budget for 1973 to provide $261 million to pay for six Boeing 747 jumbo jets complete with all desirable equipment for Presidential use. Associated Press so reported on January 25, 1972. We know too that a mere $60,000 of taxpayers' money was spent to erect a windscreen around the President's swimming pool at his San Clemente estate. So stated *Look* magazine for May 24, 1970.

The world does not always act as Richard Nixon wishes it to. When this happens it is not beyond his dignity to react with something approaching violence. He became enraged, we are told, over the defeat of his friend Yahya Khan. He was, as he himself told the world, "shocked" at the United

Nations when its delegates voted Chiang Kai-shek out of membership. He stormed at the Senate of the United States when it refused to confirm his Supreme Court nominees, Haynesworth and Carswell. And *Newsweek* quotes a "top insider" as to the President's remarks about the treatment of the dollar on international exchanges. The "insider" reported: "In these meetings he was very animated. He would pound on his desk, wave his arms, and say "God damn those so-and-so's. We'll fix those bastards."

There is no room for dissent in the Administration of Richard Milhous Nixon. Whoever does not agree completely with the Chief of State is, according to stated, clear policy, subject to dismissal. Conformity to the President's wishes must be complete.

James Allen, once Commissioner of Education under Mr. Nixon, found this out when he questioned the invasion of Cambodia.

Walter Hickel, Secretary of the Interior, found it out when he wrote a letter suggesting that the Administration had lost its capacity to communicate with young people. And when, too, he fought the oil companies too hard trying to protect the Santa Barbara channel from pollution.

Lieutenant Fitzgerald found it out when he dared tell a Congressional Committee the scandalous story of the C5A air transport—and was fired by the Pentagon the very next day. So did an indeterminate number of junior officers in the Navy who dared to differ ever so slightly with official policy on the war.

Leon Panetta, Civil Rights Chief for HEW Department, lost his job when he said "leadership is not exercised through false promises."

Frank W. Render, ranking Black civilian in the Pentagon, resigned under pressure when he spoke of racial discrimination in the armed services.

Peter Henle and Harold Goldstein, top career analysts in the Bureau of Labor Statistics, were forced out of their jobs in September 1971 for having given an objective interpretation of the facts about unemployment and consumer prices.

And so on. The list is too long to include here.

Mr. Nixon's dislike of dissent from his opinions extends to the Supreme Court. He has had the almost unprecedented opportunity of appointing four new justices. Just one more and he will control the court. Unlike previous Presidents, Richard Nixon frankly states that he intends to appoint no one to the

Supreme Court simply on merit. He will appoint only those who hold the same views as he does about the Constitution, about civil rights, about crime, protest, and punishment and, above all, about the extension of power of the Chief Executive. Criticism which has necessarily come from the American Bar Association regarding the way in which the Chief Executive has handled Supreme Court nominations has drawn from Mr. Nixon colorful comment.

Conformity throughout the government is not quite enough. There must also be appropriate praise of the Chief Executive. A memorandum sent to officials of the HUD department by its director of public affairs in 1970 read:

> I have been asked to forward the enclosed material together with a White House request that favorable references to the President's recent Vietnam statement be included in all public speeches delivered in the immediate future.

And there is standard and well-organized procedure whereby Republican organizations led by the national committee, set in motion a nationwide fan of telephone messages whenever the President speaks on television. The messages call upon people throughout the country to listen to the President and then send approving messages to the White House.

The founders of our country who framed the Constitution had had a bad experience with the English king. They were determined so to fashion the structure of the government of the United States that no President would be able to exalt himself to a position resembling that of a monarch. This was the reason for the system of "checks and balances" under which our nation has prospered for almost 200 years. The genius of the system of checks and balances is that there are three *co-equal* branches of the United States government—legislative, executive and judicial. That is the Congress, the President, and his cabinet, and the courts.

The Constitution does not countenance a president—not even Richard Nixon—trying to make the Supreme Court agree with him. It certainly does not countenance a President trying to reduce the Congress to a secondary role in the conduct of governmental affairs. Richard Nixon has tried, in his drive for power, to do both of those things.

As to the relationship of Richard Nixon to the Congress, Mr. Nixon has built within the White House walls his own personal center of power beyond the reach of Congressional inquiry. He has, of course, appointed a cabinet and changed its membership from time to time. But the cabinet plays a decided "second fiddle" to the White House staff. It is in that staff, if not in the mind of the Chief Executive alone, that decisions are being made that affect the destiny, life, and welfare of 200 million Americans and indeed all the rest of the world. Except for Henry Kissinger, the White House staff is composed of people scarcely known even by name to most of the American people—shadowy figures at best. And they are there for just one purpose, to do their Chief's bidding and to ask no questions why. The trouble with the cabinet departments is that they contain career people, professionals in their fields. Their minds are not to be made up by someone else—not even a President. Therefore, to a President who seeks untrammelled power, the departments become a sort of nuisance. Mr. Nixon has treated them as such.

The inner circle of advisors which meets often with the President does not contain a single member of the cabinet. Perhaps because cabinet members can be called to testify before committees of Congress, whereas, at least in this Administration, White House aides can refuse to do so. Henry Kissinger has consistently refused to testify, even when asked to do so by important Congressional committees. Why? Rather obviously because he and Mr. Nixon propose to deal with the world as the two of them see fit and without interference from the Congress, the American people, or anyone else.

As he has felt his executive power grow, the Chief Executive has not hesitated to take on judicial powers as well. He pronounced Charles Manson guilty before his trial was half over, thus violating a fundamental principle of Anglo-Saxon common law. He once declared that the killing at My Lai was a "massacre," but when Lieutenant Calley was convicted of murder by court martial and a wave of public sympathy seemed for a time to sweep the country, President Nixon declared that he himself would decide Lt. Calley's fate. And since opposition to school busing appears to be a popular election issue, Mr. Nixon has not hesitated openly to criticise and seek to circumvent the courts regarding that matter.

All of which makes the prospect of a Nixon-controlled Supreme Court the more ominous.

Only the Congress, therefore, stands in Richard Nixon's way as he drives toward inordinate and unprecedented power over the life and government of the United States, which may explain why the Chief Executive has dealt with Congress as he has.

The freezing, by the President's office of Management and Budget, of funds appropriated by Congress for pressing domestic needs, as mentioned earlier, has been a flagrant and probably unconstitutional violation of the will of Congress. It has been an assumption by the Executive of essentially legislative powers—an invasion, that is, of the clear province of one of the other supposedly co-equal branches of the American government. And it has been done on no small scale.

Congressman Evins of Tennessee, has said of Mr. Nixon's action: "Communities are being deprived of safe and adequate water supplies and sanitation systems, families are being deprived of housing, children are being deprived of nutrition and milk assistance and education, entire regions are being deprived of needed water-resource developments."

Senator Mansfield has urged a court action to affirm the right of Congress to control its own appropriations. But all to no avail. Only as it suited Richard Nixon's personal political advantage has any of the frozen $12 billion and more been released.

Few Presidents in history—if any—have thwarted the will of Congress with as many vetoes of as many important measures as has Richard Nixon. Most of those vetoes have been discussed. Among them are:

January, 1970—Health, Education and Welfare appropriation bill—vetoed because it contained, in Mr. Nixon's opinion, "too much" for clean water, "too much" for model cities, "too much" for education.

June, 1970—Hill-Burton Hospital Construction Act.

August, 1970—Education appropriation bill.

August, 1970—Housing and Urban Development and Veterans' Appropriation bill.

October, 1970—Bill to limit campaign expenditures for television and radio time.

December, 1970—The Nelson-O'Hara bill that would have trained some 500,000 unemployed people for badly needed public service work and employed them.

December, 1970—Bill to provide aid to medical schools for the training of more family doctors.

January, 1971—Bill to include firemen in hazardous-employment retirement program.

June, 1971—Public Works Employment Bill aimed at reducing unemployment.

243

August, 1971—Employees disability retirement plan.

December, 1971—The entire bill for continuance of the Office of Economic Opportunity which contained provision for day care centers for children of working parents, thus enabling them to escape from welfare rolls.

In a theatrical gesture to carry out campaign promises to cut federal spending, Mr. Nixon vetoed, in just a few days in October, 1972, a large group of bills. The primary target was the Health, Education and Welfare-Labor Fund Bill ($30 billion), but there were numerous smaller appropriations for vocational rehabilitation, public works, flood control, airport development. Many of these were valuable bills, economical and carefully estimated.

Mr. Nixon has failed to invite the Congressional authors of important bills to witness the signing thereof in order that he alone might appear to be responsible for the legislation. This kind of action is unprecedented in the history of relations between presidents and congresses.

He invited no member of Congress to accompany him to China. The Chinese Premier, not the American President, corrected this slight by himself inviting two Senators to come. No members of Congress were consulted or even given advance notice of the Chief Executive's decision to visit China or to order the invasion of Cambodia. For the first time in history, President Nixon failed to invite any member of Congress to attend the formal meetings of the Organization of American States. Previous presidents have always done so.

Nixon has repeatedly failed to give his own party leaders in Congress advance notice of what he was going to do, even where those Congressional leaders had to defend his action. He gave Republican leaders no notice that he was going to veto the Hill-Burton Act. Senator Scott, Republican leader in the Senate, has complained that he was given no more than an hour's notice by the President about the nomination of Powell and Rehnquist to the Supreme Court, and less than that when Earl Butz was nominated to be Secretary of Agriculture.

When Congress was considering Mr. Nixon's nomination of Harold Carswell to be a supreme Court Justice, the President wrote to Senator Saxbe of Ohio the following:

What is centrally at issue in this nomination is the constitutional responsibility of the President to appoint members of the court— and whether this responsibility can be frustrated by those who wish to subject their own philosophy of their own subjective judgment for that of the one person entrusted by the Constitution with the power of appointment.

Apparently Richard Nixon either had not ever read the Constitution of the United States or he was prepared to demand the prerogative of violating it deliberately. For the Constitution provides that the President may *nominate* but the Senate must *consent* before a Supreme Court appointment can be made.

Repeatedly President Nixon has refused to give Congress information about his plans to provide arms to foreign countries.

We have already noted that when the Senate voted 72 to 6 to urge Nixon to propose to the Soviet Union a mutual moratorium on development of nuclear weapons, he declared such a vote to be "irrelevant."

When Congress refused to provide taxpayers' money for Mr. Nixon's hoped-for gift to Boeing Aircraft Company to get his pet SST built, the President declared he would get it done anyway.

We have also noted that Mr. Nixon violated time-honored precedent and decent observance of the Constitutional division of powers when he flatly declared he would disregard the Mansfield Amendment for withdrawal of U.S. forces from Vietnam, even though he himself had signed the bill containing that Amendment. Such contemptuous defiance of the Congress —co-equal branch of the government with Richard I—had never happened before in American history—at least not within living memory.

In other instances, attempts on the part of Congress to exercise its legislative function have not always been successful. On February 7, 1972, President Nixon signed the foreign aid appropriation bill. The bill contained a Congressional prohibition against the giving of more armament to the dictatorship in Greece. On February 17, 1972, the President issued an executive order which provided $72 million worth of arms to the Greek government.

Throughout Richard Nixon's reign, evidence has accumulated to show that the Justice Department and the Army have been engaged in surveillance of members of Congress. This has included the monitoring of the meetings attended by members of Congress. It has included wire taps, according to several Congress members—among them conservative Senator

245

Joseph Montoya of New Mexico. The Army has admitted to having built up dossiers on such prominent Democratic Senators as Edmund Muskie, George McGovern, and Sam Ervin. That all this has been and is official policy and practice of Mr. Nixon and his Administration was made plain indeed by William Rehnquist when, as assistant Attorney General, he testified to a Senate committee. Rehnquist said: "The Executive has the right to collect and store data on the affairs of any citizen so long as those affairs are relevent to a subject in which the Federal Government has a legitimate interest."

So much for the main outlines only of the attempts of Richard Milhous Nixon to denigrate the Congress of the United States and take from it and to himself the powers which the Constitution specifically bestowed upon the national legislature. Columnist D. J. R. Bruckner of the *Los Angeles Times* summed it up by writing that "humiliation, intimidation and retribution have become refined instruments of the Executive Branch."

There is, after all, no use having power unless one uses it. And what better way than for the benefit of one's own friends and supporters. And on occasion one's self. The record of the Nixon Administration is replete with instances of this.

Mr. Nixon's law partner and Attorney General, John Mitchell, did not, apparently, forget that their firm had received fees amounting to three-quarters of a million dollars from El Paso Natural Gas Company while both of them were active in the firm. Six days after he was sworn in as Attorney General, Mr. Mitchell approved what is generally termed a "sweetheart deal," whereby El Paso Gas got an anti-trust action against it dismissed. The Attorney General could have let the case go on through the courts. It involved virtual monopoly by El Paso of delivery of gas to the Far West of the nation. But instead, Mr. Mitchell approved the dismissal.

The law firm of Nixon, Mudge, Rose, Guthrie, Alexander, and Mitchell has prospered well during the term of office of its erstwhile senior partner. The Nixon and Mitchell names were technically withdrawn from the firm's designation when those two gentlemen moved into control of the U.S. government. But the firm added substantially to its Washington staff and no one, it can safely be assumed, has exactly forgotten the relationship of Nixon and Mitchell to it. Including Nixon and Mitchell.

In September 1971 Congressman Morris Udall of Arizona, chairman of a subcommittee of the House Post Office Committee revealed that the "Nixon-Mitchell" law firm had been hired to act as bond attorneys for the sale of U.S. Postal Service bonds. This was lucrative business. Chairman Udall quoted an official of the new Post Office Corporation who stated that the bond underwriters had told the Corporation that the law firm of which the President and Attorney General had been partners "had to be hired." It *was*. Congressman Udall also pointed out that the decision of the Post Office Corporation to sell its bonds on the open market instead of through the U.S. Treasury would cost the taxpayers an estimated additional $125 million in interest charges.

In the summer of 1970 Mr. Nixon's Defense Department tried to make a $200 million loan to the Penn Central Railroad. Just what business this was of the Defense Department was extremely unclear. Why the White House apparently wanted the deal done this way was very clear. For it was a way whereby it was hoped that Congress would not find out about the matter until it was an accomplished fact. But the House Appropriations Committee did find out, committeemen "hit the ceiling," hearings were held, and the loan was not made. Fortunately. For a very short time thereafter Penn Central filed for bankruptcy.

In October, 1971, Deputy Attorney General Richard Kleindienst blocked his own anti-trust division from opposing the merger of two giants in the drug business, Warner-Lambert and Parke-Davis. It turned out, quite incidentally, that the board chairman of Warner-Lambert was a long-time financial backer of President Nixon and a client of the "Nixon-Mitchell" law firm. The Washington Post reported as follows: "One of the President's closest friends and leading campaign contributors—Elmer H. Bobst—revealed this month that he talked with aides of Mr. Nixon about a controversial merger involving the drug company in which he is the largest single stockholder."

On October 23, 1971, Walter Cronkite, ace television newsman, reported that President Nixon and his close friend, Bebe Rebozo, had profited handsomely in Florida land transactions. Cronkite said that the two friends had sold shares in a land company back to the company at $2 a share when the market price was $1. It was obviously worth much more than that to the company to have associated with it the name of the President of the United States.

The stories about Mr. Rebozo and the favored treatment he has received from the Federal Government are long and many.

Suffice it to say that the gentleman on one occasion was given no less than four chances to become the lowest bidder on a contract to handle land-title services in connection with sale of land in the Everglades National Park.

Of note in the strange case of Richard Milhous Nixon is his almost incredible willingness to place accolades upon his own brow. A few examples follow.

When Richard Nixon paid his visit to Pope Paul VI, he made a speech to the Pontiff, which was carefully released to the press. Richard Nixon told the Pope these things:

> Tonight after I leave the Vatican I will be flying to sea and there I shall see the mightiest military force which exists in the world on any ocean.
>
> Speaking very humbly as President of the strongest nation in the world, with more power perhaps than any leader in the world, I can say with all the power I have, you have something, you and your colleagues, that the world needs and particularly the young people of the world need very much today.
>
> Great as is the power of the Presidency of the United States, the power that can make the difference between war and peace in great crises, the power that can be used to help those nations of the world that need help and assistance to gain a decent standard of living and to help people within our own country who haven't had an equal chance, the power that can bring better programs for housing, health, transportation and all those material things of life that are so important to the good life.

The President put forth his welfare reform program with the modest statement that it was the most far-reaching such proposal in all history.

He presented his proposal in the field of environment with the claim that it was "the most costly and comprehensive such plan ever proposed."

When it came time for Game Plan II, Mr. Nixon introduced it as "the new American Revolution" and said its purpose was "Power to the People." On examination, it looked much more like a plan that would lead to more power to the President.

He made his announcement that the United States was prepared to raise the dollar price of gold at the conclusion of his summit meeting with French Premier Pompidou. Mr. Nixon said, "It is my great privilege to announce the conclusion of the most magnificent monetary agreement in the history of the world."

The President, happening to be in power at the climax of long, long years of scientific effort, labelled the first moon walks as "The greatest week in the history of the world since the Creation." Whereupon the *Christian Science Monitor* commented cryptically that "Christians would give higher importance to several events in the life of Jesus of Nazareth."

Of his 8-point proposal to the "other side" in the Vietnam war, Richard Milhous Nixon said that it was "the most generous peace offer in the history of warfare."

And when the Head of State of the United States went to China to meet with the heads of that nation's Communist government, he described his seven days in China as "the week that changed the world."

Almost the only remaining statement which, it seemed, could logically emanate from the Presidential lips would be to nominate himself as Richard I of the American Empire and expect a subservient Senate promptly to confirm the nomination.

17. THE COMING OF THE GARRISON STATE?

It would be an exaggeration to say that the United States is a garrison state, but none to say that it is in danger of becoming one.

—Henry Steele Commager

In the spring of 1970 a gentle, 80-year-old Quaker lady joined in a peace march in a small California city. Two days later an FBI agent called at her home, identified himself and asked if she and her husband were not asociated with a plot to assassinate President Nixon. Needless to say she was stupefied. And frightened.

How many other marchers for peace received similar calls we do not know. We do know that this lady never took part in a peace demonstration again. Which was, of course, the purpose of the FBI call.

On July 14, 1970, *Look* magazine published a penetrating article by the distinguished political scientist, Henry Steele Commager. Its title was "Is Freedom Dying in America?" Three passages from the article will convey its impact.

If repression is not yet as blatant or as flamboyant as it was during the McCarthy years, it is in many respects more pervasive and more formidable. For it comes to us now with official sanction and is imposed upon us by officials sworn to uphold the law: The Attorney General, the FBI, state and local officials, the police, and even judges. In Georgia and California, in Lamar, S.C., and Jackson, Mississippi, and Kent, Ohio, the attacks are overt and dramatic; on the higher levels of the national administration it is a process of erosion, the erosion of what Thomas Jefferson called "the sacred soil of liberty." Those in high office do not openly proclaim their disillusionment with the principles of freedom, but they confess it by their conduct, while the people acquiesce in their own disinheritance by abandoning the "eternal vigilance" that is the price of liberty.

The thrust is everywhere the same, and so too the animus behind it: to equate dissent with lawlessness and noncomformity with treason. The purpose of those who are prepared to sweep aside our ancient guarantees of freedom is to blot out those great problems that glare upon us from every horizon, and pretend that if we refuse to acknowledge them, they will somehow go away. It is to argue that discontent is not an honest expression of genuine grievances but of willfulness, or perversity, or perhaps of the crime of being young, and that if it can only be stifled, we can restore harmony to our distracted society.

It would be an exaggeration to say that the United States is a garrison state, but none to say that it is in danger of becoming one.

Was Dr. Commager justified in his fears? Did he exaggerate the danger to American freedoms? Is our country threatened with becoming what Dr. Commager calls "a garrison state"? Are we, in fact, part way there already? There have been alarms like this sounded before, of course. But thus far the people have recognized the danger before it was too late—and reacted against it effectively. Will we, in our time, follow that good example? Or are we—a "silent majority" of us at least—too affluent to care? No sure answer can be given to those questions. Certainly those who still believe in government of the people by the people and for the people have cause for concern. Our country is in the midst of a period of profound crisis. And it is fundamentally a moral crisis.

The United States once held a position of moral leadership in the world which was almost unique in history. We hold such a position no longer. We have traded it for military might, for power politics, and for national affluence. We can regain that moral leadership only by acting, as a people and as a nation, in a moral way. We can regain it only when we recapture that sense of high moral purpose which once marked our country's course. That purpose must include a relentless search for peace instead of power, a relentless drive for justice for all our fellow citizens, especially the poor and the minorities among us, instead of comfort and security for ourselves, a relentless drive toward tolerance and understanding, instead of prejudice and repression of dissent.

What America needs perhaps more than anything else today is a revival of what was best in that most typical of all American political movements—Populism. The slogan of that late-19th-century philosophy was a simple and powerful one. It was: "Equal opportunity for all, special privilege to none."

We have drifted far from that slogan today. We harbor at the center of our political life an opposite concept. It is the concept of the "great silent majority." For what that concept actually means is the assembly of a political majority composed of the comfortable, the complacent and the conformist —a majority of people who want to be protected in their affluence from the restless idealism of the young, the protests of the poor, and the drives, sometimes revolutionary, of the distressed millions of the world.

If such a majority is ever formed and those who appeal to it for votes kept in power for any length of time, then freedom will inevitably be eroded away in the name of a false "order" and "security" and the days of government of, by, and for the people will be numbered.

The basic danger to the America of tradition is inherent in the policies of the Nixon Administration. It arises from the commitment of the Administration to the politics of the "great silent majority." The essential ingredient of that policy is fear. Tragically enough there is good reason for deep concern if not actual fear on the part of everyone. For rising crime rates, drug abuse, decline of moral standards and evidence of social irresponsibility are facts of life today. So is a rising tide of violence. In 1969, major crime increased by 12%; in 1970 by another 11%; and in the first six months of 1971 at an annual rate of 12%, with a 17% increase in violent crimes in the previously crime-free suburbs. In 1971, willful murders increased by 21% in California, robbery by 20% and burglary by 17%.

A study by the International Association of Police Chiefs

251

showed that in the year 1971 all previous records for bombing were shattered in the United States. There were 2,054 such crimes recorded, resulting in 18 killed and 207 injured.

At one point in late 1971, all prisons in the state of Florida were closed to the admission of any more convicted inmates because prisoners were already sleeping on floors and there wasn't room for any more. What was to be done with those newly sentenced was not clear.

In his 1972 State of the Union Message, President Nixon claimed that crime in the District of Columbia was increasing less rapidly than before. But closer examination of the facts by the conservative *Washington Star* showed that the only reason the President could make such a claim was because crimes against property—burglary and auto thefts—had declined enough to cover up the fact that crimes of violence—murder, rape, robbery and aggravated assault—had continued to increase as much as before. One of the gravest reasons for concern about the condition of life in the nation's capital was the alarming statistic that 36% of the young men in a three-square-mile area around the capitol building were hard heroin addicts. The President did not mention this.

A poll conducted by *Life* Magazine in January, 1972, showed that 78% of its readers felt unsafe in their homes, and 30% said they kept guns under their pillows.

Newsweek Magazine remarked mildly in its January 24, 1972 issue that: "Although President Nixon made law and order a central theme of the 1968 campaign, his Administration can point to no decline in the nation's crime rate to help his re-election bid."

In March, 1972, the entire fleet of TWA airplanes was threatened with destruction by bombs unless the airline paid a "ransom" of $2 million.

The causes of the crime wave in the United States are many. One is that professional crime pays—handsomely. Congressman Claude Pepper, Chairman of the House Select Committee on Crime, estimates the annual "take" of professional criminals at $7 billion. Another—and deeper—cause of crime was set forth by former Attorney General Ramsey Clark who wrote:

There is a clear, common thread among such seemingly unrelated phenomena as the firebombing of Dresden in 1945, our military expedition in Indochina, the use of B-52's in Cambodia, Laos, and Viet Nam, the deaths of prisoners and guards at

Attica and San Quentin, the police killings of Black Panthers Fred Hampton and Mark Clark, the 12 percent rise in violent crime in the first six months of 1971, our glorification of guns, the shooting of students at South Carolina and Jackson State colleges, and the deaths of four young Americans at Kent State.

The thread is more than the presence of violence. It is more than the Government's use of violence. It is more than the unquestionable excessiveness and lawlessness of the violence used. It is the acceptance of violence by the people. Is violence an acceptable problem-solver for Americans? Is violence the American way of having its way? The qualities of character that call for shooting looters, condone shooting students. As we live by violence, so shall we die by it.

This kind of condition in a nation is the very seedbed from which "garrison" states have grown. People prefer "order" to freedom when they become sufficiently frightened. What has been done to remove that fear? Or is the continuance of the fear an important ingredient in certain political programs?

Back in the early days of the Nixon Administration, Senators Hart of Michigan and Ervin of North Carolina introduced legislation which would have provided increased pay and better training for policemen, though federal grants to states and cities. These same Senators introduced another bill to provide $1 billion to improve law enforcement, to increase the number of courts and judges, and thus, to bring about speed in trials and speedier justice.

Another group of Senators—Eagleton, Brooke, Saxbe, and Mondale—all of them former Attorneys-General of their states—have developed a piece of legislation known as the Model Criminal Justice Reform Act. This bill would offer 90% federal financing to any state or local government which would agree to undertake a full-scale upgrading of its entire criminal justice system. Legislation of this kind certainly represents the most constructive approach to the problem of crime in the United States. The Administration has not supported it. Why not?

Fundamental to any other measures should be a massive national effort to enable all Americans to live in decent, clean houses, in decent, clean neighborhoods with well-lighted streets and equal protection from the law. It is the people of the ghettos, the barrios, and the slums who suffer most from the absence of "law and order." It is in neighborhoods of dimly lighted streets and sub-standard housing where the drug business has its field day and even becomes a principal line of "business." Until these conditions are corrected there will be neither liberty nor justice for all Americans.

The danger to freedom—the danger that we may drift into a repressive or "garrison" state—comes from too little, not too much, fair, effective, and univertal law enforcement.

There is another approach to the problem of crime. It has not yet been effective against the professional criminal. It threatens basic liberties and the Bill of Rights of our Constitution. It is the approach apparently preferred by the Nixon Administration. It has not yielded the results which its advocates claimed for it. It has not checked the alarming increase in crime in the United States.

About five months after he became Attorney General in the Nixon Administration, John Mitchell advanced the doctrine that the Attorney General needs no authorization from a court or anyone else before wiretapping or other eavesdropping on any person suspected of subversive or unlawful acts. This expanded the practices used against foreign agents to include any person of whom the Attorney General or anyone in his department felt suspicious.

The *Washington Evening Star* commented editorially on the Attorney General's doctrine: "No one man—not the President nor his designated agent—should have such unilateral authority. He must act under the authority of a court warrant." But the counsel of the *Star* has not been followed.

From his early beginning the Attorney General did not retreat. On the contrary, he advanced. Representing the Nixon Administration in such matters, he succeeded in getting through Congress a preventive detention law under which law-enforcement agencies can arrest and hold in prison for 60 days without bail any person suspected of being about to commit some unlawful act—even if that person had no previous criminal record.

Mr. Mitchell also got from Congress laws permitting police to enter private dwellings or other premises without warning or identification of themselves. He obtained passage of a law allowing 25-year sentences to be imposed on "dangerous special offenders," whatever exactly that language means. The same law permits expanded jail terms for people refusing to testify before grand juries and removes much of the immunity formerly allowed them when they do testify.

The question arises as to why Congress would pass such laws. The answer is the crime wave. If Congress had failed to do the Attorney General's bidding then, from that day, every crime committed would have been blamed upon the Congress, as surely as the sun shines. Furthermore there were no doubt many members who voted for these laws because they sincerely believed that they would curb crime. Perhaps if coupled with measures like the Hart-Ervin or the Eagleton legislation, this could happen.

The Attorney General did not seek a law to authorize his unlimited surveillance and wire-tapping of anyone suspected by him. He claimed he did not need it. Some courts ruled otherwise but the "Justice" department appealed their decisions and went right ahead with its program.

When hearings were held by Senator Ervin's committee on Civil Rights, the man who was then Assistant Attorney General, William H. Rehnquist, now a Supreme Court Justice, testified for the Justice Department about abuses resulting from its program of surveillance. Mr. Rehnquist said:

> Given the far-flung responsibilities of the executive branch for law enforcement, and the large complement of personnel required to discharge these responsibilities, it would scarcely be surprising if there were not isolated examples of abuse of this investigative function.

> But it will come as no surprise, I am sure, for me to state that the department will vigorously oppose any legislation which, whether by opening the door to unnecessary and unmanageable judicial supervision of such activities or otherwise, would effectively impair this extraordinarily important function of the federal government.

The "extraordinarily important function of the Federal Government" to which Mr. Rehnquist referred was that of spying upon its own citizens, deciding freely, without court order, upon whom to spy, conducting investigation of citizens' activities, and storing data concerning them for possible future use against them. These and other measures instituted by the Nixon Administration will be recognized as measures typical of a very different kind of government from what we have known in the United States. Are such measures justified as a means of combatting the crime wave? Perhaps, though they have thus far proved of small effect. But they have been used, not only by the Federal Bureau of Investigation but also by the Army in ways reminiscent of "witch-hunts" not only against criminals but against people who disagree with the policies of the Nixon government.

Attorney General Mitchell's point of view toward certain

people and certain activities sheds a good deal of light on where the primary focus of the "law enforcement" activities of the Justice Department lies.

A quarter of a million people marched in almost perfect order through the streets of Washington in October, 1969. They marched in protest against the war policies of the Nixon Administration. The Attorney General said the march reminded him of the Russian Revolution. Shifting his ground from left to right, Mr. Mitchell said that the May Day, 1971, marchers reminded him of Hitler's Brown Shirts. He told reporters that every anti-war march was led by people with "Communist-related-oriented backgrounds."

We may be sure that the files of the Justice Department are bulging with information about every aspect of the lives of anyone identified as having dared to march down a public street in free America to express his disagreement with the policies of what is supposed to be his own government.

Mr. Mitchell was not working alone. Neither was the Justice Department. For the U.S. Army was hard at work along the same lines. The story was first "broken" by *Chicago Today*, once Chicago's *American*, now owned by the conservative *Chicago Tribune*. It showed that the Army had deployed thousands of its men, not to fight or even to spy upon a foreign enemy, but to collect "information" about its own fellow countrymen who might be critical of the party in power. *Life* magazine did a feature story about this military activity. And Senator Sam Ervin called it "a deterrent power over the individual rights of American citizens." As indeed it was precisely intended to be. And is intended to be. For there has been no cessation of this activity. Nor will there be as long as Richard Nixon is President. It has been played down a bit. But that is all.

The Army's description of the people against whom its spying is carried on is "Persons of Interest." The name of the surveillance project is CONUS INTEL, meaning Continental United States Intelligence. Some of the Persons of Interest are legitimate objects of surveillance—the Weathermen for example. But they form a minor fraction of the people about whom the Army has stored information and continues to do so. On the list of suspected "subversives" are anyone who writes a letter to a Congressman in opposition to the Southeast Asia War, anyone who marches in a demonstration, anyone who signs a petition, almost any priest or minister,—since they might be spreading the teachings of Jesus which are clearly anti-war and hence "subversive." Others on the list are anyone who dares to say the ecology is in danger, who advocates birth-control or—worst of all—who believes in civil liberties.

Millions of dossiers against millions of citizens now repose in Army Intelligence files, ready to be used should "Der Tag" ever come. How many? No one knows and the Army, of course, refuses to tell. But *Life* magazine has estimated that 25 million citizens are now "booked" in Army files. One agent testified to Senator Ervin's committee that the U.S. Army has already developed "the intelligence apparatus of a police state."

John M. O'Brien, who described himself as a "domestic spy for the Army" and who worked out of the Chicago office of the 113th Military Intelligence Group testified that his unit kept dossiers on some 800 persons, including Congressman Abner Mikva and Senator Adlai Stevenson III.

Here is where the matter becomes even more deadly serious than it is in the case of private citizens. For both Mikva and Stevenson are members of the United States Congress. Both of them are members of the opposite political party to that of Mr. Nixon, Mr. Mitchell, and—apparently—the military. Both of them have opposed Nixon policies on numerous occasions. For the Executive to carry on spying against political opponents is to follow exactly in the footsteps of every dictator in history.

Nor did it stop with Mikva and Stevenson. Senator Ervin's Committee found that he himself, the governors of several states and Senators Muskie and McGovern, leading candidates for the Democratic nomination for President, had all been subject to Army surveillance. The Senator on February 29, 1972, asked the Supreme Court to declare such activity a violation of the Constitution.

In a Senate speech Senator Ervin declared: "The Army has no business meddling in civilian politics or conducting surveillance of law-abiding American citizens or maintaining data banks on civilians who had no business with the Defense Department. Vast networks are being developed throughout the land by government and by private industries. In these systems, where they contain the record of the individual's thoughts, beliefs, habits, attitudes and personal activities, there may well rest a potential for political control and for intimidation which is alien to a society of free men."

The FBI is in the act too. And probably jealous that the Army is elbowing its way into its activities. One object of its special interest seems to be "Earth Day" rallies where speakers are monitored and those attending catalogued. Senator Muskie, leader in Congress for a clean environment, found himself in the suspect category because he spoke at an Earth Day rally.

Conservative Senator Joseph Montoya of New Mexico, speaking at a Jefferson Day dinner in March, 1971, said that the Nixon Administration was encouraging and participating in "frightening invasions of citizens' rights and privileges." The Senator added that, "Even the United States Senate is not immune. More than a few members have plainly stated that they believe their conversations have been monitored."

Even people doing business with the government have been warned not to do anything contrary to its wishes. On orders from above, no doubt, the Rural Electrification Administration in mid-1971 issued a directive prohibiting "political activities by REA borrowers." Those borrowers included more than 1,000 rural electric cooperatives, certainly all their directors and managers and probably even their six million members.

Perhaps the most revealing and frightening evidence of activities exactly paralleling those of the secret police in a "garrison" state came to light when someone invaded the FBI office in Media, Pennsylvania. The order had gone out a short time before to numerous FBI agents to infiltrate college classes to gather information on students who might be "plotting against the government." And the FBI was driving hard against young dissenters from the war. A memorandum found in the Media office files reads as follows:

There was a pretty general consensus that more interviews with these subjects and hangers-on are in order for plenty of reasons, chief of which are it will enhance the paranoia endemic in these circles and will further serve to get the point across that there is an FBI Agent behind every mailbox. In addition, some will be overcome by the overwhelming personalities of the contracting agent and volunteer to tell all—perhaps on a continuing basis. The Director has okayed PSI's and SI's age 18 to 21. We have been blocked off from this critical age group in the past. Let us take advantage of this opportunity.

The PSI's and SI's referred to are hired informers for the FBI, people paid to spy on others in the groups or organizations to which they belong or to infiltrate those to which they have not belonged.

The FBI told the Catholic Archbishop of Boston to cancel a peace rally scheduled for a Catholic hall because such activities were potentially dangerous and subversive.

And when a young woman in Philadelphia undertook the writing of a book about the FBI, her apartment was raided and all her material taken from her.

Government by secret police has never been American government—until now.

Mr. J. Edgar Hoover went before a Congressional Committee to ask for 1,000 additional agents. His justification was based largely upon his report of a plot, headed by the Berrigan brothers, both Catholic priests, to kidnap Henry Kissinger and blow up tunnels under the city of Washington. Mr. Hoover made this accusation before any trial or even an indictment of the Berrigans or others accused of being involved with them had been made. He, in effect, condemned them without trial— a Gestapo tactic pure and simple—no matter the outcome. Why did Mr. Hoover do this? A partial explanation is given by a Catholic writer, Francine du Plessix Gray, in these sentences:

> I can't think of any men who have been a more profound embarrassment than the Berrigans to the Nixon Administration and to the FBI and to the Catholic Church.
>
> The Catholic community in the United States, since its beginning, has always been a community remarkable for its docility, its conservatism, its often blind patriotism, its political predictability. . . . You need not stretch your imagination far to realize the shock and discomfiture on the part of our government when all of a sudden . . . it found that the most profound dissent movement to have rocked the United States since the slavery issue—the anti-Vietnam war movement—was being led, to a great extent, by Irish Catholic priests.

Crime and protest are not the same thing.

The reason Attorney General Mitchell, Richard Nixon's campaign manager, demanded and got from the Congress a law making it possible to throw into jail anyone refusing to testify before a federal grand jury has become clear. Grand juries are now being used not only for their legitimate purpose of indicting criminals but also to "probe, expose, and punish the exercise of political freedom by its immediate targets and chill dissent by all but the hardiest" in the words of a report from the Center for the Study of Democratic Institutions. The *Christian Science Monitor* asks: "Are grand juries being used as 'fishing expeditions' to gather material on and harass members of the anti-war left, rather than to investigate specific crimes? If witnesses refuse to testify they can be jailed for the life of the grand jury—up to 18 months."

This practice, instituted by the Nixon Administration, involves issuing subpoenas to any person believed to have knowledge of a matter of interest to the government—such, for example, as a peace demonstration. The person subpoenaed can be required to bring with him any personal papers or records. He is questioned by a government attorney before the grand jury but is not allowed to have an attorney of his own. Questions may or may not have anything to do with a specific crime or any kind of criminal action, but may simply involve "fishing expeditions" seeking to build a case against some organization or group. The entire proceeding is secret— a "star chamber" session. And unless the witness testifies in answer to all questions he can be thrown in jail.

In addition to all this, the President has sought to reorganize all the "intelligence" activities of the government and to put in charge of them Henry Kissinger, his own personal staff man. The transparent reason for this is that Mr. Kissinger, being a member of the White House staff, is exempt from testifying before Congressional Committees on the grounds of "executive privilege." Thus Mr. Nixon and Mr. Kissinger can carry on any kind of surveillance over American citizens they choose to and there is no way for anyone to know what is being done. Senators Symington and Fulbright bitterly attacked this action by the President. But to no avail.

In May, 1971, a peace march took place in Washington D.C. It was not particularly well organized and it appeared to be almost leaderless. The May Day march itself was orderly and without incident. But when some thousand persons assembled on the steps of the Capitol building to hear a speech by a member of Congress who had invited them there they were summarily arrested by Washington police. Out of all the 1,000 people arrested in this action not a single one was convicted of any crime or misdemeanor. The eight who were brought to trial were all acquitted. Charges against the rest were dropped.

This was, however, only the beginning. A group of protesters decided to remain in Washington and on a certain day to attempt to block traffic to government buildings. They bore no arms and they committed no acts of violence. They were of course in violation of the law in their interference with the flow of traffic. Considerable crowds gathered as spectators of what was going on.

The Washington police moved in. Not merely to arrest the admitted law violators. But to arrest some 13,000 persons who were anywhere near the scene. The vast majority of those arrested were people on their way to work, sightseers or simply the curious. Except in a few cases, these people were arrested without any charges being made against them—for the obvious reason that they had committed no offense. They were arrested in flagrant violation of the most basic concepts of the American Constitution.

Washington jails were so overcrowded that hundreds of people were injured or rendered seriously ill. The overflow that could not be crowded into the jails were herded into a football arena and kept there over night without food or means of keeping warm. Only when the authorities got ready to do so was anyone released. Some were held for as long as 36 hours. The prisoners were not told what crime they had committed, nor allowed legal aid. The *New York Times* commented in an editorial which read in part:

> The police may have feared that they were going to be in combat with tough urban guerrillas. In fact, the Mayday demonstrators were mostly feckless and leaderless. They did not generally taunt the police; they tried to engage in friendly dialogue with them, they did not resist arrest. Incidents of violence against property were comparatively few and well within the power of the police to contain.
>
> For Mr. Mitchell to compare these demonstrators to Nazi Brown Shirts is absurd. For him to paint this lurid picture of Washington, caught up in a terrifying struggle against "mob rule" is deliberately to mislead the public. His motives appear to be blatantly political. Mr. Mitchell seems to think there are votes to be won by being "tough" with long-haired radicals. Instead of trying to maintain the delicate and difficult balance between the necessary maintenance of public order and the protection of individual rights, he has made a vulgar and inflammatory appeal to prejudice and passion.

Later in a class-action suit, 1,200 persons sued the Department of Justice and the District of Columbia police for false arrest. This was not some sporadic incident. It was not a mistake in tactics by Washington policemen. What happened in Washington on that day in May was official policy of the Nixon Administration. The Chairman of the Washington Human Relations Commission stated, "Every source I have been able to check shows the mass arrest decision was made by the President of the United States, passed on to the Attorney General, to Kleindienst, to Chief of Police Wilson."

Not only so. Both the President of this supposedly free

nation and its Attorney General made repeated statements that they approved whole-heartedly of what had been done and that they hoped other cities would follow the example set by Washington, the nation's capital.

It is not wise for anyone to protest the policies of the Nixon Administration, peacefully or otherwise. It is not wise even to be in the vicinity where others are protesting. For the Constitutional rights of people may mean absolutely nothing if it pleases those who now rule America to make them so. Such practices and policies are exactly the kind which are used by those in power in totalitarian states. But they may very well be popular with that fearful "silent majority" which Mr. Nixon and his colleagues seek to develop.

There have been times when political opposition to the policies of President Nixon has itself been equated with treason to the United States. The outstanding example of this was when Mr. Nixon's right hand man H. R. Haldeman declared on the "Today" show that "the only conclusion you can draw is that the critics now are *consciously* aiding and abetting the enemy of the United States." This Mr. Haldeman said after Mr. Nixon had revealed his 8-point program for settling the war in Southeast Asia and called upon everyone to support that program. As a matter of fact, criticism of it by political opponents had been mild, and in most cases the critics had added expressions of hope that the plan would open the way to peace, despite their disagreement on certain points. But even this, in the opinion of White House insiders, was equivalent to treason. In their opinion, Mr. Nixon *is* the state. So was Louis XIV. The President in a later address softened Haldeman's charge. But he did not repudiate it.

President Nixon has made no concealment of his purpose to remake the Supreme Court into a body that agrees with him. Already he has appointed four of the nine justices. And the record shows that those four have voted consistently in accordance with the President's wishes.

Neither is it any secret that what Mr. Nixon is most interested in is a court that will uphold the measures extending executive power and reverse the trend of the Warren court which spelled out in practical terms the concept of civil liberties contained in the Bill of Rights of the Constitution. Just how far Mr. Nixon is ready to go in these directions is made quite clear by his nomination of William H. Rehnquist. Mr. Rehnquist is now a Justice of the Supreme Court, though 26 Senate votes were cast against his confirmation.

Mr. Rehnquist goes to the Court without having in any way repudiated his testimony to the Ervin Committee that the Executive has unlimited license to spy upon any citizen, including members of Congress, whenever the Executive decides that such action would promote the national security. Mr. Rehnquist goes to the Court having fully endorsed the mass-arrest policy of the Nixon Administration—mass arrests involving detention in prison without charge. The new Justice is the author of the doctrine that any employee of the Executive Department who disagrees with the President should be fired. He has advocated and upheld the unlimited right of the Executive to use wire-tapping and other electronic devices against any citizen whom it suspects, without authorization from any court.

The sharpest criticism of Mr. Nixon's nomination came not from a Democratic or a labor source but from a respected Republican one. The Ripon Society, progressive wing of the Republican Party, published an editorial in its official organ *The Ripon Forum*. Excerpts from that editorial follow:

> We want to register our opinion that he (Rehnquist) is Nixon's most dangerous nominee yet.
> Approval of William Rehnquist's nomination will for the first time give credence to what has until recently seemed an alarmist fear: that we are moving into era of repression, in which the U.S. democracy gives up its most noble enterprise—the maintenance of a free and open society.
> His voluminous public statements and his private comments of which we are aware show him to be a thorough-going authoritarian, a nearly absolute believer in executive supremacy over the legislature and a slack reconstructionist of the Constitution.

If in any country a considerable proportion of the comfortable, propertied people belonging to the dominant ethnic group can be made fearful of change, fearful of the strivings of minorities, fearful of the "strange ways" of the young, fearful of foreign enemies and "ideologies"—then these people may be ready progressively to sacrifice freedom for the sake of order and a false security. And then too a political constituency which may be called a "great silent majority" can be developed.

This is not a process of creating social or national unity. Far from it. It is a process which divides the people of a nation into hostile camps, fearful of one another. And it inevitably challenges the outcast minorities to protest—if they can. So the excuse—the apparent need—for repression of dissent arises naturally enough out of the political strategy of the fearful "great silent majority." It is the old, old maxim of "Divide and rule."

President Nixon kept the members of the "Black Caucus," consisting of the thirteen Black members of the House of Representatives, waiting for a whole year before he "found time" to see them. And then he rejected most of their requests.

Fair Employment Practices are important to Mexican-Americans, Black, and other minority groups alike. The Nixon Administration has supported legislation, narrowly defeated in the Senate, which would have required FEPC Commissioners to obtain court orders before they could enforce any of their decisions.

There appeared in the press for February 6, 1972 a United Press story about a young Mexican-American. He had been recruited by the Alcohol, Tobacco, and Firearms division of the Internal Revenue Service. His assigned task was to infiltrate Mexican-American organizations and, as a member of them, to foment violence and disorder that could be blamed on the Chicano Organization. This he had done in a number of instances in both California and Texas. He quit his "job" because when he was arrested for doing what he had been told to do the agency refused to protect him. The Alcohol, Tobacco, and Firearms division refused to comment to UPI reporters on this story. It is hardly an encouraging one. It is the kind of story calculated to arouse the fears of the "great silent majority" just as the policies of the Nixon Administration are calculated to gain its support.

A companion story, also carried in the nation's press, concerned a veteran of the U.S. Marine Corps by the name of Robert W. Hardy, who had been the principal government witness against 28 persons, one of them his own parish priest. They were accused of raiding the Selective Service offices in Camden, New Jersey.

But, apparently unable to live with himself, Hardy made affidavit in March, 1972, stating that he had been hired at $60-a-day by the FBI to provoke the raid. His affidavit quoted the FBI as stating that "someone in the Little White House in California wanted the raid actually to happen" whereas his agreement when he accepted the assignment was that arrests would be made on conspiracy charges before the raid could take place. Hardy further stated that he furnished and paid for nearly all the tools necessary for the raid, and that he was reimbursed by the FBI.

Why, why should a thing like this be done? Why indeed, unless it is necessary to have instances such as draft board raids to point to if someone is interested in justifying, through fear, the measures of repression that are the stuff of which "garrison" states are made?

Is Henry Steele Commager right when he says, "It would be an exaggeration to say that the United States is a garrison state, but none to say it is in danger of becoming one?" There are reasons, all too many, to believe that he is right. The very kind of laws needed to repress dissent of any kind are on the statute books.

The Department of Justice, the Army, the FBI and other agencies have already assembled dossiers on thousands of people—just as the secret police do in totalitarian countries. This practice has been extended to "cover" members of the National Congress.

Executive power has been concentrated in the White House staff beyond the reach of even Congressional inquiry.

Congress has been attacked and denigrated by the Executive and we have at least one Supreme Court Justice who believes as do the Department of Justice and the President that the Executive has an unlimited right to spy on members of the National Legislature.

The press and television have been attacked repeatedly and, to an extent at least, intimidated.

Dissent from the policies of the Administration has been equated with treason to the country.

A huge military-industrial complex is being built ever stronger and richer by the policies of the Administration.

Control of the Supreme Court by President Nixon is nearly an accomplished fact.

Industrial monopoly increases its power, pours millions into the campaign coffers of the party in power, shuts the door to participation in our economy in the face of small business, and even invades agriculture with corporation farming.

The Administration appears to prefer to carry on the government of the people with a minimum of knowledge of what it does reaching those same people. And when courageous men dare to reveal the facts to the people they are fired from their jobs or—in Daniel Ellsberg's case—arrested and prosecuted.

Wars are started by the President without consent of Congress, and carried on with a minimum of reporting to the people about them.

All foreign policy decisions are taken away from the State Department, made personally by the President, and carried out by him and his secret White House advisors. And when Congress passes a law to try to bring an end to an immoral war the President blandly declares he will disregard it.

Absolute conformity to the will of the President is required of everyone in government positions and those who step out of line are subject to dismissal.

Most serious of all, the fears of the people are played upon, fears of one group as against another, and fears of foreign countries. So an arms race is accelerated in the name of a national "defense" which cannot any longer defend but which takes an even greater toll in taxes from the people.

We may hope that Henry Steele Commager is mistaken. But there is ample evidence that he may be right. The hope we have rests on the voices of warning and dissent which come now from many sources.

Evangelist Billy Graham acknowledges: "I don't guess anybody loves the flag more than some of the people that are against the war."

Senator Frank Church warns: "For the first time in history, there has come into view the possibility of our President becoming a Caesar, because the principles of a free constitution are irrevocably lost when the legislative power is dominated by the Executive."

Senator Percy, Republican of Illinois, has said: "There are those in political life today whose statements leave no doubt that they would curb dissent and limit freedom of expression. As the fabric of our society undergoes unprecedented strains, the danger that our dominant politics might become what I would term a 'politics of fear' increases."

The *Christian Science Monitor,* in introducing a series of articles, sent out fliers which read:

In this super-computerized world of ours, the government and private firms may well know more about you than you can remember yourself. Federal intelligence arms—FBI, CIA, NSA, IRS—all are gathering and storing great quantities of highly personal data about individual citizens. And a national data bank is now in the active planning stage.

Your Social Security number could soon become the "code" for anyone in government, and possibly in private enterprise, to obtain your file for whatever purpose they deem necessary.

And two soldiers who served in Vietnam speak. The first, the son of an average citizen wrote to his parents: "Our greatest asset, our youth, is being wasted in a senseless, brutal war in Asia. At home, young people are denied the very freedoms of protest and free speech our soldiers are dying for. America is rapidly becoming a stratified, segregated society in which our minority groups are refused the chance for a decent life. Our air and water are polluted to the point where it will take generations to repair the damage. It is past time for us to think in concrete terms of people. . . ."

The second soldier is the son of a Republican Senator. Part of a letter to his father reads: "The government has made a strong effort to polarize the country into two hostile camps with no middle ground. The people who are demanding the peace they were promised for 10 years are being portrayed as traitors in order to alienate them from the silent majority. The real danger is not the takeover by anarchy but the introduction of repressive measures followed by the use of force that would make our country little different from the totalitarian governments we abhor."

The end result of the "police"-state tactics of the Nixon Administration and of the attempt to develop a fearful "silent majority" among the comfortable, complacent and conformist is tragically illustrated by two events.

The first of these was the action of the special state grand jury convened in Ravenna, Ohio in connection with the killing of four Kent State University students by the Ohio National Guard on May 4, 1970. There was ample evidence that the shooting of those four students, two of them girls, was "unnecessary, unwarranted and inexcusable" to use the exact words of the Commission on Student Unrest appointed by President Nixon himself. There is evidence that some rocks had been thrown. And what had started out as an orderly protest against President Nixon's invasion of Cambodia did turn to disorder, partly caused by the very presence of the Guard. But it has not been the practice in America to impose a penalty of death upon rock throwers. Furthermore it is a supposedly unbreakable rule for soldiers engaged in riot control that if they shoot at all it is never "shoot to kill." The rule is to shoot first over people's heads and as a last resort at their legs. The Ohio Guard shot to kill.

A New York City insurance executive, Peter Davis by name, was commissioned by the United Methodist Church to assemble and study all the evidence in the case. After fourteen months of painstaking examination of all the evidence that could be assembled, Mr. Davis concluded that the guardsmen seeking to punish the students for their protest of the Cambodia invasion deliberately fired into the student ranks. The Board of Christian Social Concerns of the Methodist Church has stated: "The killing of four students at Kent State now stands as a classic example of justice delayed, circumvented and mocked. . . . We have an almost step-by-step (photographic) record of what happened on May 4, 1970, and this record suggests that the shooting began as the result of a planned and prearranged act involving a certain number of guardsmen . . ."

One of the guardsmen himself wrote to Attorney General Mitchell saying: "As a guardsman who was present at Kent State, I cannot wholly dismiss the possibility of collusion. Just as I know many fellow guardsmen who were appalled at the murders, I know others who welcomed the deadly confrontation."

The FBI itself, reporting its investigation stated: "We have reason to believe that the claim by the National Guard that their lives were endangered by the students was fabricated after the event." The report also said that there was no evidence of sniper fire.

And yet when the grand jury, composed of supposedly decent, middle-class, good, average Americans made its report and returned its indictments, it declared that the guardsmen had acted in self defense and were blameless. It also endorsed the use of live ammunition in such situations. But in a veritable diatribe of invective against students and faculty of the university, the grand jury indicted 25 of them for "deliberate criminal conduct." One of those indicted for "second-degree rioting" had been present only because he went out to try to stop the trouble. He was Student-body President. The charge of "second-degree rioting" means failing to stop a riot once it has started. Most of the accused were indicted on unspecified charges. No one was named until all had been arrested. The report placed all the blame for the killings on the Administration of the University and the students, including apparently those who had been killed. Perhaps the grand jury recalled President Nixon's off-hand comment to the effect that "when dissent turns to violence it invites tragedy." Perhaps *excuses* it?

President White of Kent State called the grand jury report "a prime example of a brewing national disaster" and said that if it were pursued in all its nuances it would eventually destroy not only Kent State but all major universities in America." And a federal district court judge, William K. Thomas, ordered the report of the grand jury destroyed because it would "irreparably injure" the right to a fair trial of the 25 accused.

The spirit in which that grand jury acted was expressed quite clearly by Seabury Ford, chairman of the Republican Party of Portage County, who was one of the prosecutors assigned to the grand jury. In an interview with the Akron *Beacon-Journal*, Mr. Ford said that the National Guard "should have shot all the troublemakers."

A petition signed by 10,380 Kent State students had asked President Nixon to order a federal grand jury investigation. He refused to do so. So did the Attorney General.

One sequel to this grim story is that only one person among the 25 indicted by that grand jury was convicted. He was sentenced to six months in jail for interfering with firemen who were seeking to put out a fire in the Kent State ROTC building two days before the fatal shooting. All the other 24 were found to have been falsely accused and were acquitted.

Another sequel to the story, however, is this. Across the country there were those who applauded the grand jury's action. There were those who said that the dead young people "got what they deserved." These were the people—how many we do not yet know—who had learned to be part of the fearful "silent majority."

Another event demonstrates even more clearly than does the Kent State case the depths of social and moral deterioration to which the mind-set of a fearful "silent majority" is carrying our country. The story is of a young man in a suburb of Kansas City, a town whose people, like those in Ohio, are supposedly decent, church-going, average, middle-class Americans. This young man, Nick Rice by name, attended military school. He tried unsuccessfully to win an appointment to the Air Force Academy. He was about to enroll in the ROTC at Kansas University. Then, on a July evening in 1970, Nick Rice, an innocent by-stander, was accidentally shot dead by a police bullet intended for some youths who had vandalized a store.

The news reached the Rices' suburban home. One would have expected expression of sympathy for the bereaved parents. But no. Their boy had been shot by police. Therefore he must have been one of those young dissenters. Within minutes after their son's death the parents began to receive 'phone calls saying "I'm glad your son was killed" and "You ought to be shot like your boy." Former friends began to shun the Rices. Mr. Rice's insurance business was boycotted.

Because their son was killed!

This is no longer the America we used to know. That America of "equal opportunity for all, special privilege to none" is being destroyed by the very people who profess to love it. Whereas those who truly love it best must be berated and accused falsely because they have the courage to try to bring their country back to the faithfulness of its traditional ideals.

The "garrison" state may not be as far away as we would like to think. If it comes it will be because the fearful "silent majority" has been brought together into a real political majority. It will be composed of otherwise decent people who have been taught by those seeking their political support to feel themselves threatened by the young, the poor, the Black, and Mexican-American. It will be composed of people taught by those seeking their political support that anyone daring to dissent from the policies of the regime in power in the United States is, by the very fact, "subversive," an advocate of violence, an enemy of the nation and undeserving of decent human treatment. If such people are killed it is because "they got what they deserved." So says the creed of the fearful "silent majority."

The tactics employed by clever politicians to bring about this kind of psychology in people are the tactics that lead to the death of freedom and the coming of a repressive, all-powerful, "garrison" state.

And the strange case of Richard Milhous Nixon is that of a man who started out to end "control of people's lives by a handful of people in Washington" but who, as he climbed to personal power for himself, created the conditions and the climate for the destruction of the very freedoms he had once said he wanted to preserve.

The drive of Mr. Nixon and his Administration toward a transformation of the American government into something alien to the nation's traditions is evident enough.

The attacks of Governor Wallace on other Democrats and his virtual avoidance of criticism of Mr. Nixon made one wonder a little about the Governor's future plans. The friendly words of Vice-President Agnew about Governor Wallace add to the evidence. The previously quoted words of John Mitchell, Mr. Nixon's campaign manager, that "this nation is going so far to the right that you won't be able to recognize it" echo louder and louder as the days pass.

The question is whether the people care—whether *enough* people care *enough*—to stop the process before it is too late.

18. THE GOLDEN ROPES

I will fight to the limits of my capacity the forces that seek to impose strangling governmental control over the lives of the people.

America's political leaders, statesmen, Senators, Congressmen, even Mayors of towns, should have no ties, knowing or unknowing to groups influenced by men politically hostile to the United States.

—Richard M. Nixon

The strange case of Richard Milhous Nixon would be quite incomprehensible were it not for two golden ropes that run through his astonishing career and bind it together into a consistent whole.

At the beginning of his career this ambitious young man gave his listeners two strident messages, quoted above.

Yet at the end of this strange case we find the same man, now President of the United States, imposing more rigid controls on the economy of the country than it had ever known except in time of major war and seeking to forge a virtual power alliance with the most populous Communist nation on the face of the globe.

There are two loyalties which Mr. Nixon has never violated —two "golden ropes." These bind together his career and are the keys to solution of his strange case.

The first of these is woven of strands of loyalty to that topmost "cream" of American society which has from the beginning supported and financed the career of Mr. Nixon. Where the interests of that social and economic stratum of our society have been involved, Mr. Nixon has not failed to serve them well and faithfully.

A man of prudence does not forget—nor neglect in action —friends who have provided what probably exceeds $150 million to advance his political career. Some of those friends came forward very early in the rise to political power of Richard Nixon. A few years later these and other friends provided a special fund to help Mr. Nixon when he was a "struggling" Senator.

And as time passed, the financing of Richard Milhous Nixon has become a well-oiled business.

From an article written by Everett R. Holles for the *New York Times News Service* published, among other places, in the *St. Louis Post-Dispatch* on February 17, 1972, we are able to glean something about one inner sanctum of Nixon support. Here is some of what that distinguished journalist said:

One of the most bountiful but least known sources of big campaign money for President Richard M. Nixon is an exclusive club of California businessmen who like to boast that, without their efforts and generosity, he would not be occupying the White House today.

The Lincoln Club of Orange County, made up largely of millionaires, carries not only great political influence but also considerable social prestige in a seaside community where sleek yachts and race horses abound and the wealthy live in walled beachfront compounds with uniformed guards at the gates.

According to former members who now oppose some of its policies, the Lincoln Club has 124 carefully screened members who pay dues of $500 a year. They say its affairs are tightly controlled by a handful of Mr. Nixon's personal friends and Orange County neighbors who sit on the board of directors. Prominent in this inner circle are four or five men who, among them, have raised several million dollars for the Republican Party.

Because many of the members are directors of large corporations throughout the country, the club serves as a finder or point of contact, influence and pressure in obtaining large campaign contributions. The donations—often split into unpretentious $5000 segments—are funneled into the party's national treasury through a variety of convenient committees set up for that purpose, in California and in the East.

All of the club's decisions are made by the 18-man board, which is presided over by the club's perennial president, Arnold O. Beckman, 72 years old, founder of Beckman Instruments, Inc., of Fullerton, and a director of Continental Airlines and half a dozen other industrial and banking corporations.

The leaders of the Lincoln Club may be publicity shy but, in the privacy of their Saturday breakfast meetings, they evidently have very little modesty about what they have done for Mr. Nixon or their importance to his political well-being.

The club's annual dinner on April 9, 1969, was a belated

celebration of Mr. Nixon's election and the minutes of the meeting show Beckman to have been in an expansive mood as he told the Lincoln club members, "without California, Dick Nixon could not have won the election. And it was Orange County, with some help from San Diego County, that provided the plurality for him to win California."

He went on to say that Lincoln club members spearheaded the Nixon-Agnew campaign in Orange County, had raised more than $400,000 to give Mr. Nixon his biggest victory anywhere in the nation—a county plurality of 166,000 votes that represented nearly one-third of the President's nationwide plurality.

Friends like these need protection. They desire national policies that will leave room for expansion of their business interests. They want the burden of taxation to be spread broadly across the population, not concentrated upon those best able to pay. They like a loose labor market with ample unemployment to sap the power of organized labor. They want no dissent against their "best of all possible worlds." And when such dissent shows itself they expect it to be dealt with in vigorous and summary fashion.

Richard Nixon, as President of the United States, has tried to stand loyally by his friends. He has done his part, and then some, to urge, approve, and advocate a practice of mass arrests of both participants and innocent bystanders whenever dissent and protest raise their heads anywhere in the nation.

By his callous comment he all but approved the killing of the four Kent State students by the Ohio National Guard.

He has berated his fellow-citizens who have had to depend on welfare; he has vetoed bill after bill that would have taken large numbers of the unemployed off the welfare rolls by providing jobs for them, and he has done all he could to liquidate the war on poverty which his predecessor conceived and started.

He has demanded ever-increasing military appropriations, thus assuring lush contracts for manufacturers of weaponry. But he has lifted not a finger to reform the wasteful favoritism with which such contracts are arranged by the Pentagon.

Anti-trust actions by the Justice Department have been dismissed or settled out of court on "sweetheart" terms. The quashing of the action that might have prevented International Telephone and Telegraph (ITT) from swallowing Hartford Fire Insurance was only the best publicized example.

The Federal Communications Commission, controlled by Nixon men, decided it "did not have money enough" to go through with an investigation of monopolistic practices by the American Telephone and Telegraph Company. Whereupon, the lone dissenter, Commissioner Nicholas Johnson remarked:

> If an unemployed inner city resident breaks into a coin phone box and takes $3.20 to feed his family he is considered an outcast, his earning potential is cut off entirely, and he is sent to the jailhouse. But if a wealthy telephone company executive succeeds in 'breaking into' 100 million private telephones, taking $3.20 from each subscriber by manipulating the law, he is hailed as a pillar of the business community, his stock goes up, and he's invited to the White House. I think it's about time that 'law and order'—not to mention wage-price control—is applied to rich and poor alike.

The biggest of all customers of AT&T is the Department of Defense. It had an arsenal of facts and 3,200 auditors to analyze and present them—something FCC lacked. Testimony was planned. Then all of a sudden, apparently on orders from "on high" the Department refused to let its expert testify about AT&T rates before the Price Commission.

Mr. Nixon has vetoed bills passed by Congress for hospitals, housing, purer water, training of family doctors and other socially-needed programs on the grounds of "economy."

During the Administration of Richard Nixon and as a result of his deliberate economic policies, interest rates have reached the highest level since the Civil War. Government deposits have been concentrated in the largest of the nation's banks. Money lenders have prospered as never before.

When, at long last, the President came forth with his health plan, it was a bonanza for the insurance companies since it would compel all employers to purchase billions of dollars of indemnity insurance from those companies.

Advisory Committees to government regulatory agencies have been filled with wealthy industrialists and financiers, often with connections with the very industries supposed to be regulated.

As almost a gratuitous insult to consumers, Mr. Nixon set up an 80-man Council for Consumer Affairs in September, 1917. He appointed to the Council only business executives with not a single bona fide consumer representative on it.

The President bestowed a $4 billion-a-year tax concession upon business in the form of fast depreciation allowance. He matched this by asking Congress for a 10% tax credit for industries spending money to buy labor-saving machinery.

When he decided to make his golden promise about re-placing the local property tax with federal funds to support the nation's schools, the only taxes which were being considered were those falling most heavily on the poor, least heavily on the rich, namely sales and value-added taxes.

Despite budget deficits of close to $90 billion in three years of his administration, despite reports of 56% average profits of military contractors Mr. Nixon has never once proposed an excess profits tax to reduce the deficit nor a single measure to close the gaping loopholes in income, gift, and inheritance taxes. A study by the Joint Economic Committee of Congress has estimated that these tax loopholes are costing the Treasury $63 billion a year.

In contrast, Senator Muskie proposed to graduate, and thus make more equitable, the Social Security payroll tax, to close tax loopholes, thereby increasing revenues by some $14 billion a year; and to use this money, in part, to relieve people of limited means of some of their property tax burdens. Under Mr. Nixon the percentage of poor people has *increased* by 5% a year. The poorest fifth of the population receives barely 3% of national income which the richest fifth gets almost half of it.

When President Nixon sprang Game Plan III upon the nation in August, 1971, he froze wages and prices but re-fused to place any limit on profits. He went to Detroit and spoke to a group of industrialists, telling them to no one's surprise, that he strongly believed that bigger profits were the answer to the nation's problems.

Even where the matter of providing the American people with a liveable environment has been concerned, Mr. Nixon has allowed industrialists to keep secret the facts about their pollution and has assured them they would not be made "scape-goats" in any attempts to save the waters of the air.

President Nixon once declaimed: "So critical is the matter of early growth that we must make a national commitment to provide all American children an opportunity for healthful and stimulating development during the first five years of life." But when Congress passed legislation that would have provided exactly that kind of opportunity for that exact age group, Mr. Nixon vetoed it. Here was his chance to perform an act appealing to his wealthy right-wing supporters. He needed, politically, to do that at that time because he had just announced his trip to Communist China. So the children of the United States paid the bill for their President's glamorous fraternization with the rulers of China. So did their mothers who would like to have gone to work with quiet minds as to the safety of their children.

So much for the first of the golden ropes. The second is dependent upon and inextricably intertwined with the first one.

Richard Milhous Nixon has done many acts, as Congressman, as Senator, as Vice-President, as candidate, and as President of the United States. Many of these acts and policies may appear to be dramatically contradictory of one another. Not so.

Whether, from one point of view or another, there has been a golden rope of absolutely loyalty about them. This time loyalty to himself and his own political advancement.

He has consistently done those things best calculated—at any cost to such "principles" as he may have appeared to hold—to win and keep on winning. Not economic conservatism, nor "defense of freedom," nor opposition to government "bureaucracy," nor anti-Communism—none of these has stood the test again Richard Milhous Nixon's one cardinal and unbreakable rule of conduct. That rule is to *win*, whatever it takes to do it.

Most politicians built their careers on the development of a certain fairly clear image themselves as conservatives, progressives, populists, radicals, reactionaries—what not. Most politicians adhere to certain basic principles, calculated, it is true, to accord reasonably well with the political complexion of their constituency. But most politicians have some sheet-anchors of consistent policy to which, however they may vary their course in minor matters, they adhere throughout their careers.

Not so in the strange case of Richard Milhous Nixon.

Armed with his remarkable flexibility and guided by his corps of public relations advisors, sensitive to the results of every poll of public opinion, Richard Milhous Nixon has been able to desert any past policy or expressed view he has ever held in order to protect his own political future. Except for his faithfulness to our first golden rope, it is quite impossible to find in Mr. Nixon's record any principles of government or any policies, social, economic, international or otherwise for which he has clearly stood.

The orchestration of the changes has been perfectly arranged. The dramatic television announcements professionally staged—usually without notice to anyone, including Republican leaders—have been the principal means.

Above all there has been the timing. What was not done —even vigorously opposed—for three years, became "policy" as election time approached.

Numberless groups of American citizens, whose problems festered meanwhile, waited and waited through the years for some attention to be paid by the Nixon administration to their problems.

Then as the time for his "necessary" re-election drew near, some part of the long-needed remedial action was forthcoming, always in terms which completely disregarded the absolutely essential action of Congress with respect to the matter and laid the accolade for the action firmly on the brow of Richard Milhous Nixon himself.

And not only did millions of Americans have to wait—unemployed, neglected, poor—for the "right time" for some relief.

The withdrawal of ground troops from Southeast Asia was scheduled so that the last of them would be coming home just before election day; this, regardless of considerations of peace, war or even military strategy.

Some people wondered why, if the troops could be withdrawn just in time for Mr. Nixon's re-election, they could not be withdrawn much sooner. Others, whose sons would be among the last to leave, wondered whether they might not be exposed to danger while the timing exactly suited the political advantage of Richard Nixon.

When the United Nations failed to do his bidding and keep Nationalist China in membership, the President flew into a rage at the action of the overwhelming majority, then after pledging he would do no such thing, he agreed with Communist China that it could have its own way with Taiwan.

When Mr. Nixon ordered the invasion of Cambodia he said it was because enemy forces were concentrating in the "sanctuaries" along the Vietnam border and preparing to attack U.S. troops. He also said the invasion was to "attack the headquarters for the entire Communist military operation in South Vietnam." But no such headquarters was ever found. Two months later the President had changed his mind about the whole thing. He said then that he had ordered the invasion because the enemy was moving out of the sanctuaries in just the opposite direction, namely, to attack the Cambodian government in Phnom Penh.

Through three long years families in need of low-cost homes they could afford waited. During 1971 the regional offices of

HUD reported very small amounts of funds indeed for the program enacted by Congress to help them out. Then, suddenly in 1972, the Los Angeles Office alone reported to applicants that it had $150 million to spend.

Congressman Anderson of Tennessee, former Nautilus Submarine Commander, declared that President Nixon "has a $3.5 billion campaign slush fund" consisting of money appropriated by Congress but frozen by the White House. These billions, said Anderson "the Nixon campaign strategists will release during the next six months for reasons other than orderly management."

Having resisted every meaningful measure proposed by Congress to put the unemployed back to work, Mr. Nixon suddenly demanded in early 1972 an appropriation of $500 million to relieve the states and localities of some of their rising welfare costs.

Mr. Nixon himself has pointed to the desperate need of the nation for more physicians. Yet he "pocket vetoed" a bill enacted by Congress for the training of more doctors, only to advocate that very thing when he got ready with his own brand of legislation.

Richard Nixon campaigned for president saying he was for abolishing the draft and having a volunteer army—only to vent considerable spleen on Congress for failing promptly to renew the draft for a two-year period.

Before his election as President, Mr. Nixon was a principal advocate of federal union with the democratic nations of the Atlantic basin. Once in office he gave no encouragement to any such movement. Instead he focused his foreign policy upon relations with China and Russia.

Having charged the Congress with "financial irresponsibility" and "causing inflation" by exceeding his budget estimates for certain programs for small amounts, Richard Nixon has won, hands-down, the undisputed title of champion deficit spender of all time.

Mr. Nixon fought bitterly against the proposal in Congress to finance political campaigns by a $1 check-off of income tax payments. He fought it, that is to say, until it was modified so it would not affect his own personal re-election campaign. Then he signed the bill.

Reading the signs of farmer opinion, the President changed his plans about the Department of Agriculture three times. First he proposed to abolish it and merge its functions with those of three other departments. Then he reversed that position and declared he would retain the Department—this to help get Earl Butz confirmed as Secretary of Agriculture. The Butz appointment accomplished, the plan was again changed. The USDA would be allowed to stand but all its functions "not directly affecting farming," would be transferred to other departments. Among the agencies he proposed to take out of the Department were the Farmers' Home Administration and the Rural Electrification Administration. The aroused storms of protest from rural America.

A cartoon, appearing in the *Los Angeles Times* for December 15, 1971, depicted two identical figures of President Nixon, facing one another. The caption read: "I will not accept wage and price controls. I will not raise the price of gold. I will not devalue the dollar." And in all cases the word "not" was crossed out.

A companion cartoon might have shown Richard Nixon accusing those opposed to him of being "knowing or unknowing tools of Communism," and another one toasting the health of the most powerful Communist leaders in the world.

Yes. Richard Milhous Nixon does, at any given time, what seems best for Richard Milhous Nixon.

When he presented his budget for fiscal 1973, he warned Congress that it must authorize no additional spending programs, however badly needed, except only those set forth in the budget message. To do so would be further evidence of "financial irresponsibility."

But Mr. Nixon himself included in that same budget message a golden promise to the older people of the country calculated to cost some $1.5 billion. And he followed a few days later with his proposal for school financing. As originally set forth by the President that proposal could involve an outlay of some $50 billion of federal funds.

The promise to the nation's senior citizens was that Mr. Nixon would recommend to Congress that older people dependent upon Medicare be no longer required to pay the monthly charge of $5.60—later $5.80—for Part B, the doctor's care part of the program.

Mr. Nixon did not explain how he proposed to finance his promised $1.5 billion reduction in income to the Medicare program. The National Council of Senior Citizens was interested and concerned. Its president, Nelson Cruikshank, found on investigation that current income to the Medicare Fund was $2.6 billion, consisting of the monthly payments of $1.5 billion from the beneficiaries and $1.1 billion from general revenues of the Federal Government. Outpayments from the fund amounted to $2.5 billion, leaving a small surplus.

But Cruikshank also found by careful study of the budget that the President had made no provision at all for compensating the Medicare Fund for the $1.5 loss involved in the attractive promise. More than that he found that the President was actually proposing to withdraw from Medicare the contribution from general revenues, thus throwing the entire burden back onto the payroll tax.

Mr. Cruikshank observed, in testimony to the Senate Finance Committee, that: "The obvious conclusion is that the loss must be made up either by raiding one of the other Social Security trust funds or by increasing the payroll tax."

President Nixon's promise to the older people was, to say the least, not all it appeared to be. For he conveniently failed to tell the senior citizens that they and others least able to do so would pay the bill for whatever relief "he" proposed to give them. They and their sons and daughters would pay that bill either through a weakening of another part of their Social Security system, or by increases in the regressive payroll taxes.

Net effect of the President's proposal was to shift, again, part of the tax burden from the progressive income tax based on ability to pay, to the payroll tax which falls with equal weight upon rich and poor alike.

The National Council of Senior Citizens summed it all up in a sentence: "President Nixon is playing games with the nation's elderly."

These were not the only games the President was playing or would play in his passionate drive for re-election.

What would come next, no one—perhaps not even Mr. Nixon himself—could predict. Of only one thing could the nation be certain. Whatever new promise could be made by Richard Milhous Nixon which would attract votes for his re-election—that promise he would not hesitate to make. He would make it however distant its practical realization might be. He would make it regardless of its violation of his own solemn warnings or commitments. And there would always be the Congress or the Courts to blame when his promises were not fulfilled.

But what he would not do was to deal with the root problem, the root injustice, in the American economy, the inexcusable and growing gap between the rich and the poor of our country.

A really just tax system could perhaps help most to mitigate this injustice. Richard Nixon's policies have made our tax system more inequitable than it was when he took office. And he proposes now with a sales tax to make it even more so. An improved Social Security system could help greatly. Mr. Nixon proposes instead to weaken it. A massive drive to change the slums of inner cities into decent places for people to raise their children could strike the blow most needed against the cycle of poverty. Nothing in the Nixon program contemplates anything approaching such a drive. A strengthening of farmer's cooperatives and a curb on the invasion of agriculture by giant corporations could help raise farmer income. Richard Nixon only proposes to throw competitive agriculture into a so-called "free market" dominated by monopolies. Even if Mr. Nixon would vigorously push his own welfare reform program, inadequate as it is, it would help some. Most important of all, from the point of view of human dignity, would be a real drive to put our unemployed to work at the jobs our society so desperately needs to have done. President Nixon has vetoed such programs when enacted by the Congress.

Only as the problems of the ghettos, the barrios and the decaying rural areas are relieved can we honestly measure progress for our country. It is there in those places and in what happens to them that the Nixon record must be judged. The record speaks for itself.

19. "REELECT THE PRESIDENT"

The Nixon record did speak for itself—but apparently not loudly enough or to enough people who cared. Most of the nation was bent on enjoying what was called "the good life" and really didn't want to be bothered.

So on November 7, 1972, Richard Milhous Nixon was re-elected President of the United States by one of the largest majorities, of those voting, in the nation's history.

Why did this happen?

Some of the reasons were evident enough. Others only came to light as a few courageous newspapers began to dig out the amazing and disheartening facts about the operations of the

White House "palace guard" and the Committee to Re-elect the President.

Mr. Nixon, as the incumbent president had little trouble winning every Republican primary. True he had opposition— from California Representative Paul McCloskey on the anti-war left and from Ohio Congressman John Ashbrook on the right. But in New Hampshire McCloskey polled only 20% of the vote and shortly thereafter dropped out of the race for lack of funds. Ashbrook made an even poorer showing in the primaries which he entered. Many of the votes that might have gone to him were being cast for Right Winger John Schmitz, the candidate of the American Independent Party, which the John Birch Society supported.

But while the Republicans were going their customary monolithic way, the Democrats were also running true to form. Their primaries were crowded with candidates and surprise after surprise was taking place.

As late as February the Gallup Poll had shown Senator Muskie of Maine in the lead with 29%, followed by Senators Kennedy and Humphrey with 24% and 23% respectively. Senator George McGovern of South Dakota trailed with an apparently hopeless 5%. Some polls were also showing Muskie running neck-and-neck with Nixon, should they face each other in the November election. Of this, we may be sure, the White House took careful and concerned note.

It was not long till the picture began to change, first in New Hampshire. There, a victory for Senator Muskie was regarded as certain and predictions had been for a 60% to 75% vote for him. But shortly before the primary the anti-Muskie and ultra-conservative Manchester *Union-Leader* published a story alleging that in a speech in Florida Senator Muskie had made derogatory remarks about French Canadians, who constitute a considerable bloc of New Hampshire voters. He was reported to have referred to them as "Canucks," a term they deeply resented. No record of such a statement could then be found, nor has it ever been. Senator Muskie bitterly and somewhat tearfully denounced and denied that he had ever said such a thing. But the damage had been done, and when the votes were counted Muskie received only 48%, a severe setback and a stunning surprise. Equally surprising was the strong showing of McGovern, who gained some 36% of the total vote. Since Muskie was the potential Democratic candidate most feared by the White House and

McGovern the least feared, New Hampshire results were, no doubt, welcome there.

Florida's primary followed. Governor Wallace of Alabama was predicted to win, largely because of his vigorous and flamboyant opposition to the busing of school children. He did win with some 42% of the vote—even more than expected. The contest was for second place. That was captured not by the supposed "front runner" Muskie, but by Hubert Humphrey, with Senator Jackson of Washington, the only outspoken Democratic "hawk" candidate in third place. Muskie trailed badly with less than 10%. One reason for his poor showing was circulation of a letter, accusing Senators Humphrey and Jackson of sexual immorality, written, apparently on Senator Muskie's stationery. Again, Muskie denied authorship of any such letter. But the damage had been done. By whom?

The Wisconsin primary became, therefore, a "must win" for Muskie if he was to have any chance of recovering his front-runner position. But in a result surprising to almost everyone—except perhaps to the White House—McGovern received 30% of the vote, leading Wallace with 22%, Humphrey with 21% and Muskie with only 10%. This was in a state with a considerable Polish population, a factor supposedly very favorable to the second-generation Muskie.

A remarkably large number of registered Republicans crossed party lines and voted in the Democratic primary instead of their own, a practice permitted under Wisconsin election law. Studies of precinct results showed that Senator McGovern had been the recipient of the largest segment of this "cross-over" vote. Why had Republicans done this? Out of ardent support of Senator McGovern? Or for some other reason?

After Wisconsin it was mostly downhill for McGovern. However, he won, or ran well in primary after primary. He had an intensely loyal following, composed in part of younger people who had been Eugene McCarthy's most ardent supporters in 1968.

For Senator Muskie it was a different story. After poor showings in several more primaries he announced he would actively campaign in no more of them.

On May 15 a tragic event took place in Laurel, Maryland which may have had crucial bearing on the outcome of the 1972 presidential election. A gunman shot Governor George

Wallace four times, wounding him critically. Repeated surgery failed to relieve a paralysis of the entire lower portion of his body which the bullets had caused. On the very next day he won 51% of the primary vote in Michigan and some 37% in Maryland, to lead the field there, giving him second place to McGovern in number of convention delegates. But his active campaigning days were at an end. Inevitably he became a less important factor in the presidential race.

No one, probably not even Governor Wallace, had believed it possible that he could be nominated as the Democratic candidate, though this was his avowed objective, but there had remained the possibility that he might once again run as an independent. Had he done so, the outcome of the 1972 election might—just might—have been different. For Wallace would almost certainly have carried a number of Southern states, every one of which went into the Nixon column. And in the North and West most of the Wallace vote, perhaps three-fourths of it, would have come from people who voted for Nixon.

Thus, once again, the good political fortune of Richard Milhous Nixon held. The murders of the Kennedy brothers had removed his two most formidable Democratic opponents. The murder of Martin Luther King removed an eloquent anti-Nixon voice. And the crippling of Governor Wallace smoothed measurably Mr. Nixon's re-election path.

The biggest Democratic primary prize was California's 271 delegate votes in the Convention. On winning this primary rested the remaining hopes of Hubert Humphrey for another try at the presidency. He campaigned with his usual vigor and effectiveness, and he openly attacked McGovern. He charged that McGovern's proposal to reduce military expenditures would cost many Californians their jobs. And, with even greater effect he held up to ridicule statements Senator McGovern had made to the effect that the "welfare mess" could be cleaned up by providing every American with a $1000 grant or tax credit. However possible mathematically such a reallocation of the tax burden might have been, the manner in which McGovern had presented his proposal had sounded like "pie in the sky" and had struck fear in the pocketbooks not only of wealthy but of middle-income taxpayers.

The polls, even as late as a week or two before the primaries were giving McGovern a 20 point lead over Humphrey. When the votes were counted that lead had shrunk to five points only. McGovern did gain California's 271 votes after some bitter maneuvering in the Convention, but the California primary contest had provided the Nixon campaign with invaluable propaganda material out of the mouth of Hubert H. Humphrey himself.

Reform of Democratic Party convention procedures, resulting from the recommendations of a committee headed by Senator McGovern, brought about what was probably the most genuinely democratic (with small D) convention in the nation's history. In the opinion of columnist D. J. R. Bruckner, writing for the *Los Angeles Times*, the delegates to the 1972 Democratic convention "were a good deal more careful, reasonable, compromising, courteous—if you will professional—than most of the old pros." Bruckner's view was widely shared.

But, while McGovern won the nomination easily and his forces controlled the convention from beginning to end, this was not without its price.

First, McGovern needed "the old pros," some of them, at least, and he never received enthusiastic backing from many of them. The process of delegate selection had eliminated many of them. In one California caucus, for example, the mayor of the largest city in the district was defeated in the caucus vote, despite his expression of all-out support for the candidate.

As the campaign progressed McGovern's ardent supporters eliminated a lot more "old pro" support which he might have had. For example, a highly respected, capable, and progressive California assemblyman offered his and his organization's support, only to be told that it was not needed and further that the McGovern organization would name its own district coordinators.

Indeed there was, in the McGovern campaign, especially at local levels, an attitude that amounted to: "We'd rather keep our Senator McGovern as far out in the left wing as we like to see him than have him beat Richard Nixon." From this point of view, McGovern's visits to Mayor Daley and Lyndon Johnson were regarded with dismay, and many a once-enthusiastic young worker lost the desire to put much effort into the campaign after all.

In other ways, the largely exemplary Democratic Convention no doubt cost McGovern millions of votes. The television cameras focused repeatedly on persons with long hair, very young persons, and advocates of "far-out" causes. Among the last named were the "gays." These homosexual activists were equipped, by whom no one at the time guessed, with large

"McGovern" badges. Middle America was somewhat more afraid of McGovern than it had been before.

Some of the nation's biggest and best-run labor unions endorsed Senator McGovern and provided valuable support to his campaign. The Teamsters on the other hand, perhaps in exchange for the parole of Jimmie Hoffa and the failure to prosecute the son of the union's president, contributed an estimated "hundreds of thousands of dollars" to the Nixon campaign chest. Officially, the AFL-CIO was neutral—between Richard Nixon, with a lifelong anti-labor record, and McGovern, against whom one or two "wrong" votes from labor's point of view might be charged. What probably rankled most, however, both among the labor leaders and the "old pros," was their inability to exercise the degree of control over the Democratic Convention to which they had, through the years, become accustomed.

The Republican Convention was planned down to the finest detail to contrast with the Democratic one. No "long-hairs" and few Black or Chicano people were in attendance. The delegates were well dressed—and indeed well heeled. Richard Nixon was nominated by acclamation. Representative McCloskey was denied even his own negative vote.

Furthermore Mr. Nixon's acceptance speech was an appeal to fear—fear on the part of middle and traditional America of the young, the poor, the "far out" and above all the Democratic Party. It was surprisingly devoid of pointing with pride to the accomplishments of his administration. It was instead a warning to the "great silent-and-comfortable majority" to rally 'round the Nixon standard lest the good life they were enjoying be swept away in a tide of left-wing extremism and "welfare chiseling."

Thus the lines were drawn. The White House and the Committee to Re-elect the President had the exact Democratic candidate they had most hoped for—the one they had decided would be easiest to beat. The stage was set for one of the cleverest—and most foul—campaigns in American history.

From beginning to end the polls favored the re-election of Mr. Nixon. A poll taken shortly after the Democratic convention showed McGovern's percentage *down*, not up as might have been expected. There were times during the campaign when the Senator made small gains, but they were limited to one or two percentage points. They were few and far between.

In fact, Senator McGovern was never able to catch on with

a majority of voters. He was never able to convince them that, if elected, he could "do the job." His sterling, sincerely religious character, so clearly evident in his work in the Senate and in his campaign against hunger, awakened, for reasons difficult to understand, little response. He went up and down the country emphasizing the problems and concerns of the people: the immoral war still raging in Southeast Asia, four years after Nixon's promise that he had a secret formula for ending it; the tragedy of the unemployed; the progressive destruction of the environment; the blight of our inner cities; the plight of the poor and the progressive destruction of the family farm and with it the invaluable and irreplaceable culture of rural America.

He repeatedly asserted that billions of dollars could be saved by cutting the fat out of the Pentagon budget, and that those billions should be used to employ people to clean the environment, to build mass transportation systems, to rehabilitate the core cities. He was right. Unfortunately not many people were listening.

McGovern campaigned feverishly. So did many of his supporters.

The President did not. He was too busy with affairs of state. He was above the battle, just as the very name of his campaign committee signified. For it was not the Republican National Committee, it was the Committee to Re-elect the President, a title implying quite clearly that the President had a certain monarchical right to his position and that it would be an act somewhat less than patriotic to deny him "four more years."

Even mild criticism of Mr. Nixon's conduct of the war or his proposals for a settlement of it was labeled, quite specifically by Mr. Haldeman on the "Today" show, as "consciously aiding the enemy," in other words a mild form of treason.

True, the President did make an occasional foray into the political hustings. He re-emphasized the trust of his administration by declaring to a select group of oil millionaires at John Connally's Texas ranch that the depletion allowance, far from relieving them of too much of their taxes, was not as big as it ought to be.

And on Mr. Nixon's behalf a very considerable campaign was being carried on. Billions of letters were mailed to citizens of every political persuasion at a cost no one could estimate. Republican speakers in California based their entire appeal on the charge that McGovern's election would mean the loss of untold numbers of jobs in so-called "defense" industries. High school audiences asked McGovern speakers if they could promise to preserve their father's jobs in case of McGovern's election. Little did they suspect that once re-elected Mr. Nixon would close down naval and other military installations in many parts of the country, shifting them in most cases from cities like San Francisco and Boston, whose citizens had voted against Richard Nixon, to places like San Diego and the South which had loyally supported him. Restaurant waitresses declared in strident tones that they would move out of the country if McGovern were elected because the economy would be sure to collapse.

Nor did pro-Nixon forces fail to contend that his visits to China and Russia, the other two "great powers" had laid the basis for a more peaceful world, nor that the President was "winding down the war" and that McGovern's election would leave our prisoners of war stranded in North Vietnam's prison camps. And ever and always there was the underlying theme of fear—fear of McGovern.

There were, indeed, grounds for such fear. Not certainly, the ones most frequently alleged by the Committee to Re-elect the President. But there were, throughout the campaign, mistakes and blunders on McGovern's part which severely hurt his chances. There was his assertion of "1000%" support of Senator Eagleton, which was to be repudiated only a few days later by asking him to step down as candidate for vice-president. There was the replacement of the invaluable Lawrence O'Brien with the inept Mrs. Jean Westwood as chairman of the Democratic National Committee. There were the confused, almost contradictory statements about Pierre Salinger's ill-fated meeting with the North Vietnamese in Paris. And there was, it is true, a certain amount of changing of the McGovern emphasis, if not the McGovern mind, as he sought to strike upon issues that would at last arouse the people.

Indeed the idea that "McGovern changes his mind too much" became a major influence in the election. The media emphasized this repeatedly, yet failed, inexplicably, to point out the 180-degree changes of course in Mr. Nixon's very actions, such as his embracing of the two greatest Communist powers on earth after a career based on accusations that his opponents were "soft on Communism."

Subtly what seems to have been happening was that a psychology was developing to the effect that the only really

288

"respectable" thing a well-placed citizen could do was to "re-elect the President". Faithfully following the polls, a majority of the people and the overwhelming majority of the press jumped on the bandwagon. Except for the *New York Times* and a few other courageous journals, the newspapers endorsed Mr. Nixon for re-election. Even the *Los Angeles Times* did so, only to become one of the second or third biggest thorns in his vulnerable side just days after his re-election.

Late in October, on the very eve of the election, Henry Kissinger appeared on television to announce to the nation that his peace negotiations had been successful and that except for the working out of a few minor details of no real consequence "peace was at hand."

The plain fact that it wasn't at hand at all never emerged until after Richard Nixon had been safely re-elected. In vain the North Vietnamese called for the signing on October 31 of the agreement worked out with Dr. Kissinger. The war went on.

Was Henry Kissinger telling the truth, based on his own knowledge? Or was he deliberately misleading the nation in order to gain votes for his chief?

Probably the world will never know. It may well be that, for all he knew at the time, Dr. Kissinger was telling the truth and did believe that only minor matters stood in the way of a cease-fire in October 1972. But if this is the case, then the only possible explanation for the fact that Dr. Kissinger's peace agreement did not end the war is that it was vetoed by higher authority. There was only one higher authority than Dr. Kissinger in American foreign affairs. Richard Nixon.

In any case the Kissinger announcement was worth millions of votes for the re-election of the President, whether or not it was a true statement as it turned out not to be.

To the casual observer of political affairs it would appear that Mr. Nixon and the Committee to Re-elect the President had enough going for them so that the history of the campaign of 1972 could have been ended at this point.

But such, at least in the Committee's opinion, and perhaps, indeed, in the opinion of Richard Nixon himself, was not the case.

There was a lot more to that campaign than appeared, at the time, on the surface.

What the campaign carried on by the Committee to Re-elect the President amounted to was nothing less than an attempt to destroy the Democratic Party as an effective force in American political life. Millions of dollars and every means, fair or foul, were devoted to that enterprise.

Senator Muskie never made a slurring statement about French Canadians, nor referred to them as "Canucks". The barefaced lie that he did so was fed to the Manchester, New Hampshire *Union-Leader* by someone who was gleefully taking part in the Committee's department of "dirty tricks." Federal investigators told *The Washington Post* that this "department" was directed by special counsel to the President, Charles Colson, assisted by later-to-be convicted Watergate conspirator E. Howard Hunt.

Very early in the campaign Donald H. Segretti was hired by Dwight L. Chapin, assistant to Robert Haldeman and Mr. Nixon's appointment secretary, to perform certain services in the campaign. Segretti was paid "some $30,000 to $40,000" out of campaign funds of the Committee to Re-elect the President by Herbert W. Kalmbach, Mr. Nixon's personal attorney. This, according to Kalmbach's own statement to the F.B.I., Kalmbach said he did not know what Segretti was supposed to do. But a Florida grand jury found out and in May 1973 Segretti was indicted on charges of having distributed literature calculated to sabotage the March 1972 Florida Democratic primary. A principal item in that "literature" was the letter forged on Senator Muskie's stationery accusing Senator Jackson of homosexuality and Senator Humphrey of having had a prostitute in his automobile. The actual forging was widely reported to have been done in the White House itself. Dwight Chapin resigned his position there in March 1973. Informed of the indictment, Senator Jackson asked, bitterly, why it had taken 14 months for the Justice Department to move on the case. He called on the Senate committee to determine whether the U.S. Attorney's office had been instructed by "someone higher up" to delay action. Questioned by reporters the White House refused to say why Kalmbach had paid Segretti. But perhaps one purpose, in addition to his Florida job, was to enable Segretti to volunteer his "services" in the McGovern campaign—a thing he attempted more than once to do!

Labor leaders and other politically important figures received imperious and sometimes insulting telephone calls, purporting to come from leaders in the Democratic campaign —but which no one in the Democratic organization ever made.

Channel 2 News broadcasts on May 14, 1973 quoted Mr. Nixon's deposed White House Counsel John W. Dean to the effect that he had helped to carry out wiretapping on anti-war groups during the Democratic Convention. And there were no denials of *Time* Magazine reports that White House Counsel Charles Colson had recruited young men to pose as homosexuals and to appear prominently at the Democratic Convention wearing huge McGovern buttons.

All of which was a long time coming out. And all of which took place before the events of the night of June 17, 1972.

On that now fateful night five men, James W. McCord, security officer for the Committee to Re-elect the President, and four Miami Cubans, were arrested in the offices of the Democratic National Committee in the Watergate Hotel in Washington D.C. They had in their pockets some 53 new $100 bills. They were equipped with rubber gloves and possessed devices for tapping telephones and installing "bugging" devices in the Democratic offices. They were charged with second-degree burglary.

This was not the first such attempt. Sometime previously a tap had been placed on the telephone of R. Spencer Oliver, executive director of the National Association of State Democratic Chairmen. The fruits of that telephone tap had been carried for several weeks to the Committee to Re-elect the President. They had given direct and valuable information about the relative strength of various Democratic candidates, and their vulnerable points as well, as reported to Oliver by the state chairmen.

Much more might have been learned had the June 17 break-in gone undetected. Some of the information might have been used for blackmail. In any case Democratic strategy, quarrels, plans and finances would have been an open book to the Nixon campaign.

Larry O'Brien, former Democratic National Committee Chairman, filed a $1 million damage suit against the Committee to Re-elect the President.

Some people, most of them Democrats, naturally, were outraged.

Some of the news reporters were also.

But White House press secretary Ziegler's official "comment" was "I'm not going to comment on a third-rate burglary attempt." President Nixon simply stated: "The White House has had no involvement whatever in this particular incident."

John Mitchell, former Attorney General and at the time Mr. Nixon's campaign manager, called the Democrat's lawsuit "another example of sheer demagoguery".

Such attempts to pass the whole sordid matter off as a mere "incident" caused respected columnist Joseph Kraft to comment in the *Los Angeles Times* of June 27 that "the absence of even an attempt to make a moral case points up the true connection between the Republican chiefs and the Watergate affair. The central fact is that the President and his campaign manager have set a tone that positively encourages dirty work by low-level operators."

Kraft went on to point out that Mitchell had claimed the virtually unlimited right as Attorney General to "bug" citizens of the United States, that he had appointed as head of the criminal division of the Justice Department a man who had almost immediately had to retire because he was involved in a Texas scandal involving fraud and bribery, and that, as Campaign Manager he had refused to report the names of his contributors to the campaign fund to re-elect Richard Nixon.

And then, with the vision of a prophet, Joseph Kraft wrote: "So there is a connection, albeit indirect, and also a lesson. Unless the President and Mitchell clean up their own operations, they are going to pay a price. They will find that they cannot get away with keeping the President above the battle. They will see themselves trapped in the miasma of disbelief and suspicion which, after almost four years of the Nixon Administration, is thicker than ever."

Less than a year after he wrote that column Joseph Kraft could, had he so desired, have written the biggest "I told you so" story in the history of the United States.

For no such "clean up" as he called for was to take place.

For reasons almost impossible to understand Watergate had little effect on the outcome of the November 1972 election. All through the months that followed it the references were to the "Watergate caper." The nation's capacity for moral outrage was, apparently, blunted by the material good life that many of us were leading. After all, a majority of the good people of the country were "afraid of McGovern," afraid of a thoroughly good man, a devotedly religious man, a man unselfishly devoted to the relief of suffering, a man almost poor in worldly goods.

The Committee to Re-elect the President went on its merry way collecting an estimated $60 million from the richest of the rich—a cool million of it from one oil tycoon, another half-million from an insurance magnate.

None of the huge contributions which were received before the April 7 date, when the new campaign spending law became effective, were reported to the nation, although every Democratic candidate except Jackson and Mills had faithfully done so.

John Gardner's Common Cause organization brought suit for violation of the *old* campaign spending law and finally got an admission from the Committee to Re-elect the President that it had been in violation of the law. But then, Common Cause agreed to a consent decree whereby the Nixon committee disclosed all contributions of $100 or more which had been made between January 1 and March 9, 1972. Whatever had been collected before January or between March 9 and April 7 remained anonymous.

Of the $60 million which financed the most expensive purchase of the Presidency in history somewhere between $1 and $2 million—no one really knows for the records were destroyed—was devoted in cold cash to the kind of espionage, sabotage and defamation operations we have just briefly described. This estimate of the untraceable and unreported cash contributed and spent came from none other than Hugh Sloan, one-time treasurer of the Committee to Re-elect the President in sworn testimony in the continuing suit brought by Common Cause.

Senator McGovern and his organization were no "pikers" themselves when it came to raising money. But it came from millions of people and in comparatively small amounts in almost all cases. All of it was faithfully reported. But it was no match for the Nixon millions.

It may be of interest to the reader that the Prime Minister of Great Britain is limited by law to an expenditure of no more than $3,000 in seeking re-election. A reason no doubt why British politics is clean and political corruption practically unknown in that country.

The British government is not for sale.

November 7 came and with it the re-election of Richard Milhous Nixon to a second term. He received slightly more than 60% of the vote to 38% for McGovern and a little more than 1% for right-winger John Schmitz. Furthermore McGovern carried only two states, Massachusetts and the District of Columbia. All the rest went to Nixon.

The Committee to Re-elect the President—not to say Mr. Nixon himself—hailed the "landslide" victory.

Not so the Republican Party.

For it was the strangest "landslide" in the nation's history. Never before had a president been elected by anything remotely resembling Mr. Nixon's margin without carrying into office with him other members of his own party. In 1936 for example, when Franklin Roosevelt lost only Maine and Vermont, his party gained, net, nine Senate and 14 House seats. In 1964 when Lyndon Johnson beat Barry Goldwater by the biggest margin in history the Democrats gained, net, 37 House seats and one Senate seat. They already had 67!

But in 1972 this kind of result did not take place. On the contrary the Democrats made net gains in both the Senate and the state houses and lost only a handful of House seats.

The reason was not far to seek. It was inherent in the very name of the triumphant "Committee to Re-elect the President." It was not a committee to promote election of Republican candidates. That was left to a comparatively poorly financed Republican National Committee. The business of the Committee to Re-elect the President was to re-elect Richard Milhous Nixon by whatever means and at whatever sacrifice of other Republican candidates. In three states, especially, the race for the Senate was very close. These were Colorado, Delaware and Iowa. In all three cases the Republican candidates, all of them incumbents and all faithful supporters of Richard Nixon, appealed to the President for some evidence of support. No such support, not even a letter, was forthcoming. And the Democrats won all three seats.

Understandably enough, Richard Nixon claimed the outcome of the election as a "mandate" for his policies. In fact, he claimed it for considerably more than that, as we shall see in following chapters.

But the "mandate" does deserve some analysis, for the fact is that it rode on the votes of almost exactly one-third of the American voters. Mr. Nixon received a little more than 60% of votes *cast*. But only 55% of the eligible voters took the trouble to vote at all. Those who could not bring themselves to vote for either candidate stayed home in droves, 45% of them, and 60% of 55% is 33%.

In the election of 1972 two-thirds of the American people did not vote for Richard Nixon.

20. "THE ARROGANCE OF POWER"

During the course of the campaign of 1972 Congressman John Schmitz, American Party candidate for president expressed his opinion that President Nixon had moved the country closer to a totalitarian state in four years than had any president in his lifetime. He joined Henry Steele Commager in that political scientist's concern for the future of Constitutional government in the United States, which concern was discussed in Chapter 17.

But probably neither Schmitz, Commager nor, certainly, a majority of the voters realized how right was their concern.

Mr. Nixon put some clear handwriting on the wall during the course of the campaign itself. He did it in his customarily deft and clever way.

In September Mr. Nixon viewed with alarm the mounting deficits of which he himself had been the principal author and demanded of Congress passage of a "spending ceiling" bill. The appeal of such a proposal to the burdened taxpayers of the country was evident, but Mr. Nixon's proposal went far beyond the imposition of a ceiling on government spending. The bill, if enacted, would have given to Richard Milhous Nixon the unlimited power to curtail as much as he liked, or even to abolish by arbitrary executive order, any program enacted into law by the Congress of the United States. Administration spokesmen conceded to Congressional committees that, under the proposal, Mr. Nixon would have power to reduce social security payments or even the salaries and allowances of members of Congress. A more blatant attempt to take from Congress its most fundamental constitutional power—control of the nation's purse—could hardly have been conceived.

A supine majority of the House of Representatives, unable apparently to read letters on the wall a foot high, passed Mr. Nixon's bill. Fortunately for the United States Constitution and for the freedom of the American people the Senate refused to go along and defeated the bill. Perhaps the Senate majority remembered that their forefathers once fought a Revolutionary

War to prevent their descendents from ever having to suffer under the arbitrary, unchecked and unbalanced rule of a monarch, particularly a monarch who controlled the nation's purse strings.

These events should have been, but apparently were not, adequate signals to the country of what was to come in case Mr. Nixon was re-elected.

Far more subtly Richard Nixon sent up repeatedly during the campaign another signal. This was his oft-intoned statement that if he was re-elected there would be no increase in taxes during the ensuing four years.

Just how Richard Nixon or anyone else could anticipate what was to take place, economically, in the nation four years hence was, of course, not gone into. The evident demagoguery of the appeal was likewise largely overlooked and the Democrats, instead of calling the Nixon promise by its right name, sought all too often simply to echo the promise. No one, at least no one within hearing of many voters, pointed out that taxation is the basic way of holding down inflation. And Mr. Nixon was, at the same time, promising to do that.

The "no tax increase" promise was of basic importance to Richard Nixon's plans, as we shall see.

A third smoke signal was sent up from the Nixon camp. It was the politically astute attack of Mr. Nixon on the busing of school children which the courts of the nation were ordering in consonance with the law as they interpreted it. There was little doubt that in some cities—notably Detroit, where Governor Wallace had piled up so surprisingly large a protest vote—the courts had required extreme busing programs, nor that parents were generally, and justifiably, up in arms when their children were sent long distances to inferior schools. Furthermore some minorities, notably the Mexican-American one, actually preferred 'their own" neighborhood schools to integrated ones outside their communities.

Politically, Mr. Nixon was on good ground, but implicit in his attacks was a willingness to have his way in defiance of the nation's judiciary.

November 7 came and with it "the mandate." The most logical interpretation of such mandate as a third of the nation's voters might have given was that it meant approval of the past actions and policies of the administration. Even this was certainly tempered by the fact that the "mandate" had stopped at the White House steps and had been accompanied by an equal "mandate" to the Democratic Congress to hold Mr. Nixon in reasonable check.

But Richard Milhous Nixon and his then faceless and unquestioningly loyal White House counsels, advisors and staff had a very different view of the mandate.

They interpreted it to mean that Richard Milhous Nixon was now, in his second term, to rule the nation exactly as he pleased and without hindrance from anyone.

Every re-elected president in memory has, during the early months of his second term, sought the cooperation of the Congress and assumed an attitude of relaxed confidence. Every other re-elected president has sought to conciliate those he has defeated and in his second and last term to unite the nation in a way that he could not do while still a partisan candidate for re-election.

Not so Richard Milhous Nixon.

Quite the contrary.

He would show the Congress, the courts, the nation, foreign governments and those recalcitrant little brown people of Southeast Asia that to cross Richard Nixon was a thing that simply could not safely be done on planet earth.

He proceeded with methodical precision to make his intentions perfectly clear.

First, he demanded letters of resignation, not only from his cabinet members as is more or less customary as presidents begin second terms, but from a vast number of number two, three and four persons in the executive department. Thus everyone who occupied any position of consequence in the executive branch was beholden to Richard Nixon and to him alone for the continuance of their careers and livelihod. This was an essential part of a program of "housecleaning," of "tightening up the team" for what lay ahead. It was, we may believe from what *did* lie ahead, a means of making sure that there were no dissident voices around the government and also no one not appropriately subservient to the will of "The President."

There were exceptions to the rule about resignations. Some people were fired outright, most notably the deeply respected Father Theodore M. Hesburgh, president of Notre Dame University and chairman of the U.S. Commission on Civil Rights, to which position he had been appointed by President Eisenhower.

With a large segment of the Roman Catholic vote safely

in his pocket Mr. Nixon could now afford to get rid of Dr. Hesburgh. For, two years before, Father Hesburgh had said that "the quality of leadership exercised by the President" was a crucial factor in achieving quiet on the campuses, national unity, and racial justice, the last of which was, and is, the principal objective of the Commission's work. Father Hesburgh went further and called the uproar over school busing "the most phoney issue in the country." He wrote that "we must be willing to shuck the status quo when it is retrogressive or unjust."

Obviously Father Hesburgh's moral leadership was the last thing that was appropriate to Mr. Nixon's plans. The Reverend Billy Graham fit in much better, since that evangelist faithfully endorsed almost anything Mr. Nixon did and refrained from suggestions that moral leadership had anything to do with the American presidency.

Father Hesburgh was not alone. When the first wave of housecleaning had subsided, only two of Mr. Nixon's original cabinet remained in office and six top Justice Department officials had lost their jobs, though Richard Kleindienst was retained as Attorney General. It was notable that in almost every case the official who was fired had been either "too independent" or "too liberal" and his replacement was either more conservative or less well-known and hence more likely to follow orders without question.

Long-time career people in the Department of Agriculture confided in hushed whispers that never in their experience had the activities and points of view of Department personnel been so completely subjected to the will of the White House. "We hardly dare to breathe. Everybody is afraid."

Gradually, and as it turned out quite temporarily, the government was restaffed, though even in these early weeks of the new dispensation there was evident reluctance on the part of really able people to accept positions in the Nixon Administration. How long would it be before their resignations might be asked for? Furthermore the odor of Watergate somehow refused to go away.

As for those who did accept appointment there was an evident pattern. Few of them were people of political experience. Fewer still had any kind of constituency of their own. Peter Brennan, the new Secretary of Labor, who always carried a hand gun, was a rare exception. He was head of New York City Building Trades. With the exception of Henry Kissinger none of the new appointees had backgrounds of any considerable distinction in fields of public service. All therefore owed their positions not to their own qualifications, but to their appointments by Mr. Nixon.

With respect to the "Health" part of the Department of Health, Education, and Welfare, the American Public Health Association complained loudly that health professionals were being replaced by political appointees and that instead of professionalization of health services, Mr. Nixon was going in for a "politicalization."

It was evident that the new "team" would speak with one voice and that that voice would be that of Richard Milhous Nixon. The people who were being hired were unlikely to deviate by thought, word, or deed from the wishes of "the President."

As we have observed in previous chapters, Mr. Nixon had made very considerable progress in the direction of downgrading the Cabinet during his first term. His White House cadre—Haldeman, Ehrlichman, Dean, Ziegler, Klein, Whitehead, Colson, Chapin, Kissinger et al.—were firmly installed, well disciplined and, in their capacity of White House staff, beyond the reach of Congressional or any other kind of inquiry. Except for Dr. Kissinger their names were known by practically no one in the nation until Watergate began to be unfolded in all its implications. Yet, at Mr. Nixon's direction, these men were making decisions affecting the welfare and destiny of the people of the United States and, indeed, of the world.

But this was not enough for Richard Milhous Nixon, as his drive for personal power mounted on the wave of his re-election majority.

He moved to recast the executive branch of the United States government. He did so by carrying out by executive decree the substance of what he had proposed to Congress, but which that supposedly coordinate branch of government had refused to enact into law. This was to concentrate decision-making power over most of the departments of government in the hands of four people, directly responsible to the President.

Mr. Nixon's original proposal (the one Congress turned down) was to group most of the functions of the executive branch of government into four gigantic agencies: one each for human resources, national resources, community development and economic development.

When Congress failed to approve his proposal Mr. Nixon

simply proceeded to carry it out anyway, in a manner much more far-reaching, and we may guess satisfying to him, than would have been his legislation.

He proceeded, in preparation for "The Nixon Era" to appoint Casper Weinberger as human resources czar, a man from Cleveland named John Lynn as community development czar, and Earl Butz, of all people, as controller of the fate of the nation's natural resources.

The last named appointment caused *The Los Angeles Times'* Ernest B. Ferguson to exclaim as follows in a feature story headed "Felony committed against U.S. National Resources":

> The operating thesis in the Nixon Administration as it begins its second term is that the President won a great popular mandate in November, so anyone in Congress or elsewhere who disagrees with him is obstructing the will of the people. . . . By appointing the secretaries of HEW, HUD and Agriculture to be his super-Cabinet officers in charge of major fields of domestic concern, Mr. Nixon is openly bypassing Congress, which has declined to enact the executive reorganization plan he asked for two years ago.

> And, specifically, unless Earl Butz is prepared to eat bales of his own words and backtrack on firm policies of his recent past, Mr. Nixon has committed a felony against America's natural resources by appointing Butz to oversee them. . . . Butz extends himself to make it clear that with him agribusiness interests come first, and all others do not exist. . . . Either the farmers use poisonous pesticides or 50 million Americans will starve, for one instance.

> At a meeting with the Natural Resources Council Butz listened to the fears of the environmental spokesmen, then went on to repeat his attitudes as if he had never heard them.

To complete the reorganization—and Nixonization—of the government, Secretary of the Treasury Shultz was given a post in domestic affairs comparable to that of Henry Kissinger in foreign relations. Shultz was to be economic czar.

There was a special advantage to this arrangement. All four of the "czars" were also heads of cabinet departments. In their special, and far more powerful, positions as overlords over vast areas of the nation's life they were part of the White House staff and hence shielded from Congressional inquiry. They were also directly under Mr. Nixon's control. Just where their status as legitimate cabinet members ended and their positions within the secret government began was conveniently unclear. In view of Mr. Nixon's insistence on "executive privilege" for everyone associated with the White House, the four titans were in position to answer such Congressional questions as they desired in their capacity as cabinet members, but then to invoke executive privilege as White House aides whenever members of Congress became too inquisitive about what was going on in the real power structure of the secret government.

The relation between Shultz as economic czar and John Ehrlichman as the President's White House Advisor on domestic matters was left undefined. So were a lot of other relationships.

And no doubt deliberately so, for now the distinctions between White House staff and Cabinet were well blurred. certainly to the detriment of the positions of cabinet members in the hierarchy of decision-making power. All that power was now centered in the person of Richard Milhous Nixon—to an extent without precedent in American history.

Steps were taken to be sure the power stayed right there. Telephones of key figures were tapped so the inner-inner circle of Mr. Nixon and his very few real intimates could know what the just-inner circle people were thinking.

Also, a practice previously undreamed of in the operation of American government was likewise put into operation. This was the direct naming of undersecretaries and assistant secretaries of the departments by the White House itself, not by the members of the cabinet.

Nor did the web of control stop there. Into each department and agency of government were injected agents of Mr. Nixon. Most of them were men who had worked and been trained in "loyalty" to "the President" in the White House before being given their "big brother" assignments. They were placed in positions where they could observe and know all that was going on in their particular agencies or departments and thus be able not only to tell the supposed heads of those departments what they should do to please the President but also to report results directly to him.

It was, we may inquire, to shield and better conrol these special agents that Mr. Nixon announced that "executive privilege," that is immunity from being called before Congress, was, by his order, extended to all present *and past* members of the White House staff. Another extension of executive power without precedent in American history.

The *Los Angeles Times* commented editorially about this. Its lead editorial for March 14, 1973 had this, in part, to say:

> President Nixon has extended the doctrine of executive privilege to former members of his personal staff, a step that could and undoubtedly will be used to shield one or more past White House employees from questioning by a Senate committee about the Watergate bugging scandal.
>
> Mr. Nixon has taken a valid doctrine and weakened its legitimacy by using it as a political tool. In choosing to prevent the appearance before a congressional committee of persons who may have knowledge of criminal activity, he has elevated an interest in avoiding political embarrassment above an interest in establishing the truth. That is not executive privilege; it is executive arrogance, and in the end it can only harm the Administration.

Most of the restructuring of the executive department of the American government was accomplished by Richard Nixon during the Christmas recess of Congress and while his bombers were raining death and destruction upon peoples far away.

That he was reaching out for a personal power such as no former president had ever done was all too evident. If these and other actions of Richard Nixon went unchallenged the predictions of our Chapter 17 would indeed be fulfilled and constitutional democracy as Americans had known it would be replaced by a virtual presidential dictatorship.

The key to Richard Nixon's plan to defy the Congress and, in effect, repeal its laws lay in the Office of Management and Budget. The director of that office had always been regarded as staff to the President and therefore not even subject to Senate confirmation.

Yet it was through this OMB that Mr. Nixon had already begun to take unto himself legislative powers which properly belonged to the Congress. He had already made a fast start in that direction in his first term. But the nation had had then only a taste of what was to come.

Consequently the person whom the President might choose to carry out his orders through the Office of Management and Budget was one of utmost consequence.

Mr. Nixon's appointment to that position was nothing short of astonishing. He named a Mr. Roy L. Ash, the president of Litton Industries, a slumping corporate giant which had, under Mr. Ash's presidency, become completely dependent upon government largesse to continue in business. Its two principal lines of business were, at the time of Mr. Ash's elevation to his high office, government subsidized shipbuilding and the manufacture of weapons of war for the Pentagon. Mr. Ash had lost practically all of Litton's unsubsidized business in the course of leading the company on a five-year toboggan from earnings of $83 million in 1967 to a net loss, after preferred dividends in 1972. At the very time of his appointment his company was in negotiation with the Pentagon, attempting to recover some very large costs on a contract to build amphibious assault ships for the Navy.

This was the man to whom Richard Nixon gave the power to impound funds for school children's milk, for clean water and air for the nation, for low-cost housing and every other program of benefit to the people. It was also the man who could readily approve payments of cost overruns, subsidies, and other large packages of taxpayer's money to favored companies like his own—provided of course that the money was available. To make sure that Mr. Ash was not disappointed in the early months of his administration of OMB an item of $192 million was earmarked in Mr. Nixon's budget for payment to Litton Industries. This item was carefully hidden from any casual survey of the budget, but Congressman Aspin of Wisconsin discovered it and spoke of it on the House floor.

Mr. Ash made no concealment of the fact that he was a five figure-contributor to the Committee to Re-elect the President.

An "upstart" civil service employee of the Navy by the name of Gordon Rule went voluntarily to Congress and opposed the Ash appointment. He had reason. His job was to monitor Navy contracts in an endeavor to keep costs from skyrocketing. In that capacity he had had experience with Litton Industries.

The next day Richard Nixon demanded Rule's resignation. Rule refused. He was promptly demoted to an insignificant job at drastically reduced salary.

One feature of dictatorial government is that no one disagrees with the top man. No one in the executive department of the U.S. government disagrees with Richard Nixon—not if he wants to keep his job.

The drive of Richard Milhous Nixon to extend his power did not stop with the attempt to subjugate the Congress. It extended to regulatory agencies, like the Federal Trade Commission, the Securities and Exchange Commission, the Interstate Commerce Commission and others. These were never intended to be subservient to the President. Rather, they were established by the Congress to be completely independent bodies carrying out specific regulatory functions assigned in the legislation creating them.

But Mr. Nixon had found a way to bring them effectively under his control.

Alarmed, the Senate held hearings on the subject based on a bill introduced by Senator Metcalf of Montana and entitled the "Regulatory Agencies Independence Act."

After the hearings Senator Metcalf told the Senate:

The hearings brought out the facts that these "arms of Congress," which Congress intended to be independent, with quasi-legislative and quasi-judicial powers, were being subjected to the executive budget-cutting process the same as executive departments and agencies, and that in many cases, notably that of the Federal Trade Commission and the Securities and Exchange Commission, their functions and effectiveness were being impaired by the refusal of the OMB to give them what they urgently need to do their investigative and regulatory work.

This, apparently was part of Mr. Ash's assignment, and as the Nixon appointments unfolded, the case of Mr. Ash appeared not as unique but rather as part of a pattern.

A Texas oil executive was chosen to be Secretary of Transportation!

Robert W. Long, a major official of the Bank of America, was named assistant-Secretary of Agriculture by Mr. Nixon. This brought vigorous protest from Congressman Jerome R. Waldie of California. Waldie pointed out that Long had publicly referred to the family farm as a "myth," "a tangle of sentiment" and "economic unreality." The Congressman said that "the Department of Agriculture is chiefly led by a secretary [Earl Butz] whose commitment to the corporation farm concept was well established when President Nixon appointed him."

Waldie also noted for the record that Bank of America had given $10,000 to the fund used to try to pass proposition 22 on the 1972 California ballot. That proposition if passed would have pretty well rendered Caesar Chavez's Farm Workers Union a helpless body.

As the editorials above quoted eloquently point out, Mr.

Nixon moved still further to insulate his personal government from Congressional inquiry and public knowledge. This he did, especially as the Watergate scandal began to unfold, by unprecedated broadening of the concept of "executive privilege."

No one presently associated with the White House, or who had been associated with it, was to testify before Congressional committees unless specifically authorized to do so by the President.

Thus the government could better be run in secret.

Doughty old Senator Ervin of North Carolina, the Senate's best Constitutional lawyer, responded in no uncertain terms. He declared that if necessary to make them testify before his committee he would have White House aides arrested by the Senate's sergeant-at-arms and brought to Capitol Hill.

But the issues lay far deeper than the battle over "executive privilege," which battle, not incidentally, the Congress was eventually to win.

The election came and went and despite the Kissinger forecast there was no peace in Southeast Asia.

Back in May the President had responded in typical Nixon fashion to the threatened military collapse of South Vietnam —and with it his "Vietnamization" program. He had ordered the mining of Haiphong harbor and the unlimited bombing of North Vietnam.

To assure the success of this bold, not to say cruel and dangerous move, the White House cadre and the Committee to Re-elect the President spent some $8,400 of unreported campaign contributors' money to bombard themselves with fake telegrams expressing support for "the President's" action. A fake advertisement costing $4,400 was placed in the *New York Times* for May 17. Purporting to be an expression of citizen opinion, the advertisement was conceived and paid for by the Nixon organization. All through the summer and fall of 1972, with the political campaign in progress, the war went on.

But now with his re-election safely in the bag, it was time for Mr. Nixon to vent his displeasure in no uncertain terms on those little so-and-sos in Southeast Asia who had not done as Richard Milhous Nixon wished.

Exactly what he wished was quite unclear, as future events were to show, but his means of realizing whatever his wishes were were plain enough, especially during the Christmas season when Congress was in recess. Richard Nixon loosed upon

305

North Vietnam—and South Vietnam, too, although for different purposes—the most devasting saturation bombing attack in the history of warfare.

Saturation bombing means the sending of large numbers of planes in formation to drop enough bombs in a given area to destroy everything within the area, whatever it may be. Thus, inevitably, villages, farms, homes, hospitals, schools may be bombed along with factories, port facilities and military installations. Of course, there is no deliberate intention to bomb hospitals or schools. They just happen "unfortunately" to be in the area marked for destruction.

Excerpts from just one eyewitness newspaper account appearing in the *Los Angeles Times* for January 7, 1973 will be enough to illustrate:

"Recent American air raids virtually razed Haiphong's western industrial zone, one of North Vietnam's biggest concentrations of factories.

Observers saw square miles that had become a desert of mud, rubble, twisted, metal, fragments of walls and heaps of debris.

Six miles from the city there are craters in the rice paddies, hundreds of yards from any building.

Then there appears a vast expanse of destruction, sometimes stretching farther than the eye can see, where nothing remains intact.

. . . B-52 strategic bombers made about 30 sorties against these areas in successive waves during the night of Dec. 22-23, and again during the night of Dec. 26-27, while fighter-bombers hit at the city proper and the port.

In another bombed district, An Duong, hundreds of houses, which could better be described as huts with mud halls, have been flattened. Next to a crater, several yards wide, a pregnant woman wearing the white turban of mourning in her hair was still crying.

Children scratched in the debris with their bare hands, against a gray background of uprooted banana and pawpaw trees."

The Los Angeles Times editorially called the bombing "beyond all reason" and said it made the United States of America appear "a barbarian gone mad."

Richard Nixon's arrogance of power was extracting a heavy price from "his" world. It had its elements of pathos as well as arrogance. While the Christmas raids were being inflicted on the people as well as the military targets of North Vietnam, Mr. Nixon chose to spend the Christmas holidays at his Florida estate rather than in Washington.

In order to guard him against possible air attacks from Cuba—a most likely event, indeed!—he ordered 100 Air Force planes and crews to fly from their California base and to patrol the skies over Key Biscayne. This meant that several hundred Air Force personnel could not spend Christmas with their families, some of whom complained out loud. But this was, perhaps, a small matter compared to the assurance of safety of Richard Milhous Nixon while he enjoyed the holidays in Florida instead of Washington.

At long last, late in January a peace agreement that satisfied Richard Nixon was concluded and the prisoners of war began to come home, praising him for their release.

What had the months of utter destruction in Southeast Asia accomplished? It was hard at first blush to see.

Mr. Nixon appeared to know. It was "peace with honor."

Others weren't so sure. The Business Executives' Move for Vietnam Peace, headquartered in Baltimore took the trouble to analyze the differences between the Kissinger agreement that had almost been signed in October and the Nixon one finally consummated in January.

No such difference of consequence could be found. Paragraph by paragraph the two agreements were compared. Such minor differences as did appear made the Kissinger draft appear, if anything, more favorable to the American position that the later and final one.

For example, the final agreement requires the United States to "remove, permanently deactivate or destroy all mines." The first one was not nearly so specific. The final agreement fails to require the freeing of prisoners in Cambodia and Laos, though the earlier agreement did provide for this. Other than such differences the two agreements were the same. It was hard to see what the two months of continued all-out war had gained, unless it were a kind of simple re-assertion of the arrogance of power. Whether the peace was "with honor" was a matter of opinion. Some felt that American honor had pretty well been destroyed in the course of an immoral war.

Whether it was peace at all remained quite clearly an open question. There were violations of the cease-fire on both sides, it being hard to determine on which side lay the major guilt.

As American ground forces were withdrawn from Vietnam the air force in nearby Thailand was kept in full strength and full alert. Arms were rushed to South Vietnam by the United States and the North continued to supply its forces still stationed in South Vietnam.

Though there was provision for non-interference by foreign powers in the affairs of Vietnam in the peace agreement, Mr. Nixon invited President Thieu to visit him at San Clemente and assured him of full United States support.

As the "peace" seemed to become more and more precarious and violations more frequent Mr. Nixon warned North Vietnam, Russia, China and the rest of the world of the possibility of resumption of full-scale war.

For the people of Cambodia there was no need of such warning. In the early months of 1973 they were in the midst of full-scale war already. American bombers were pounding that little country without let up or hindrance on the excuse, once again, that it was being invaded by a foreign foe, North Vietnam. But a report, quickly squashed by censorship, came from the U.S. Embassy in Phnom Penh itself to the effect that the war in Cambodia was a civil war, with foreign troops playing no significant part in the fighting.

Persistent reports of civilian casualties on a sickening scale came from Cambodia and were the result of American bombing. The excuse: the essentially American puppet regime of President Lon Nol was tottering before the attacks of increasingly strong rebel armies. The morale of so-called "government troops" was at a low ebb.

So Richard Nixon ordered Cambodia bombed. After all, it was his particular country. For he, by arbitrary presidential action, had brought Cambodia into the Southeast Asia war some years before.

Prince Sihanouk, for whose restoration to power the Khmer Rouge—Cambodian rebels—were fighting, declared that his forces would capture Phnom Phenh at once and take over control of the country were it not for American bombing.

Members of Congress as well as sections of the press began to speak out. They pointed out that Mr. Nixon had no more justification or authorization to bomb Cambodia, if as much, as he had had to order the invasion of that country. Senator Mansfield, Senate majority leader, and other peace-minded Senators threatened action.

Mansfield said that Mr. Nixon was endeavoring to "keep in power a regime in Cambodia that does not have the confidence of the people, and doing |so| with the power of B52 bombers." He warned that we were close to getting into another Vietnam.

There were many who agreed with Senator Mansfield—many who had thought the United States was really getting out of Southeast Asia, many who saw clearly how utterly impossible it was to compel other peoples to think as we do by killing them. It was long past the time to leave the people of Vietnam, Cambodia and Laos to determine their own destiny and their own form of government free of the influence of American bombs.

But as of April there were only threats from Congress. In fact, the Pentagon demanded from Congress the right to transfer half a billion dollars from "other funds" to the carrying on of the war in Southeast Asia! The war for the supposed ending of which so much acclaim had been accorded to Mr. Nixon. To the utter amazement of thoughtful people a House subcommittee approved, tentatively, a grant of $150 million dollars for this very purpose. Perhaps the committee did this because the very temporary Secretary of Defense, Elliott Richardson, was telling Congress in good Nixonian fashion that it didn't matter very much what Congress did, the Pentagon would find ways to keep up the bombing anyway.

After all, where would Richard Milhous Nixon's place in history be if his puppet regime in Cambodia were to fall? The lives of Cambodian villagers were, it appeared, a small sacrifice toward protecting that place in history. Furthermore, Mr. Nixon had told the Pope in all modesty that he was the most powerful individual in the world. It would never do to let a bunch of Cambodian rebels becloud that image.

Richard Milhous Nixon's arrogance of power was perhaps most evident in his treatment of the Congress of the United States and his debonair attitude toward laws on the statute books of the nation. He waited in late October 1972 for Congress to adjourn, then pocket-vetoed no less than a dozen bills, some of them important ones, which the Congress had enacted in its closing days. It is, of course, a president's constitutional right to veto acts of Congress, but Mr. Nixon was using his veto power far more extensively than his predecessors had done.

Among the bills killed in this instance were the total appropriation bill for the Departments of Labor and Health, Education and Welfare, the Public Works and Economic Development Act of 1972, calculated to put several hundred thousand unemployed back to work; an airport safety bill; a flood protection bill; amendments to the Older Americans Act, which would have expanded services to the elderly; expansion of health care for war veterans; and a measure to continue the long-established program of vocational rehabilitation of handicapped people.

Mr. Nixon's justification for his vetoes was that they were "necessary to prevent a tax increase." This was true only if no other expenditures, such as those for military weaponry or space exploration were to be held at levels desired by Mr. Nixon.

The fact that all this legislation was "pocket vetoed" made the action of the President all the more objectionable to the Congress. In all the nation's history the pocket veto had been used only sparingly by presidents; Mr. Nixon seemed to be using it rather ruthlessly. Democratic members of Congress promised to revive the vetoed measures when the new Congress assembled in January.

If there was resentment against the President's extravagant use of his veto power, there was open outrage over other actions which he took during the Christmas holidays of 1972.

As noted at the beginning of this chapter the Senate had voted down Mr. Nixon's proposal that he be given carte-blanche power to curtail without limitation or even to abolish any government program he saw fit in order to keep total spending within the limits of a spending ceiling.

This however did not deter Richard Nixon in the least. As he was doing in the matter of restructuring of the government, so in this case he began to act exactly as if Congress had in fact passed his particular kind of spending ceiling bill. He would do as he pleased anyway, regardless of the action or even the existence of the Congress of the United States.

Accordingly in December 1972 Mr. Nixon announced that, by executive decree, he was wiping some laws off the statute books, suspending others, and curtailing the operation of still more. Among these laws virtually repealed by arbitrary presidential action were the Rural Electrification Act, the Soil Conservation Act, the Urban Renewal and Model Cities Acts, disaster loans to farmers and others. All low-cost housing programs, some which had been in effect for many years, were, so said Mr. Nixon, suspended for a period of 18 months. The Office of Economic Opportunity was to be virtually eliminated, the War on Poverty brought to an abrupt end.

As to other laws which Mr. Nixon did not like he "merely"

proposed to curtail their operation. A case in point was the Water Quality Act of 1972 which the 92nd Congress in its closing days had passed by substantial margins over another Nixon veto. Here Mr. Nixon announced that he was impounding $6 billion from the $11 billion-dollar program enacted by the Congress to give the nation clean water over a period of years.

Indeed it was by impoundment of funds that Mr. Nixon was preparing to abolish, suspend or curtail operation of the laws of the land. So the gauntlet was laid down and the issue drawn.

Democratic members of Congress were openly furious, many Republican members privately so. They were beginning to see that the Congress was going to have to fight for its very existence as the coequal branch of the United States government which the Constitution says it shall be.

But there was more to come. Impoundment was one way of trying to abolish socially helpful laws. Another way was the President's budget, and Richard Nixon's budget for fiscal year 1973-4 was an incredible blow to the hopes of millions of people.

He proposed in that budget to abolish, for want of funds, no less than 70 programs of the federal government and to sweep the New Deal, the Fair Deal and the Great Society legislation of his Democratic predecessors into hoped-for oblivion. Almost all of those programs were aimed at improvement of the health, education and welfare, to borrow a governmental term, of the American people, particularly the disadvantaged among them. In a word they were what had come to be known as "social programs." Cities, towns and states as well as untold millions of citizens relied on these programs for the progressive solution of their problems.

The Middle Americans, especially the jobless among them, the poor, the disadvantaged, the small farmers, the sick, the elderly and the children—these would be required, if Richard Nixon had his way, to pay the entire price to enable him to keep his promise of no tax increase for four years. And, it must be added, no significant tax reform.

Some 20,000 people rallied in Washington in protest at the killing of the War on Poverty, and a little group of women and children gathered outside the San Dimas, California Post Office in order to mail packages of broken dolls to President Nixon. The dolls, they said, were "symbols of broken dreams and promises." It was the murder of the Head Start program that hurt them most, for it had meant a chance at an equal start in school for thousands of children in their valley.

The only bright spot for the average American, and then only for some of them, was the 20% increase in social security benefits, passed by Congress in summer of 1972—over the vigorous protests of Mr. Nixon.

It was true that in partial compensation for these monumental losses Mr. Nixon proposed revenue sharing. But what this meant was throwing back to city councils, county boards of supervisors and state legislature the problem of beginning all over at the very beginning of social action and re-enacting, if they wished to, programs more or less similar to the federal ones Mr. Nixon was determined to destroy.

This the local agencies simply were not doing. It was sobering to recall that it was the national government, not local ones, that freed the slaves, extended women's rights, wiped out child labor, enacted social security and medicare, started to protect natural resources including the precious soil, brought electricity to rural America, and began to fight pollution of the environment. In most cases it has been only national government that could do these things, for the simple reason that the problems are national in scope.

But these considerations were not, it seemed, what Richard Nixon was interested in.

There was no attempt on his part to conceal his intentions for his second term. He was going to return to the first "principles" of his political career. He was going to make his two "golden ropes" the pattern for the United States. He was gonig to force the nation back to the time when "rugged individualism" was an American creed and when "states rights" was an unanswerable appeal, when hand-outs were the answer to unemployment, and when the rich, well-heeled and powerful ruled the nation, its government, and its economy.

In his inaugural address he had told people to see what they could do for themselves. Some of them were doing very well. But others, in fact millions, were being shut out of the so-called "free enterprise system."

When history books were written they were to record the years 1973 to 1977 as "The Nixon Era," the era when America was made over and "made back" in the image of Richard Milhous Nixon and his very wealthy supporters.

Time Magazine for January 22, 1973 summed up the situation in the following paragraph:

"What was success doing to Richard Nixon? The early evidence was disturbing. Silent, secretive and still suspicious, he seemed to be reaching, in a mood strangely compounded of euphoria and truculence, for greater power. . . . Yet all of Nixon's post-election actions suggest that he is determined to subdue his opponents, defy rather than reason with the Democratic Congress and run the executive branch by decree, brooking no contrary advice by strong-willed Cabinet subordinates."

The fundamental issue was the Constitutional one. Could the President override the will of Congress as expressed in law in the manner he was attempting to do?

His defense was stated by him in these words: "The Constitutional right for the President to impound funds and that is not to spend money when the spending of money would mean either increasing prices or taxes for all the people, that right is absolutely clear."

Others were not so sure. Even Roy Ash conceded in hearing before Senator Ervin's committee that there is "no explicit law that says the President has the authority to impound funds." And Senator Ervin for his part and speaking as a universally recognized and respected expert in Constitutional law declared that he could find "not a syllable in the Constitution to support the President's claim." The Senator said that Mr. Nixon had far exceeded any possible precedents by withholding funds from programs he personally disliked.

As expected, administration witnesses faithfully defended Mr. Nixon's power thrust. Their testimony was characterized by Congressional critics as "a blueprint for presidential rule of the government."

Very early in the game, Senator Mansfield, the Democratic majority leader, had taken up the Nixon challenge. Even before the new Congress met he had pointed out that whatever precedent there was for a president's impounding of funds appropriated by Congress could only be found in minor and temporary action of the sort and that never in history had impoundment been used "to such a degree as by this Administration."

Never before, indeed, had impoundment been used to repeal—to violate—the laws of the land.

Mansfield declared that "the intent of Congress has been flouted and this question must be faced up to even if it means going to the Supreme Court to do so." He said the conflict had other aspects as well as that of impounded of funds, among them the growing practice of the withholding of information vital to the legislative process by the executive, and abuse of executive privilege.

Mansfield's statement was the more significant because he had more than once came to Mr. Nixon's defense and had repeatedly expressed the desire to cooperate with the Administration.

Action by the Congress took a number of forms. Seventeen Senate committee chairmen filed a lawsuit to restrain the President from impounding funds duly appropriated by the Congress. And Senator Ervin, as well as other members of the Senate and the House, introduced legislation aimed at preventing the impounding of funds. The Ervin bill provided that such impoundment must cease and the funds be duly used, as directed by the law, unless Congress by positive action approved the impoundment. As the controversy increased in intensity the Senator considered strengthening his bill in a number of ways.

Senator Nelson of Wisconsin declared that Mr. Nixon was proceeding with full knowledge reported to him by his own Justice Department that his actions were supported "by neither reason nor precedent."

The reasons for the coming of the constitutional crisis were rooted not only in Richard Nixon's drive for personal power but in the conflict between the President and the Congress over the economic and social policies of the United States government. This became clear as Mr. Nixon attempted to defend his actions. Over and over he attacked the Congress as a "spendthrift" body, devoid of financial responsibility. He declared that the laws he was, in effect, repealing and the programs he was curtailing or abolishing had proved to be "failures." Interestingly, and perhaps significantly, all these programs had been initiated by Administrations other than that of Richard Nixon.

The problem faced by the Congress was that of getting its side of the story told to the American people. The President could get for himself prime radio or television time simply by demanding it. But when Democratic leaders of Congress asked for equal time to answer Mr. Nixon, the networks, perhaps out of fear of Administration displeasure, consistently refused to give it to them.

Many members of Congress agreed with Mr. Nixon about the desirability of fixing an overall limit to government spending in any given year. Some of them were able to point to an effort they themselves had made to impose a ceiling on spending by the Pentagon. They could also remind Mr. Nixon that he and his administration had violently opposed any such ceiling. Congressmen were also able to say that the President's proposed budget for 1973-4 was estimated by him to be $19 billion out of balance, that it was the fourth straight deficit budget and was therefore not exactly an example of fiscal frugality. They readily conceded that Congress had an evident duty to improve its own procedures in order to exercise better overall control over the relationship between revenues and expenditures. And they gave credit to Mr. Nixon for having pushed them into action that should have been taken some time ago.

But, said members of Congress, the spending limit legislation, since it was legislation, was the business of Congress and not a matter for presidential dictatorship.

Democratic Senators proceeded to take definitive action. They worked out legislation to impose an overall spending ceiling actually lower than the one Mr. Nixon had demanded, and they coupled with this a prohibition against presidential impounding of funds duly appropriated by the Congress. In late March this bill was ready for introduction and action by the Congress. When reporting this to the nation, Senator Proxmire of Wisconsin also predicted the Congress would trim Mr. Nixon's budget for the Pentagon by $4 billion and his foreign aid request by $1 billion.

Congress was trying to say that Richard Nixon must not succeed in his effort to rewrite the Constitution by executive order.

None of these facts or actions deterred Richard Milhous Nixon. There loomed something that might deter him but it was only beginning to surface as a threat. He went right on vetoing and impounding, showing his power as the days passed. Program after program on which the people of the nation had relied, sometimes for decades, became suspended at least, terminated at worst.

Revenue sharing, which Mr. Nixon had represented as a means of enabling local politicians to do what they wished about these programs was of little help, partly because the amount of money dished out to local authorities was far too little and more especially because that money was being used for new city halls, the balancing of local budgets, additions to the police force or other similar purposes. After all, it was a good deal to expect city, county, even state governments to

315

replace in a moment of time a process of legislation and implementation which had occupied years of careful conception by the federal government.

So, some protest began to be voiced, especially from the Christian community. The moderator of the United Presbyterian Church declared that President Nixon had committed "one of the most immoral acts ever done by a President of the United States" in impounding welfare funds. He went on to say that Mr. Nixon had a "Charles de Gaulle complex" and that the President was "doing an arrogant, unconstitutional act imposing his personal judgment against the judgment of the Congress of the United States."

Bishop Charles F. Golden, newly elected President of the United Methodist Church, second largest religious body in the nation, went farther. He asked: "Who is to say that there will be a national election in 1976, or that if there is one, the people will have a presidential choice if this apparently calculated sabotage of the constitutional process is continued." Bishop Golden confirmed that the White House had failed even to reply to a request from the 45-man Council of (Methodist) Bishops for an appointment with the President.

Early attempts by the Congress to redress the balance and reclaim some of its lost position fell considerably short of success. The bill which Mr. Nixon had pocket-vetoed and which provided for continuance of the long-established program of vocational training for handicapped people was revived and passed by both Houses of Congress. It passed the Senate 86 to 2. It was promptly vetoed again by the President, who declared, somewhat extravagantly it seemed, that its passage would cause a 15% increase in taxes. The Senate attempted to override the veto. But astonishingly failed to do so. Twenty-five Republicans and five Southern Democrats switched positions and voted to sustain the veto.

The nation's press recorded a major victory for Mr. Nixon. His drive for power was unchecked.

A next test came on a bill which would have required the President to spend $120 million for grants to smaller communities so they could provide themselves with clean water. This was vetoed with a somewhat surprising presidential message alleging that the action of Congress was unconstitutional!

But, this time in the House, the veto was again sustained.

It might not have made a great deal of difference, however, even had these vetoes been overridden. The nation had seen what happened when the Clean Water Act was passed over the veto and more than half its funds were promptly impounded by the White House.

The planning for Richard Milhous Nixon's assumption of supreme power in the United States had been well and carefully laid.

Meanwhile a good deal was happening to the economy of the United States. It was hardly distasteful to the people who had contributed some $60 million toward Mr. Nixon's re-election.

Why so much, when all indications were consistently that Mr. Nixon would be re-elected easily?

Probably because experience had taught that the bigger the contribution the bigger the reward. Probably too because the nation's wealthiest of the wealthy had learned that Richard Nixon had never let them down.

He didn't this time either.

The first golden rope was holding firm.

Back in the summer of 1972 the grain exporting companies had been informed well ahead of time of the impending huge grain sale to Russia. This had come about by the simple device of two high officials of the Department of Agricule, one of whom had actually negotiated the wheat deal, going to work for a couple of the big grain exporters. Those exporters were able then to buy wheat at a low price from the uninformed farmers and sell it at handsome profit at the much higher fixed price to the Soviet Union. (Incidentally, that deal had much to do with the escalation of food prices which began in the winter of 1972-3.)

While big business had done reasonably well under Phase II of Game Plan III, there were constant demands for the taking off of controls, once Mr. Nixon had been re-elected.

Accordingly, on January 11, 1973 Phase III of the economic "control" program was inaugurated. The wage and price boards were abolished on that day and the economy turned loose to develop as the market-place decided, subject only to "voluntary restraints."

One trouble was that there was little inclination in the big business community to exercise restraints. Another trouble was that for many commodities there was no "market place" in any real sense of that word. Monopoly or near-monopoly had usurped the field.

So inflation of living costs went clear through the roof in the first quarter of 1973 and kept right on thereafter, if at a somewhat slower rate.

Compared to Mr. Nixon's goal of a 2.5% inflation rate the price increases were almost astronomical. For all commodities the rate of increase in 1972 was 6.5%. In the first quarter of 1973 it was 21.5%. For processed foods it was 53%. Even for industrial commodities it was 10.3% and going up, not down.

Now inflation is a hidden tax on every paycheck and every fixed income. So the promise of no tax increase became a bit hollow. It became hollower still when wage and salary earners looked at their payroll deductions. For payroll taxes in 1973 were paying 26% of the federal tax bill, compared to just 14% ten years before, while corporation taxes were paying 14% compared to 20% ten years before.

Furthermore the payroll taxes weighed far more heavily on people with small incomes than on those with big incomes. For example, as Richard Strout pointed out in the *Christian Science Monitor*, a bachelor earning $25,000 pays no more payroll tax than a married couple with five children who earn $11,000. The payroll tax supports good things. But it badly needs reform.

The Nixon Administration opposes such tax reforms.

It also opposes closing the loopholes, largely because of favored treatment of capital gains that enable unearned income to pay far less tax than does earned income. This is manifestly unfair and wrong.

To its credit, the Administration did propose repeal of the $100 deduction for dividends received by individuals. But the Nixon Administration adamantly opposes any change in the highly favored tax position which has been accorded to corporations. This might be justifiable if the corporations were in distress. But, in general, that was far from the case.

On top of an increase in overall profit rates of some 23% in the fourth quarter of 1973, corporate profits jumped by some $11.6 billion in the first quarter of 1973. This was more than double the rate of increase of the year previous and the fastest rise in more than 20 years. Automobile company profits, led as usual by General Motors, were up substantially, yet the companies were asking and getting a go-ahead for price increases from the Administration.

These profit increases were one obvious cause of the inflation of living costs. Others were, as always, high interest rates, which were rising sharply again in 1973, as well as gigantic military expenditures and monopoly pricing.

Concerning the last named cause, Senator Philip Hart of

Michigan proposed that huge corporations be broken up in an attempt to save what was left of "free enterprise" in America. He got, unfortunately, little support either from his Senate colleagues or from the public.

Senator Proxmire pointed out that 100 "defense" contractors were showing profits of from 50% to 500% on their government business. That business produced not a penny's worth of anything the people could buy.

While profits were going up, spendable income of the people was dropping. In the first quarter of 1973 it was no higher than it had been in 1972, this is the face of the spiraling cost of living.

Due in part at least to the galloping inflation as well as the largest trade deficits in history, the battered United States dollar fell and fell in money markets, until the price of gold soared to more than $100 an ounce. Already the dollar had been devalued twice by Mr. Nixon. The question was whether another devaluation might be in the offing.

Meanwhile, Mr. Nixon was doing nothing to check the hidden tax increase which the people were paying for the escalating cost of living.

He was pulling hard on both his golden ropes.

In a few short months Richard Milhous Nixon had taken measures to completely control the executive bureaucracy, to defy the Congress and usurp its Constitutional legislative power, to take to himself control of the nation's pursestrings, and to further assert his power by continuing, without any constitutional grounds for doing so, the war in Southeast Asia. He was moreover only one appointment away from control of the Supreme Court of the United States.

But there was one more force that lay across his path. This was American public opinion, moulded as it is to a large extent by mass media—the newspapers, television, and radio. Already during his first term, as related in Chapter 14, attacks had been launched against the media, some of which, such as the attempt to prevent publication of the Pentagon Papers, were quite logically branded as attempted censorship.

These were, however, only the beginning. They were, so to speak, "before the mandate."

William L. Shirer, author of the famous best seller *The Rise and Fall of the Third Reich*, and eminent foreign correspondent, recently wrote an article for *The Nation* (January 22, 1973) in which this passage appears:

Assaults on the freedom of the press, First Amendment guarantees, dissent. Obviously we have not fallen as far as Nazi Germany, but are we not on our way? Have not Nixon and his minions carried on for four years an assault on our press freedoms and on the right to dissent—and not without success? They have intimidated the networks, threatened TV station owners with loss of their licenses if they do not, in effect, censor network news critical of the Administration, and successfully gone to court to induce the Supreme Court to rule by five to four that the First Amendment does not give reporters the right to protect their confidential sources—a telling blow to our press freedoms. On the other hand, the Administration, by propaganda, deceit, evasion, playing favorites, and by expert use of the power of the White House to make news and control it, has done very well in putting its own story over in the press. But this has not satisfied Nixon.

On November 27, 1972, William Farr, a reporter for the *Los Angeles Times*, was sentenced to jail. His offense was his refusal to break a confidence and reveal the source of information contained in an article he wrote in 1970. Reporter Farr spent many days in jail. So did other reporters for the same "offense."

This was something new under the American sun. It appeared to be part of a broad attempt to circumscribe the people's "right to know." For if reporters could be forced to reveal sources of their information when given in confidence, almost no one in a government position or any other job which might be jeopardized would be willing to provide information even of the most vital sort. Certainly this would be true of anyone working for the Nixon Administration. It would also be true where a reporter might obtain information from a disgruntled member of an organized crime ring provided that member was sure he would not be exposed to probable death.

This jailing of the reporters was mainly the result of a five to four Supreme Court decision in June 1972 which denied the right of *New York Times* reporter Earl Caldwell to protect his sources.

Senator Alan Cranston, of California, on opening day of the 93rd Congress introduced a bill to protect reporters' rights. So did Senators Ervin of North Carolina, and Kennedy of Massachusetts. Cranston, testifying for his bill S.158 told the Senate Judiciary Committee that "it is my view that Congress' aim should be to protect explicitly all of the newsgathering rights which many people had all along assumed were implicit in the First Amendment, until the Court told us otherwise. Newsmen exercise the privilege on behalf of the public. The public itself is beneficiary."

Senator Cranston's bill, and all others like it, was vigorously opposed by the Nixon Administration on the ground that such protection of reporters might somehow endanger the "national security."

Senator Ervin countered by speaking to the press at the March convention of the National Association of Broadcasters. He declared: "I think the Nixon Administration has been the most repressive administration as far as basic rights are concerned since John Adams had the Congress pass the Alien and Sedition Act."

Republican Governor Tom McCall of Oregon, on signing an unqualified "shield" law protecting reporters, called the law "a shield of the public's right to know." He said further: "I never thought I would have to sign a bill authorizing freedom of the press. However the U.S. Supreme Court has said, temporarily, I think, that the United States Constitution does not say what it clearly says."

The Nixon Administration, perhaps having in mind its failure to exercise prior censorship against publication of the Pentagon Papers, was, by April, urging passage of a bill of its own. This bill, S.1400 was authored by Conservative Senator Roman Hruska of Nebraska. Its principal purpose was strictly to control news media when they attempted to dig into government affairs. The President sent a special message to Congress in support of the bill. He described it as only a technical measures designed to bring together in one place in the criminal code certain bits and pieces of espionage and "security" laws already on the statute books.

But others found much more in S.1400 than that. The St. Petersburg, Florida *Times* printed an editorial about the matter which contained these passages.

The Watergate has been breached. The resulting flood threatens to wash some of President Nixon's aides into jail. And Mr. Nixon finds himself in the preposterous role of asking Congress for new power to keep things under wraps. He couldn't have picked a worse time. And probably he wouldn't have sent up his request for a new official secrecy law had he realized the political crime of the century was about to be laid right at his door.

Now, at least, the lawmakers should have warning enough to

throw the request back. The President, of course, didn't say anything about secrecy when he sent Congress his March 14 message asking "codification" of existing criminal laws. The White House pictured this proposed legal rewrite as technical stuff, interesting only to lawyers.

It seemed unlikely that S.1400 would be passed by Congress. It was more likely to take the advice of the St. Petersburg *Times*.

But this was not the only way in which Richard Nixon and his White House cadre were trying to gain power over the channels of communication.

One method was described by columnist Joseph Alsop, ordinarily one of the staunchest of Nixon defenders. Mr. Alsop wrote in one of his syndicated columns:

> Consider, for example, the extraordinary dragnet subpoenas issued to the publisher of *The Washington Post,* Katharine Graham, three members of the *Post* staff and assorted other newspapermen. They are part of the huge crop of subpoenas sprouting from the maze of suits and countersuits born of the ugly Watergate case.

> The particular suit in question is a civil one, brought by former Secretary of Commerce Maurice H. Stans against the former chairman of the Democratic National Committee, Lawrence O'Brien. The dragnet subpoenas were issued at the behest of Kenneth Parkinson, lawyer for Stans and also lawyer for the Committee for the Re-election of The President.

> The dragnet subpoenas amount to a demand for full disclosure of the inner workings of the newspaper business, including reporters' sources and everything else.

> The demand originates in a civil, not a criminal proceeding. The subpoenas will rightly be resisted up to the Supreme Court, if necessary, but at heavy expense for all the incidental costs of resistance.

> For these reasons, the dragnet subpoenas constitute an unquestionable, gross and unjustifiable invasion of the freedom of the press. Worse still, this is an invasion that the White House could easily have prevented, or at least have called off. No one can suppose that Parkinson would have issued his subpoenas, or have persisted in them, if the President had sent down the necessary order.

On December 18, 1972, the same day the city of Haiphong was bombed, Walter Cronkite, ace television commentator, devoted most of the time of his regular evening report to a discussion of the Administration's attack on broadcasters. He said that such attacks were being stepped up markedly ever since Mr. Nixon's re-election. He called attention to an ominous speech by 34-year-old Clay T. Whitehead, director of the White House Office of Telecommunications Policy. In that speech Mr. Whitehead had set forth a new policy and a new doctrine. Henceforth *local* radio and television stations would be held responsible, on pain of loss of licenses, for any network programs which they aired. This to replace network responsibility. Mr. Whitehead had gone farther and said that the Administration was prepared to submit legislation which would give the government broad powers to combat what he called the "consistent bias" of network programs. The Federal Communications Commission would hold each station responsible for balancing or removing the "ideological plugola" (Mr. Whitehead's words) of the network programs. And, to quote Mr. Whitehead directly: "Station Managers and network officials who fail to act to correct imbalance or consistent bias in the network, or who acquiesce by silence can only be considered willing participants to be held fully accountable at license-renewal time." Stations were to be expected, said Mr. Whitehead, to "eschew elitist gossip in the guise of news analysis."

There could be little doubt what Mr. Whitehead really meant by "elitist gossip," remembering Vice-president Spiro Agnew's frequent use of those same terms when he attacked the media for unfavorable comments about the Nixon Administration. Nor could any reasonable person doubt that when Whitehead spoke of "bias" he meant comment unfavorable to the Nixon Administration.

Here then was the most direct, the foreboding threat to what *Newsweek* Magazine called "broadcasting's traditional but legally fragile liberties and privileges."

It was little wonder that Mr. Cronkite was alarmed.

But the plans of Mr. Nixon did not end with attempted intimidation of commercial television. There was public television to be considered, the Corporation for Public Broadcasting or CPB which had been conceived by Congress as a forum for bringing significant programs into American homes free of commercialism or the influence of advertisers.

Mr. Nixon was moving to make of CPB an agency of the White House, controlled by the White House, and used primarily for broadcasting programs approved by the White

House. He put in charge of Public Broadcasting a man named Henry Loomis, who admitted that he had almost no familiarity with public television, and whose sole qualification seemed to be that he once worked for the U.S. Information Agency. Mr. Nixon then appointed conservative and recently defeated Republican Congressman from suburban St. Louis, Thomas B. Curtis as chairman of the board.

Since its establishment the programming of public television had been decided by the 240 stations which make up the public broadcasting network.

But no longer.

They were informed early in January, as inaugural day drew near, that henceforth all decisions regarding their programs would be made by the board of CPB meeting in Washington and firmly controlled by Nixon appointees.

One of the first acts of this board was to announce discontinuance of practically all of the public affairs programs— programs that local station managers and program directors considered essential public service features. Among the programs marked for oblivion were William Buckley's "Firing Line," "Black Journal," "Bill Moyer's Journal," "Behind the Lines," "World Press," "America '73," and "Washington Week in Review."

Significantly, one public affairs program was *not* to be taken off the air. This was Elizabeth Drew's interview program "Thirty Minutes with . . .," the program on which many prominent Nixon supporters have frequently appeared.

Robert MacNeil, a former BBC and NBC newsman and a reporter for "Washington Week in Review" described the situation in a speech to the Consumer Federation of America's Annual Assembly in late January. MacNeil said that "bias in the minds of CPB board apparently is an attitude which does not indicate permanent genuflection before the wisdom and purity of Richard Milhous Nixon."

In the early months of 1973 the controversy between the public broadcasting stations and the CPB board grew hotter and hotter. An attempt at compromise was worked out by a group representing both sides, but it was rejected by the board on a 10 to four vote.

Chairman Curtis thereupon resigned. He gave his reasons in an interview with the *New York Times* in which he charged that White House pressures had so undermined the integrity of the CBP board that he could no longer remain as its chairman. He said that he had accepted the appointment with the understanding that it would not be "made a propaganda arm of the Nixon Administration."

The clear implication of the former congressman's remarks was that that was precisely what was happening.

Perhaps it was part of the power drive of Richard Nixon to use the public broadcasting network in place of the press conferences he was not holding. For as the months passed he exposed himself less and less frequently to the questioning of the press conference. He withdrew more and more often from the White House to Camp David, San Clemente or Key Biscayne, and he consulted less and less with anyone other than his White House intimates.

But the drive for power went on in Richard Nixon's behalf and by his own actions right up to the time that Watergate became a scandal instead of a caper.

Step by step Richard Nixon was taking to himself powers that belonged to Congress. He was making the entire bureaucracy afraid to dissent in the slightest degree. He was killing the programs of government which he did not like. He was developing a well-paid professional army, trained in riot control and suppression of public protest. He was punishing with unauthorized bombing the people of Southeast Asia who would not bend to his will. He had actually advanced along the road of public opinion itself.

Richard Milhous Nixon was, in the early weeks of his "mandate," gaining for himself a position which was far more akin to that of a dictator than of a responsible and constitutional President of the United States.

21. WATERGATE: TIP OF AN ICEBERG

Despite official claims to the contrary the crime wave was not abating as 1972 gave away to 1973. Indeed serious crimes, murder and forcible rape, were increasing at an alarming 20% a year. Homicides were greater in proportion to population in the United States than anywhere in the world except El Salvador. And a Gallup Poll revealed that one person out of every three in the inner cities had either been mugged or rolled in the proceeding 12 months.

President Nixon's reaction was stern. He announced in a radio address late in February that he was proposing to Congress severe legislation requiring the death penalty for treason, sabotage, espionage, hijacking and kidnapping, all of which are federal crimes. For second heroin "pusher" offenders he proposed mandatory life imprisonment, and he spoke harshly of "soft-headed judges" and probation officers who he said seemed more concerned about criminals than about their victims.

Elsewhere Mr. Nixon had placed those young men who fled to Canada or otherwise evaded the draft squarely in the criminal category. He had said: "We cannot provide forgiveness for them. They must pay their price. The price is criminal penalty for disobeying the laws of the land."

None disagreed with Mr. Nixon that it was high time for a vigorous drive against lawlessness. Many agreed with his death penalty proposal.

The only trouble was that the President who spoke so sternly about punishment of draft evaders and criminals was the same one who was raining death and destruction on Southeast Asia, and himself violating the laws of the nation by arbitrarily ordering their suspension or refusing to fund their carrying out.

It was also the same President whose administration was day-by-day being shown to have been deeply involved in a thing called Watergate.

All through the months of the election campaign, from June 17 to November 7 Richard Nixon's luck held firm. Watergate was still a "caper" and "incident" or a "third-rate burglary." And the President announced on August 29: "I can say categorically that his [John Dean, his chief counsel's] investigation indicated that no one in the White House staff, no one in this administration was involved in this bizarre incident."

No trials were held before the election, not of the seven men indicted for the Watergate break-in, nor of Democratic Chairman O'Brien's lawsuit for $1 million damages from the Committee to Re-elect the President.

Even after the election Richard Nixon was able to restructure the executive branch of the United States government, to defy its Congress and its courts, to virtually end all controls on the economy, to pursue with frightfulness the war in Southeast Asia, and, in sum to launch a series of actions aimed at transforming American society through his own personal power. He was able to do all this without more than a shadow of Watergate hanging over him.

But while Richard Milhous Nixon was reaching with such apparent success for his pinnacle of power a little band of relentless and courageous newspaper reporters were digging away at Watergate. They worked, most of them, for three outstanding newspapers: *The Washington Post*, the *New York Times* and the *Los Angeles Times*.

It was the *Los Angeles Times* that found a former FBI agent, Albert C. Baldwin 3rd, and, defying threat of suppression from the White House and Justice Department, published his account of his electronic eavesdropping on Democratic headquarters long before, and perhaps in preparation for, the Watergate break-in. Baldwin told the *Times* he had regularly delivered his transcripts to "someone" at the Committee to Re-elect the President.

We now know that reporters', as well as government officials' telephones were tapped from the time of Mr. Nixon's first election. We know this because the files of the F.B.I., which recorded the taps, were found in the office of John Erlichman, Mr. Nixon's advisor on domestic affairs. The files had been taken by White House action from the F.B.I. because of fear that J. Edgar Hoover might use the information they contained against Nixon officials. The White House seemed able in this administration to do exactly as it pleased, at least up until the spring of 1973.

The reporters and their papers worked under difficult conditions. They were harassed by the Administration and dragnet subpoenas were issued, attempting to require them to reveal all their sources of information about Watergate.

But they kept on.

Other factors, too, were at work. According to Roy Wilkins, respected Black leader of the National Association for the Advancement of Colored People, it was "the cavalier attitude of the White House, the attitude that the king's household could do no wrong" and the Nixon Administration attacks on the newspapers that stirred the people.

Perhaps, too, it was reports of the gigantic sums of money that had been contributed to the Committee to Re-elect the President that raised questions about its use. There were lots of $100 bills floating around, like the ones that Watergate's Bernard Barker had gotten, $10,000 worth, from a Florida bank and like the 50 or more of them that were in the pockets of the men who were caught in Watergate. There was the mysterious $89,000 which had travelled to Mexico and back into Barker's bank account and another $25,000 that went there too from grain tycoon Wayne Andreas of Minnesota who asked for, and got, a charter for a new bank in a remarkably short time. This $114,000 was supposed to have been contributed for the campaign to re-elect the President.

It seemed strange that John Mitchell, Nixon's campaign manager and closest associate should suddenly have resigned "for family reasons" just two weeks after the Watergate break-in.

Mitchell's successor as attorney general, Richard Kleindienst, had promised "the most thorough and comprehensive investigation" of Watergate. Then why had the Justice Department gone out of its way to announce gratuitously that it simply was not possible that anyone other than the seven indicted men could have had anything to do with the crime? Who then had financed it—the seven themselves? Hardly likely.

Perhaps all this was rankling in the public mind as the trial of the Watergate Seven began at last on January 8, 1973. The Nixon Administration refused to name an independent prosecution saying, in effect, that its own Justice Department could honestly prosecute a group of people, two of whom had until recently been White House aides of Mr. Nixon, and one of whom was at the time of his arrest security director of the Committee to Re-elect the President.

Judge John L. Sirica was to think very differently, and to say so, before the trial was ended.

When they were indicted on September 15, 1972 all seven of the accused had plead not guilty. But for some reason E. Howard Hunt, Jr., former White House consultant and the four Cuban refugees, who were the pawns in the game, changed their pleas to guilty once the trial began, thus avoiding their being questioned or given opportunity to testify. James W. McCord, security director of the Committee to Re-elect the President and G. Gordon Liddy, one of the Committee's counsels plead not guilty. Liddy refused from that day forward to answer any questions, even when ordered by a court; McCord became a key witness in investigations to follow.

It took the jury just 90 minutes to come to a verdict of guilty against McCord and Liddy.

But Judge Sirica was openly and caustically angered at the failure of the prosecution effectively to prosecute. He declared as the trial ended that he hoped a grand jury and the Senate investigating committee would do a far more thorough job than had been done in his court. He furthermore offered to those who had plead guilty and to McCord to hold their sentences in abeyance if they would promise to testify honestly before those two bodies.

Thus, perhaps it was Judge Sirica more than any other single person who "blew the lid" off Watergate. He did it on February 2, 1973 just a few days after Richard Milhous Nixon had been safely (?) inaugurated for a second term.

Judge Sirica was helped by the newspapers and by James W. McCord.

Almost as soon as the trial was over and he was freed on bail McCord began to talk. Some of the things he said were challenged. But those who heard him could not doubt his sincerity or his deep distress. Once McCord began to talk so did many other people—if for no other reason than to answer McCord. There began to flow a veritable flood of confessions, charges and countercharges among dozens of people.

And the "Watergate caper" became, along with other revelations not even directly related to it, the most serious crisis for the American presidency in history.

It would be both redundant and needless to repeat here all the details of the story, as yet unfinished. For those details were front-page headlines every day for weeks on end. And the deep involvement of Richard Nixon's White House, his Administration, and the Committee to Re-elect the President was revealed piece by piece.

Increasingly it became evident that the Watergate break-in was only the tip of an iceberg of planned intrigue, illegal political espionage and dishonest practices carried on, as the editor of the conservative Republican Walla Walla, Washington *Union-Bulletin* put it "in the name of, if not under the direction of, the office of the President of the United States."

So widespread were resignations, firings and just plain departures from Administration and White House posts that by May Mr. Nixon was left with a bare skeleton of people to carry on the business of government.

There was John Mitchell, departed only days after the Watergate break-in. At first the former chief law enforcement officer of the United States declared that he had had no prior knowledge of Watergate. But he later admitted that he had attended no less than three meetings where it was discussed, where, he contended, he had spoken against it.

But he did nothing to expose the plot. Why not? Why did he not tell his intimate friend, the President? Or did he perhaps? And why had he resigned? These questions might find answers in time.

But Mr. Mitchell was involved in more than Watergate. And on May 10, 1973 he and Maurice Stans, Mr. Nixon's chief money raiser and former Secretary of Commerce were indicted with financier Robert L. Vesco. The charges stemmed from Vesco's trouble with the Securities and Exchange Commission over his having milked mutual funds of an estimated $224 million. Three days after the date when the new campaign spending law went into effect, $200,000 had been delivered to the Committee to Re-elect the President in cash from Mr. Vesco. Thereupon Mitchell and Stans interceded on Vesco's behalf with the S.E.C. After all one good turn seemed to deserve another, especially when Vesco's administrative assistant had been a young man named Donald Nixon who happened to be a nephew of the President of the United States.

The $200,000 was returned to Vesco, who promptly fled to South America. But the damage had been done. L. Bradford Cook, recently appointed by Mr. Nixon, abruptly resigned as S.E.C. chairman on May 16, leaving another major government position vacant.

Presumably Stans did not particularly miss the $200,000. For in his safe was kept an estimated $700,000 to $1 million in unreported cash, from which friend Stans approved payments to the Watergate Seven, among others.

For what purpose?

It became clearly evident that the purpose was to keep the convicted men quiet. It was the pay-off for the plea of guilty by five of them. John J. Caulfield, White House aide to Ehrlichman till March 1972, admitted tearfully to Senator Ervin's committee that it was he who tried to persuade McCord. He did it, he declared because he felt he "was doing something for the President." He testified that he had promised McCord executive clemency if he would keep quiet and while he, Caulfield, could not recall the actual use of Mr. Nixon's name he did remember assuring him that the promise came from "the highest levels" in the White House.

L. Patrick Gray proved the tragic figure in the drama. Nominated by Mr. Nixon to succeed J. Edgar Hoover as head of the F.B.I., Gray testified quite honestly before the Senate Judiciary Committee. He said he had believed he should do whatever the President or his White House aides asked him to do. So he had let Mr. Nixon's chief counsel John Dean sit in on FBI questioning of White House personnel about Watergate; he had given the White House copies of FBI investigative interviews; and he had obediently destroyed damaging evidence at the suggestion of Dean and Ehrlichman.

This was evidence of the long-range objective of the Nixon forces, destruction of the opposition party. For it was a collection of carefully forged fake "State Department" documents calculated to besmirch the memory of President John Kennedy by linking him to the assassination of President Diem of South Vietnam. According to grand jury testimony the forgeries were done by Watergate burglar E. Howard Hunt on orders of Charles Colson, special White House counsel. This was the same Colson who brought Hunt into the White House staff, who reportedly telephoned to get Jeb Stuart Magruder to ask why Watergate was being delayed, and who planted the fake "homosexuals" in McGovern's corner at the Democratic Convention.

But to return to Gray. He offered to let the Senate Committee see the FBI's Watergate files, whereupon President Nixon publicly criticised him and on April 6 withdrew his nomination. On April 27 Patrick Gray resigned as acting head of the FBI. On May 12 he revealed that in July 1972, just three weeks after Watergate, he had warned the President that White House aides might be involved and that, in any case, they were interfering with the FBI's investigation of Watergate. More than a year later Mr. Nixon was to confess to the truth of Gray's warning, but it was not till April 17, 1973 that the President openly acknowledged that "serious charges" had come to his attention, that he was beginning new inquiries, and that if anyone in the government was indicted he would immediately suspend them. Press Secretary Ziegler declared, thereupon, that this was the "operative" position of the President and that all previous denials of White House involvement were "inoperative."

On April 30 Richard Nixon made the first of what may be called his "justification" statements to the nation—this time on television. He told nothing that was not already known about Watergate. He said he had been deceived by those around him. He took "responsibility" 'but he made no acknowledgment that any blame fell on his own shoulders. He even at-

331

tempted to excuse the whole sordid business by saying that "both of our great parties have been guilty of such tactics," an accusation for which he offered no proof.

Then he announced the resignations of his two closest White House confidants, H. R. Haldeman his chief of staff and John Ehrlichman, and of another attorney general, this time Richard Kleindienst. John Dean, his chief counsel, who had declared he would not be a "scapegoat," Mr. Nixon had fired. Of Kleindienst it was simply said that he had resigned because the investigation of Watergate and related matters might "implicate individuals with whom he had had close personal and professional relations." This was the same Kleindienst however who had failed in Judge Sirica's opinion to conduct a thorough or effective investigation or prosecution in the Watergate case. There were "little people" in the office of the Committee to Re-elect the President who had asked, but not been given, opportunity to make statements privately, away from their superiors in the office. It was also the same Kleindienst who had argued before Congress that the FBI should not be independent or non-political but subject to control by the President, as indeed had been the case.

As for Haldeman and Ehrlichman, Mr. Nixon had only the highest praise. They were, he asserted, guilty of no wrongdoing and charges to the contrary were unfair and unfounded. But this was the same Haldeman who, as long ago as 1962, had been Nixon's campaign manager against Pat Brown for governor of California. It was the same Haldeman who, with Mr. Nixon himself had been found guilty, by Republican Judge Byron Arnold, of conjuring up an imaginery "Committee for the Preservation of the Democratic Party in California" and sending out with Nixon campaign money thousands of letters in the bogus committee's name to conservative Democrats alleging that a postcard poll had shown "overwhelmingly" that California Democrats rejected the "extremist views" of Governor Brown. It was also the same Haldeman who had directed the political sabotage campaign aimed to eliminate Senator Muskie and bring about the nomination of McGovern. According to *Time* Magazine Haldeman controlled some $350,000 of campaign funds which he was apparently to use to try to keep the Watergate Seven quiet.

It was the same Ehrlichman who had asked Gray to destroy evidence, who assigned Watergate's Hunt and Liddy to investigate the moral and personal life of Daniel Ellsberg, who knew of their burglary of Ellsberg's psychiatrist's office and who was to convey to the judge in the Ellsberg case the offer of a virtual bribe in the form of appointment as FBI chief.

John Dean's case was different. After Mr. Nixon fired him he denied that President Nixon had ever even asked him to make the "investigation" on the alleged basis of which Mr. Nixon had made his flat denial that anyone in the White House was involved in Watergate. Dean also removed from the White House and put in a safe deposit box, open to Judge Sirica, certain documents that reportedly outline a complete plan of political sabotage, burglary, wire-tapping, infiltration and provocation to violence aimed at destroying opposition to the Administration. Desperately the Administration tried to prevent Judge Sirica from ever opening the envelopes.

Against Mr. Nixon's charge that no one in the Administration should seek immunity from prosecution and thus be free to testify before Senator Ervin's committee, Dean defiantly did just that. He asked and got at least limited immunity before his testimony took place.

Other heads fell right and left, many of them because of accusations from others of what had been the tight Nixon team of young faceless men. There was Jeb Magruder who had brought Liddy into the White House staff and, according to *Time* Magazine, attended meetings where, in Magruder's words, John Mitchell had "given a go-ahead." Magruder resigned a top position in the Commerce Department. There was Gordon Strachan, aide to Haldeman and general counsel of the U.S. Information Agency, who was White House contact with Segretti-type "agents provocateurs," recruited by White House people as early as 1969 or 1970 to spy upon, disrupt, discredit, and if need be burglarize opponents of the Administration. There were Mississippi millionaire Frederick La Rue and Robert Mardian who destroyed records of the Committee to Re-elect the President that would have shown its involvement in Watergate. There were Dwight Chapin who hired Segretti, Caulfield, Magruder, Krogh, Hunt and Liddy—all at one time or another on the White House staff, most of them reporting to Haldeman, all of them involved in one way or another in the pattern of illegitimate political sabotage of which Watergate was a part.

As will be seen, the list includes two attorneys general, supposedly the nation's chief law enforcement officers. It includes a one-time head of the FBI. It includes twelve men who were at one time or another members of the intimate White House staff of Richard Nixon and two of whom, Haldeman and Ehrlichman, were at his elbow daily. Among this number are four of the men who, having been trained in the White House, were sent out into the departments of the government to be sure that those department heads acted as Richard Nixon wished.

It appears that either Richard Milhous Nixon is the poorest judge of human character who has ever served in public office in America—as mayor of a small city, let alone as President of the United States, that he was over a period of more than a decade completely deceived as to their true character by his most intimate associates, including almost his total White House staff—or that, astute and crafty politician as he has universally been regarded to be, he deliberately chose to surround himself with people who believed in and were ready to carry out a total program calculated to destroy all opposition to Richard Nixon and to bring to a virtual end the two-party system in the United Sattes.

How much, exactly, Mr. Nixon knew beforehand about Watergate is comparatively unimportant. That he approved, or at least that his subordinates knew he *would* approve the well-financed plan to persuade the Watergate burglars to plead guilty, keep their mouths shut and rely on executive clemency to shorten their sentences seems too logical to be disbelieved. Whether he knew of the attempt on the part of his staff to persuade the CIA to try to stop FBI investigation of the funneling of campaign funds through Mexico or of the more far-reaching attempt to put the blame for Watergate on the CIA we could only guess. He almost seemed to confess as much in his statement of May 22. But that is what the record now clearly shows to have been the intent of Richard Nixon's entire organization. And not of himself? The reader can answer that question as he will.

One thing that is clear is that Richard Nixon tried his best to hush up Watergate, that he acted in the case only when events forced his hand.

He tried to extend the concept of "executive privilege" to prevent any present or past employees of the White House from answering questions not only of Congressional committees but of grand juries and the FBI. It was hard to believe that he "had nothing to hide."

As Senator Ervin and his special committee began hearings there were hints from White House Press Secretary Ziegler that "informal procedures might be worked out" to enable Nixon staff people to testify "within limits."

It was, however, too late. The hearings went on in professional, careful manner. Witness after witness was called. And the story of Watergate in all its ramifications was told to an astonished and deeply concerned world. The once tightly controlled team of conspirators fell apart. They began to accuse one another. Cover-up was at an end.

It was up to Elliott Richardson, pulled out of his three months tenure in the Department of Defense to succeed Kleindienst, to try to show that the Justice Department could and would conduct an objective prosecution of the Watergate case. To the fury of President Nixon, Republican Senator Percy of Illinois had got through a sparsely attended Senate a resolution calling for an independent prosecutor. He and others on Capitol Hill would, Richardson said, have their way, though he would keep "ultimate responsibility." Richardson named, and the Senate approved, respected Harvard professor Archibald Cox as special prosecutor.

On May 17, the San Francisco *Examiner* published a United Press International story which was based on findings of *The Washington Post*. That story quoted men who had been participants in "illegal and quasilegal undercover operations" conducted on President Nixon's behalf ever since 1969. Those men told the *Post* that Watergate was "a natural action that came from long existing circumstances." Those circumstances, they said, were a large-scale and continuing campaign aimed at student demonstrators, radicals, newspaper reporters, "leaking" White House aides and above all Democrats. The methods used included bugging, infiltration, burglary, spying and sabotage. Continuing to quote some of the very people who had done these things, the *Post* story said that the FBI, the Secret Service and special teams working for the Justice Department and the White House were all engaged in the "campaign." Among the results obtained were information on the private lives of Democratic presidential candidates, the encouragement of violence at anti-war demonstrations, and successful spying on "persons regarded as opponents of the Nixon Administration."

It has been said on the best authority that the love of money is the root of all evil. It might be added that the possession of too much money can be even worse.

The Committee to Re-elect the President had money running out of its ears. The General Accounting Office reported repeatedly to the Justice Department violations by the Committee of the Campaign Spending Law. For millions of dollars were not reported. One such report of the GAO said that Herbert Kalmbach, President Nixon's personal lawyer, had received more than $500,000 of such unreported funds, at least half of which, according to Kalmbach's own statement, had been paid to Watergate defendants.

This was the fourth such report delivered to the Justice Department by the GAO. But Justice had not acted.

The $500,000 of Kalmbach's was of course only a tiny fraction of the total funds of the Committee.

And Hugh Sloan, one time Committee treasurer, testified under oath that the amount devoted to the "dirty tricks" department of the campaign was probably $1 to $2 million, all in cash and all unreported. Sloan had resigned in the midst of the campaign because, as he put it, he "wouldn't do some of the things they wanted me to do."

Watergate was the tip of an iceberg.

The iceberg consisted of the kind of campaign tactics employed by Richard Nixon from the beginning of his career. It was, unfortunately not very far out of line.

It was of a piece with the quick settlement of three antitrust suits for I.T. and T., exchanged for a promise to finance the Republican convention.

It was of a piece with the dairy farmers' purchase with $400,000 and more for the Committee to Re-elect the President, of a reversal by the Department of Agriculture of a decision not to increase the support price of milk.

It was of a piece with the forged documents, the wiretapping, the harassment of the press, the spying on Democratic members of Congress and a lot more.

Watergate was akin to some even worse events. One of them was exposed to a degree in the spring of 1973. We told in our Chapter 17 how a reluctant FBI agent, posing as an anti-war zealot, had made all arrangements for a break-in by peace-minded Catholic priests, among others, at a draft board in Camden, New Jersey. The intruders were, of course, all caught and charged. But the jury, when it heard the story acquitted every one of them.

This, however, was only one instance. For on May 24, 1973 the *Los Angeles Times* reported revelations about the violence committed by the radical Weatherman organization in 1969 and 1970. An agent provocateur for the FBI was reported to have himself instructed the Weathermen in the manufacture of bombs and even to have actually participated in bombing. He was quoted as having told his "fellow" Weathermen that "true revolutionaries had to be ready to kill people."

The not-too-well-concealed purpose of such nefarious acts by a supposed law-enforcement agency is to demonstrate the need for repressive measures against violence.

On May 23 President Nixon issued, through a subordinate, a long and tortuous statement. In it he attempted to explain and excuse many actions on the ground that they were done for the sake of "national security." In July 1970 he said he had approved a plan which "included authorization for breaking and entering on specific categories of targets in specific situations related to natural security." He said that plan was never put into effect because J. Edgar Hoover objected to it.

But the plan sounded very much like the campaign of sabotage and spying revealed in *The Washington Post* article referred to above. Was it national security or the security of the Nixon Administration that was at stake? Maybe the two were a bit confused in some minds.

In the statement Mr. Nixon also admitted that Patrick Gray had indeed warned him on July 6 that some "people higher up" might be involved in Watergate, but he did not explain why after that he had made categorical statements that no one in the White House or his Administration was involved.

The President also tried to explain why he had issued orders to limit the Watergate investigation. He did not want it to interfere, he said, with other undercover activities of the FBI and CIA. He said he had done this for reasons of "national security." That was why, also, he had ordered his subordinates to delve into the private life of Daniel Ellsberg. But Ellsberg's only offense was giving the American people much-needed information about what more than one President had been doing to them. It was hard to understand why the Nixon Administration was trying him for something like treason. It was harder still to understand how "national security" was involved.

Commenting on what the President had said United Press released a story containing these paragraphs:

The President clearly thinks that illegal, unethical and covert activities for national security are more acceptable to the public

337

than similar actions undertaken for partisan political purposes. He confirmed his part in the former but denied any participation in the latter.

But at the edges, the line seems to blur despite Nixon's effort to draw it sharply. After all, G. Gordon Liddy and E. Howard Hunt employed their burglar's tools on behalf of both causes.

Nixon's orders apparently inhibited the FBI's Watergate investigation although he insisted that was not his purpose.

It seems to be a short step from telling the FBI to limit its investigation and ordering it to cover up the whole mess. A Senate committee and a U.S. grand jury are now trying to determine if that step was taken by Nixon or any of his aides.

But most revealing and in a grim way encouraging were these statements of Mr. Nixon's: "It is clear that unethical as well as illegal activities took place in the course of the 1972 presidential campign." And "To the extent that I may have contributed to the climate in which they took place I did not intend to."

Could it be that Richard Milhous Nixon was really sorry about all this? Only his future actions could answer that question. But even the possibility was reason to arouse a kind of pity, and for some, hope.

One of the most respected scholars of American history and government is Professor Arthur S. Link of Princeton University, co-author of *The American Epoch* and winner of the Bancroft Prize for his biography of Woodrow Wilson. Recently, the *Los Angeles Times* published an interview with Professor Link by its Associate Editor Robert J. Donovan. Professor Link said:

This is the greatest moral crisis of the Presidency. It is unprecedented. There is nothing analagous to it in the past, nothing.

The only way we can preserve the two-party system is by observing certain definite rules of the political game. These rules are pretty wide and allow a great deal of latitude for things that ought not happen.

Heretofore, however, the rules have been observed. The parties have been like two great organisms fighting each other. They will engage in all kinds of antics, like the war dance of whooping cranes, and all kinds of rhetoric. Yet instinctively they seem to know that some things you can't do and still preserve the two-party system.

You can't attempt to destroy the other party. You can't attempt to subvert the other pary's decision-making and choice of candidates. That never happened before. This is a rather fundamental right if you are going to have a two-party system. And, most fundamentally, the leaders of the two parties have to remain within the laws and not engage in wiretapping, burglary and so on.

The program of which Watergate became, we hope, a climax, was aimed to destroy the political opposition to Richard Nixon, to pervert the election laws, and, in the words of Stewart Alsop, writing in *Newsweek*, "to alter the very nature of the ancient American political system."

The *Los Angeles Times* called it, perhaps recalling how Richard Nixon built his political career, "An Un-American Activity."

But the real tragedy of Watergate and related criminal acts of the Committee to Re-elect the President lay deeper. It lay in the fact that it took revelations of this lurid kind to arouse the conscience and the alarm of the nation to what was happening to their government.

That conscience and that alarm should long since have been aroused to white heat. The personal decision of Mr. Nixon to invade Cambodia should have aroused us. Subservience of our government to the military-industrial complex should have aroused us. The merciless bombing of Southeast Asia and the refusal to conclude an early peace should have aroused us. Mr. Nixon's vetos of every significant piece of Congressional legislation calculated to reduce welfare rolls and enable unemployed people to go back to work—this surely should have aroused us. So should his callous veto of the Child Care Center bill of 1971. The policy of mass arrest proclaimed by the President and attorney general and carried out in Washington in May 1971, with not one of 13,000 arrested being convicted of even a misdemeanor, should have caused us to wonder about the future of American civil liberties. The impoundment of billions of dollars of funds appropriated by Congress to meet outstanding needs of people, $12 billion in Mr. Nixon's first term, should have angered everyone who values, even respects, the nation's Constitution. And the concentration of power in secret, claudestine White House "government" should have scared us to death.

But the nation and the Congress did not wake up until a couple of alert Washington cops caught agents of the Committee to Re-elect the President in the act of burglarizing and

339

attempting to plant spying devices in the headquarters of the Democratic National Committee.

All of which speaks ominous volumes about the tragically irresponsible apathy of the people of the United States.

The "good material life" had taken its toll. As long as most of us were physically comfortable, as long as profit rates were rising we were building to dismiss the plight of the nation's poor by blaming them and "welfare chiselers" for increasing the tax burden. As long as it was "only" little brown people, some of whom were Communists, whom American bombs were slaughtering, we were not disturbed.

Only a dramatic criminal act brought the nation to its senses.

Maybe we should, in a tragic sort of way, thank God for Watergate.

22. HOPE OR DESPAIR

As spring mellowed into summer the worst spat of tornados in history struck the South and the Middle West. Floods subsided but left desolution in their wake. The economy lost momentum, began to register no gains. Administration economists faithfully hailed this as a favorable sign that inflation could more easily be dampened. Other independent voices feared out loud that this was the danger signal of a first class depression in the offing. The dollar continued to take a beating throughout the world; the price of gold rose to an unbelievable $100 an ounce; gold mining fever struck our country. This was partly due to the continued unchecked inflation, partly to Watergate and the concern of other nations that Mr. Nixon had lost the respect necessary to enable him to govern.

The "energy crisis" deepened. Some cities suffered severe curtailment of natural gas supplies. Some gas stations closed, and independents in the oil business were being eliminated. Questions arose as to whether the shortages were genuine or contrived by the major oil companies. And Speaker "Bob" Moretti of the California Assembly pointed out that whether or not the crisis was real, the majors had everything to gain from it. For example: the Alaska pipeline, drilling again in Santa Barbara Channel, defeat of the environmentalists, escalating prices, elimination of the competition of independents, bigger profits, and support for a continuing "American military presence" in Southeast Asia. All this, said Speaker Moretti, could be reason enough why the major oil companies would like an "energy crisis."

Public opinion polls showed sharp decline in the percentage of people believing Mr. Nixon was doing a good job as President. They also showed that more people believed he knew about Watergate and other schemes from the beginning than thought he didn't. And an overwhelming majority indicated they thought he knew all about the attempts at "cover up."

Outwardly the White House assured everyone that Mr. Nixon was carrying on business as usual, that, in fact, he was engaged in matters far more important than the scandals that swirled around him. He was, we were assured, going to continue to pursue his goals, despite Watergate or any other such influences.

The President continued an almost secretive life, absenting himself from Washington frequently, conferring seldom with Congressional leaders or even his staff or leaders of the Republican party. Needless to say, there were no press conferences.

General Alexander Haig, a military man completely subject to orders of his Commander-in-chief, the President, was appointed head of the White House Staff. Some found such an appointment somewhat ominous.

That Nixon practices had not changed was signalled by the dismissal of Dr. Jerome Jaffe as head of Office of Drug Abuse Prevention. For Dr. Jaffe had expressed reservations about Richard Milhous Nixon's proposed anti-drug bill. Conformity with the President was still the order of the day.

There were occasions when Mr. Nixon emerged into the limelight. One was when the "biggest dinner in White House history" was tendered to former prisoners of war and their wives. For this, Richard Nixon was in excellent form. He enjoyed standing ovations given him—especially when he declared that the nation must stop making heroes out of those who steal government secrets. Mr. Nixon had repeatedly declared that he "had nothing to hide." But his defense of secrecy was indeed a classic one. He even went so far as to contend that, but for secrecy the P.O.W.s would still be in prison! And Mr. Nixon asked for help in his battle against the newspapers.

There were those who, like the author, thought they detected, in his late May statement a note of regret on the part of Richard Nixon for the illegal acts that had been committed on his behalf. Such delusions were compleely dispelled at that biggest of all White House dinners.

A note of sheer tragedy was struck in the midst of the Senate hearings on Watergate. Republican Congressman William O. Mills of Maryland was found dead, an apparent suicide, on May 24. His motive, if indeed he was a suicide, was clear enough. For the General Accounting Office had reported that the $25,000 Mills had received from the Committee to Re-elect the President was part of the millions the Committee had failed to report. The reason so very large a campaign fund was provided to Mills was not disclosed. His death underlined in tragedy the depth of the nation's troubles.

Mr. Nixon's long and belabored statement of late May left members of his own party divided sharply. Some defended him and accepted his excuse that he had acted to protect "national security." More seemed to feel a deep uneasiness because the President had not even yet "come clean" with the nation.

The business of government went on, but haltingly. Mr. Nixon, attempting to restaff his riddled executive branch, found, as a rule, only moderately equipped people with which to do so. He and such Administration spokesmen as remained attempted day by day to divert attention from Watergate by talking about foreign policy and making proposals such as that American Presidents should be limited to one six-year term. But Watergate held the headlines.

There were some signs and many rumors to the effect that Mr. Nixon did not intend to "take Watergate lying down," that he was preparing to go on the attack in good Chotiner fashion and to inject accusations as of old against his opponents and detractors. This could have the effect of further dividing the already deeply confused and splintered nation, but it would be quite "in character," and those who had seen how the President acted when frustrated or disappointed feared that some extreme reaction might be forthcoming.

Meanwhile revelations about Watergate and related illegal actions on the part of high Administration officials continued to fill the newspapers and television commentaries. Senator

Symington's Armed Services Committee was coming upon evidence that led the Senator to observe that he did not see how Mr. Nixon could have failed to know what was going on at his very elbow. Samplings of public opinion indicated that most people believed the press was doing an objective and fair job of ferreting out the facts and that its efforts were not directed at Mr. Nixon but would have been carried on in the same manner whoever had been President.

Talk of impeachment there was, and increasingly, but most of it stopped short of advocating so drastic a step. "It would tear the country apart for a period of months" was the most persistent comment.

Mr. Nixon's resignation was another matter. Members of his own party openly suggested this course. It was probably the one thing that could best restore people's fading trust in their government, but the White House vigorously denied, as in fact did Mr. Nixon himself, that he had the slightest intention of resigning. Nor did those who knew his Strange Case best have any real expectation that he would resign and save the nation further agony. The basic danger grew, danger of the nation becoming virtually leaderless and "rudderless."

There was, indeed, a gospel of despair abroad in the land. It was expressed in such terms as "What's all the big deal about Watergate? They all do it. It's part of American life and politics."

Those who spoke or thought in such terms sometimes declared that they would never again cast a ballot. All they wanted was to be left alone so they could find some enjoyment in life. They hoped the "energy crisis," real or imaginary, wouldn't make it impossible for them to take that vacation trip.

If this type of "thinking" grew then the outlook for the United States was grim indeed. For it represented a lethal cynicism about human nature and about the quality of the nation's leadership which could render reform all but impossible. It could drive even those who knew better to despair, those who saw Watergate as an attack on the fundamentals of the American political system and who were determined to see that such venal action in high places could never occur again.

Fortunately not everyone was thinking or acting or failing to act in this cynical fashion. There were increasing numbers of people who felt that deep disgrace had shrouded the

343

American presidency and hence the nation, and that it was up to them to do all they could to restore integrity in government and moral purpose to our nation's course.

Obstacles were enormous, however.

The *Los Angeles Times* in a series of extensive articles revealed penetration of the Mafia into Southern California and a nefarious triangle between it, the Teamsters' Union leadership and the Nixon Administration.

Even "Skylab" was not operating properly and people feared for the astronauts' safety.

Ugly rumors began to surround the tragic crash of the United Airlines plane with Mrs. E. Howard Hunt among those killed, with $10,000 in $100 bills in her purse, and a tremendous insurance policy covering her death.

Threatening crop failures threw doubt on the Nixon-Butz program of huge agricultural exports; and the refusal of oil companies adequately to supply farmers cooperatives' endangered farmers' ability to harvest even the crops they were able to raise.

The executive department of government was in a shambles. Few indeed of Mr. Nixon's White House intimates had escaped either resignation or dismissal. The departments of government had lost a number of their officials by the same process and for the same reason, Watergate and the rest of the "iceberg." The President was critically short of capable people untouched by the scandals who could conceivably fill positions of major responsibility. This was dramatically illustrated by the bewildering shuffling of two men. Elliot Richardson occupied no less than three cabinet positions in a short three months—Health, Education and Welfare, Defense, and Justice. James R. Schlesinger had been head of the Atomic Energy Commission, director of the Central Intelligence Agency, and Secretary of Defense in almost the same three months time. A man who by experience was hardly qualified at all for the position was heading the FBI on a temporary basis, William Ruckelshaus, pulled out of his job as head of Environmental Protection Agency.

Genuine high-quality men of unimpeachable integrity were for some strange reason reluctant to be associated with the Nixon Administration.

But government in the United States is more than the executive department, Richard Milhous Nixon to the contrary notwithstanding.

There are two other branches of our government and as

the executive tobogganed in public trust and effectiveness, the legislative and judicial branches of government showed unmistakable signs of awakening to the crisis and acting in the best of American traditions.

Even the almost-Nixon-controlled Supreme Court had voted 8 to 0 that the "Justice" Department could not wiretap, eavesdrop or spy upon citizens without a court order, as Mitchell and Rehnquist had claimed it could.

In decision after decision judges were ruling that Mr. Nixon could not legally freeze funds duly appropriated by Congress for specific purposes. No less than four such decisions were reported by Channel 4 television on May 11 alone. Notable were the words of Federal Judge William B. Jones who ruled:

An Administrator's responsibility to carry out the Congressional objectives of a program does not give him the power to discontinue that program, especially in the face of a Congressional mandate that it shall go on.

The Minnesota Farmer's Union won a class action suit against Mr. Nixon's attempt to abolish disaster loans to farmers by executive order.

The judge said: "Defendant's [that is the President's] action of December 27, 1972, which terminated, without notice, the Emergency Loan Program is unlawful."

Judge Matt Byrne, resisting the virtual bribe offered him at San Clemente, threw the Ellsberg case out of court.

In Camden, New Jersey, all defendants were acquitted in the draft board break-in which an FBI agent had engineered.

Indictments began to be returned by grand juries—such as those against Mitchell and Stans.

And, spurred by the remarks of Judge Sirica as well as by revelations of Congressional committees, even the Justice Department appeared to be moving toward something like effective prosecution of those involved in Watergate and its iceberg. Appointment of the distinguished Harvard Professor Archibald Cox as special prosecutor was a dramatic omen for this.

And at long last the Congress began to act as if it recognized the dangers posed by Richard Nixon's grab for personal power.

Wise Chairman Senator Sam Ervin was steering his investigation along low-key judicious lines, building his case step by step toward "higher-up" witnesses to be called after groundwork had been laid. In many people's minds Senator Ervin was emerging as the arch defender of their Constitution.

It was Senator Ervin's bill to forbid impoundment of funds unless approved by Congress that passed the Senate on the same day in May when the state of Georgia brought suit before the Supreme Court to force the President to stop impounding funds appropriated by Congress. It was also Senator Ervin's bill to fix by Congressional action a ceiling on government spending that was passed by the Senate along with the anti-impoundment measure. The Senate ceiling was somewhat less than the one proposed by President Nixon.

Significantly on that same historic day in May, Mr. Nixon announced that he was abandoning his super-czar plan for running the government and would begin to recognize his cabinet as a respected and even a decision-making body.

On a discordant note it was announced at the same time that John Connally was coming back into the White House as an unpaid counselor who would continue his lucrative Texas law practice at the same time. Mr. Ziegler was less than convincing in assuring reporters that no conflict of interest was involved—even with respect to big oil.

Congress continued to hammer away. Responding no doubt to public opinion polls which showed the people three to one against the bombing of Cambodia without Congressional approval, both Houses of Congress voted, again in May, to cut off funds for any kind of military action in or over that beleaguered little nation. This was the first time the House had passed such an anti-war measure. The vote was 219 to 118.

The members of Congress for World Peace through Law, a large and growing group of Senators and Congressmen, announced in April that their research showed that a reduction of $10 billion in the Pentagon budget could be effected without any weakening of the nation's actual military requirements.

By an almost unprecedented 15 to 0 vote the Senate Committee on Foreign Relations approved for floor debate the Javits-Stennis bill restricting the war powers of the President. And a House subcommittee took similar action. The House action was the more important of the two since the bill had passed the Senate in the 92nd Congress only to fail in the House.

As expected Mr. Nixon vetoed the bill passed by both Houses of Congress that would have required confirmation by the Senate of the Director of the Office of Management and Budget. The Senate overrode the veto, by a 62 to 22 vote. But it was sustained in the House, 236 votes to override against 178 against, 40 votes short of the required two-thirds majority.

Memories were being refreshed daily about the election campaign of 1972.

The Private Fair Campaign Practices Commission headed by Republican Charles P. Taft termed the tactics of the Committee to Re-elect the President "a conscious conspiracy to violate laws, to manipulate voters, and to make a mockery of the democratic system of self-government." It said that in 20 years of its existence "no campaign tactics comparable in extent or in potential damage to a free society "had ever been employed.

Rather lamely, it seemed, Richard Nixon asked that a commission be set up to study the problem and recommend reforms.

But the Senate was in no mood to wait for that. Its Commerce Committee approved a bill which would fix top limits on overall spending on behalf of any candidate, thus plugging the biggest loophole in present law. And Republican Senator Marlow Cook of Kentucky succeeded in attaching a rider that would forbid any agency except the duly established National Committees of both parties from receiving campaign contributions—an obvious slap at the Committee to Re-elect the President.

Senator Percy, Republican of Illinois, wanted an even stronger bill which would include a blanket prohibition against cash contributions of more than a token amount and a strict limitation on the amount any single individual could contribute, together with abolition of dummy fund-collecting committees such as had been so freely used to collect the $400,000 contribution to Mr. Nixon by one dairy farmers' organization.

The actions of Senators Cook and Percy were symptoms of a growing resentment within his own party against Richard Nixon's high-handed and questionable practices. It was reported by columnists Evans and Novak that a powerful group of Republican leaders had delivered a virtual ultimatum to the President demanding that respected Republican leaders be included in the White House staff and that Mr. Nixon listen to Republican members of Congress and give them a significant role in policy formation.

Two Republican House members formally joined the Democratic Party giving as their reasons that they could not conscientiously support the Nixon policies.

Support for Mr. Nixon dropped markedly in the polls.

The British and French governments expressed a resounding lack of enthusiasm for the projected visit to Europe of the President.

Richard Nixon on his own account issued a flat denial of rumors that he might be willing to testify before Senate Committees investigating Watergate or, rather astonishingly, before any grand jury. At the same time Mr. Nixon achieved a new high point of executive arrogance by ordering the supposedly independent prosecutor, Professor Cox, immediately to find out who had leaked a rumor that he would testify!

Mildly put, none of this helped relations between White House and Capitol Hill, and if anything it was relations within the Republican Party that were hurting most.

The Democrats meanwhile were wisely "playing it cool." There was a commendable absence of chortling over the discomfiture of the opposite party. There were instead appeals for national unity and for determination to heal the nation's wounds by moving to alleviate domestic problems and by a restoration of Constitutional government.

There were those who soberly pointed out that Watergate and the rest of the iceberg should have come as no surprise. They were after all entirely consistent with the political tactics employed by Mr. Nixon and his close supporters over a quarter of a century. Richard Whalen writing in the *Los Angeles Times* discussed the tragic events in terms of the kind of arrogant men with whom Mr. Nixon had surrounded himself and wound up his article by saying that the American press should ask itself "why a police beat story was needed to break the truth about what had been going on in the White House for four years."

More important, was the feeling of deep concern over what had been done to the United States of America. More specifically, what had been done to the Presidency as the nation's highest office, the one from which challenging moral leadership should come. What could happen now to restore the severely damaged credibility of the nation's highest office and indeed of government in general?

Some of the answers to those questions were already being given in the firm adherence to duty of the nation's judiciary and the newly found determination of the Congress to fight to recover its proper role in the scheme of government.

There were some calls for impeachment and indeed such drastic action might be forced upon the Congress if revelations went much farther in the President's direction. But the consensus in and out of Congress seemed to be that the very process of impeachment would so further rend the already battered nation that it should be avoided if at all possible.

More frequent were calls, from Republican as well as Democratic and independent sources, that Mr. Nixon resign, in a truly noble and selfless gesture of sheer patriotism. But these calls were, as expected, brushed aside by him with further demands that the persons who had "leaked" such a rumor be brought to task.

Perhaps the best available solution was a projection of the reported demands of Republican leaders for a decent respect from the White House. Perhaps Congressional leaders of both parties might make clear to Mr. Nixon that unless he began to act like a Constitutional President and treat the Congress, the courts, and the American people with decent consideration, the Congress might exercise the one power he could not possibly veto—the power *not* to appropriate funds for the White House or other pet projects of the President.

Among the people there were unmistakeable signs of hope. The Gallup Poll showed their listing "Corruption in Government-Watergate" as a major issue facing the nation. There was praise for the press instead of castigation that Mr. Agnew once had led. The Pulitzer Prize for Public Service was appropriately and with a touch of "divine retribution," awarded to *The Washington Post,* arch gad-fly of the Nixon Administration for its coverage of Watergate. There seemed to be a growing spirit of national humility and a quiet commitment to see that right was done in high places and among all of us just because it was right. If "honest confession is good for the soul," this was another sign of hope.

The hope was tempered, for many people, by a deep conviction that the Nixon imperialism should have been effectively challenged by the Congress, the courts, the media, and the people, before the Watergate deluge descended and for different reasons.

These people had long been profoundly worried over the clear and present danger to the American constitutional form of government which the Nixon policies and actions had presented throughout his presidency. His crass defiance of any limitations on his war-making power, his cavalier violation by executive order of the duly enacted laws of the land, his attempted destruction of programs helpful to poor and middle Americans, his intemperate attacks upon he courts, and his attempts to cow the media into subservience—these it seemed to many had constituted ample ground for determined resistance long ago by the Congress, the press, and the people. Spirited defense of our basic governmental institutions against the Nixon thrust toward something akin to dictatorial rule should have been mounted long before Watergate brought it forth.

Hope remained that the flood of Watergate, if not more basic considerations, had begun the process of cleansing the political life of the United States of America. As Shana Alexander put it, in *Newsweek*, "the ship hâd begun deserting the rats."

Hope remained that the spirit of the nation's better self was about to restore the balance of our tripartite form of government.

There was hope that at long last the nation had awakened to the strange willingness of Richard Nixon to use, or to have used on his behalf, any means, methods, or tactics that would enhance his personal power and prestige.

It was high time for this to be the case.

For the strange case of Richard Nixon had, it appeared, not been changed even by Watergate. The golden ropes had not been severed. The Ashes, the Connallys, the oil companies and the war contractors still ruled the executive department.

And the Nixon loyalists were returning to the attack, an attack on all those who revealed "secrets" to the people, all those who thus threatened "national"—or was it "Nixon?"—security, all those who, like the Ervin Senate Committee, were trying to give the nation the whole truth.

The tactics were appropriately altered to fit the situation, but the drive for preservation of Richard Nixon's personal power remained the golden rope that gave its grim consistency to the Strange Case of Richard Milhous Nixon.